7-NIGHT LOAN

Due Back
Anytime on the eighth day

Fine for Late Return
£2.50 per day

Short Loan Items
... cannot be renewed or reserved
... are not due back at the weekend

Opening Hours
Email
Telephone

MULTICULTURAL EDUCATION

MULTICULTURAL EDUCATION

Major Themes in Education

Edited by
David Gillborn

Volume II
Identities and Intersections

Routledge
Taylor & Francis Group

LONDON AND NEW YORK

First published 2015
by Routledge
2 Park Square, Milton Park, Abingdon, Oxon OX14 4RN

and by Routledge
711 Third Avenue, New York, NY 10017

Routledge is an imprint of the Taylor & Francis Group, an informa business

Editorial material and selection © 2015 David Gillborn; individual owners retain copyright in their own material

British Library Cataloguing in Publication Data
A catalogue record for this book is available from the British Library

Library of Congress Cataloging in Publication Data
A catalog record for this book has been requested

ISBN: 978-0-415-50017-3 (Set)
ISBN: 978-0-415-50019-7 (Volume II)

Typeset in Times
by Book Now Ltd, London

Publisher's Note
References within each chapter are as they appear in the original complete work

Printed and bound in Great Britain by
TJ International Ltd, Padstow, Cornwall

CONTENTS

CONTENTS

ACKNOWLEDGEMENTS

The publishers would like to thank the following for permission to reprint their material:

Perseus Books Group for permission to reprint Derrick Bell, 'The Rules of Racial Standing', in *Faces at the Bottom of the Well: The Permanence of Racism* (New York: Basic Books, 1992), pp. 109–126.

The American Anthropological Association for permission to reprint Margaret A. Gibson, 'Complicating the Immigrant/Involuntary Minority Typology', *Anthropology & Education Quarterly*, 28, 3, 1997, 431–454.

Taylor & Francis for permission to reprint Crain Soudien, 'Certainty and Ambiguity in Youth Identities in South Africa: Discourses in Transition', *Discourse: Studies in the Cultural Politics of Education*, 22, 3, 2001, 311–326.

Taylor & Francis for permission to reprint Deborah Youdell, 'Subjectivation and Performative Politics—Butler Thinking Althusser and Foucault: Intelligibility, Agency and the Raced–Nationed–Religioned Subjects of Education', *British Journal of Sociology of Education*, 27, 4, 2006, 511–528.

Taylor & Francis for permission to reprint Nicola Rollock, 'The Invisibility of Race: Intersectional Reflections on the Liminal Space of Alterity', *Race Ethnicity and Education*, 15, 1, 2012, 65–84.

Taylor & Francis for permission to reprint Ricky Lee Allen, 'What About Poor White People?', in W. Ayers, T. Quinn and D. Stovall (eds), *Handbook of Social Justice in Education* (New York: Routledge, 2009), pp. 209–230.

The American Sociological Association for permission to reprint Annette Lareau and Erin McNamara Horvat, 'Moments of Social Inclusion and Exclusion: Race, Class, and Cultural Capital in Family–School Relationships', *Sociology of Education*, 72, 1, 1999, 37–53.

Teachers College Record for permission to reprint Michael W. Apple and Thomas C. Pedroni, 'Conservative Alliance Building and African American Support of

Vouchers: The End of *Brown's* Promise or a New Beginning?', *Teachers College Record*, 107, 9, 2005, 2068–2105.

T. Elon Dancy II and M. Christopher Brown II, 'Race, Class and Education: Lessons for School Leaders from Hurricane Katrina and the Gulf Coast', in Linda C. Tillman and James Joseph Scheurich (eds), *Handbook of Research on Educational Leadership for Equity and Diversity* (New York: Routledge, 2013), pp. 517–536.

Sage Publications for permission to reprint Heidi Safia Mirza and Diane Reay, 'Spaces and Places of Black Educational Desire: Rethinking Black Supplementary Schools as a New Social Movement', *Sociology*, 34, 3, 2000, 521–544.

Journal of International Women's Studies for permission to reprint Avtar Brah and Ann Phoenix, 'Ain't I A Woman? Revisiting Intersectionality, *Journal of International Women's Studies*, 5, 3, 2004, 75–86.

Sage Publications for permission to reprint Pedro A. Noguera, 'The Trouble with Black Boys: The Role and Influence of Environmental and Cultural Factors on the Academic Performance of African American Males', *Urban Education*, 38, 4, 2003, 431–459.

Taylor & Francis for permission to reprint Lance Trevor McCready, 'Some Challenges Facing Queer Youth Programs in Urban High Schools: Racial Segregation and De-Normalizing Whiteness', *Journal of Gay & Lesbian Issues in Education*, 1, 3, 2003, 37–51.

Sage Publications for permission to reprint Alfredo J. Artiles, 'Toward an Interdisciplinary Understanding of Educational Equity and Difference: The Case of the Racialization of Ability', *Educational Researcher*, 40, 9, 2011, 431–445.

Wanda J. Blanchett, 'Telling It Like It Is: The Role of Race, Class & Culture in the Perpetuation of Learning Disability as a Privileged Category for the White Middle Class', *Disability Studies Quarterly*, 30, 2, 2010.

Taylor & Francis for permission to reprint Gregg D. Beratan, 'The Song Remains the Same: Transposition and the Disproportionate Representation of Minority Students in Special Education', *Race Ethnicity & Education*, 11, 4, 2008, 337–354.

Teachers College Record for permission to reprint Zeus Leonardo and Alicia A. Broderick, 'Smartness as Property: A Critical Exploration of Intersections Between Whiteness and Disability Studies', *Teachers College Record*, 113, 10, 2011, 2206–2232.

Disclaimer

The publishers have made every effort to contact authors/copyright holders of works reprinted in *Multicultural Education (Major Themes in Education)*. This has not been possible in every case, however, and we would welcome correspondence from those individuals/companies whom we have been unable to trace.

Part 6

RACE, RACISM AND IDENTITIES

22

THE RULES OF RACIAL STANDING

Derrick Bell

Source: *Faces at the Bottom of the Well: the Permanence of Racism*, New York: Basic Books, 1992, pp. 109–126.

"I AM A TRAVELER in a strange land, and during my journey I approach a tall mountain. Though it will take me out of my way, I am drawn irresistibly to climb it. There is a narrow path leading to the top, but the mountain is very steep. As I reach its summit, I am exhausted and disoriented and, at first, do not recognize a strange sound I hear. It seems like a voice. Then, unmistakably, it is a voice: not near, not far and, despite the other-worldly atmosphere, deep and resonant.

"It is a little scary, but I can't help noticing that the voice sounds suspiciously like the actor James Earl Jones doing one more TV commercial voiceover. It really riles me how even one of the country's finest actors cannot escape the exploitative practice of overlaying the actions of the whites portrayed on the screen with the warm, rich voices of blacks. Damn! I thought. If Langston Hughes were now writing his famous poem, whose first line is, 'You've taken my blues and gone,'[1] he'd have to include black voices as well as black music—both shamelessly employed by whites for the usual reason: profit.

"But James Earl Jones or not, while I can see no one in the vicinity, the voice is now unmistakable: 'WELCOME, FRIEND. WE HAVE BEEN WAITING FOR YOU. ALL IS IN READINESS.'

"Surprised, as well as amused, I look around for the source of the voice. There is no one. But nearby has materialized a glass-walled office, and on a desk in the very center of the room stands the most elaborate desktop computer I have ever seen. I enter the room and sit down at the computer. Immediately its screen flashes a command: 'SPEAK UP, IKE, AN 'SPRESS YO'SE'F!'

"I smile as I recognize the directive from one of Paul Lawrence Dunbar's dialect poems.[2] Though I've never felt autobiographical, my first hesitant words lead to a flood of sentences, paragraphs, pages about my life, my work. The longer I type, the faster come the pages. Time passes, but I feel neither weariness nor want. Finally, many hours later, I finish. I gather up the printed pages, which the computer produced silently and swiftly as I typed. As I walk from the room, I see

3

before me a great light. I recognize the voice that greeted me on my arrival. It answers my questions before I have formed them:

"You Are Here Because You Are Deemed Worthy. We Have Read These Pages and Discerned in Them Your True Mission. Approach the Light.'

"There is a loud but melodious sound like a crashing of celestial cymbals. The light disappears but, in some strange way, remains with me.

"The Light You Saw, and See No More, Is Now Yours. You Have Been Granted to Know the Rules of Racial Standing. Take the Pages with You. The Essence of Your Work Is Now Transformed into a Description of Your Gift. Use It Wisely. Guard It Well. And Remember, No Gift Comes Without a Price.'

"There is silence. Computer room and voice are gone. I come down from the mountain and continue my trip. Arriving home, I turn to the pages. Sure enough, my lengthy text has been reduced to five rules engraved in gold on bound parchment pages."

As I finished, I reached into a desk drawer for a small sheaf of bound pages and handed them to Geneva. "I dreamed the story I just told you and the next morning found these pages. I assume both the dream and the rules are your gift."

Geneva didn't confirm my assumptions, but the devilish look in her eye gave her away. "Why don't you read and consider the first of the rules. Then let me know your thoughts."

First rule

The law grants litigants standing to come into court based on their having suffi-cient personal interest and involvement in the issue to justify judicial cognizance.[3] *Black people (while they may be able to get into court) are denied such standing legitimacy in the world generally when they discuss their negative experiences with racism or even when they attempt to give a positive evaluation of another black person or of his or her work.*[4] *No matter their experience or expertise, blacks' statements involving race are deemed "special pleading" and thus not entitled to serious consideration.*

"Isn't this the point of *Invisible Man,*" I asked, "where Ralph Ellison depicts blacks as a category of human beings whose suffering is so thoroughly ignored that they, and it, might as well not exist?"[5]

"Quite right. Ellison's novel was published forty years ago," Geneva replied, "and despite all the acclaim it received, the number of black people suffering because of racism—and virtually ignored in their suffering—has increased."

"In particular" I said, "the First Rule accurately reflects the special discounting of black views when we recommend other blacks for a position or for promotion. When not ignored entirely, the unconvinced response from whites will contain the scarcely concealed question 'Who else likes this person?' Both parties know *who* 'who else' is.

"Misunderstanding, though, poses the real danger—a lesson I learned without the gift of a special rule. When back in 1957, as my first lawyering job I went to work at the Justice Department, only a few of the thousands of lawyers there were black. One of them, Maceo Hubbard, a man of broad experience, taught me a lot I had not learned in law school. 'When white folks ask you for an evaluation of another black,' he warned me, 'you have to remember one thing. However carefully you say it, you can hurt the brother, but you can't help him.' Maceo's sage advice, unhappily, is still valid."

"I understand," Geneva said, "that, as a matter of course, some minority law teachers simply do not read and evaluate the work of other minority teachers."

"I don't go that far. For one thing, my failure to comment when asked is taken as a negative recommendation. But when law schools request—as they frequently do—that I evaluate the scholarly work of another black law teacher being considered for promotion or tenure, I approach the task with great caution. I remember all too well an instance when, younger and less wise, I wrote a generally favourable letter for a black teacher. I noted—I thought in the interest of objectivity—that because the piece under review had been prepared for a conference presentation, the paucity of its footnoting was acceptable. I was certain, I said, that the author would provide more support for his statements when the speech was revised for publication. The upshot was that not only was the professor denied tenure, but in explaining his supposed deficiencies to others—and to him—the faculty reported that they had no choice: 'Even another black law teacher said this man is not scholarly.' It was a painful application of Maceo Hubbard's warning. The candidate didn't speak to me for some years afterward."

Geneva shook her head sadly. "Great profession you're in."

"It goes with the territory of being black, not of being a law teacher," I said, turning to the Second Rule.

Second rule

Not only are blacks' complaints discounted, but black victims of racism are less effective witnesses than are whites, who are members of the oppressor class. This phenomenon reflects a widespread assumption that blacks, unlike whites, cannot be objective on racial issues and will favor their own no matter what. This deep-seated belief fuels a continuing effort—despite all manner of Supreme Court decisions intended to curb the practice—to keep black people off juries in cases involving race.[6] Black judges hearing racial cases are eyed suspiciously and sometimes asked to recuse themselves in favor of a white judge—without those making the request even being aware of the paradox in their motions.[7]

I pointed out to Geneva that this rule is applicable far beyond black jurors and judges. It is no accident that white writers have dominated the recording of race relations in this country: they are considered the more objective commentators on racial issues. For example, the litigation leading up to the Court's decision in

Brown v. *Board of Education*[8] has been well documented by Richard Kluger's *Simple Justice*[9]—as has the life and work of Dr. Martin Luther King, Jr., by David Garrow[10] and Taylor Branch,[11] among other white writers,[12] whose work covers the protest aspects of the civil rights movement. Black writers who have covered similar ground, however, have not received the attention or the rewards of their white colleagues.[13] The writer Gloria Joseph summarizes the problem as, having commended as exemplary a white writer's essay on feminism and racism, she then acknowledges that the white writer "reiterates much that has been voiced by black female writers, but the acclaim given her article shows again that it takes whiteness to give even Blackness validity."[14] The black writer and poet bell hooks articulates the frustration resulting from this phenomenon when she complains: "We produce cultural criticism in the context of white supremacy. At times, even the most progressive and well-meaning white folks, who are friends and allies, may not understand why a black writer has to say something a certain way, or why we may not want to explain what has been said as though the first people we must always be addressing are privileged white readers." Later on the same page, though, she acknowledges a deeper dimension to her frustration: "And [yet] every black writer knows that the people you may most want to hear your words may never read them, that many of them have never learned to read."[15]

"I think bell hooks speaks for all of us," I said, "and the worst aspect of our frustration is that the pressure to perform primarily for those for whom we care less is less part of some invidious scheme than an economic necessity so long repeated it is now a cultural component of life as blacks in a nation that is—despite all—determined to be and remain white."

"The black writer," Geneva suggested, "is not unlike the black mother who, to sustain herself and her children, must work all day taking care of white children while her own are neglected."

"These rules seem more like revelations of distilled woe than gifts. Let's see what comes next."

Third rule

Few blacks avoid diminishment of racial standing, most of their statements about racial conditions being diluted and their recommendations of other blacks taken with a grain of salt. The usual exception to this rule is the black person who publicly disparages or criticizes other blacks who are speaking or acting in ways that upset whites. Instantly, such statements are granted "enhanced standing" even when the speaker has no special expertise or experience in the subject he or she is criticizing.

"Right on the mark again, Geneva!" I said, thinking of President Bush's nomination of Clarence Thomas to the Supreme Court in the summer of 1991 as—the President claimed—the most qualified person for the position. Given Thomas's modest academic background, relative youth, lack of litigation experience, and undistinguished service in appointive government positions, only his 'enhanced standing,' in accordance with the Third Rule, as a well-known critic of affirmative action and civil rights policies and leaders in general could have won him priority over the multitude of lawyers, white and black, with more traditional qualifications for a seat on our highest Court.

Indeed, the Thomas appointment is a definitive, but far from the sole, example of the awards awaiting blacks who gain enhanced standing. Black scholars have watched in angry frustration while blacks like Thomas Sowell, Walter Williams, Glenn Loury, and Shelby Steele gain national celebrity as experts on race owing to their willingness to minimize the effect of racism on the lowly status of blacks.

"The fact that, in line with the First Rule, most blacks dispute these assessments is generally ignored," I explained to Geneva. "Of course, some white people will scoff at your rules of racial standing, dismissing them as merely an exemplar of the old adage 'Dog bites man: no news. Man bites dog: news.' And where criticism or whistle blowing by an insider wins immediate attention, any laudatory statement by a person affiliated with a product or an institution is viewed, to some extent, as special pleading."

"Shouldn't," Geneva asked, "all but the most insensitive be able to distinguish a peoples' plaintive efforts to protest racism from a company's product-enhancing puffery?"

"Perhaps—but, distinguishable or not, it galls me that black scholars who labor in relative obscurity can leap to instant attention and acclaim by criticizing their black colleagues. This happened when Professor Randall Kennedy at Harvard Law School asserted that minority scholars have no special legitimacy in writing about race, and that their scholarship, measured by traditional standards, is flawed.[16] Had Kennedy been lauding black legal scholars, his article would have been treated as just another piece of special pleading."

"But wait!" Geneva interrupted. "The several pieces I have read by Professor Kennedy are well done and tend to give white folks hell."[17]

"Precisely my point. None of those articles have been covered by the *New York Times*.[18] But don't get me started, Geneva. Examples abound. In the fall of 1991, Professor Stephen Carter published *Reflections of an Affirmative Action Baby*,[19] in which he—who in 1985 had become the first black person to gain tenure at the prestigious Yale Law School—expressed serious reservations about the value of affirmative action for himself and others. Immediately, the book soared to national attention, and Carter began to frequent the television talk shows."

Geneva sniffed significantly. "Do I discern the distinct aroma of sour grapes?"

I threw up my hands. "Could be, but let me just say in my defense that the phenomenon of enhanced racial standing set out in the Third Rule is, while not called by that name, certainly well known. I think it's cause for wonder and more than a little credit to our integrity that more black scholars don't maim one another in a wild scramble to gain for ourselves the acclaim, adulation, and accompanying profit almost guaranteed to those of us willing to condemn our own."

"Are you suggesting," Geneva asked in feigned dudgeon, "that after all my effort your book will not leap to the top of the best-seller charts?"

"No outrageous attacks on blacks, no explicit sex, and no revelations of how bad black men treat black women! No, Geneva, I'm afraid you'll have to be content with your small, but very devoted audience."

Now she was genuinely indignant. "Wait just a minute, sir. Do you equate black women writers who describe the ill treatment black women have received at the hands of black men, with the black scholar-opportunists who reap fame and fortune by denying that racism is the cause of blacks' distress?"

"I do not. Nor do I suggest that black scholars who gain enhanced standing because of the anti-black or anti–civil rights tone of their writing have taken their positions for personal gain. Some, perhaps all, actually believe what they're saying. What I criticize is their refusal to come to grips with the effect of their statements.

"As to black women writers who set out in fiction or factual terms the distressing treatment some of them have suffered at the hands of black men, the truth of their writing is self-evident. But I wish they'd make clearer the point that much of this ill treatment is the result of black male frustration with having constantly to cope with the barriers of racism, including systemic job discrimination that is the direct cause of the brutal circumstances in which so many blacks live their lives."

"Are they," Geneva asked, with only slightly disguised scorn, "obligated to insert caveats reminding readers that abusive behavior by black men is often motivated by frustration with the constraints racism imposes on their lives?"

"Of course not. But they should know that since at least the 1975 publication of Ntozake Shange's *For colored girls who have considered suicide when the rainbow is enuf,*[20] there has been a market for writing by black women on this subject—and, as you know, some of that writing has been the cause of debate and accusations.[21] I think, though, that the criticism and the potential for harm of black women writing adversely about black men is not as damaging to the black community as the black scholars' writing against blacks. Actually, there's a more dire form of black self-criticism which may be covered in the next rule."

Fourth rule

When a black person or group makes a statement or takes an action that the white community or vocal components thereof deem "outrageous," the latter will actively recruit blacks willing to refute the statement or condemn the action. Blacks who respond to the call for condemnation will receive superstanding status. Those blacks who refuse to be recruited will be interpreted as endorsing the statements and action and may suffer political or economic reprisals.

"Pretty Strong stuff!" I exclaimed.

"Meaning?" Geneva asked.

8

"Well, perhaps the best contemporary example of the Fourth Rule involves the adverse reaction of many whites to the Muslim minister Louis Farrakhan. Smart and superarticulate, Minister Farrakhan is perhaps the best living example of a black man ready, willing, and able to 'tell it like it is' regarding who is responsible for racism in this country. In this regard, he's easily a match for all those condescending white talk-show hosts who consider themselves very intelligent, certainly smarter than *any* black man.

"All these TV pros seems anxious to put this outspoken black man in his place. They have big staffs to do their research and prepare scripts filled to the brim with denigrating questions. And they have film clips carefully edited to make Farrakhan look as outrageous and irresponsible as possible.

"On camera, these self-appointed defenders of a society senseless enough to put them in their highly paid jobs, attack Farrakhan with a vengeance. Clearly, destruction and not discussion is their aim. But there's no contest. Minister Farrakhan, calm, cool, and very much on top of the questions, handles these self-appointed guardians with ease. I love it!"

"I gather," Geneva broke in, "that many black people do not concur in your assessment of the Farrakhan phenomenon."

"It doesn't matter. Whatever their views on the controversial Black Muslim minister, every black person important enough to be interviewed is asked to condemn Minister Farrakhan—or any other truly outspoken black leader. Reporters generally ask, 'Have you heard what Farrakhan said and what are *you* going to do about it?' Note that, with Farrakhan, it's not what do you have to say, but what are you going to *do* about what he said? And don't make the mistake of telling a reporter ten positive things about Farrakhan and adding one criticism. You guessed it, the story will be headlined: 'LEADING BLACK SPOKESPERSON CONDEMNS FARRAKHAN.'"

"But," Geneva objected, "Farrakhan is a Black Muslim, which most blacks are definitely not."

"It's not his faith we're asked to deal with, Geneva. It's his race and his mouth."

She laughed. "On the surface, this is strange, kind of crazy. Remember the biblical story of how little David killed the mighty Goliath, David left his sheep in the field, journeyed to the impending battle, and convinced King Saul of the Israelites to allow him to be their champion. The armor they put on him was so heavy, he took it off, and went to meet Goliath with his staff, a slingshot, and five smooth stones in his pouch. And David was not modest or shy as he told Goliath what the Philistine giant least wanted to hear:

> This day will the LORD deliver thee into mine hand; and I will smite thee, and take thine head from thee; and I will give the carcases of the host of the Philistines this day unto the fowls of the air, and to the wild beasts of the earth; that all the earth may know that there is a God in Israel.[22]

"For many people," Geneva continued, "Minister Farrakhan is a black David going one on one against the Philistines who bestride the land, abusing their power and generally messing over black folk. But when Farrakhan issues his challenge, no Goliath comes forth. Rather, some of the Philistines come running, not up to Farrakhan, but to any black person of substance they can find, asking, 'Did you hear what that man said about us? What are *you* going to do about it?' "

"That's the question I've been asking myself, Geneva," I responded. "Why must I do something about Minister Farrakhan? Those he condemns are not without power, not without money, not without guns. A sad history serves as proof that they know how to use all three against us. Why me?

" 'Oh,' I am told, 'that man is hurting your cause.' But the cause of black people has been under attack for three hundred years, not by one black man but by the dominant white society. The suggestion that our current plight would be relieved if Farrakhan would just shut up is both naïve and insults our intelligence. It also reveals more about those who would silence him than they likely want uncovered."

I went on with how, in 1985, when Farrakhan was scheduled to speak in New York City's Madison Square Garden, black officials came under heavy pressure to speak out and denounce him because of earlier statements of his deemed anti-Semitic and anti-white.[23] Some black officials spoke out. Others, while not condoning some of Farrakhan's comments, complained in interviews that they were repeatedly expected to condemn fellow blacks for offensive remarks or behavior, while whites are not called upon to react to every such indiscretion by white officials. Typical of this position, Representative Charles B. Rangel (D., N.Y.) told a reporter that Farrakhan's statements about Judaism being a "dirty religion" were "garbage," but added, "it's easy to come down heavy on Farrakhan." Rangel expressed the hope that matters had not reached the point that, just as blacks in South Africa have to carry a passbook to go from place to place, "black Americans have to carry their last statement refuting Farrakhan. I would not, if someone said Jesus Christ is a phony, go around asking Jews to sign a statement to condemn him."[24]

In a similar vein, the Reverend Calvin O. Butts, pastor of the Abyssinian Baptist Church in Harlem, refused to condemn Farrakhan, and pointed out that the Muslim minister criticizes many groups in strong terms, including black churches and black ministers. Butts acknowledged that many Jewish people "look askance at any slight breeze of anti-Semitism. However," he added, "if in response to Israel's refusal to impose sanctions on South Africa to protest its policies of racial separation, I jumped up and said all Jewish leaders in the United States should denounce Israel, how many Jewish people would join me in that? I don't think many."[25]

"I agree, Geneva," I said, "with both Congressman Rangel and the Reverend Butts. Anti-Semitism is a horrible thing, but just as all criticism of blacks is not racism, so not every negative comment about Jews—even if it is wrong—is anti-Semitism. Were I a Jew, I would be damned concerned about the latent—and often active—anti-Semitism in this country. But to leap with a vengeance on inflammatory comments by blacks is a misguided effort to vent justified fears on black targets of opportunity who are the society's least powerful influences and—I might add—the most likely to be made the scapegoats for deeply rooted anti-Semitism that they didn't create and that will not be cured by their destruction."

"Fear is not rational," Geneva observed. "Jews understandably feel that they must attack anti-Semitism whenever it appears. Farrakhan, being a frightening figure for most whites and thus vulnerable, becomes a symbol—even though, as you point out, an inappropriate one of the nation's anti-Semitism. Jews and white people generally hope that criticism by blacks will diminish his credibility, if not in the eyes of his followers, at least in the minds of those who believe that the threat he represents can be defused by our responding to their urgent pleas for black condemnation of an out-of-control black."

"It's not set out in the Fourth Rule, Geneva, but have you noticed that those blacks who utter 'beyond the pale' remarks are never forgiven. Thus, when Farrakhan attempts to explain that his statement was aimed at Israel as a state and not at Judaism as a religion, his explanation is rejected out of hand. The attitude seems to be: 'You said it, and thus you must be condemned for all time.' "

Geneva agreed. "The Reverend Jesse Jackson has experienced a similar 'life-time renunciation' notwithstanding his frequent and fervent apologies for the regrettable 'Hymie and Hymietown' remarks he made during his 1984 presidential campaign.[26] As I indicated earlier, I understand why a group is upset by what it deems racial or religious insults, but I doubt that I'm alone in not understanding why blacks who lack any real power in the society are not forgiven while whites, including those at the highest levels of power, are pardoned. For example, many Jewish spokespeople complained bitterly when President Reagan went to lay a wreath at the Nazi cemetery at Bitburg in Germany,[27] but they do not continue to harass him about the issue everywhere he goes. No one denounced Reagan as anti-Semitic for going. More significantly, neither President Bush nor the whites who support him are called on to condemn Reagan in order to prove that they are not anti-Semitic.

"We boast that, unlike communist countries, there is no censorship of the press here. But blacks like Jesse Jackson, who are subject to an unofficial but no less effective 'renunciation,' are simply not heard."

"Your renunciation isn't limited to controversial political figures," I interrupted. "The writer bell hooks complains that 'often radical writers doing transgressive work are told not that it's too political or too "left," but simply that it will not sell or readers just will not be interested in that perspective.'"[28]

"Similarly," she continued, "one need not agree with Farrakhan that African Americans need to separate from this country to understand that, after three hundred years of trying and not yet having the acceptance here that non-English-speaking white immigrants have on their first day on this soil, we need to be thinking of (if not yet doing) something other than singing one more chorus of 'We Shall Overcome.' Whatever his rhetorical transgressions, Minister Farrakhan and his church are giving the most disadvantaged black folk reason to hope when most of the country and more than a few of us blacks have written them off. His television hosts give him credit for cleaning up a neighborhood in Washington, D.C.,* and yet question his motives for accomplishing what few government officials have even seriously tried."

Thinking of Geneva's earlier statement about blacks who do not agree with our position on Farrakhan, I recalled a black friend who was unmoved when I discussed Farrakhan's abilities, and said, "Even if everything you say about him is correct, he is still a bigot. Why can't I call him what I think he is?" In effect, my friend was asking, "Even given the perverse weight white society gives to black-on-black criticism, must persons of color remain silent if they strongly disagree with statements or actions by other blacks?"

"The whole racial standing phenomenon, Geneva, raises a troublesome dilemma for many black scholars. How can blacks criticize other blacks or civil rights policies with which they disagree? Must they sacrifice their academic freedom, even their First Amendment right to free speech, in order to prevent whites from endowing with super standing their assertion of anti-black beliefs they have held all along?"

"The answer," Geneva said, "is that a burden of blackness, particularly for the black scholar, is racial awareness. Black academics must weigh the value of their statements, their writings, against the fact that, like it or not, their criticism of other blacks—whether or not accurate, or fair, or relevant—will gain them enhanced or super standing. In some instances, they may feel so strongly about an issue or an individual that there is no alternative to speaking out—despite the predictable consequences."

"I don't disagree," I responded, "but those who decide that, despite all, they must speak out against blacks who are threatening to whites, must not be surprised when blacks subjected to public criticism, cry 'Foul.' And when the black critics are later criticized themselves, this is not intended to—and certainly does not—silence the black speakers, as is claimed by Professor Stephen Carter.[30] After all, they now have enhanced or super standing. White people want to hear their views, almost ad nauseam. Rather, some of the rest of us are saying, 'Now, see what you have done. Knowing the consequences, you should have communicated your criticism in some other way.' "

"Is there an inconsistency," Geneva inquired, "in your opposition to blacks who gain enhanced standing by telling white people what they want to hear about blacks, and those like Minister Farrakhan who gain, if not standing, a kind of notoriety by telling whites what they least want to hear?"

"A good point," I conceded, "but I think the statements by Louis Farrakhan and other outspoken black militants are bold, impolitic, and sometimes outrageous precisely because they are intended for those blacks whose perilous condition places them beyond the courteous, the politic, even the civilities of racial and religious tolerance. These blacks need to hear their rage articulated by those able and willing to do so. They need reassurance that others, not they, are the cause of the wretched circumstances in which they live. Professor Lucius Barker makes this point when, while noting the large differences between whites and blacks

12

regarding attitudes toward Farrakhan, he warns: 'Sooner or later whites must understand that this type of rhetoric and behavior has been fostered by their own ongoing maltreatment of blacks in the American political-social order. As long as such conditions exist, blacks understandably find themselves more receptive to many types of rhetoric and promises of deliverance than would otherwise by the case.' "[31]

"The real paradox here," said Geneva, "is that while whites fear spokespersons like Minister Farrakhan, the risk posed by the Farrakhans in this country is as nothing compared with the risks to all arising from the conditions against which those Farrakhans rail in uncompromising terms."

"I have not talked to him, Geneva, but I rather imagine that Minister Farrakhan understands the rules of racial standing. He knows that abstract condemnation of racism and poverty and the devastation of our communities is inadequate and ineffective. He has decided that the only way to be heard over the racial-standing barrier is to place the blame for racism where it belongs. Using direct, blunt, even abrasive language, he forthrightly charges with evil those who do evil under the racial structure that protects them and persecutes us, that uplifts them regardless of merit and downgrades us regardless of worth."

Looking again at the final page of the text, I remembered the voice's warning that every gift has a price—a price confirmed in the Fifth Rule.

Fifth rule

True awareness requires an understanding of the Rules of Racial Standing. As an individual's understanding of these rules increases, there will be more and more instances where one can discern their workings. Using this knowledge, one gains the gift of prophecy about racism, its essence, its goals, even its remedies. The price of this knowledge is the frustration that follows recognition that no amount of public prophecy, no matter its accuracy, can either repeal the Rules of Racial Standing or prevent their operation.

I read the Fifth Rule, read it again, and then looked up at Geneva. "One more dilemma confronting black people and their leaders," I observed.

"It is that," Geneva agreed, "but notice that it reinforces rather than contradicts the admonition on the mountaintop computer screen: 'SPEAK UP, IKE, AN 'SPRESS YO'SE'F!'"

Notes

* In 1991, the Nation of Islam and its Abundant Life Clinic received a citation from the City of Washington, D.C., for expunging Washington's Mayfair Mansions of violent crack dealing. The Nation of Islam continues to patrol the area.[29]

1 Langston Hughes, "Note on Commercial Theatre," in *Selected Poems of Langston Hughes* (1990), 190.

2 "Encouragement," in *The Complete Poems of Paul Lawrence Dunbar* (1970), 296.

3 *Valley Forge Christian College* v. *Americans United*, 454 U.S. 464, 472 (1982) (organization dedicated to separation of church and state failed to identify any personal injury suffered by them as consequence of alleged constitutional error in transfer of federally owned property to religious organization without financial payment therefor).

4 Actually, the standing doctrine has often served as a barrier for blacks seeking relief from undeniable racial abuse: for example, in *Allen* v. *Wright*, 468 U.S. 737 (1984), the Court denied standing to black parents who contended that the Internal Revenue Service had not carried out its obligation to deny tax-exempt status to private schools practicing discrimination based on race as approved the year before in *Bob Jones University* v. *United States*, 461 U.S. 574 (1983). The Court in *Allen* cited *O'Shea* v. *Littleton*, 414 U.S. 488 (1974); *rizzo* v. *Goode*, 423 U.S. 362 (1975); and *City of Los Angeles* v. *Lyons*, 461 U.S. 95 (1983). In these cited cases, plaintiffs sought injunctive relief against systemwide law enforcement practices, but were denied standing for failing to allege a specific threat of being subjected to the challenged practices.

5 Ralph Ellison, *Invisible Man* (1947).

6 See *Batson* v. *Kentucky*, 476 U.S. 79 (1986) (enabling a criminal defendant to make out a prima-facie case of jury discrimination solely on the evidence concerning the prosecutor's exercise of the peremptory challenges at the defendant's trial).

7 *Commonwealth of Pennsylvania* v. *Local Union 542, International Union of Operating Engineers*, 388 F. Supp. 155 (E. D. Pa. 1974).

8 *Brown* v. *Board of Education*, 347 U.S. 483 (1954) (holding segregated schools unconstitutional).

9 Richard Kluger, *Simple Justice* (1975).

10 David Garrow, *Bearing the Cross: Martin Luther King, Jr., and the Southern Christian Leadership Conference* (1986); David J. Garrow, *The FBI and Martin Luther King, Jr.* (1983).

11 Taylor Branch, *Parting the Waters: America in the King Years, 1954–63* (1988).

12 Philip H. Melanson, *The MURKIN Conspiracy: An Investigation into the Assassination of Dr. Martin Luther King Jr.* (1989). Other important biographies include James A. Colaiaco, *Martin Luther King, Jr., Apostle of Militant Nonviolence* (1988); and Lionel Lokos, *House Divided: The Life and Legacy of Martin Luther King* (1968).

13 James H. Cone, *Martin & Malcolm & America* (1991); Vincent Harding, *Hope and History* (1990); Bernard C Watson, *We Shall Overcome: Martin Luther King, Jr., and the Black Freedom Struggle* (1990); C. Eric Lincoln, *Martin Luther King, Jr.: A Profile* (1985); Vincent Harding and Walter E. Fluker, *They Looked for a City* (1989); David L. Lewis, *King: A Biography* (1978); Lerone Bennett, Jr., *What Manner of Man: A Biography of Martin Luther King, Jr.* (1968); Louis E. Lomax, *To Kill a Black Man* (1968); and L. D. Reddick, *Crusader Without Violence: A Biography of Martin Luther King, Jr.* (1959).

14 Gloria Joseph, "The Incompatible Ménage à Trois: Marxism, Feminism, and Racism," cited in bell hooks, *Feminist Theory: from margin to center* (1984), 51.

15 bell hooks, *Yearning: Race, Gender, and Cultural Politics* (1990), 11.

16 See Randall Kennedy, "Racial Critiques of Legal Academia," *Harvard Law Review* 102 (1989): 1745.

17 See, for example, Randall Kennedy, "Race Relations Law and the Tradition of Celebration: The Case of Professor Schmidt," *Columbia Law Review* 86 (1986): 1622; "Commentary: Persuasion and Distrust: A Comment on the Affirmative Action Debate," *Harvard Law Review* 99 (1986): 1327; "Colloquy: A Reply to Philip Elman," *Harvard Law Review* 100 (1987): 1938; "McCleskey v. Kemp: Race, Capital Punishment, and the Supreme Court," *Harvard Law Review* 101 (1988): 1388.

18 Charles Rothfeld, "Minority Critic Stirs Debate on Minority Writing," *New York Times*, 5 January 1990, sec B, p. 6, col. 3.

19 Stephen L. Carter, *Reflections of an Affirmative Action Baby* (1991).

20 Ntozake Shange, *For colored girls who have considered suicide when the rainbow is enuf* (1975).

21 For a discussion of the criticism surrounding Alice Walker's 1982 book, *The Color Purple*, particularly criticism of the Steven Spielberg film based on the book, see bell hooks, *Yearning* (1990), 70–71, 176–79. See also Jack Matthews, "Three Color Purple Actresses Talk About Its Impact," *Los Angeles Times*, 31 January 1986, sec. 6, p. 1; Jack Matthews, "Some Blacks Critical of Spielberg's Purple" *Los Angeles Times,* 20 December 1985, sec. 6, p. 1; Clarence Page "Toward a New Black Cinema," *Chicago Tribune*, 12 January 1986 sec. 5, p. 3.

22 I Samuel 17:46.

23 Sam Roberts, "Blacks and Jews in New York Condemn Farrakhan's Views," *New York Times*, 4 October 1985, p. A1 , col. 2.

24 Ibid.

25 Ibid.

26 Lucius J. Barker, *Our Time Has Come: A Delegate's Diary of Jesse Jackson's 1984 Presidential Campaign* (1988), 62–87.

27 Bernard Weinraub, "Reagan Joins Kohl in Brief Memorial at Bitburg Graves," *New York Times*, 6 May 1985, p. A1.

28 hooks, *Yearning*, 11.

29 Nancy Lawson, "Paradise Revised: Development of a Drug-Free Success Story," *Washington Times*, 5 July 1991, sec. B, p. 3.

30 Stephen L. Carter, *Reflections of an Affirmative Action Baby* (1991).

31 Lucius J. Barker, *Our Time Has Come* (1988), 84.

23

COMPLICATING THE IMMIGRANT/INVOLUNTARY MINORITY TYPOLOGY

Margaret A. Gibson

Source: *Anthropology & Education Quarterly*, 28, 3, 1997, 431–454.

Drawing on both international and U.S. studies, this article takes stock of what recent ethnographic research on immigrant and involuntary minority youth reveals about variability in school performance. Empirical reality proves to be far more complex than what can be explained through dichotomous typologies of accommodation and resistance, success and failure, or immigrant and involuntary minorities. Moreover, minority youth do better in school when they feel strongly anchored in the identities of their families, communities, and peers and when they feel supported in pursuing a strategy of selective or additive acculturation.

Ogbu's typology and the five cases

In terms of the cases described in this issue, the findings are mixed with respect to the usefulness and applicability of John Ogbu's typology of immigrant and involuntary minorities (Ogbu 1983, 1987, 1991). The typology works better in what might be characterized as "new nations," traditional immigrant-receiving countries where a colonizing population from Europe conquered or displaced an indigenous group and subsequently has accepted and encouraged immigration. Countries of this type include Canada and Israel (Cummins this issue; Eisikovits this issue), as well as the United States, Australia, and New Zealand (Barrington 1991; Inglis 1992; Ogbu 1978, 1991). In each of these countries, the overall patterns of school achievement conform in certain key respects to what may be predicted from Ogbu's framework.

In Canada, immigrant students perform on the whole as well as or better than the dominant Anglo-Canadian group, while the First Nations and francophones, both involuntary minorities by Ogbu's criteria, perform less well (Cummins this issue). Not all Canadian groups fit the typology, however. Portuguese-speaking and Spanish-speaking students in Canada (both immigrant minorities) perform poorly in school, as do African Canadian students, who share attributes with both the immigrant and the involuntary minority groups.

The Israeli case is another example in which the involuntary minority group (Israeli Arabs) does significantly less well in school than the immigrant population as a whole. Eisikovits explains this disparity mainly in terms of the unequal nature of the two school systems, Jewish and Arab. In spite of the inferior quality of their schools, Arab students in fact do as well academically and persist in school longer than some of the immigrant Jewish groups, particularly those from North Africa and the Middle East. Moreover, although an involuntary minority, the Arab students have not formed an oppositional identity, nor are they resisting schooling. Their positive attitudes toward schooling may be due, Eisikovits suggests, to the fact that Arab students attend their own schools that are staffed by Arab teachers, contributing to an educational environment where Arab identity is reinforced. This relationship between minority-run schooling and identity reinforcement merits closer investigation and may have implications in other countries where members of a subordinate minority group attend their own separate schools.[1]

In the "old nations" of Europe—which once were the colonizers and only quite recently have themselves come to receive large numbers of immigrants from outside of Europe—the immigrant/involuntary minority typology fits less well. This is, in part, as van Zanten (this issue) points out, because the complex histories between European countries and their former colonies have blurred the distinctions between immigrant and involuntary minorities. Indeed, an immediate question arises as to whether migrants from former colonies are, by Ogbu's typology, to be considered immigrants or involuntary minorities. Each of the European articles includes one or more cases of this sort, where migrants from a former colony, now an independent country, have immigrated to and settled permanently in the country that formerly dominated them. In each case, namely the African Surinamese in the Netherlands, the Algerians in France, and the South Asians and African Caribbeans in Britain, the group's relationship to the host society is shaped by its colonial history. There emerges from these several cases no clear pattern with respect to school performance (as I will discuss further below).

Types of immigrants

Ogbu has suggested that immigrant minorities may have an adaptive advantage over those who have been incorporated involuntarily into the society in which they now reside (Ogbu 1978, 1991), and, as noted, in countries where both types of minorities reside, the quantitative findings do indicate that *in the aggregate* immigrant minorities are more successful in school than involuntary minorities. However, Ogbu's analysis has centered on one particular type of immigrant minority, namely those who have migrated voluntarily to a new country to enhance their economic opportunities and who enter the new country with full rights of permanent residence, and he has given less attention to how well his model pertains to other types of immigrants. Although a number of recent U.S. studies indicate that school success patterns for the children of refugees, undocumented aliens, and temporary workers may be similar to those of economic immigrants (Caplan et al. 1991; Gibson 1983a; McNall et al. 1994; Rumbaut 1995; Suárez-Orozco 1991a; Zhou and Bankston 1994), there is also evidence of great variability in the school performance of immigrant students. A number of different factors, including the immigrant group's reasons for leaving its homeland, its status in the new country, the context it encounters on arrival, and the nature of the resources available to the group, interact together to shape immigrant students' performance in school.

Economic immigrants

Those who immigrate primarily for economic reasons may be more willing than political refugees to adopt the ways of the new country, and they may view their children's adaptation as a necessary strategy for achieving their economic goals (Eisikovits this issue; van Zanten this issue). Even when economic immigrants view the socialization function of schooling to be at odds with the home culture, they may encourage their children to become competent in the ways of the dominant group so long as they do nothing to bring shame to their family's reputation. This strategy has been characterized as one of *accommodation and acculturation without assimilation* (Gibson 1988).

Refugees

Refugees, on the other hand, who at least initially may believe their stay in the new country to be only temporary, are less driven by economics and job aspirations. Anticipating a return to their homelands, they generally have less incentive to adopt the ways of the new country or to encourage their children to do so. In addition, the kind of schooling provided to refugees is influenced by host country assumptions regarding the nature and duration of the refugees' stay. In the United States, for example, the first waves of Cuban refugees attended special schools staffed by Cuban teachers where they received their instruction in Spanish. Government officials assumed that the Cubans needed to maintain their language and community so that they would be ready to return home when the time came. With the Indochinese refugees, the U.S. government pursued an entirely different policy. From the start, IndoChinese children were pressured to assimilate; schools set up at the resettlement camps were staffed by American teachers, the curriculum explicitly emphasized the teaching of American culture, and children were punished for speaking their home languages (Kelly 1981).

Guest workers

Guest workers, like refugees, although moving to the new country mainly for economic rather than political reasons, generally do not expect to remain permanently, and they may therefore have little incentive to integrate themselves into the larger society. As with refugees, the nature of schooling provided to the children of guest workers is influenced by whether or not the host country wishes these workers to settle permanently. In Belgium, for example, the status of Moroccan and Turkish workers has become increasingly problematic, with ultra-rightists calling for their repatriation and urging that their children be educated separately in their own languages to ready them for their return home (Roosens 1992). In France, too, there is increasing unease with immigrants who wish to retain their distinctive cultural identities (van Zanten this issue). In the United States, we are experiencing a similar backlash with mounting pressure to cut educational and other services to immigrants, both documented and undocumented (Macias 1996).

Undocumented workers

There is little social science literature on the school performance of undocumented immigrants, since, understandably, students without legal residence keep a low profile. My own early work in the U.S. Virgin Islands (Gibson 1983a, 1991a), where "aliens" in 1974 comprised nearly 40 percent of the total public school enrollment and where the work permits of many alien workers were known informally to have expired, offered some evidence that the children of undocumented workers sought to take full advantage of the educational opportunities available to them. They also manifested many of the attitudes and behaviors that have come to be characterized in the literature as an "immigrant orientation" to schooling (Gibson 1995a; Ogbu 1987, 1991). At the same time, because of their lack of papers, immigrant children are always at risk of exposure, and this reality influences their school experience. Furthermore, without the proof of legal residence that is required to enter college and to receive financial aid, both the academic effort and the career aspirations of undocumented students may show a decline as they approach the end of high school (Suárez-Orozco 1989, 1991a).

Migrants from former colonies

As previously noted, those who migrate from former colonies to the country that formerly colonized or conquered them cannot readily be classified as either immigrant or involuntary minorities. Moreover, based on the cases presented in this issue, we do not find that the group's prior colonial history has led necessarily to a conflicted or oppositional relationship between students and teachers. Nor do we find that the students whose parents and grandparents migrated from former colonies are necessarily disadvantaged in school when compared to other types of immigrant students. In fact, the evidence from the Netherlands and to a lesser degree from France indicates just the opposite: that the African Surinamese and Algerian students are doing better than some other immigrant groups and that these young people have benefited from their parents' prior knowledge of the language and culture of the host country.

In the Surinamese case, the children already speak Dutch fluently upon entering school, and for most it is the only language spoken at home. This is in sharp
contrast to the Turkish children, who speak mainly Turkish at home, and the
Moroccans, who speak mainly Berber or Arabic. Thus, the Turkish and Moroccan
children begin school with little competency in the Dutch language, placing them
at an early disadvantage in school compared to both the indigenous Dutch and the
children of Surinamese immigrants (Eldering this issue).

Other factors have assisted the African Surinamese in their adaptation to Dutch
society. Most important, perhaps, the first wave of Surinamese to come to the
Netherlands were members of an elite, free colored group who, following the
patterns of the white plantation owners, sent their children to the Netherlands for
higher education. They arrived with considerable resources at their command,
both economic and social, and, with university credentials and civil service eligibility in hand, those who remained have been able to obtain employment commensurate with their qualifications.

The more recent arrivals from Suriname, who now form the majority and who
came from far less privileged backgrounds than the initial wave, enjoyed the advantages of moving into a community where their compatriots had established a successful ethnic enclave. In addition, they arrived already understanding the Dutch
language and culture, and were familiar with the Dutch system of schooling.
Although not as successful as the indigenous Dutch, these later arrivals have done
comparatively well in school and better than immigrants from Turkey and Morocco.

It appears, based on the evidence at hand, that they have also been more
successful than immigrants from Aruba and the Netherlands Antilles. Like the
African Surinamese, the Arubans and Antilleans come from former Dutch colonies, are therefore familiar with the Dutch language and culture, and have prior
experience with Dutch schooling (Kromhout and Vedder 1996). While at the
primary level the mean reading and mathematics scores for Aruban and Antillean children are similar to those of the Surinamese, Kromhout and Vedder offer
evidence that some of these children are facing serious adjustment problems in
school that seem to be related to the oppositional nature of their relationship
with their former Dutch colonizers. Kromhout and Vedder point to the persistence of a "strong anti-Dutch sentiment" in the islands, forged throughout colonial history, which influences student attitudes toward the Dutch educational
system. Aruban and Antillean immigrants carry these anti-Dutch attitudes with
them to the Netherlands, where they are reinforced by fresh experiences of racism and discrimination (Kromhout and Vedder 1996:573).

Like the African Caribbeans in Britain (Gillborn this issue), but unlike the Surinamese (Eldering this issue), the Arubans and Antilleans are confronted by a host
society that views their presence in a negative light. Furthermore, the dynamics
at work in the school environment appear to reinforce negative attitudes held by
each group about the other. In addition, the most recent arrivals from Aruba and
the Antilles face severely limited opportunities for jobs. While the Surinamese
enjoy relatively full employment, close to the norm for the indigenous Dutch,

nearly 60 percent of the Antilleans and Arubans who have arrived since 1990 are currently unemployed (Kromhout and Vedder 1996).

Thus, while knowledge of the dominant language and culture is clearly an advantage for students who emigrate from former colonies, this alone is not sufficient to promote academic achievement and upward mobility. Conversely, beginning school with little or no knowledge of the new language and culture, while clearly an obstacle, is not a predictor of low achievement in school. Individual and family variables, as well as the specific context in which the immigrants find themselves on arrival, work together to shape the differing patterns of adaptation represented in this issue. The South Asians in Britain, for example, provide a case where many children, at least in the earlier years of immigration, arrived at school speaking only the home language, yet their performance on average has surpassed that of the African Caribbeans for whom English is the first language, and is similar to that of white British students of similar class backgrounds. As Gillborn suggests, an explanation of these differences lies in part in the nature of the racism and discrimination directed at each group, how these are experienced by the group, and by individual student responses to them.

Generational influences

In Ogbu's typology, a group is classified as immigrant or involuntary according to its initial terms of incorporation into a society, and variability from one generation to the next is not a focus of analysis. There is increasing evidence, however, that one's generation can have a major influence on perceptions of social identity, ethnic relations, and views of the opportunity structure. For the first generation, school performance is directly influenced by such factors as age on arrival, length of residence, the nature of previous schooling, and the support received in schools in the host country (Eisikovits this issue; Eldering this issue; Gibson 1991b; Macias 1990; Tomlinson 1991). The needs and vulnerabilities of the first generation, particularly those who began their schooling in another country, differ significantly from those of the second generation and beyond.

The ethnographic literature on immigrant youth depicts at least two distinctive patterns of adaptation. In the case of first-generation immigrants, researchers have focused on explaining how it is that large numbers of immigrant children are able to transcend the oftentimes very substantial cultural, linguistic, social, and economic barriers that stand in the way of their success in school (Caplan et al. 1991; Gibson 1983b, 1987b; Gibson and Ogbu 1991; Ogbu 1983,1987; Suárez-Orozco 1987, 1989; Sung 1979). As partial explanation, researchers have noted that immigrants often see formal education in their new country as more accessible, less expensive, and of higher quality than the education available to members of their social class in the old country. Newcomers, for a time at least, may also rationalize prejudice and discrimination as problems that could be anticipated when one moves to a new country, and that need not block their opportunity for improving their economic circumstances.

The second pattern concerns the immigrant and second-generation children who are experiencing the greatest difficulties in school. This body of research is more recent and has emerged in part as a response to the studies that show immigrant minority students to be more academically successful than involuntary minority students. Critics of these comparative studies suggest that findings on immigrant student success contribute to false stereotypes of immigrants as "successful" and of involuntary minorities as "unsuccessful." In actuality, of course, there is great variability within each category. Moreover, contrary to what may be inferred from Ogbu's model, the educational barriers faced by the children of immigrants are not always transitory in nature. Rather, as indicated in recent studies on the "new second generation," many U.S.-born children of immigrants are at risk of marginalization, delinquency, and school failure (Portes 1994).

These children generally endure the same economic hardships and discrimination as their parents, but they may not perceive the longer-term benefits of their sacrifice and hard labor in the same fashion (Suárez-Orozco and Suárez-Orozco 1995). In addition, there is increasing evidence that children of immigrants face the same kinds of vulnerabilities documented in the literature on involuntary minorities. Stacey Lee (1994) describes first-generation Asian immigrants whose negative experiences in U.S. schools have influenced them to reject all behaviors that would lead to academic achievement. Goto (1997) describes Chinese American students who empathize with the misbehavior and resistance of African American and Latino "homeboys." Hayes (1992) presents a case where the children of Mexican immigrants state that school offers them nothing; their behavior and attitudes in school resemble the patterns more typically associated with low-achieving involuntary minority students. A similar pattern has been documented in Europe. For example, Pieke (1991) describes circumstances in which Dutch Chinese students come to doubt the practical use of education and drop out of school. European scholars also speak of the children of immigrants as "involuntary immigrants" and "involuntary migrants," both because they did not choose to migrate and because these second-generation youths, in some instances, become absorbed into patterns of behavior that more generally have been associated with involuntary minorities (Eldering and Kloprogge 1989; Suárez-Orozco 1991b).

Segmented assimilation

Several recent studies indicate that among some immigrant groups school performance may actually decline across generations (Gibson 1995b; Portes and Rumbaut 1996; Suárez-Orozco and Suárez-Orozco 1995), and we can no longer assume a linear relationship between time spent in the United States and upward mobility. Rather, as the cases in this issue suggest, while some immigrants are following the traditional immigrant path of upward economic and social mobility, others may be headed into a permanent underclass. Alejandro Portes has coined the term *segmented assimilation* to characterize three contrasting assimilation patterns (Portes 1995; Portes and Rumbaut 1996; Portes and Zhou 1993).

22

The first pattern is the traditional model of linear assimilation upwards, whereby the immigrant group advances economically and is integrated socially and politically into the middle class. Cuban exiles in Miami are an example of this pattern (Portes and Stepick 1993); the African Surinamese in the Netherlands (Eldering this issue) provide another. A second type of assimilation leads downward into permanent poverty and assimilation into the underclass. Some Haitians in Miami risk this fate, as do some Mexican immigrants in California (Portes and Rumbaut 1996). The Moroccan and Turkish immigrants described by Eldering (this issue) fit this pattern as well, as do the Antilleans and Arubans who have only recently arrived in the Netherlands (Kromhout and Vedder 1996). The third pattern Portes characterizes variously as "selective acculturation" or "selective assimilation" or, following Gibson (1988), "accommodation and acculturation without assimilation." Primary features of this type are a strong ethnic enclave coupled with the deliberate preservation of the immigrant culture. A pattern of selective acculturation can lead, as with the traditional model of linear assimilation, to rapid mobility into the middle class. The Punjabi Sikhs in both Britain and the United States provide an example of this type (Gibson and Bhachu 1991); the Vietnamese in New Orleans and southern California provide another (Portes and Rumbaut 1996; Zhou and Bankston 1994).

To explain the pattern of downward assimilation, Portes and Rumbaut point to three risk factors that distinguish today's immigrants to the United States from those who arrived at the turn of the century: first, the changes that have occurred in the U.S. labor market; second, the skin color of the new immigrants; and third, the geographic location where the immigrants settle. As in the past, many immigrants arrive with few job skills and little formal education. Today, however, as a result of our postindustrial economy, unskilled workers can no longer move readily into factory jobs, receive training, and advance into higher-paying positions. Nor, due to the hourglass nature of today's economy, can we assume that the second generation will do better than their parents if only they learn English, persist through twelve years of school, and earn a high school diploma.

With respect to the second factor, nearly half of the children of immigrants residing in the United States today are nonwhite, which places them at risk of discrimination. As Portes and Rumbaut (1996) note, racial differences appear to be characteristics of individuals, but the meanings attached to these differences are created by the host society. Thus, for many of today's immigrants from Asia, Latin America, and the Caribbean, it has only been as a result of their moving to the United States that their skin color has become cause for stigmatization and discrimination. The third factor, geographic location, becomes a risk for those immigrants who, due to their initial poverty, are forced to settle in urban ghettos where they find themselves surrounded by crime, poverty, and high unemployment rates. As a result, their children may see few role models who offer an alternative to permanent poverty and membership in the underclass.

Contributors to this issue have identified similar risk factors. In the French and Dutch cases, van Zanten and Eldering describe how immigrants arriving in Europe today face a restructured economy that offers little hope for upward mobility to those lacking job skills. In addition, both cite the unequal and generally inferior nature of the schools attended by immigrant children. Gillborn describes how Caribbean and Asian children in Britain are made targets for discrimination based on the color of their skin. Van Zanten, on the other hand, indicates that in France acceptance of the high culture is a more important determinant of social acceptability than one's ethnic ancestry or racial features. In Canada the picture is more varied; although the African Canadian children suffer discrimination based on skin color, francophone children, who are white, also suffer discrimination (Cummins this issue).

Several other aspects of Portes and Rumbaut's (1996) framework bear on our analysis. Most notably, students who have neither the support of a strong ethnic enclave nor the support of parents who are themselves acculturating to their new surroundings at a pace similar to their children are at risk of "dissonant acculturation." As described by Portes and Rumbaut,

> Generational *dissonance* occurs when second generation acculturation is neither guided nor accompanied by changes in the first generation. This situation leads directly to role reversal in those instances when first-generation parents lack sufficient education or sufficient integration into the ethnic community to cope with the outside environment and hence must depend on their children's guidance. [1996:241]

Children particularly at risk of generational dissonance are those who live in poor neighborhoods, generally in urban areas, and who come into daily contact with alienated native youths. Very often the children of immigrants, wishing to be identified as "American" and not foreign, acculturate into the oppositional subcultures developed by marginalized minority youth (Portes and Zhou 1993:83). Examples of this pattern include some of the Haitian children in Miami, who feel pressured to choose between remaining "Haitian" and being looked down on by their African American peers on the one hand, or adopting an African American identity on the other hand, which in inner-city Miami generally carries with it counterschool attitudes and behaviors. Similar patterns have been documented in some Mexican American communities in California, where immigrant students who wish to be accepted by native-born Mexican peers may adopt a *cholo* identity and the antischool attitudes characteristic of many cholo youth (Matute-Bianchi 1991; Portes and Rumbaut 1996).[2] Dissonant acculturation need not always lead to poor school performance and a pattern of downward assimilation but, as Portes and Rumbaut observe, it increases the likelihood.

In sum, what this body of work suggests is that the children of immigrants are at increased risk of school failure and downward assimilation when they feel pressured to Americanize more rapidly than their parents and when their parents and ethnic community lack the cultural and social resources needed to guide their educational progress and to steer them away from a deviant path. However, where immigrant parents acculturate at the same pace as their children, which is more likely to happen in middle-class households, or where selective acculturation occurs while children remain strongly tied to the ethnic community, as was the case with the Punjabi Sikhs described by Gibson (1988), the likelihood for school success is enhanced. In other words, the best course for second-generation immigrant youth appears to be one that encourages them to remain securely anchored in their ethnic communities while pursuing a strategy of paced, selective acculturation.

Crossing cultural borders

Previous studies have indicated that immigrant students have an easier time than involuntary minorities in crossing language and cultural borders, which in turn facilitates their successful adaptation to school. To explain this phenomenon, Ogbu makes a distinction between "primary" and "secondary" cultural differences, primary differences being cultural traits that developed before contact, while secondary cultural differences are those that arise after contact as part of a minority group's adaptive response to its subordinate situation. Primary cultural differences, according to Ogbu's schema, are more readily transcended because they have not evolved, as in the case of secondary cultural differences, as "boundary-maintaining mechanisms in opposition to equivalent features in the culture of the dominant group and the schools they control" (Ogbu 1987:327).

The ethnographic literature does lend support to the conclusion that academically successful immigrants are aided in navigating across cultural borders by an additive view of acculturation. In other words, the children of immigrants often regard the acquisition of school knowledge and competence in the dominant culture as *additional* skills to be drawn upon as appropriate rather than as a replacement for their primary culture (Gibson 1988,1995a; Hoffman 1988; Matute-Bianchi 1991; Suárez-Orozco 1989; Vigil 1997; Vigil and Long 1981). Likewise, there is evidence that involuntary minority students experience the pressures placed on them in school to conform to the dominant culture as a threat to their identities. Forced, as some feel they are, to choose between conformity in school and the maintenance of their language and identity, they may elect to resist teacher authority and school rules (Deyhle 1991; Fordham and Ogbu 1987; Gibson 1982; Kleinfeld 1983; Kramer 1983; Matute-Bianchi 1991; Ogbu 1987,1991; Petroni 1970).

While these portrayals of involuntary minority youth feeling pressured to choose between loyalty to their home culture and academic success may be accurate, they can lead all too readily to faulty and potentially stereotypical conclusions. First, without looking at the full range of variability that occurs within a particular group, it can appear that only the involuntary minorities experience conflict between home and school cultures or have difficulty moving back and forth across cultural borders. Second, such a conclusion can lead us to link student resistance with involuntary status and accommodation with voluntary status

(Goto 1997; S. Lee 1994), and in similar fashion, to link student resistance with failure and accommodation with success. Neither is accurate.

Empirical reality is far more complex than what can be explained through dichotomous typologies of accommodation and resistance, success and failure, or immigrant and involuntary minorities. In actuality, many involuntary minority students do well academically and many immigrant students do poorly. Similarly, we find accommodating behavior among involuntary minorities (Mehan et al. 1994) and resistant behavior among immigrants (Goto 1997; Ima 1995; Kromhout and Vedder 1996; S. Lee 1994; Pieke 1991). We also find qualities associated with one type or the other, immigrant or involuntary, exhibited by the same student (Gillborn this issue) or by siblings in the same family.

Moreover, primary cultural differences, while neutral to begin with, can become politically charged in their meanings and can become grounds for serious conflicts between immigrant students and school authorities. For example, Muslim children in Europe resist school rules and school authority when pressured to conform to the dominant culture and to set aside symbols of their ethnic and religious identities such as the *heijab* (headscarves) worn by Muslim girls (Eldering this issue; Roosens 1992; van Zanten this issue). The critical factor for the Muslim students seems not to be the origin of the differences—whether the cultural trait developed before or after contact—but rather that the differences are viewed as markers of identity. Because they are viewed by Muslim students as important symbols of their identity, not to be compromised or sacrificed, they become a source of conflict in school if teachers pressure students to conform to the dominant culture as, for example, in removing the headscarves. Thus, Muslim children may come to experience transitions between home and school not as neutral acts of switching between two cultural systems but as politically charged border crossings that all too readily can become the source of intergroup tension and lead to acts of student defiance and resistance.

Resistance within accommodation

In the British case, Gillborn (this issue) looks specifically at student strategies for dealing with assimilationist and racist pressures in school. Drawing on his own research and that of other British ethnographers, he notes that minority students can be successful academically without being conformists and without rejecting their ethnicity. Adopting Mac an Ghaill's (1988) term, Gillborn describes their strategy as one of *resistance within accommodation,* a concept similar to my notion *of accommodation and acculturation without assimilation* (Gibson 1988) although more focused on individual than group agency. As Gillborn rightly points out, a simple dichotomy between "resistance" and "conformity" overlooks the complexity of student behaviors and responses. Accommodation is not the only path to success in school, nor does opposition necessarily lead to failure (Davidson 1996). Students may resist what they perceive as acts of oppression within school while at the same time pursue strategies that enable them to be academically successful. High academic performance need not imply conformity, nor must it entail the rejection of one's identity.

Gender differences

Neither Ogbu's typology of immigrant and involuntary minorities nor Portes's model of segmented assimilation takes sufficient account of the role that gender plays in shaping student identity, school experience, and academic performance. Yet there is mounting evidence that in some ethnic groups girls remain in school longer and receive higher grades than boys, while in others their performance lags behind that of their brothers (Gibson 1991b; Rumbaut 1994, 1995; Tomlinson 1991). As cases in this issue suggest, the girls who persist in school often have a strong rationale for doing so.

In Israel, first-generation immigrant girls, regardless of their age at immigration, are more likely to complete high school than boys. This pattern is related to the fact that the girls cannot obtain employment without a high school diploma while boys can (Eisikovits this issue). Likewise, in the Netherlands, African Surinamese girls state that a diploma is their "most reliable husband," and they persist in school as an avenue to economic independence (Eldering this issue). I have described a similar pattern for African Caribbean girls in the U.S. Virgin Islands (1983a, 1991a), and there is evidence that the pattern holds as well for West Indian girls in the continental United States (Waters 1996).

For young Asian Indian women, we find that school qualifications prove instrumental not only in leading to employment but also in helping to arrange "good" marriages (Eldering this issue; Gibson and Bhachu 1991). Similarly, in Belgium, the strong academic performance of Spanish girls has been attributed to the very high instrumental value that girls, as well as their parents, accord to schooling (Roosens and Martin 1992). School may also be viewed as a liberating force, influencing girls to remain in school even when they are not strong students, as is the case for some North African girls in France (van Zanten this issue).

Other groups have different strategies for "getting ahead" that may not place the same high value on educational credentials. For example, Portuguese girls in France and Moroccan and Turkish girls in the Netherlands expect to take up more traditional roles in the home after they leave school and therefore have little motivation to pursue the tougher academic classes that will prepare them for university admission (Eldering this issue; van Zanten this issue). In both Belgium and the Netherlands, Moroccan girls are discouraged by parents from remaining in school past their mid-teens (Cammaert 1992; Eldering this issue; Roosens n.d.). Instead, they are pressured to invest their energies into becoming successful within the traditional Islamic culture and to marry at an early age. As a result, many girls lose their motivation to succeed academically, believing they will be unable to continue with their studies.

These differing school-adaptation patterns highlight the influence of family and community forces on the decisions that girls make with respect to their course of study and the effort they invest in their studies. In addition, they underscore the dynamic nature of student success strategies and how they change over time and in response to new circumstances. In the Netherlands and Belgium, where traditional values have persisted among Moroccan Berbers and "too much" schooling for girls is seen as conflicting with family responsibilities, some of the girls negotiate a path that enables them to remain in school (Eldering this issue). Likewise, in France, Moroccan and Algerian girls today persist in school because it is for them a means of "liberation," helping them to forge new identities separate from those of their mothers (van Zanten this issue).

Several cases in this issue suggest that boys may have a more difficult time than girls in accommodating themselves to school rules while simultaneously seeking to secure and maintain their reputation within peer networks. There is some evidence in France, for example, that North African males are deliberately resisting school. Although perceived as individual acts of student defiance, the boys' actions may in fact represent their collective opposition to unequal treatment in school and to the devaluing of their distinctive identities by school authorities (van Zanten this issue). A similar pattern has been observed in Belgium, where North African males who resist the forces for cultural assimilation are those who come into greatest conflict with school authorities (Roosens n.d.). Other studies point to a pattern of classroom misbehavior among Italian schoolboys that may represent their opposition to pressures placed on them to give up their home cultures and distinctive identities (Malhotra 1985; Ware 1935).

Among lower-class African Caribbean youths in Britain, Canada, and the United States, there is evidence that the behaviors that bring males into conflict with their teachers are also those that gain males respect with their peers (Gibson 1982, 1991a; Gillborn this issue; Solomon 1992). Similar patterns have been documented among African American males (Fordham 1996). Like the North African boys in France and Belgium, African American and African Caribbean boys may have a harder time than their sisters crossing cultural borders and accommodating themselves to school rules, particularly when they feel their identities are being devalued (Fordham 1996; Waters 1996).

More research is needed in this area, but the evidence suggests that in some school settings young black and brown men are viewed as a greater threat by teachers than young black and brown women, and thus, the school experiences of boys may be qualitatively different. Feeling their identities threatened, boys may be more likely than girls to resist school authority and to manifest symbols of an oppositional identity, actions which in turn place them at further risk of failing in school (Solomon 1992, quoted in Cummins this issue). Boys, at least in some contexts, may also experience more peer pressure to reject school achievement than girls (Fordham 1996; Gibson 1982).

School effects

Drawing on findings from a major study of 20 multiethnic schools in Britain, Sally Tomlinson has suggested that "the school a child attends makes more difference to performance and attainment than ethnicity" (1991:121). Although the cases included in this issue were not similarly focused on school effects, each of the authors has pointed to the impact of educational policies and programs on the school performance of immigrant and minority students, citing as explanations for poor performance the all-too-familiar problems of unequal schools in ghetto neighborhoods, white flight, "dustbin classes," teacher prejudice, academic tracking, discontinuities between students' home and school lives, and inadequate instructional placements for newly arrived immigrant students. All these factors work to devalue student identities and contribute to their generally low academic performance.

Receiving countries, as Eisikovits (this issue) observes, often adopt a compensatory model for newcomers, lumping all of them together in common classes and overlooking the very important differences in students' cultural and educational histories. Van Zanten (this issue) notes that immigrant children are often placed in schools with poor facilities, inadequate instructional materials, and unmotivated teachers, all factors that contribute to poor performance and student resistance. Eldering (this issue) observes that the children of immigrants are frequently concentrated in schools attended mainly by immigrants and staffed by teachers who lack adequate training for working with these populations. Cummins (this issue) likewise points to school factors, including teachers' low expectations, their insensitivity to issues of ethnic and racial diversity, and a curriculum that fails to reflect the cultural worlds of the students, as explanation for the poor performance of certain groups of minority students. Gillborn, as earlier noted, identifies teachers' racist attitudes as a major factor contributing to the poor performance of some minority students.

The authors also discuss how educational policies in their respective countries have shifted over time in response to their increasingly diverse populations. Although, as in the United States, past policies have emphasized cultural assimilation, there appears to be an increasing crossnational awareness of the shortcomings of this approach and a recognition of the need for educational programs and policies that are responsive to cultural and ethnic diversity. In the Netherlands, ideological discourse now centers on the dual goals of "equality of opportunity" and the "equivalence of cultures" (Eldering this issue). Likewise, in Israel, educational programs have become increasingly concerned with the social and cultural adjustment of students, as well as with their academic attainments. In keeping with these twin goals, Israeli educators now give explicit attention to how immigrant children experience the acculturation process in an effort to cause the least possible damage to students' cultural identities (Eisikovits this issue).

Identity, power relations, and school performance

A group's original terms of incorporation, while significant, are but one of the variables that shape the school-adaptation patterns of immigrant and involuntary minority students. Academic engagement, as indicated by the cases in this issue and by other recent studies, depends not only on historical, political, and economic realities facing students and their families, but also on their day-to-day experiences at school (Davidson 1996). Thus, to focus on whether a particular ethnic group should be categorized as voluntary or involuntary is not the appropriate question and is probably not one that can be answered for many groups. A more productive approach is to take stock of what the comparative research on immigrant and involuntary minorities reveals about the factors that serve either to promote or to impede success in school and to determine how this knowledge can be utilized in our efforts to improve educational practice.

A major finding to emerge from the international cases presented here, as well as related U.S. studies, is that minority students do better in school when they feel strongly anchored in the identities of their families, communities, and peers and when they feel supported in pursuing a strategy of selective or additive acculturation. Attention to additive or selective acculturation, or what Hoffman (1988) characterizes as "cultural eclecticism" in her study of Iranian students, emerged initially in discussions of the school success patterns of first- and second-generation immigrant students (Gibson 1987a, 1988). More recently, a similar strategy has been documented among involuntary minorities (Deyhle 1995; Mehan et al. 1996). In her research on Navajo youth, Deyhle has found that the most academically successful students are those who feel most securely rooted in their traditional culture (Deyhle 1995:408). Conversely, those at greatest risk of failure in school are those who "feel disenfranchised from their culture *and* at the same time experience racial conflict" (Deyhle 1995:419–420, emphasis added). Deyhle notes moreover that differences between home and school cultures become sources for conflict in the school setting because of the unequal and coercive nature of power relations.

Cummins speaks directly to the issue of unequal power relations in the Canadian case (this issue). Noting that education is a political as well as a cultural process, he observes that it is the legacy of coercive power relations that leads to persistent problems in school for minority students. This is because schools tend to perpetuate inequalities that exist in the larger society through school environments that reinforce for minority students the unequal nature of power relations and the subtractive and antagonistic modes of acculturation that generate both resistance to school authority and disengagement with academic learning. Lewis made a similar observation more than two decades ago, noting that if multicultural education is to serve the needs of minority students, it must address issues of group subordination and the ways in which "differential power relations influence the individual's acquisition of culture" (1976:33).

Like Lewis, Cummins calls upon educators to transform the structure of interactions at school, including the ways that knowledge and power are distributed, as a means to enhancing academic achievement (see also Erickson 1987). What is needed are learning environments that support additive or empowering forms of acculturation and teacher-student relations based on collaboration rather than coercion. Moreover, we need to create environments in school that encourage students to build upon and add to their current cultural repertoires and that support

30

student identities while also encouraging students to put forth the effort necessary to be succeed academically (Davidson 1996; Gibson 1995c).

Cultural-identity formation for minority youth is not simply a matter of pre-serving a cultural tradition handed down from one's parents. Nor are student iden-tities and responses to schooling determined by one's status as either a voluntary or involuntary minority. Rather, student identities are constantly negotiated and transformed through the experiences that students have in school and in their lives outside of school (S. Lee 1996). In fact, as adolescents move between their home, school, and peer worlds they need opportunities in which to create multiple identi-ties and to "play" in creative ways with these identities (Hall 1995; Phelan et al. 1993). For minority youth, this process of identity formation and transformation is an inherently political one because of the unequal nature of power relations that exist in schools.

Thus, our efforts to build better schools need to be informed by a fuller under-standing of the relationships that exist between youth identities, the structure of power relations within school settings, and students' academic engagement. In addition, efforts to create classroom environments that support both collaborative and additive forms of learning need to be accompanied by a paradigmatic shift in the way school success is defined. Rather than viewing cultural and linguis-tic differences as "inputs" to be accommodated in school programs, we must, as Eisikovits (this issue) suggests, measure school success in terms of the plurality of cultural "outputs" and the ability of students to move successfully between their multiple cultural worlds.

Notes

1 The wider implications of this finding were pointed out to me by Kathryn Anderson-Levitt.
2 Matute-Bianchi was referring to several categories of alienated Mexican-descent stu-dents who "tend not to participate in school activities, exhibit poor attendance and per-formance in class and are usually described by teachers and staff as being unsuccessful or uninterested in school.... Often they will call themselves 'homeboys' or 'homegirls'" while their more academically-inclined Mexican peers are referred to as "schoolboys" and "schoolgirls." Cholas and cholos, who are distinguishable by their manner of dress, walk, and speech, are often viewed as gang members or gang sympathizers, although, as Matute-Bianchi points out, not all those who manifest the stylistic symbols of the cholo are in fact members of a gang (Matute-Bianchi 1991:218–220).

References cited

Barrington, John M.
1991 The New Zealand Experience: Maoris. *In* Minority Status and Schooling: A Com-parative Study of Immigrant and Involuntary Minorities. Margaret A. Gibson and John U. Ogbu, eds. Pp. 309–326. New York: Garland Publishing.
Caplan, Nathan, Marcella H. Choy, and John K. Whitmore
1991 Children of the Boat People: A Study of Educational Success. Ann Arbor: University of Michigan Press.

Cammaert, Marie-France
1992 Fighting for Success: Berber Girls in Higher Education. *In* The Insertion of Allochthonous Youngsters in Belgian Society. Eugeen Roosens, ed. Theme issue. Migration 15:83–102.

Davidson, Ann Locke
1996 Making and Molding Identity in Schools: Student Narratives on Race, Gender, and Academic Engagement. Albany: SUNY Press.

Deyhle, Donna
1991 Empowerment and Cultural Conflict: Navajo Parents and the Schooling of their Children. International Journal of Qualitative Studies in Education 4(4):277–297.
1995 Navajo Youth and Anglo Racism: Cultural Integrity and Resistance. Harvard Educational Review 65(3):23–67.

Eldering, Lotty
1989 Ethnic Minority Children in Dutch Schools: Underachievement and Its Explanations. *In* Different Cultures, Same School: Ethnic Minority Children in Europe. Lotty Eldering and Jo Kloprogge, eds. Pp. 107–136. Berwyn, PA: Swets North America.

Eldering, Lotty, and Jo Kloprogge, eds.
1989 Different Cultures, Same School: Ethnic Minority Children in Europe. Berwyn, PA: Swets North America.

Erickson, Frederick
1987 Transformation and School Success: The Politics and Culture of Educational Achievement. *In* Explaining the School Performance of Minority Students. Evelyn Jacob and Cathie Jordan, eds. Theme issue. Anthropology and Education Quarterly 18:335–356.

Foley, Douglas E.
1991 Reconsidering Anthropological Explanations of Ethnic School Failure. Anthropology and Education Quarterly 22:60–86.

Fordham, Signithia
1996 Blacked Out: Dilemmas of Race, Identity, and Success at Capital High. Chicago: University of Chicago Press.

Fordham, Signithia, and John U. Ogbu
1987 Black Students' School Success: Coping with the "Burden of Acting White." Urban Review 18(3):176–206.

Gibson, Margaret A.
1978 Down Islander Responses to Schooling in the United States Virgin Islands. *In* Perspectives in West Indian Education. Norma A. Niles Gardner and Trevor Gardner, eds. Pp. 50–67. East Lansing: West Indian Association, Michigan State University.
1982 Reputation and Respectability: How Competing Cultural Systems Affect Students' Performance in School. Anthropology and Education Quarterly 13:3–27.
1983a Ethnicity and Schooling: West Indian Immigrants in the United States Virgin Islands. Ethnic Groups 5(3):173–198.
1983b Home-School-Community Linkages: A Study of Educational Opportunity for Punjabi Youth. Final Report. Washington, DC: National Institute of Education.
1987a Playing by the Rules. *In* Education and Cultural Process. 2nd edition. George D. Spindler, ed. Pp. 274–281. Prospect Heights, IL: Waveland Press.
1987b The School Performance of Immigrant Minorities: A Comparative View. *In* Explaining the School Performance of Minority Students. Evelyn Jacob and Cathie Jordan, eds. Theme issue. Anthropology and Education Quarterly 18:262–275.

1988 Accommodation without Assimilation: Sikh Immigrants in an American High School. Ithaca, NY: Cornell University Press.

1991a Ethnicity, Gender and Social Class: The School Adaptation Patterns of West Indian Youths. *In* Minority Status and Schooling: A Comparative Study of Immigrant and Involuntary Minorities. Margaret A. Gibson and John U. Ogbu, eds. Pp. 169–203. New York: Garland Publishing.

1991b Minorities and Schooling: Some Implications. *In* Minority Status and Schooling: A Comparative Study of Immigrant and Involuntary Minorities. Margaret A. Gibson and John U. Ogbu, eds. Pp. 357–381. New York: Garland Publishing.

1995a Additive Acculturation as a Strategy for School Improvement. *In* California's Immigrant Children: Theory, Research, and Implications for Educational Policy. Rubén G. Rumbaut and Wayne A. Cornelius, eds. Pp. 77–105. La Jolla: Center for U.S.-Mexican Studies, University of California, San Diego.

1995b Whither the Class of '95: Mexican-Origin Students in a California High School. *In* Latinos in California: Report of Activities Funded by the University of California Committee on Latino Research, 1990–1995. Kathryn L. Roberts, ed. Pp. 58–60. Riverside, CA: University of California Institute for Mexico and the United States (UC MEXUS).

1995c Promoting Additive Acculturation in Schools. Multicultural Education 3(1):11–12, 54.

Gibson, Margaret A., and Parminder K. Bhachu

1991 The Dynamics of Educational Decision Making. *In* Minority Status and Schooling: A Comparative Study of Immigrant and Involuntary Minorities. Margaret A. Gibson and John U. Ogbu, eds. Pp. 63–95. New York: Garland Publishing.

Gibson, Margaret A., and John U. Ogbu, eds.

1991 Minority Status and Schooling: A Comparative Study of Immigrant and Involuntary Minorities. New York: Garland Publishing.

Goto, Stanford T.

1997 Nerds, Normal People, and Homeboys: Accommodation and Resistance among Chinese American Students. Anthropology and Education Quarterly 28:70–84.

Hall, Kathleen

1995 "There's a Time to Act English and a Time to Act Indian": The Politics of Identity among British-Sikh Teenagers. *In* Children and the Politics of Culture. Sharon Stephens, ed. Pp. 243–264. Princeton, NJ: Princeton University Press.

Hayes, Katherine G.

1992 Attitudes toward Education: Voluntary and Involuntary Immigrants from the Same Families. Anthropology and Education Quarterly 23:250–267.

Hirschman, Charles

1994 Problems and Prospects of Studying Immigrant Adaptation from the 1990 Population Census: From Generational Comparisons to the Process of "Becoming American." *In* The New Second Generation. Alejandro Portes, ed. Theme issue. International Migration Review 28(4):690–713.

Hoffman, Diane M.

1988 Cross-Cultural Adaptation and Learning: Iranians and Americans at School. *In* School and Society. Henry T. Trueba and Concha Delgado-Gaitan, eds. Pp. 163–180. New York: Praeger.

Ima, Kenji

1995 Testing the American Dream: Case Studies of At-Risk Southeast Asian Refugee Students in Secondary Schools. *In* California's Immigrant Children: Theory, Research, and Implications for Educational Policy. Rubén G. Rumbaut and Wayne A.

Cornelius, eds. Pp. 191–208. La Jolla: Center for U.S.-Mexican Studies, University of California, San Diego.

Inglis, Christine
1992 Variability in Minority Students' Educational Attainment in Australia. Paper presented at the American Anthropological Association's Annual Meeting, San Francisco, December.

Jacob, Evelyn, and Cathie Jordan, eds.
1987 Explaining the School Performance of Minority Students. Theme issue. Anthropology and Education Quarterly 18.
1993 Minority Education: Anthropological Perspectives. Norwood, NJ: Ablex Publishing.

Kao, Grace, and Marta Tienda
1995 Optimism and Achievement: The Educational Performance of Immigrant Youth. Social Science Quarterly 76(1):1–19.

Kelly, Gail
1981 Contemporary American Policies and Practices in the Education of Immigrant Children. *In* Educating Immigrants. Jotti Bhatnagar, ed. Pp. 214–232. New York: St. Martin's Press.

Kleinfeld, Judith
1983 First Do No Harm: A Reply to Courtney Cazden. Anthropology and Education Quarterly 14:282–287.

Kramer, Betty Jo
1983 The Dismal Record Continues: The Ute Indian Tribe and the School System. Ethnic Groups 5(3):151–71.

Kromhout, Mariska, and Paul Vedder
1996 Cultural Inversion in Afro-Caribbean Children in the Netherlands. Anthropology and Education Quarterly 27:568–586.

Lee, Stacey J.
1994 Behind the Model-Minority Stereotype: Voices of High- and Low-Achieving Asian American Students. Anthropology and Education Quarterly 25:413–429.
1996 Unraveling the "Model Minority" Stereotype: Listening to Asian American Youth. New York: Teachers College Press.

Lee, Yongsook
1991 Koreans in Japan and the United States. *In* Minority Status and Schooling: A Comparative Study of Immigrant and Involuntary Minorities. Margaret A. Gibson and John U. Ogbu, eds. Pp. 131–167. New York: Garland Publishing.

Lewis, Diane K.
1976 The Multicultural Education Model and Minorities: Some Reservations. Anthropology and Education Quarterly 7:32–37.

Mac an Ghaill, Mairtin
1988 Young, Gifted and Black. Milton Keynes, England: Open University Press.

Macias, Jose
1990 Scholastic Antecedents of Immigrant Students: Schooling in a Mexican Immigrant-Sending Community. Anthropology and Education Quarterly 21:291–318.

Macias, Jose, ed.
1996 Racial and Ethnic Exclusion in Education and Society. Theme issue. Anthropology and Education Quarterly 27.

Malhotra, M.K.
1985 Research Report: The Educational Problems of Foreign Children of Different Nationalities in West Germany. Ethnic and Racial Studies 8(2):291–299.

Mar'i, Sami K.
1978 Arab Education in Israel. New York: Syracuse University Press.

Matute-Bianchi, Maria Eugenia
1986 Ethnic Identities and Patterns of School Success and Failure among Mexican-Descent and Japanese-American Students in a California High School. American Journal of Education 95(1):233–255.

1991 Situational Ethnicity and Patterns of School Performance among Immigrant and Nonimmigrant Mexican-Descent Students. In Minority Status and Schooling: A Comparative Study of Immigrant and Involuntary Minorities. Margaret A. Gibson and John U. Ogbu, eds. Pp. 205–247. New York: Garland Publishing.

McNall, Miles, Timothy Dunnigan, and Jeylan T. Mortimer
1994 The Education Achievement of the St. Paul Hmong. Anthropology and Education Quarterly 25:44–65.

Mehan, Hugh, Lea Hubbard, and Irene Villanueva
1994 Forming Academic Identities: Accommodation without Assimilation among Involuntary Minorities. Anthropology and Education Quarterly 25:91–117.

Mehan; Hugh, Irene Villanueva, Lea Hubbard, and Angela Lintz
1996 Constructing School Success: The Consequences of Untracking Low-Achieving Students. Cambridge: Cambridge University Press.

Ogbu, John U.
1974 The Next Generation: An Ethnography of Education in an Urban Neighborhood. New York: Academic Press.

1978 Minority Education and Caste: The American System in Cross-Cultural Perspective. New York: Academic Press.

1983 Minority Status and Schooling in Plural Societies. Comparative Education Review 27(2):168–190.

1987 Variability in Minority School Performance: A Problem in Search of an Explanation. In Explaining the School Performance of Minority Students. Evelyn Jacob and Cathie Jordan, eds. Theme issue. Anthropology and Education Quarterly 18:312–334.

1991 Immigrant and Involuntary Minorities in Comparative Perspective. In Minority Status and Schooling: A Comparative Study of Immigrant and Involuntary Minorities. Margaret A. Gibson and John U. Ogbu, eds. Pp. 3–33. New York: Garland Publishing.

1995 Understanding Cultural Diversity and Learning. In Handbook of Research on Multicultural Education. James A. Banks, ed. Pp. 582–593. New York: Macmillan Publishing.

Ogbu, John U., and Herbert D. Simons
n.d. Voluntary and Involuntary Minorities: Toward a Cultural-Ecological Theory of School Performance: Some Implications for Education. Unpublished MS submitted to *AEQ*.

Olneck, Michael R.
1995 Immigrants and Education. In Handbook of Research on Multicultural Education. James A. Banks, ed. Pp. 310–327. New York: Macmillan Publishing.

Petroni, F.A.
1970 UncleToms: White Stereotypes in the Black Movement. Human Organization 29(4):260–266.

Phelan, Patricia, Ann L. Davidson, and Hanh Cao Yu
1993 Students' Multiple Worlds: Navigating the Borders of Family, Peer, and School Cultures. In Renegotiating Cultural Diversity in American Schools. Patricia Phelan and Ann L. Davidson, eds. Pp. 52–88. New York: Teachers College Press.

Pieke, Frank N.

1991 Chinese Educational Achievement and "Folk Theories of Success." *In* Migration, Minority Status, and Education: European Dilemmas and Responses in the 1990s. Marcelo Suárez-Orozco, ed. Theme issue. Anthropology and Education Quarterly 22:162–180.

Portes, Alejandro

1995 Segmented Assimilation among New Immigrant Youth: A Conceptual Framework. *In* California's Immigrant Children: Theory, Research, and Implications for Educational Policy. Rubén G. Rumbaut and Wayne A. Cornelius, eds. Pp. 71–76. La Jolla: Center for U.S.-Mexican Studies, University of California, San Diego.

Portes, Alejandro, ed.

1994 The New Second Generation. Theme issue. International Migration Review 28(4).

Portes, Alejandro, and Ruben G Rumbaut

1996 Immigrant America. 2nd edition. Berkeley: University of California Press.

Portes, Alejandro, and Alex Stepick

1993 City on the Edge: The Transformation of Miami. Berkeley: University of California Press.

Portes, Alejandro, and Min Zhou

1993 The New Second Generation: Segmented Assimilation and Its Variants among Post-1965 Immigrant Youth. Annals of the American Academy of Political and Social Science 530:74–98.

Romo, Harriett

1984 The Mexican Origin Population's Differing Perceptions of their Children's Schooling. Social Science Quarterly 65(2):635–650.

Roosens, Eugeen

n.d. Young "Newcomers" in Belgium: School Experience and Social Integration. Unpublished manuscript Centre for Social and Cultural Anthropology, Catholic University of Leuven, Leuven, Belgium.

Roosens, Eugeen, ed.

1992 The Insertion of Allochthonous Youngsters in Belgian Society. Theme issue. Migration 15.

Roosens, Eugeen, and Aldo Martin

1992 Ethno-Cultural Orientation and School Results. A Case Study: Spanish Youngsters in Antwerp. *In* The Insertion of Allochthonous Youngsters in Belgian Society. Eugeen Roosens, ed. Theme issue. Migration 15:17–37.

Rumbaut, Rubén G.

1994 The Crucible Within: Ethnic Identity, Self-Esteem, and Segmented Assimilation among Children of Immigrants. *In* The New Second Generation. Alejandro Portes, ed. Theme issue. International Migration Review 28(4):748–794.

1995 The New Californians: Comparative Research Findings on the Educational Progress of Immigrant Children. *In* California's Immigrant Children: Theory, Research, and Implications for Educational Policy. Rubén G. Rumbaut and Wayne A. Cornelius, eds. Pp. 17–69. La Jolla: Center for U.S.-Mexican Studies, University of California, San Diego.

Solomon, Patrick

1992 Black Resistance in a High School: Forging a Separatist Culture. New York: SUNY Press.

Suárez-Orozco, Marcelo M.
1987 "Becoming Somebody": Central American Immigrants in U.S. Inner-City Schools. *In* Explaining the School Performance of Minority Students. Evelyn Jacob and Cathie Jordan, eds. Theme issue. Anthropology and Education Quarterly 18:287–299.
1989 Central American Refugees and U.S. High Schools: A Psychosocial Study of Motivation and Achievement. Stanford, CA: Stanford University Press.
1991a Immigrant Adaptation to Schooling: A Hispanic Case. *In* Minority Status and Schooling: A Comparative Study of Immigrant and Involuntary Minorities. Margaret A. Gibson and John U. Ogbu, eds. Pp. 37–61. New York: Garland Publishing.
Suárez-Orozco, Marcelo M., ed.
1991b Migration, Minority Status, and Education: European Dilemmas and Responses in the 1990s. Theme issue. Anthropology and Education Quarterly 22:99–120.
Suárez-Orozco, Carola, and Marcelo Suárez-Orozco
1995 Transformations: Migration, Family Life, and Achievement Motivation among Latino Adolescents. Stanford, CA: Stanford University Press.
Sung, Betty Lee
1979 Transplanted Chinese Children. Report to the Administration for Children. Youth and Family. Washington, DC: Department of Health, Education and Welfare.
Tomlinson, Sally
1991 Ethnicity and Educational Attainment in England—An Overview. Anthropology and Education Quarterly 22:121–139.
Trueba, Henry T.
1988 Culturally Based Explanations of Minority Students' Academic Achievement. Anthropology and Education Quarterly 22:270–287.
1991 Comments on Foley's "Reconsidering Anthropological Explanations of Ethnic School Failure." Anthropology and Education Quarterly 22:87–94.
Tuan, Mia
1995 Korean and Russian Students in a Los Angeles High School: Exploring the Alternative Strategies of Two High-Achieving Groups. *In* California's Immigrant Children: Theory, Research, and Implications for Educational Policy. Rubén G. Rumbaut and Wayne A. Cornelius, eds. Pp. 107–130. La Jolla: Center for U.S.-Mexican Studies, University of California, San Diego.
Valverde, Sylvia A.
1987 A Comparative Study of Hispanic High School Dropouts and Graduates: Why Do Some Leave School Early and Some Finish? Education and Urban Society 19(3):320–329.
Vernez, Georges, and Allan Abrahamse
1996 How Immigrants Fare in U.S. Education. Santa Monica, CA: RAND Corporation.
Vigil, James Diego
1997 *Personas Mexicanas:* Chicano High Schoolers in a Changing Los Angeles. Fort Worth, TX: Harcourt, Brace and Company.
Vigil, James Diego, and J. M. Long
1981 Unidirectional or Nativist Acculturation—Chicano Paths to School Achievement. Human Organization 40(3):273–277.
Ware, Caroline F.
1935 Greenwich Village 1920–1930: A Comment on American Civilization in the Post-War Years. Boston: Houghton Mifflin.

Waters, Mary
1994 Ethnic and Racial Identities of Second Generation Black Immigrants in New York City. *In* The New Second Generation. Alejandro Portes, ed. Theme issue. International Migration Review 28(4):795–820.
1996 The Intersections of Gender, Race and Ethnicity in Identity Development of Caribbean American Teens. *In* Urban Girls: Resisting Stereotypes, Creating Identities. Bonnie Leadbeater and Niobe Way, eds. Pp. 65–81. New York: New York University Press.
Zhou, Min, and Carl L. Bankston III
1994 Social Capital and the Adaptation of the Second Generation: The Case of Vietnamese Youth in New Orleans. *In* The New Second Generation. Alejandro Portes, ed. Theme issue. International Migration Review 28:821–845.

24

CERTAINTY AND AMBIGUITY IN YOUTH IDENTITIES IN SOUTH AFRICA

Discourses in transition

Crain Soudien

Source: *Discourse: Studies in the Cultural Politics of Education*, 22, 3, 2001, 311–326.

Presented in the person of Mr Nelson Mandela, a progressive constitution, and its new government, South Africa has made immense strides away from its apartheid past. Responses to the new South Africa have varied. Although most South Africans are positive about the new democracy (Henry J. Kaiser Family Foundation, 2001, p. 10), there is in some quarters an apparent nostalgia, not so much for apartheid itself (few in the country would admit to that), but for the certainty that the old order provided. Even among subordinate groups that were victims of apartheid, notably those who have come to be known as Zulus, Indians and coloureds, there is evidence—manifested repeatedly in recent elections where Indian and coloured voting patterns seemed to suggest an intense anxiety at the prospect of being lumped with African people—of a yearning for the idyllised identities and the social positions that it is claimed have been displaced by the developments of the new South Africa (see Jensen & Turner, 1995; Bickford-Smith *et al.*, 1999; Pullen, 1996). Among those who are more positive, there is a growing trend towards a new Africanism. The African Renaissance movement, for example, has called on all South Africans to commit themselves to the African continent (Mgxashe, 2000).

How young people are thinking their way through these identity conundrums and the role of the school in these processes are of crucial importance for the new South Africa. This paper explores the thinking of senior high school students in the Cape Town area in regard to the debate around identity and the role of the school in shaping identity.

The paper is based on observations and discussions with young people in a number of different school settings. It arose out of an awareness that very little empirical work was being done on the impact of the apartheid and the post-apartheid school on young people's identities. Aside from Pam Christie (1990) and Margie Gaganakis (1991) in the apartheid era and Nazir Carrim and Crain Soudien (1999) in the post-apartheid period, there is little published work on the relationship between school and identity. There is, what is more, little work that seeks to understand how young people are coping in their new settings, in particular how young people are dealing with integration. Some of the students in this study were attending an integrating school. There are, therefore, a whole range of school contexts to be studied in South Africa, namely, the continuing African school, the integrating white, Indian and coloured schools, and those schools that remain predominantly white, Indian or coloured. The consequence of this shortcoming is that a limited understanding of the relationship between school and identity dominates the discussion and has been reproduced in a range of analyses (see Dube, 1985; Dean et al., 1983; Mokwena, 1992). Central in this understanding is the idea that the apartheid school reproduces the identities and dispositions required by capitalism and the apartheid system (see Hlatshwayo, 2000, p. 7).

This paper seeks to make the argument that the relationship between school and identity is more complex. This complexity applies to both the period of apartheid and the post-apartheid period. In the apartheid era, young people emerged from schools clearly marked by the experience of racial separateness. They were the whites, the coloureds, the Africans and the Indians that the system wished them to be, but they were also more than that. The official ideology of the post-apartheid government is to promote non-racialism and a new inclusive South Africanism. The identity construction tensions in the new system, however, have not disappeared. The argument I wish to make in this contribution is that schools in the new South Africa, and the students and teachers inside them, continue to struggle with the disparate messages about who they are and who they ought to be.

The approach I use here to show how the apartheid and the post-apartheid systems operate as sites of both reproduction and contestation is based on the use of what I call 'discourses'. I use 'discourses' in the Foucauldian sense as regimens that both shape and are shaped by thought and action. Discourses provide a working interpretive space for individuals and groups and are fluid and changeable. I talk in this paper about three kinds of discourses, the Official, the Formal and the Informal. None of these discourses is stable or internally consistent and coherent. The Official discourse, as an example, is the product of intense contestation and arises out of the struggle for political hegemony. It is dominated, however, at any one moment in time, by the ideologies, views and perspectives of whichever political group is in power. When this study was begun, South Africa was still in the grip of apartheid. The Official discourse of apartheid was embodied in the prescribed curriculum, in the official policy laid down by the government and the physical ordering of everyday life through a range of policing, regimenting and hierarchalising mechanisms. Schools created as African, coloured, white and Indian schools physically embodied this discourse. When the new anti-apartheid government came into power in 1994, it sought to rewrite the Official discourse. This it did through promulgating a human-rights-framed constitution and a series of laws aimed at outlawing all forms of discrimination. Schools could no longer

40

discriminate on racial grounds. Significantly, however, much of the physical land-scape and the curriculum remained in place after the new government came into power. The Official discourse thus changed but it did so within the context of the physical and curricular grip of the old order.

Hegemonic as official discourses are, they are always surrounded by other, often less effective, discourses, some of which are oppositional and many of which complement the hegemonic discourse. These discourses lurk as potential points of contradiction within the dominant discourse itself, but are more often outside of the Official order and represented in a range of public and private forms of behaviour and thought. Two such discourses that are relevant here arise in schools and are referred to as the Formal and the Informal discourses. The Formal discourse of a school is that to which the school as a community seeks to commit itself. The Formal is distinct from the Official in that it is a stance or an approach that the school itself develops as a mission for its educational work. The Informal is the world of social relationships which young people inhabit, associated with their social, cultural and leisure interests. Although elements of both the Formal and the Informal may be oppositional, they may also collude with the Official discourse, thus producing dis-cursive complexes made up of a variety of ideals, aspirations and desires, which are seldom stable, continuous or seamless. The discursive map of South Africa is thus a complex web of sometimes discrete and discontinuous themes, sometimes overlap-ping and synchronous ideals, and frequently contesting and contradicting notions of self and other. Although I speak of the Formal and the Informal discourses as singular structures, I do so only in so far as they are arenas or environments. Inside of those arenas or environments are nuances and subdiscourses and even contesting discourses. I speak, for example, of the Formal discourse in the school. This Formal discourse is, however, a contested ideology and is frequently dominated, as is the case in the Southern Suburbs, by racial chauvinists who overturn more open-minded approaches inside the schools. Similarly, the Informal discourse has a diverse range of mindsets and dispositions.

In this paper I try to show how dominant and oppositional forms of identity are reproduced in young people. I work with their experiences of school and attempt to show how the different moments of the school experience, the Official embod-ied in the symbolism of the state, the Formal as represented by the curriculum and regimen of the school, and the Informal where young people operate outside of the Formal structures of school, offer intensely complex opportunities for young people to receive and make identity. This process of receiving and making, the paper will try to show, generates identities that are profoundly heterogeneous, contradictory and susceptible to change.

The research context

The bulk of the material for this study is drawn from interviews I and research asso-ciates have conducted over a period of more than seven years (1993–2000) with young people between the ages of 16 and 19. These interviews were transcribed and coded in an iterative process that produced expansive coding categories. These coding categories emerged essentially from an analysis of the transcripts.

The study began as a doctoral dissertation and has since evolved into an ongoing research project (see Soudien, 1996). With the assistance of two colleagues I conducted over 50 interviews with students drawn largely from two schools. I worked with children classified 'African' entering a formerly coloured school and with another cohort of largely coloured students in a formerly coloured school. I had also conducted interviews with small groups of students outside of these two schools, including a number of white students. The perspectives of the white students, however, are not included in this paper.

The students were for the most part what the old apartheid government, and, indeed, many in the new government, would classify as 'African' and 'coloured'. I use the racial terminology that is familiar to South Africans and those who know South Africa. The terms 'white', 'African', 'Indian' and 'coloured' have an ambiguous status in the country. Although their validity as scientific categories has been repeatedly shown to be dubious (see Hall, 1988; Miles, 1989), and although I concur unconditionally with the point of view that race does not exist, racialisation as a social process is a reality. I recognise that in using the terms 'African', 'coloured', 'Indian' and 'white', I am complicit in entrenching the racial meanings surrounding their use.

The students who were interviewed for the study were evenly divided in terms of gender. Although I have begun to orientate my recent interviews to include a gender analysis, this was not the case at the beginning of the study. Gender, thus, does not form a significant part of the reporting of this study. The focus of the work is racial identity.

It seeks to follow the development of young people's assessment of their place in the new South Africa.

The context in which this work has taken place has changed significantly between 1993 and 2000. As I indicated above, the apartheid school officially ceased to exist in 1994 when the new government was elected (although, it must be said, schools had already begun to open up during the last few years of the apartheid era). The new government passed the South African Schools Act in 1996. This Act laid down the policies, frameworks and modalities for the new non-racial, non-sexist and equitable education system on the basis of equal funding for all schools. Crucially, however, although the policy terrain changed, the material realities of race, class and gender remained in most schools. Schools for the poor, for the most part, remained mired in their pre-1994 difficulties.

The two schools surveyed for this study were both previously disadvantaged schools serving the coloured community. Both had impeccable records as 'struggle schools'. One, the poorer of the two, called 'Southern Suburbs High' in this study, was located in a working class coloured area near False Bay. This school was heavily involved in the student uprisings of the 1970s and 1980s. Many students went on to become well-known student militants. The school was the first coloured school in the Western Cape to introduce isiXhosa as a subject. It was for this reason that many African students chose to go there when schools started opening up in the mid-1980s. These students came from outlying African townships such as Gugulethu, Nyanga, Langa and Khayelitsha by train journeys that began early in the morning and often ended late in the afternoon.

The other school in the study, 'City Central High', a more middle class school, served a community that had been broken up by the Group Areas Act of 1950. City Central students also travelled. They came from middle class coloured suburbs dotted around the city, such as Walmer Estate, Woodstock and Kensington. The school had a formidable staff with impeccable academic and political credentials. Many members of staff occupied leadership positions in the city's political and cultural organisations. The school produced young men and women who went on to become outstanding leaders in many areas of life in the city and the country.

It is important to make the point, however, that although both schools had a strong presence of anti-apartheid teachers, there were still many teachers who supported the apartheid order, particularly in Southern Suburbs.

Ironically, the opening up of schools during the late 1980s and the early 1990s had a major negative impact on both schools. Parents who could afford to do so removed their children from City Central and Southern Suburbs and chose to send them to formerly white schools. The exodus of middle class families from the schools introduced strains into the schools that they had not previously had to deal with.

Youth identity: certainty and ambiguity

The essential argument of this paper is that the identities young people develop are internally divided; that their subjectivities are unavoidably the products of a series of intersecting encounters with the Official, the Formal and the Informal, which leave them, in Jane Flax's (1993, p. 95) terms, in a number of different positions at different times and places. Their identities are, by definition, incoherent and discontinuous. They are of their apartheid pasts, but simultaneously against it. Identity formation in school is a process in which young people bring resources, find new ones and constantly work to make sense of their positions relative to others. In the apartheid school this work is conducted as a series of rhetorical manoeuvres in which young people constantly engage with that which they are racially, and in other ways, supposed to be. It is this engagement which produces what Homi Bhabha (1994) calls recognition and disavowal. The very act of going to school is a form of recognition or, in my terms, owning up to the racial labelling of the social system. At a particular level, children own up to being the coloureds or the Africans or the whites or the Indians the apartheid order or the social environment says they have to be to attend that particular school. The act of owning up is, however, never a straight admission but a response to a series of social compulsions. Young people are forced to acknowledge the call of apartheid in their lives, much as, as Louis Althusser (1971) explained, one was forced to acknowledge ideology. Some of the compulsions carry more authority than others, and so one ignores them at one's peril. One ceases to exist, for example, if one chooses to operate outside the Official order. It is the strategic and rhetorical manoeuvres around these compulsions that are explored below.

Owning up to the official

The official order of apartheid encompassed and embodied the everyday world in which the subjects of South Africa found themselves. This order continued to permeate the new South Africa and has a material existence in many schools today. It continues to confront young people as they seek to establish their identities. When the South African Human Rights Commission (SAHRC) commissioned a study of desegregation in 1998–1999, it discovered that at least 15 formerly white schools had no black learners or only what it called a 'token few' (Vally & Dalamba, 1999, p. 28). Many features of these schools sought to reinforce their whiteness. The report makes the assertion that '[a]lmost all the learners questioned in this school [referred to as School 206 in the study] expressed similar sentiments'. The sentiment referred to may be illustrated by a quote from a learner who said, '[t]here is too much racial mixing. I do not like this. Go back to apartheid' (Vally & Dalamba, 1999, p. 29). At the same time, of course, most schools in the country which were established as African schools ('integration' is only happening in Indian, white and coloured schools) continue to be so and the students in them know only those schools' racially exclusive realities. Owning up to these realities is for young people, African and coloured, a complex and continuing experience of ambiguity. For African children, the act of going to integrating schools outside of their townships is both a break with and an acknowledgement of their apartheid subjectivities. In leaving their township schools, they are signalling their rejection of the ensemble of meanings associated with their apartheid pasts. Leaving is leaving behind Bantu Education for the previously forbidden vistas of the white or the half-way-white coloured world. The process of leaving is profoundly decisive. It has the impact, as Gaganakis (1991, p. 87) has said, of separating themselves, culturally and spatially, from those with whom they grew up.

With respect to their pasts, their entry into formerly white or coloured schools is thus a complex statement of betrayal and recognition—betrayal of the township in leaving it and recognition of their affiliation with it in meeting racist coloured children. At the same time, for a few students, and the significant division of opinion within their number must be emphasised, going to a white or coloured school is unequivocally the expression of a desire to relinquish the township altogether. Township students thus stand before and in relation to the Official discourse with considerable ambiguity. It seeks to have them acknowledge their African separateness, and in ways that remind them of their subordinate status; their response, however, is to emphasize why they are taking this step of moving away. They want the status that comes with going to a 'better' school. Their identities are very much divided between the attractiveness of the outside world—the new school—and the familiarity of their inside worlds—the township. A divided self thus manifests itself in its participation at school.

Coming to a school that was not African was for many of the students from the township initially a distressing experience. Against the background of their apartheid organised lives, making the social adjustment proved to be emotionally painful.

A student, Phyllis, who had previously attended a coloured school in the city of Port Elizabeth on the southeastern seaboard of South Africa made the following remark about what she had felt like when she first arrived at Southern Suburbs High in 1992:

> It's like I was a visitor here. A visitor now here. It's like the blacks are the visitors, but the coloured children are not all . . . but the coloured children are not all . . .The coloured children some of them are all right to the black children. They are not doing funny stuff to them. (Cape Town, 1995)

Several features of the school were intimidating for the students, not least of all having to speak in a language that was not their own. Two young women from Gugulethu, Naledi and Nomsa, were particularly vocal about this experience. Naledi's lack of Afrikaans placed her at an immediate disadvantage. She suspected people of gossiping about her. Nomsa found having to speak in class particularly frightening because the coloured children laughed at her English. The structured environment of her English class, for example, made her particularly anxious:

> Sometimes it will happen at . . . in English class, because there we talk. So it happened there and teacher didn't like that. He usually shout at them, but now they stop. But they don't do it in front of the teacher . . . [i]t's not so bad now, like the first time I saw it. (Cape Town, 1995)

With time most of the students came to accept Southern Suburbs High as *their* school. They had learned to live in it. Their membership of the school community remained, nonetheless, brittle. In their experiences in the classroom and in their encounters with teachers outside of the classroom they learnt, like Lindi, who also came from Gugulethu, that attendance at Southern Suburbs High called for social navigational skills that they had to acquire quickly. In the course of being a student they came across repeatedly, perhaps not every day but certainly regularly, both minor and traumatic incidents in which they either had to assume a particular status themselves or to accept a status conferred upon them by the Official discourse.

The contexts in which status assumption and status referral occurred at the school were varied. Embedded in many of these ordinary experiences, however, was an ideology of 'othering' both camouflaged and obscured in the cultural and linguistic presumptions of the official curriculum of the school. As Zukiswa, also from Gugulethu, explained in describing her difficulties with Afrikaans, teachers were frequently oblivious, through the assumptions they made, to the differences of students, particularly their linguistic competencies and cultural backgrounds. The teachers unconsciously premised their work on the model of what they understood a coloured child to be. Obviously, many thought, Southern Suburbs High children had to be able to speak Afrikaans. Zukiswa said:

> Ja. My Afrikaans teacher doesn't explain anything. He just, I mean, I speak Xhosa, so I find it difficult to speak Afrikaans, because Afrikaans is a very difficult language for me. He just tells us the page in the textbook, and do this work, and then he sits there . . . He doesn't explain, and then one day he was checking our books and found that I didn't do much work. He asked me why, and then I told him that I didn't understand the work . . . Sometimes, you're scared of him. You just don't go to his classes. (Cape Town, 1995)

The full weight of the old Official discourse lay on the African students in situations such as these. Even though the students were in a post-apartheid school, the school still operated as a coloured school. Its teachers were coloured and most of the students were coloured. This experience, of having to cope with a world in which different assumptions about student competence were the rule, was one that many students had gone through. Not all of those experiences were as culturally veiled as Zukiswa's. Andile, whose English was even weaker than Zukiswa's, spoke of trying to ask a question in a class:

> [a]nd teacher don't understand me. Now I start to think . . . I ask the teacher, né [you know]? I ask the teacher to . . . I don't, I ask the teacher . . . [he cannot find the word and then speaks in Xhosa] . . . [Long pause] . . . hey, this name . . . And the teacher don't want to [word in Xhosa]. And then shout [at me]. (Cape Town, 1995)

Behind much teacher talk appeared to lie the Official ideology of apartheid. This the students were aware of. Thabo, backed up by his fellow students, made the point that:

> They . . . let's say with the school fees, with school fees, issues like that. They don't tend to look like what's the situation at home and all that. But they will rather tell the child in the class, 'you must bring your school fees'. But they don't know what's going on at home. So they must help us more on that also. In that because now the child feels, 'This teacher thinks I don't want to bring the money. I don't have the money, she doesn't even ask.' Okay, maybe she ask, but in front of the whole class, 'why don't you bring your money?' How can I tell her then? (Cape Town, 1995)

It was hard for students to avoid being bruised by the encounter with the racial-ideological discourse within the school. Although individual teachers were aware of this discourse, coming as many did from anti-apartheid histories, and deliberately raised the matter when it was appropriate to do so, the discourse of the 'other' tailed African students' every move in the school. Many teachers used, in language and gestures that the students did not fail to notice, approaches that had the effect of setting these students apart. The students did not accept this othering. They often simply avoided going to the classes of those teachers who were particularly offensive or, when they felt that the school was being blatantly racist, challenged these forms of behaviour. By 2000 little had changed in the school. The new Official discourse certainly had made inroads into the school. The school had a new principal who was a popular anti-apartheid activist in the Southern Suburbs of Cape Town, and he was acutely aware of the situation in the school. In 2000, concerned with the extent of the problem, he asked that I come back into the school to work with issues of racism among students and staff.

The engagement of coloured students at City Central during the 1990s with the Official discourse is considerably different to that of their African counterparts. Although the Official discourse of the apartheid era placed them somewhat higher up the hierarchy of social privilege, their encounter with hegemonic thinking in the country was no less complex than that of their African colleagues. Central in this engagement, for many, but certainly not for all, was a rejection of what the official stood for. This Official discourse in its old apartheid form, and even in some ways in its post-apartheid form—President Nelson Mandela, for example, came to City Central in 1995 to honour the 'contribution of coloureds' to the struggle—sought to create among people described as 'coloureds' a sense of their separateness as a race. The curriculum developed by the apartheid Coloured Affairs Department (which had administrative responsibility for coloured matters) sought to instil in people a coloured identity. Students at City Central rejected this identity in its official manifestations. This rejection derived from the strong nonracial Formal discourse of the school.

During the dark days of apartheid, and even after the new government came into power in 1994, the school had assumed a fierce non-racial stance with respect to the curriculum and the everyday politics of education. When the apartheid government introduced separate schools and separate educational departments for coloureds in 1964, many of the teachers in the school participated in protests against the racialisation of schooling. In line with this, the school rejected racial attributions of any form. The teachers made it clear that they were teaching under protest and refused to collaborate with the apartheid government. Only where it was absolutely essential for the 'good' of their students did they acknowledge the Coloured Affairs Department. The school, as a result, worked hard to banish racial talk in the school. When the new government came into power in 1994, most teachers in the school remained critical of the continuing valence of race and racial designations within the new state's policies. Some members of staff, for example, boycotted Mandela's visit because of its racial overtone. This approach to South African social and political life had a powerful impact on students. Many students emerged from City Central with strong ideals about issues such as equality and racism.

Consistent with this powerful Formal discourse, students claimed that race was not an important feature in the making of their judgements about social relations. Many rejected the 'coloured' label. Tasneem, an 18-year-old student interviewed in 2000, commented, 'We don't use that term around here. We're not coloureds.'

In reality, the situation was a good deal more complex. Race pervaded the students' everyday worlds. Although racial names such as 'kaffir'—a highly obnoxious term—were taboo in the school, the reach of race was something from which the students could not escape. Deirdré, a girl from Walmer Estate who was much admired for her style, when asked whether racism still existed in South Africa said:

> [d]efinitely. A lot . . . [Take] myself for example. If I sit in the bus and a so-called coloured, old woman or aged, comes into the bus then I automatically get up. But if it's a so-called black woman then I don't. Sometimes, without me really wanting to do it, then I'd like hesitate to get up because it's as if, because it's been put to us so that black people . . . aren't human. (Cape Town, 1995)

Try as they might, students had difficulty in dismissing the label 'coloured' that was placed on them. Although many rejected the term, they found the certainty and familiarity it offered hard to ignore. Their teachers were largely coloured. They came from townships and suburbs that were constructed for only people described as 'coloureds'. Even when they saw their teachers playing out their non-racial beliefs, they saw them doing so, as André, a leading student in the school in 1995, said, as 'courageous *coloured* leaders, willing to stand up for their communities'. This is not how those leaders themselves might have chosen to be seen, but the power of the apartheid state's social engineering surrounded the students. Alan, from the township of Kensington, commented:

> Yes, I would [describe myself as coloured]. The reason being that—me and [indistinct noise on tape] had endless arguments about this. And actually that girl Michelle . . . she'll tell me, 'but you're black, man', and I say, 'no, I'm coloured'. So then she'd tell me 'why?', and I'd say like, because they're [politicians] always telling you that coloureds and blacks fall under the same . . . coloureds fall under blacks, right. But here too. You're not black, and you're not white. You're coloured. You're in the middle . . . I don't think I'd want to be called black actually. And I don't think I'd ever be called white, so coloured is fine. (Cape Town, 1995)

André was to make an even stronger intellectual argument for using the term 'coloured'. Prefacing his comments in the politically correct formal address of City Central by describing himself as South African, he then switched the line of his thought:

I look at myself as a South African, as a human being. I don't look at myself as coloured. Okay, I admit it, I've grown up used to being called coloured. I'm coloured. And my neighbourhood [is a] coloured neighbourhood. I've grown up with it. What can I do? It's going to be in me, no matter . . . It's no use I'm going to try and get it out of me, like some people are trying. Also, there are things that I am proud of as a coloured person. (Cape Town, 1995)

The school's Formal understanding of race clearly played a big role in moving young people beyond the limitations of this discourse, but even this non-racialism could not ignore the deep imprint and the pervasiveness of the discourse of race. Even though the Official discourse of apartheid was displaced after 1994, the depth in which the education system and its schools were rooted in racial terms made it difficult for the school to fully live up to its non-racial ideals. In 1998 the school employed a teacher who would have been classified as an African in the apartheid era. The school struggled to find ways of making her feel accepted. It sought to introduce a class where the teacher could teach isiXhosa. The teacher left after little more than a year. A student interviewed in 2000, Serina, described the reactions of students to the teacher:

I liked her a lot. I know they were hoping to have her teach a Xhosa class, but the students weren't interested. I suppose that was a definite race issue . . . There was still the issue not only in our school but everywhere of no, I'm not going to speak their language. Even though I was open to the idea, I didn't go to the classes. (Cape Town, 2000)

What these experiences in these two schools show is how difficult it was for students to evade the racialising structures in which they found themselves. These structures constantly served to remind students that they were Africans and coloureds. Students were strongly aware of what the Official discourse wanted them to be and would have been able to describe how this discourse had changed after 1994. The response of the African students at Southern Suburbs was essentially that of strategic compliance with this discourse. They took the insults but made it clear that they did not accept them. They refused to be the kind of Africans the apartheid-minded school wanted them to be. The students at City Central also reject the Official discourse that brands them as coloureds but struggle to shake off its effects entirely.

Owning up to the formal and the informal at southern suburbs

The Official discourse with its strong racialising thrust does not operate unimpeded in schools. It is important to emphasize how much, in fact, it has to operate alongside of and to accommodate other discourses that influence and shape young people's perspectives and identities. It is in the interplay between the Formal and the Informal discourses, in particular, that one can see how much of a mistake it would be to read off student identity from the Official discourse.

The argument that I want to make here is that these discourses function alongside of and in articulation with the Official discourse in complex ways. For African children at Southern Suburbs and indeed at other schools, elements of the Formal and Informal discourses collude in pushing them to acknowledge their inferior and subordinate positions. This collusion takes place in the context of anti-apartheid discourses that seek to take them towards more open identities. For coloured children at City Central the relationship between the Formal and the Informal discourses is also structured in contestation. The Formal addresses them in the oppositional tones of 'the Universal Human' who stands above apartheid, whereas much of the Informal grounds them in the separate lived reality of apartheid requiring them to accept their colouredness.

At Southern Suburbs, the Formal and Informal discourses constitute a medium, or media, in which young Africans are called upon to signal and affirm their relative position to the coloured children they meet at school. They are constantly called upon to accept the fact that their histories are signs of an inferiority that is irremediable. Their blackness is testimony of it. Their responses to these invocations, however, reveal the full range of their rhetorical strategies. Sometimes they are submissive and acquiescent; at other times they are strident, defiant and proud.

Many of the African students deliberately sought to project themselves beyond the stereotypes framed by the official environment of the apartheid order. Monde, a student at Southern Suburbs in 1994, said of his coloured peers' attitudes to his being African:

> I mean they don't accept the name 'African'. They don't regard themselves as African. They always say 'Monde, African man'. And I told them, 'no, we are all Africans because our roots is here in Africa, whether we're white, whether we're coloured, whether we're black'. (Cape Town, 1995)

Another student, Zukiswa, went out of her way to cultivate friends beyond the African community. She explained her relationship with a coloured friend, 'she's always with me, and wherever I go, she's there. We go to outings, and she also comes with us . . . We went to Sandvlei [a waterside area] I remember, for the school holidays.' Although such events in the lives of most other students were not frequent, students were undoubtedly keen to move beyond the limits of their traditional circles. They enjoyed the same music their coloured friends liked. In a group discussion with students in Grade 12 at a Gugulethu high school the students explained that their favourite music included modern pop icons such as Mariah Carey.

Of all the students, Petrus spoke most fluidly and easily about his friendships at school. For him, with whom he associated was entirely a matter of choice. He said,

'I've always been involved in these school things, school teams. I won't say that I've been lonely at this school. I've never been rejected at school. Besides that, I've excluded *myself* [his own emphasis].' There were teachers at the school who played a big role in shaping these attitudes. Miriam explained:

> Altogether, like at our school there's a lot of nice teachers who under-stand the students. And always tries to . . . om humanity in hulle in te preach en so aan [to instil humanity into them, and so on] . . . Really, I like them. I like die activities wat hulle somtyds het, al is dit so baie min. But dis fine, dis lekker. Hulle stel belang in 'n . . . like, me now. Hulle sal altyd vir my—like [I like the activities they organize, even if they are rare. But it's fine, it's enjoyable. They take an interest in me. They'll always, like—] like I'm involved in drama and that—they'll always like encourage me, like in my schoolwork. (Cape Town, 1995)

Mathakhoza's story confirmed Miriam's:

> they're always . . . and if maybe there's something that you don't under-stand, they can . . . they help you out. Ja. There's this teacher I actually like. Out of all of these teachers, my Afrikaans teacher . . . he can maybe provide extra classes for you so that . . . so he can help you out with your work. Even on Saturdays, she'll ask you to come to school, just to come and help you. And she'll take you back home. [As a second-language English speaker Mathakhoza substitutes male and female pronouns on occasion.] (Cape Town, 1995)

Mathakhoza explained, 'actually, the only thing I like is to go to school with a different person. Different colour, like [she means 'to'] mine, . . . so that we can communicate, for communication. To learn how to speak her language, and so she also or he also must make an effort to understand my language.' Zukiswa's explanation for this was similar, '[y]es, it is exciting, because I'm around differ-ent people. I just love the people.' Phyllis continued the theme, '[w]e get to know other people which we didn't even know, then to make friends with'.

Teachers, however, who say things like 'you people', leave them feeling deeply frustrated because they want to make friends. Rebelling against school and teachers is, however, not an option that is able to gain them ground. Occasion-ally, of course, the agenda becomes unbearable and they either take a stand by themselves, as Mathakhoza did, or they rally together, as the boys did when they were about to be punished for an infraction that they considered not to have been their responsibility. As the work of Kapp (2000) makes clear, the desires of young African young people, particularly their preference for English over their home languages, are complex, but, as Mgxashe (2000, p. 11) says, there is a conscious debate taking place among many African youth about their exposure to 'foreign' cultures. He quotes Lindi Jordan, who says:

when we start talking about the African Renaissance we are not necessarily talking about living strictly in accordance with our traditional
values . . . we are more bent towards African values which are a kind
of hybrid of all our exposures and experiences. (Mgxashe, 2000, p. 11)

What it means to be African in the city is thus bound up with young African
men and women working out new ways of expressing their Africanness. This
Africanness, as the Henry J. Kaiser Family Foundation report (2001) points out,
cannot be separated from their wish to be modern young men and women. The
report, though not constructed as a report on the attitudes of youth to modernity,
is suggestive of how much young Africans invest in being modern. To be sure,
there is much that reminds them that they are African, but they are remaking this
Africanness as they spend much of their time tuning into popular radio and television shows. The work of Ngwane (1999) on the development of new cultural
forms and styles among African youth is even more emphatic. He talks of how
young men leaving the city to go to the rural areas for initiation ceremonies are
using their education to displace older more oral-based traditions and practices
during initiation. In these situations young men are rejecting the tradition of
their elders as the traditions of what they call 'the ignorant' and investing them
with new forms of masculinity based on the ability to argue and reason. Nolita,
a young woman from Langa, interviewed late in 2000, commented that living in
the city placed a heavy strain on young people's sense of being African, 'because
they don't care. They just throw away their traditions.' The point, however,
is not that young people are throwing away their traditions, but that they are
remaking them.

Most of the students interviewed at Southern Suburbs between 1993 and
1995 and those whom a research associate interviewed in 2000 make it emphatically clear that they want a 'better life'. For Nolita this better life is simple
and no different to that of young people elsewhere. She says, 'I want to see
myself get educated, and having my own house, and having my own family.'
At the same time many, like Nolita, remain attached to their African past: 'we
must know about [our] ancestors, and [our] traditional things'. Being an African
in the city is thus about living with complexity. For many of the young people in this study this complexity is bound up with who they are. African students choose to make the long journey across the city each day. They want to
go to schools such as Southern Suburbs because they believe that it will help
them improve themselves. They anticipate the difficulties they will encounter
in entering schools such as these and so come to the conclusion that they must
deal with the slights and hurts they will receive. Many students say to themselves, like Monde, a student from Gugulethu interviewed in 1995, that 'I like
school because it keeps me away from bad things.' Monde explained that when
bad 'things' happened to him at school, 'I just ignore things like racism. Only
what I'm concerned about is my studies.' African students had learnt to live
with the racism around them.

Owning up to the formal and the informal at city central

For coloured children the play between the Formal and the Informal is equally complex, but has different and also ambiguous results. The formal environment of their school tries hard to get them to the point of rejecting the salience of race. Mohammed a student at City Central in 1999 explained:

> we were taught all these terms, we didn't actually experience them first hand. We know about it. And if you say that a class is multiracial means your accepting the fact that there is more than one race. And that more than one race issue has brought along too many problems . . . The issue of multi-race we don't accept it any more. (Cape Town, 2000)

Ironically, six years into the new era, the Informal environment in which many young people classified 'coloured' operated appeared to have shifted. Whereas earlier nonracialism occupied a strong space in the perspectives and the lives of young people, this appeared to have receded by 2000. In the middle of the 1990s the Informal environment at City Central was represented by almost equal numbers of students whom I describe as the 'Cools', the 'Straights' and the 'Floaters'. These students operated in a lively space in which the Cools sought to assert their dominance with their interests in nightclubbing and partying. The Straights, by contrast, epitomised the ideals of the school, dominated the Student Representative Council and contributed to the intense ethos of non-racialism at the school. Floaters moved in and out of both groups as their interests dictated. Critically, however, the Straights served to hold the hegemony of the school's Formal commitment to its political ideals in place. André, the student referred to earlier, speaking of the influence of his history teacher, demonstrated this commitment:

> I can point to one person, Mr A, my History teacher. He actually made me feel good about myself, because I have a great knowledge of general things . . . I read the newspapers a lot. And he told me that . . . that didn't actually make me a nerd, and I shouldn't be afraid of expressing things. (Cape Town, 1995).

Students used these relationships to build a vibrant cultural life at the school. Students wrote poetry, performed and danced, and sustained, themselves, a strong presence in the school. Shahiema, another student in 1995, explained what she found inspiring about the informal culture at City Central:

> what inspired me was the dedication of a lot of the people at the school. Especially the students where the SRC [Student Representative Council] was concerned. These people were totally committed to the SRC and I admired them. I mean, for a long time, I wanted to be part of the SRC . . . they went out there and they wanted to be secretary of the SRC. (Cape Town, 1995)

Although Straights certainly did not have everything their own way in the school and had to deal with the allure and easy authority that the Cools commanded, they offered strong role models in the school. Their fellow students looked up to them.

By 2000, the situation in the school had changed. Political activity in the school, as in the rest of the country, had shifted away from the strident protest of the early 1990s. Students were beginning to enter City Central in less awe of the place. Also, perceptions had begun to take root in the coloured community, as in the white community, that their skin colour counted against them. They were not dark enough when it came to the job market. These perceptions provided the space for the balance of forces in the Informal environment at the school to change. Being political and accepting the ideals of non-racialism were now less attractive. In these circumstances, a sense of colouredness grew in the student community. Although the teachers remained committed to the high-minded ideals of the Formal discourse, the students were more aware of the racialising process than ever before. The Informal discourse, as Feroza, a City Central student of the 1999 cohort, explained, had the effect of holding their colouredness in place:

> we just had coloureds in our school . . . So there was one way of think-ing and one way of acting . . . we all had the same way of acting . . . I was one of them you know [and] you had this sense of belonging. (Cape Town, 2000)

Another student Asheeqa, interviewed in 2000, concurred with Feroza and explained how a fashion show held at the school brought out the small-mindedness of some of the students. She said, 'I went to the fashion show . . . a few months ago. And they were playing this African song and people were like really laughing at it and stuff' (Cape Town, 2000). A friend, Zulfa, interviewed with her, agreed and said, 'we all had the same social norms and we were common [like that] with just about everyone at the school' (Cape Town, 2000).

The school principal had tried to deal with the fact that African students sat apart from the other students during intervals but found it difficult to change students' attitudes. Zulfa commented,

> I think like no matter what, there is still subconsciously in everyone's mind that apartheid is still kind of there and like its not just something that you can think of it as the laws are gone, and everyone would be equal to each other. That's why I think that a lot of the coloureds' minds . . . maybe they've been thinking . . . different cultures should be separate from each other. (Cape Town, 2000)

Resurgent, though, as this coloured identity was in the school, there were many students who continued to hold fast to a broader sense of their identity. Rukshana, a student from the 1999 cohort, explained that she and her friends did not subscribe to colouredness; 'yeah', she said:

we don't use words like that. We try to avoid them. We care more about character. People in our class were different but it was based on character that people liked them or not. This issue of many races, it caused some of our best teachers to be taken away from us. We don't accept that stuff. (Cape Town, 2000)

In students' discussions about music Serina explained that her culture was mixed:

I think it's a mixture, it's like I'm going through things, I'm just borrowing. I feel that I should try and be as unique as I want to be. You know I don't want . . . to be the stereotype of a coloured person who goes to clubs with coloured people . . . I'm into the alternative types of music. (Cape Town, 2000)

It is in working with these different interpretations of the world around them that students develop what Flax (1993, p. 95) called 'troubled identities'. 'Troubled' in Flax's terms refers to the persistence of doubt in people's minds about what is important in working out who they are and where they belong culturally, racially and in a variety of other ways.

At the heart of this trouble is the considerable weight of the Formal discourse, which requires young people to own up to a universalism that the school constantly flourishes in front of them. Against this stands the Informal discourse, which insistently calls on them to cut loose and concentrate on being themselves and even being coloured.

What this at-homeness or familiarity with the Informal discourse of colouredism set up was that City Central students were able to present themselves as subjects able to project two distinct sides to their subjectivities. They were unmistakably the products and the producers of both the Formal and the Informal discourses. Evident in their lives were the clear signs and markers of these discourses. Students reveal themselves to be, like people with multiple subjectivities elsewhere, adept in several, often discontinuous, environments.

Conclusion

It is important to recognise how differently the discourse configuration serves the African and coloured students observed at Southern Suburbs and City Central Schools. The discourses that swirl in and around African students' lives offer them constrained and qualified opportunities in the new South Africa. They are constantly reminded of their blackness as a sign of inferiority. The discourses that serve coloured students provided them with more space. They are able to invoke a sense of the inclusive new South African identity more easily than their African counterparts. They remain, however, unsure of their place in the new polis. The essay has tried to argue that school is an important site for symbolic work, and that it is not just a conduit for ruling class aspirations. What the work has shown is how complex school is as an experience for young people. It has not only argued that school is a contested terrain, it has tried to show up the nature of the discursive contestation as a dialectic in which collusion, contestation, agreement and dissonance constantly operate in people's lives.

Paul Willis (1977, p. 146) talks of the 'unintended and contradictory importance of the institution of the school'. He says that aspects of the dominant ideology are defeated there, but that the defeat is pyrrhic. This work seeks to argue that elements of the apartheid ideology and residues of this apartheid ideology in the new South Africa are, to be sure, defeated on the school campus. African children find in school the material for their dreams of a better life. Coloured children see themselves painted differently to the portraits embossed for them on their birth certificates. But, in equal measure, apartheid and the racialising ideology of apartheid that continues to exist in the new South Africa have more than held their own. Their ways and tastes remain evident in the behaviour of children. The children emerge with identities that are the end products of a form of social compromise. They are manifestly, therefore, the products of their oppositional worlds. But they are also the children of apartheid; their parentage is unmistakably imprinted with its characteristics.

What this conclusion points to is how difficult it is to read off from the school a meaning of the larger society. School and education are sites in which young people, as active subjects, measure what they can and cannot do. In making strategic choices, they explore dimensions of their subjectivities which the racial order seeks to close down. They emerge from their schooling experience with the ethnic badges of coloured and Xhosa culture, and invariably they are profoundly conscious of the racial hierarchies that surround them. They are, however, considerably more than the stereotypes that the hegemonic racial discourse prepares for them. The African students in this study find themselves invited inside the social order and often shut out. In dealing with it, they are, simultaneously, submissive and combative. In reading their environments they make strategic decisions about when they will comply with the order around them and when to resist. The configuration of discourses holds them in a constant tension. For coloured students the complexity is of a somewhat different order. The discourses that circulate around them position them as 'in-between' people. Their responses to this, interestingly, are those of a profound ambiguity of self.

The imperative of most of the discourses that inhabit the South African ideological terrain is to name, point and fix using phrases that are deemed to be reality in and for eternity. The intention is to produce a 'synchronic essentialism', based on 'signifiers of stability', such as Africanness or colouredness and so on. Stable as the projection of these signifiers might be, instability and ambiguity are their persistent features, as Stuart Hall (1988) has shown. 'Black,' says Hall (1988, p. 28), 'is essentially a politically and culturally constructed category, which cannot be grounded in a set of fixed and trans-cultural or transcendental racial categories and which therefore has no guarantees in nature.' In this study, what the testimony suggests is that terms such as 'African' and 'coloured' (and also, I venture to suggest, those of 'Indian' and 'white') are recognisable at particular levels of meaning. The effect of the discourses operating within South Africa is to construct median categories such as 'white', 'coloured', 'African' and 'Indian' but always to provide opportunities for those categories to subvert themselves.

References

ALTHUSSER, L. (1971) *Lenin and Philosophy and Other Essays* (New York, New Left Books).

BHABHA, H. (1994) *The Location of Culture* (London and New York, Routledge).

BICKFORD-SMITH, VIVIAN, VAN HEYNINGEN, E. & WORDEN, N. (1999) *Cape Town in the Twentieth Century* (Cape Town, David Philip).

CARRIM, N. & SOUDIEN, C. (1999) Critical antiracism in South Africa, in: S. May (Ed.) *Critical Multiculturalism: rethinking multicultural and antiracist education* (London, Falmer Press).

CHRISTIE, P. (1990) *Open Schools: racially mixed Catholic schools in South Africa, 1976–1986* (Braamfontein, South Africa, Ravan Press).

DEAN, E., HARTMANN, P. & KATZEN, M. (1983) *History in Black and White: an analysis of South African school history textbooks* (Paris, UNESCO).

DUBE, E. (1985) The relationship between racism and education in South Africa, *Harvard Education Review*, 55 (1), pp. 86–110.

FLAX, J. (1993) *Disputed Subjects: essays on psychoanalysis, philosophy and politics* (London, Routledge).

GAGANAKIS, M. (1991) Opening up the closed school, in: D. Freer (Ed.) *Towards Open Schools: possibilities and realities for non-racial education in South Africa* (Manzini, Swaziland, Macmillan Boleswa).

HALL, S. (1988) New ethnicities, in: *ICA Document 7* (London, ICA).

HENRY J. KAISER FAMILY FOUNDATION (2001) *Hot Prospects, Cold Facts: portrait of young South Africa* (Parklands, South Africa, Love Life).

HLATSHWAYO, S. (2000) *Education and Independence: education in South Africa, 1658–1988* (Westport, CT, Greenwood Press).

JENSEN, S. & TURNER, S. (1995) A place called Heideveld identities and strategies among the coloureds in Cape Town, South Africa. MA thesis, Roskilde University.

KAPP, R. (2000) 'With English you can go everywhere': an analysis of the role and status of English at a former DET school, *Journal of Education*, 25, pp. 227–259.

MGXASHE, M. (2000) The youth and the African renaissance, *New Agenda*, 1, pp, 8–14.

MILES, R. (1989) *Racism* (London, Routledge).

MOKWENA, S. (1992) Living on the wrong side of the law, in: D. EVERATT & E. SISULU (Eds) *Black Youth in Crisis: facing the future* (Johannesburg, Ravan Press).

NGWANE, Z. (1999) Apartheid under education: schooling, initiation and domestic reproduction in post apartheid rural South Africa. Unpublished paper.

PULLEN, E. (1996) Race and self: a community study of self-identity among women classified as 'coloured' in Cape Town. Paper delivered at University of Cape Town, History Department Seminar.

SOUDIEN, C. (1996) Apartheid's children: student narratives of the relationship between experiences in schools and perceptions of racial identity in South Africa. PhD dissertation, State University of New York, Buffalo.

VALLY, S. & DALAMBA, Y. (1999) *Racism, 'Racial Integration' and Desegregation in South African Public High Schools: a report on a study by the South African Human Rights Commission (SAHRC)* (Johannesburg, SAHRC).

WILLIS, P. (1977) *Learning to Labor: how working class kids get working class jobs* (Farnborough, UK, Saxon House).

25

SUBJECTIVATION AND PERFORMATIVE POLITICS— BUTLER THINKING ALTHUSSER AND FOUCAULT

Intelligibility, agency and the raced–nationed–religioned subjects of education

Deborah Youdell

Source: *British Journal of Sociology of Education*, 27, 4, 2006, 511–528.

Judith Butler is perhaps best known for her take-up of the debate between Derrida and Austin over the function of the performative and her subsequent suggestion that the subject be understood as performatively constituted. Another important but less often noted move within Butler's consideration of the processes through which the subject is constituted is her thinking between Althusser's notion of subjection and Foucault's notion of subjectivation. In this paper, I explore Butler's understanding of processes of subjectivation, examine the relationship between subjectivation and the performative suggested in and by Butler's work, and consider how the performative is implicated in processes of subjectivation—in 'who' the subject is, or might be, subjectivated as. Finally, I examine the usefulness of understanding the subjectivating effects of discourse for education, in particular for educationalists concerned to make better sense of and interrupt educational inequalities. In doing this I offer a reading of an episode of ethnographic data generated in an Australian high school. I suggest that it is through subjectivating processes of the sort that Butler helps us to understand that some students are rendered subjects inside the educational endeavour, and others are rendered outside this endeavour or, indeed, outside student-hood.

Introduction

This paper considers the usefulness for education of Judith Butler's thinking between Althusser's notion of subjection and Foucault's notion of subjectivation and the possibility for discursive agency and performative politics that this thinking opens up. While concerned with the broad utility of these conceptual tools, the paper illustrates their usefulness by deploying them to analyse the processes of raced–nationed–religioned subjectivation at a 'Multicultural Day' event in a Sydney high school. In doing this, the paper proceeds from a series of what might be termed 'left' or 'critical' concerns centred around the differentiating and exclusionary effects of schooling, and, with a focus here on the subjectivation of 'Arabic' students, on the operations of race, racism and Whiteness.

These may seem unlikely points of departure for a paper offered as a post-structural piece. But as Foucault's (1988a) discussion in 'Critical Theory/Intellectual History' points out, 'left' thinkers have for some time been looking for tools for understanding and strategies for interrupting material inequality through an engagement with language; a decentred subject; and an unstable truth. Rather than asking what structures and institutions (economic, social, or linguistic) produce material inequality, this move reconfigures this concern and asks how the self comes into being, what the costs of the self might be, and how the self might be made *again differently*.

A central project has been developing tools and strategies for interrogating the 'nature of the present' (Foucault, 1988a, p. 36), an interrogation that seeks to expose the relationship between 'the subject, truth, and the constitution of experience' (Foucault, 1988b, p. 48). These efforts are wholly political in that they focus upon those aspects of the present that Foucault finds 'intolerable'. Foucault seeks to develop understandings of how the present is made, and so how it might be unmade, by 'following lines of fragility in the present', trajectories that might allow us to 'grasp why and how that-which-is might no longer be that-which-is' (1988a, p. 37). Butler takes this further and posits a performative politics in which she imagines discourses taking on new meanings and circulating in contexts from which they have been barred or in which they have been rendered unintelligible, as performative subjects engage a deconstructive politics that intervenes and unsettles hegemonic meanings (Butler, 1997a).

In exploring these conceptual tools and putting them to use, the paper focuses on the subjectivation of a group of Lebanese and Turkish young. The analysis suggests a series of political, educational, popular and (sub)cultural discourses that circulate in this school setting and beyond, and which provide the discursive terrain on and through which these students are subjectivated. Specifically, the paper explores how Lebanese and Turkish students (collectively called 'Arabic' in this setting) are subjectivated in ways that render apparently incommensurable constitutions of the good-Arabic-student-subject and the bad-Arabic-subject through the citation and inscription of an Orientalism (Said, 2003) reinvigorated by post-9/11 anti-Islamic discourse (Lipman, 2004). This, then, is the intolerable present I want to interrogate. The paper also considers how these students render themselves through the possibilities for practices of self, or discursive agency, that subjectivation brings. This is a consideration that demonstrates the capacity of Butler's performative politics to maintain in view simultaneously a sense of the context of constraint in which these performatively constituted subjects are effected and the potential for these subjects to act and to act with intent.

Methodology

My experiences of 'Multicultural Day' in an Australian high school are situated in the conduct of a school ethnography during 2001. There has been significant debate about the implications, and even the possibility, of undertaking ethnography in a post-structural or Foucauldian frame. Critical, interpretive and feminist traditions in school (and other) ethnography have long emphasized the multiplicity of meanings and perspectives that exist within contexts; the complexities of and tensions within the roles and status' of the researcher and the researched, as well as relations between them; and the potential and limits of reflexivity (see, for instance, Carr & Kemmis, 1986; Lather, 1991; Stanley & Wise, 1993; Skeggs, 1994; Delamont & Atkinson, 1995; Hammersley & Atkinson, 1995). These methodological insights have been usefully supplemented and, indeed, scrutinized in the light of post-structural ideas and adaptations of qualitative methodology informed by these ideas (see, for example, Miller, 1997; Prior, 1997; Silverman, 1997; Stronach & MacLure, 1997; Britzman, 2000; Lather, 2000; McCoy, 2000; St Pierre, 2000; Harwood, 2001; Alvesson, 2002; Maclure, 2003).

In doing ethnography in school framed by a concern to interrogate the subjectivating effects of an intolerable present, I make use of the usual methods of interview, observation, collection of artefacts and texts. I am not, however, asking the researched to explicate their understanding of the context and relations within it. Rather, I am looking for moments in which subjects are constituted and in which constituted subjects act. I am looking for discourses and their subjectivating effects. I ask myself what discourses might be circulating inside and/or across school contexts, how these are being deployed, what their effects might be. While at times it seems that discourses and their effects are clearly evident, more often it seems that these are subtle and oblique, needing to be teased out, to be deconstructed. Ultimately, I want to know whether thinking in terms of the subjectivating effects of discourse can help me to understand how students are made within particular constraints and how these constraints might be breached. This is not the collection of 'real' or 'actual' discourses, but is wholly constrained by my own discursive repertoire—the discourse that I see and name—and my capacity to represent these. I am, then, absolutely entangled in the data I generate and the representations I produce.

These data are inevitably simulacra (Baudrillard, 1994) of my own creation, copies without original that cannot reflect any 'real' moment in a field that is itself inaccessible without the mediating discursive frames that fill it with meaning. In this way the ethnographic data offered bear a heavy interpretive burden. I am not seeking to describe the nuances of the context and tease out what is happening within it. Rather, I am seeking to construct compelling representations of moments inside school in order to untangle the discursive frames that guide meaning and render subjects within it. My research process is unavoidably implicated in the very subjectivating processes about which it speaks. Yet these data are recognizable. They do not contain, expose or reflect any universal truth, but these *petite narratives* do resonate.

Given the focus on subjectivation in this paper, the place of the subject deserves some further consideration here. Serious attention is increasingly being paid to the problematic relationship between the 'knowing' subjects implicit to empirical research and the 'troubled' subjects of post-structural writing (see, once again, Britzman, 2000; Lather, 2000; St Pierre, 2000). Yet there is no easy solution. Understanding the researching and researched subject to be perpetually but provisionally constituted through discourse means that research practice is wholly implicated in processes of ongoing subjectivation (of both the researcher and the researched) even as these subjectivities form the objects of study. Replacing sovereign agency with the notion of discursive agency (Butler, 1997a)—which I will explore in some detail later—goes some way to illuminate and relieve these tensions, offering an ethnography that retains agency and intent in the context of discursive constraint without implicitly casting this subject a sovereign.

Understanding the subjects who inhabit schools and school ethnography in this way suggests that the discourses deployed by students and teachers (and researcher) may be both intentional and unintentional: discourses intentionally deployed may escape or exceed the intent of the subject who speaks or acts, and/or the subject may unwittingly deploy discourses whose historicities and/or intersections assert unanticipated meanings. Indeed, discursive practices may entail the deployment of complex combinations of intentional and unintentional discourses and their discursive effects. Taking up Butler's notion of discursive agency, this analysis assumes multiple degrees of both intent and understanding among subjects in terms of the embedded meanings and effects of discourses. On the one hand, it suggests that subjects do not necessarily regurgitate discourse unwittingly. On the other hand, however, it suggests that discourses are not necessarily cited knowingly and that they are not necessarily known explicitly to the subject and/ or audience. As such, subjects need not be self-consciously alert to the discourses deployed in order for their familiar and embedded meanings to be inscribed. Furthermore, the analysis suggests, again after Butler (1997a), that discourses do not need to be explicitly cited in order to be deployed. Rather, multiple discourses are referenced through the meanings, associations and omissions embedded in the historicity of apparently simple and benign utterances and bodily practices.

As I have explored elsewhere (Youdell, 2005), these discussions render indeterminable the question of whether I should offer an account of myself as the researcher. The risk of slipping into an inadvertent essentialism tempts me to avoid such an account; however, the risk of assuming a disembodied authorial authority by not doing so seems much greater. Given the centrality of visual economies to prevailing discourses of gender and race (see Jacobson, 1998; Seshadri-Crooks, 2000), my own location within these discourses (woman, White) is undoubtedly 'visible' to and taken as immutable by the students involved in my research. Yet my social class, sexuality, subcultural and age locations are perhaps less singular or 'obvious' and, therefore, less tightly constrained. For instance, in the context of prevailing hetero-normative discourse, it is likely that students locate (constitute) me as heterosexual—the unspoken Same of the heterosexual/homosexual Same/

Other binary—as long as an alternative sexuality is not asserted. And as a British ('English') woman doing school ethnography in Australia, nationality was an explicit axis of my subjectivation: students who had speculated privately that I might be 'very posh' or 'from England' (but not both) were reassured by my Englishness (in ways that posh-ness may not have been reassuring in this low-income locale), and at the same time this Englishness was constitutive of my position as an outsider whose lack of knowledge of the context was acceptable and whose interest in it was comprehensible (or just about).

Performative subjects, subjectivation, performative politics

As my discussion so far has indicated, this paper is concerned with two inter-related threads—understanding (some of) the intolerable effects of education as well as the contribution that can be made to this by Judith Butler's work on the subject, the subject's potential to act willfully, and politics. For me, it is in Butler's return to Althusser via Foucault that an understanding of subjection/subjectivation, agency, and the political is most usefully developed (Butler, 1997a, b, 2004).

Judith Butler begins by adopting Foucault's notion of discourse as productive and uses this alongside the notion of the performative to consider the production of sexed and gendered subjects (Butler, 1990, 1993). This is not the performativity, after Lyotard, of the marketized and corporatized education workplace that Stephen Ball (2003) writes about. Rather, this performative is borrowed from a debate between Derrida (1988) and Austin (1962) concerning the nature of language and its relationship to the world in which a performative is: 'that discursive practice that enacts or produces that which it names' (Butler, 1993, p. 13). Butler suggests that:

> Discursive performativity appears to produce that which it names, to enact its own referent, to name and to do, to name and to make. . . . [g]enerally speaking, a performative functions to produce that which it declares. (Butler, 1993, p. 107)

Butler argues that the subject must be performatively constituted in order to make sense *as* a subject. While these subjects appear, at least at the level of the everyday or commonsense, to precede their designation, this apparently pre-existing subject is an artefact of its performative constitution. A key contribution made to debates concerning the function of the performative is Derrida's (1988) assertion that any performative is open to misfire and so might fail or doing something unintended or unexpected. And Foucault's (1990a) account of discourse insists that no discourse is guaranteed—while particular discourses prevail in some contexts and endure over time, the potential for the meanings of these to shift and/or for subordinate discourses to unsettle these remains.

Developing this notion of the performatively constituted subject, Butler (1997a, b, 2004) takes up Althusser's notion of subjection and Foucault's notion of subjectivation to elaborate a nuanced understanding of production and constraint.

For Althusser (1971), 'subjection' is achieved through the action of 'ideological State apparatuses' (p. 136). These *ideological* State apparatuses are understood as representations of ideas, outlooks and beliefs that are imaginary or 'distortions' of a scientifically accessible 'real' (p. 153) (in Althusser's terms, the 'real' conditions of production and consumption). As these ideas are translated into actions and social practices and come to be embedded in social ritual, ideology is given a material existence that is at once a distortion and implicated in the production of this distortion. These ideological state apparatus are both at stake in and the site of struggle, with the school identified as a key site.

For Althusser, ideology, and ideological State apparatuses, are inextricably linked with the subject (Althusser, 1971). The subject, Althusser argues, is constituted by ideology that constitutes the individual as a subject. The subject is hailed as an individual, even as she/he is constituted a subject. This transformation of the individual into a subject, and the 'obviousness' of subjecthood, are key functions of ideology.

Recognition is central to these processes. The subject recognizes herself/himself as she/he is hailed. Furthermore, she/he recognizes herself/himself reflected in/by the Subject—Althusser's 'Subject *par excellence*' (1971, p. 167; original emphasis) who occupies the centre of ideology—by whom/on whose behalf the subject is hailed. This is Althusser's 'mirror-recognition' (1971, p. 168). It is through this recognition that the subject is 'recruited'—subjecthood is freely taken and subjection is freely accepted by the good subject. In Althusser's neo-marxist Science this recognition is, in fact, a mis-recognition—the subject is not a reflection of the Subject, but *subject to* the Subject: '*there are no subjects except by and for their subjection*' (1971, p. 169; original emphasis).

This recognition of the hail and transformation of the individual into a subject is simultaneous and inseparable. In Althusser's account there is no 'before' subjection when the subject was an individual—as Althusser asserts, 'individuals are always-already subjects' (1971, p. 164). Nevertheless, just as ideology suggests real knowledge free from distortion, the individual/subject binary does seem to retain an implicit sense of an individual free from subjection. Freedom, albeit constrained, is suggested again by the idea that the subjecthood is freely taken up, even as this is a freedom taken *inside* subjection. Althusser argues the intrinsic ambiguity of the subject:

> In the ordinary use of the term, subject in fact means: (1) a free subjectivity, a centre of initiatives, author of and responsible for its actions; (2) a subjected being, who submits to a higher authority, and is therefore stripped of all freedom except that of freely accepting his [sic] submission. This last note gives us the meaning of this ambiguity, which is merely a reflection of the effect which produces it: the individual *is interpellated as a (free) subject in order that he shall submit freely to the commandments of the Subject, i.e. in order that he shall (freely) accept his subjection*, i.e. in order that he shall make the gestures and actions of his subjection 'all by himself.' (1971, p. 169; original emphasis)

A foreshadowing of Foucault's notion of the individual constituted in discourses and through the technologies of disciplinary power (Foucault, 1990a, 1991) or through practices of the self (Foucault, 1990b, 1992) is evident in Althusser's account of ideology and subjection. I am provoked to wonder, much as Judith Butler has, what would 'happen' if I were to think of ideologies (as well as the 'undistorted truth'), and ideological State apparatuses, and the subjection that ideological State apparatuses effect, as discursive, as performative.

According to Foucault, the person is *subjectivated*—she/he is at once rendered a subject and subjected to relations of power through discourse. That is, *productive power* constitutes and constrains, but does not determine, the subjects with whom it is concerned. Yet while Foucault indicates a concern with the subject at the centre of his work, he says relatively little directly about the notions of subjection and subjectivation.

Foucault says of the relation between productive power and the subject, and the subject's location in productive power:

> This form of power applies itself to immediate everyday life which categorizes the individual, marks him [sic] by his own individuality, attaches him to his own identity, imposes a law of truth on him which he must recognize and which others have to recognize in him. It is a form of power which makes individuals subjects. There are two meanings of the word subject: subject to someone else by control and dependence, and tied to his own identity by a conscious self-knowledge. Both meanings suggest a form of power which subjugates and makes subject to. (1982, p. 212)

In a similar vein, in 'Critical Theory/Intellectual History', Foucault' suggests that:

> If I tell the truth about myself, as I am doing now, it is in part that I am constituted as a subject across a number of power relations which are exerted over me and which I exert over others. (1988a, p. 39)

Here the echoes of Althusser's model of subjection resonates through Foucault's thinking about the subject, despite the very clear divergence of these thinkers in relation to the status of science, knowledge, Truth and so on.

In Foucault's final interview he offers a direct account of his understanding of subjectiv(iz)ation. He says:

> I will call subjectivization the procedure by which one obtains the constitution of a subject, or more precisely, of a subjectivity which is of course only one of the given possibilities of organization of a self-consciousness. (Foucault, 1988c, p. 253)

While the operations and constraints of productive power remain evident, here power relations appear in the background, with the self, and the possibility of (contingent) self-knowledge and volition foregrounded. This is more clearly stated by Foucault in 'An Aesthetic of Existence', when he says of the subject:

> the subject is constituted through practices of subjection, or, in a more autonomous way, through practices of liberation, or liberty, as in Antiquity, on the basis, of course, of a number of rules, styles, inventions to be found in the cultural environment. (1988b, p. 51)

Here, the self-conscious practices of the subject, and her/his involvement in her/his own constitution, are indicated as (potentially) 'practices of liberation' *at the same time as* the constrained context in which this subject acts is indicated by 'practices of subjection'. The subject acts, but she/he acts within/at the limits of subjection.

Perhaps more significantly, processes of subjection/subjectivation are demonstrated through Foucault's specific contextual studies in which the subject is a key field of concern at the same time as the subject *as* a field of concern is interrogated. In particular, *Discipline and Punish* (Foucault, 1991) and *History of Sexuality Volume 1* (Foucault, 1990a) show how the subject is subjected to relations of power as she/he is individualized, categorized, classified, hierarchized, normalized, surveilled and provoked to self-surveillance. These are technologies of subjection brought into play within institutions. This is not because such institutions are ideological State apparatuses as in Althusser's account, but because institutions improvise, cite and circulate discursive frames and coterminous technologies that render subjects in relations of power. As Althusser notes the simultaneity of subjection and the making of a 'free' subject, so Foucault notes the non-necessary effects of discourse and the disciplinary technologies it makes meaningful and the persistence possibility of resistance intrinsic to productive power (Foucault, 1990a). It is to the potentialities of being otherwise or, to adapt a construction of Foucault's, that-which-is-not, that Foucault's *Uses of Pleasure* (1992) and *Care of the Self* (1990b) turn. Here the aesthetics, self-care, the technologies of self, allude to the possibilities of being otherwise, not through lessons of/from resistance but from the self-conscious practices of subjects, even if these subjects come into being through the condition of subjection, or subjectivation.

Considering these Althusserian and Foucauldian accounts of subjection together, Butler asserts that:

> 'subjectivation' . . . denotes both the becoming of the subject and the process of subjection—one inhabits the figure of autonomy only by becoming subjected to a power, a subjection which implies a radical dependency. [. . .] Subjection is, literally, the *making* of a subject, the principle of regulation according to which a subject is formulated or produced. Such subjection is a kind of power that not only unilaterally *acts on* a given individual as a form of domination, but also *activates* or

forms the subject. Hence, subjection is neither simply the domination of a subject nor its production, but designates a certain kind of restriction *in* production. (Butler, 1997b, pp. 83–84; original emphasis)

Likewise:

It is important to remember at least two caveats on subjection and regulation derived from Foucaultian scholarship: (1) regulatory power not only acts upon an preexisting subject but also shapes and forms that subject; moreover, every juridical form of power has its productive effect; and (2) to become subject to a regulation is also to be brought into being as a subject precisely through being regulated. (Butler, 2004, p. 41)

Butler develops these ideas to detail how subjectivation as an effect of discourse and, more specifically, the performative offers political potential. She engages with Althusser's understanding of interpellation (Althusser, 1971)—the turn to the hail of authority—to think about how the hail might be understood as a performative and how the performatively constituted subjects might engage in the sorts of insurrectionary acts of which Foucault speaks. She suggests that while the subject needs to be named in ways that make sense in discourse in order to be '*recognizable*' (Butler, 1997a, p. 5; original emphasis), by being subjectivated the subject can subjectivate another. Butler writes:

the one who names, who works within language to find a name for another, is presumed to be already named, positioned within language as one who is already subject to the founding or inaugurating address. This suggests that such a subject in language is positioned as both addressed and addressing, and that the very possibility of naming another requires that one first be named. The subject of speech who is named becomes, potentially, one who might well name another in time. (1997a, p. 29)

Butler calls the capacity to name and so constitute that results from subjectivation 'discursive agency' (Butler, 1997a, p. 127). By thinking of agency as discursive—as being the product of being inaugurated in and by discourse and so able to join its citational chains—Butler moves past an understanding of intent and agency that is the property of an *a priori*, rational, self-knowing subject, but *retains* a subject who can act with intent. Discourse and its effects ultimately exceed the intent or free will of an agent, but, like Foucault's practices of self, the performatively constituted subject can still deploy discursive performatives that have the potential to be constitutive.

Butler suggests that as a politics these practices involve:

decontextualizing and recontextualizing . . . terms through radical acts of public misappropriation such that the conventional relation between [interpellation and meaning] might become tenuous and even broken over time. (Butler, 1997a, p. 100)

This 'performative politics' (Butler, 1997a, p. 127) offers significant promise for a post-structural politics of change. Through such practices, Butler insists, the sedimented meanings of enduring and prevailing discourses might be unsettled and reinscribed; subordinate, disavowed or silenced discourses might be deployed in, and made meaningful in, contexts from which they have been barred; and challenges to prevailing constitutions of subjects might be deployed self-consciously through the discursive practices of subjects who are themselves subjectivated. Butler sets out, then, a possible method for Foucault's struggles against subjection.[1]

These ideas have massive implications for education. With this understanding of subjectivation, the school student is so because he/she is designated as such. Indeed, while these designations appear to describe pre-existing subjects, understanding these designations as performative reveals that *it is the very act of designation that constitutes these subjects* as if they were already students. Simultaneously, the practices of these discursive agents amount to a politics that insists nobody is necessarily anything, and what it means to be a teacher, a student, a learner might be opened up to radical rethinking. The political challenge, then, is to intercept these subjectivating processes in order to constitute students *again differently.* Butler's performative politics offer tools for thinking how this might be done. These are understandings that I put to work in the analysis of school data that follows.

Subjectivating practices at 'Multicultural Day'

Multicultural Day, Plains High, Sydney, Australia, December 2001

It is an extremely hot, sticky day—even for Sydney's outer-west at the top of summer. Set up around Plains High's outside spaces there are stalls, dance and drama events, sports activities, and a ducking pool (offering up the male PE teachers for a dunking). Students and their family and guests mill around, visiting stalls, socializing and watching performances.

The Deputy Principal and a team of 4 male teachers, all White Australians aged around 40, patrol the school grounds, communicating with each other on walkie-talkies. I—a White English woman invited to experience an 'Australian Multicultural Day' by some of the students who have been participating in my research—watch the Deputy Principal and his team watching the students and their guests as I wander around the school grounds from one event site to another.

As well as being a multicultural 'celebration', this is also a school fundraiser and a key part of this is the stalls provided by students, parents, family and friends. These stalls are set up under a covered walkway that surrounds 3 sides of the school's main quad. These have hand-written A3 size signs: *'International Hotdogs'*; *'International Food'*; *'Italian Food'*; *'Hair Braiding'* and *'Hair braiding started in Africa but is now popular around the world'*; *'Flower Lais'*; *'Make your own beads'*; *'Philipino Food'*; *'German Cafe'*; *'Arabic Food'* and *'Kebabs'*.

White chalk on the fascia board above the Arabic Food stall reads *'Lebanon'* and *'Lebs Rule'*. *'Lebs Rule'* has been crossed out, but not erased, and *'Turks Rule'* chalked next to it. A half moon has also been drawn there.

The Arabic Food stall is constantly surrounded by a press of students, as well as guests and teachers, who wait for kebab rolls or chat with friends. The stall staff—a group of 14 and 15 year old students and a small number of slightly older young men and women—work hard to keep up with demand. The atmosphere around the stall is buzzing, and it continues to trade long after the other stalls have sold-out.

The Deputy Principal, or a member of his walkie-talkie team, regularly stands in the quad in front of the Arabic Food stall watching.

Around the middle of the afternoon I see the Deputy Principal standing with two Arabic boys (aged roughly 16–18) who have been hanging out at the Arabic Food stall on a BMX bike. The Deputy Principal tells the boys to 'leave the school premises immediately'. One motions towards a students on the stall and replies 'you told him to invite his family and friends, well I'm his friend so I can be here'. The Deputy Principal responds 'No, we say who can be here, now please leave'.

A while later, the Deputy Principal ejects another Arabic boy, also on a BMX, who has spent the afternoon at the stall. The Deputy Principal says to him 'You were going to light up on the premises—now leave'. The boy cups an unlit cigarette in his hand. One of the students from the stall asks: 'Sir, what if I personally vouch for him?'. The Deputy Principal does not respond to this offer and directs the boy away. The Deputy Principal watches me watching.

Later in the afternoon I walk past the car park behind the quad and see a police van parked there. The Deputy Principal stands nearby with one of his walkie-talkie team and says to him 'the thing they have to realize is that we decide who comes onto the premises'. His colleague replies 'they don't realize that'. (Fieldnotes)

Critical multiculturalism, critical anti-racism and, more recently, critical race theory in education offer significant criticisms of the sort of pluralist multiculturalism that appears to frame Multicultural Day at Plains High. These critical accounts argue that pluralist (as opposed to political or critical) multiculturalism presents cultural difference as naturally occurring and neutral, and race/ethnic harmony (tolerance) as following on from a recognition and celebration of these differences. This version of multiculturalism is criticized for ignoring the persistent (discursive) constitution of race/ethnicity as axes for differentiation and stratification, erasing historical and contemporary exploitations and subjugations, and failing to note, let alone challenge, the enduring supremacy of the majority race/ethnicity. There is not scope within this paper to explore these criticisms as fully as might be justified, but see Gilroy (1986), Gillborn (2004), Ladsen-Billings (2004), McCoy (2000) and Rizvi (1997) for excellent accounts.

Work in these areas has also extended significantly our understandings of race and racism. In particular, critical analyses of Whiteness and the mechanisms whereby White supremacy (Gillborn, 2005) or White hegemony (Youdell, 2003) are secured, White Noise becomes overwhelming (McCoy, 2000) and Whiteness is reproduced as at once normative and invisible (Leonardo, 2004), offer extremely fruitful tools for interrogating the discourses that circulate in school settings and the subjectivating effects that these discourse might have. Also particularly useful for the analysis offered here are Lipman's (2004) account of how anti-Islamic discourses are pervading educational discourse and settings 'post-9/11' and McCoy's (2000) reminder of the sense of 'epidemic' and being 'out-of-control' that infuses official and popular discourses (including pluralist multiculturalism) and so frames the terms in which difference might be intelligible.

The data that I produce and analyse here offer a series of moments from 'Multicultural Day' at Plains High. These readings are tentative and inevitably incomplete. They are also contentious and unsettling. The 'tokenism' of one-day-only ethnic food and craft stalls, wearing of traditional dress, and ethnic music and dance that form the focus of many such days of 'celebration' is evident (Solomos & Back, 1996). And the inclusion of the traditional 'Aussie' dunking pool and cricket match underscores the refusal of Whiteness and its cultural forms to be shifted from the centre for even this token day. This, then, seems to be a very typical example of a (pluralist) 'Multicultural Day'. Also evident, and the focus of this analysis, are struggles over the place and meaning of the 'Lebanese', 'Turkish' and 'Arabic' subject within this contemporary Australian high school.

Edward Said's works *Orientalism* (2003) and *Representing Islam* (1992) usefully identify the peculiarity of the 'Orient' and the 'Oriental', and later Islam, in the western imagination. For Said, the problematic is the gap between how the Orient, the Oriental, Islam, and the 'Arab' actually are, and how these are envisioned and represented in western ideas and media. While Said's work stresses heterogeneity and change, what is at stake for him is the distance between the real and the imagined. Taking a Foucauldian approach to these ideas, in particular approaching them through Butler's conceptions of performativity and subjectivation, radically unsettles this real/imagined divide. It does this by underscoring the discursive construction of this real and, therefore, exposing Orientalism(s)

70

as constitutive of subjects, as performative, as subjectivating. Thinking about Orientalism as discourses steeped in historicity and sedimented meaning helps to expose how the scientific rationale of colonial north Africa; the religious rationale of Crusades in the near and middle east; and the Empire's deployment of these in the construction of the Orient as the Occident's exotic Other and the Oriental/Arab as in the proper service of his (sic) colonial master, all suffuse contemporary western discourses of the Orient and of Islam. The 'Savage Arab' once in need of taming and Christianizing comes, in contemporary discourse, to be in need of westernizing, 'democratizing'. And these are needs heightened to epidemic levels in post-9/11 discourses of 'terror'. As Butler (1997a) notes in *Excitable Speech*, such discourses do not need to be made explicit or spoken to be cited and to have performative force. On the contrary, discourses that go unspoken, that are silent or silenced, remain constitutive. Furthermore, Butler's suggests that the subjectivated subject acts her/his place in the discourses through which she/he has been rendered intelligible, through which subjecthood, albeit subjectivated and subjugated, is effected. In a discursive frame in which Whiteness (synonymous with western-ness) is normative and these enduring (but mobile) discourses of the Orient/Islam continue to be cited, the White/Anglo/ Aussie and the Arab act their respective place in discourse (but not necessarily always). And in a discursive frame of school authority in which a teacher/student binary is a fundamental subjectivating divide, the teacher and the student act their respective place in discourse (but, again, not always).

These conceptual tools, then, help us to identify these discourses as they are deployed, resisted, recuperated and deployed again in the events of Multicultural Day. This is not an exhaustive account of the discourses that frame this setting (such an account is surely impossible). Further discourses are also clearly at play, intersecting the prevailing discourses of the Orient/Arab that I have already sketched; for instance, adult and youth heterosexual-masculinities, street/youth subculture, national and religious pride. This partial account, then, is offered as fragments of a porous network of discourses that are particularly significant to the subjectivations I am exploring here.

In the school's acceptance of the Arabic students' donation of an Arabic Food stall, the school constitutes 'Arabic' as a legitimate axis of minority cultural difference and subjectivates the Arabic subject as a good student. And in donating the stall and participating in Multicultural Day, this good-Arabic-student-subject takes up this subjecthood. In doing this, just as the school cedes the good-Arabic-student-subject, so this subject cedes the authority of the school institution by which she/he is subjectivated. And the students gain the rights of the student (to invite guests) but also subjection to teacher authority (to have their guests ejected).

The stall, the food it sells, and so the students and others who staff it, are named (by the students?) 'Arabic'. This collective performative interpellation is particularized by the further performative names 'Lebs' and 'Turks'. And nationalism meets competitive team sports (or in another discourse something more sinister) in the chalked proclamation (performative?) 'Lebs Rule' and 'Turks Rule'. The crossing out, without erasure, of 'Lebs Rule' (by the author of 'Turks Rule'?) does not lessen the constitutive effect of this textual practice. That the crossing out, the replacement of one 'ruling' nationality with another, is left for public display continues to cite the claim as well as the erasure and the overthrow that calls up. It seems that this is not a battle but a playful skirmish—Lebanese and Turkish students have organized and are staffing the 'Arabic Food' stall together under that collective given and taken name: 'Arab'. Indeed, there is a collectivity evident in these claims. Rather than erasing each others' self-constituting performatives, then, each claim in this apparent contest acts to render the other intelligible (Butler, 2004), even if this is also a subjectivation.

In a discursive frame of normative Whiteness, the claim that Lebs or Turks rule cannot have performative force. The subjectivating practices of the school render the Arabic subject (the Leb or the Turk), but she/he remains (reviled?) 'ethnic'[2] in this context—in the school and the wider social context of contemporary Australia, Lebs and Turks certainly do not rule. Yet this practice of self, made possible through the prior subjectivation of these raced-nationed-regionalized subjects, is simultaneously felicitous. That is, Lebs and Turks may not rule, but the statement is not empty. Instead it silently calls up once again the threat of the savage Arab Other. What might be read as (invisibly) written on the fascia board is 'Arabs Rule'. And the crescent moon of Islam drawn alongside these claims interpellates collective regional identity in religious terms—these good-Arabic-student-subjects also silently constitute themselves Islamic. And the constitution 'Islamic' alongside a proclamation of ruling calls up that deepest of post-9/11 western/White fantasies—that Islam aims to Rule. And the spectre of 9/11, anti-western 'terror' silently rises. In this discursive frame, the Lebs and Turks (Arabs and Islamist) do not rule, but they would. And so these once good-Arabic-student-subjects are potentially subjectivated (through the coalescence of performative practices as external as the US media and as intimate as their own) as Islamic-Fundamentalist and even potential terrorist threats—and in urgent and absolute need of surveillance. And as the Arab/Islamist threatens to burst out of the confines of service and studenthood, this is not the surveillance of the panopticon, but a very immediate and visible coercive surveillance—the White, male, senior teacher stands in the quad in front of the stall, walkie-talkie in hand.

This, then, is a moment in which the 'Arabic' students in the school gain public recognition as legitimate, and this subjectivation opens up the opportunity for self-constitution. But, given the discursive terrain of this subjectivation and practices of self, this self-constitution is one that threatens to slide back into injury and the constraint of the Savage Arab/Islamist threat.

It appears from this reading that it is the students' practices that have suggested confrontation, a possible risk or danger—the wider discourse of Arabic threat is implicit in the claim that Lebs/Turks rule. Yet it is likely that the discourse of Islamic/Arabic threat would permeate this context at this moment without these chalked claims, that it would be 'on the lips' of White teachers—it was already one of the discourses of the Other that effect Whiteness and its normativity long before 9/11 happened. Again, Said's reading of the relation between the Occident and the Orient, inflected with a notion of discourse and the performative, is pertinent. These long-established discourses echo in contemporary contexts without ever being spoken. Indeed, perhaps the absence of the need to explicitly cite a discourse in order for it to be cited goes to its endurance and performative force. But the appearance that this discourse was deployed by the students and only *responded to* by the school renders 'legitimate' the teachers' apparent diagnosis of cultural discontent or threat and makes their move to police this threat not a raced and racist subjectivation but a necessary response. This is not to say that the squad of senior teachers armed with walkie-talkies is a response to this constitutive chalked claim—the establishment of this squad and the procurement of walkie-talkies to facilitate the best government of this population surely dates back to the students volunteering to mount the kebab stall, their arrival in the suburb, the school, the White Australia Policy, the refusal of Orientals at nineteenth-century colonial ports?

Butler's theoretical tools, then, enable us to see how the teachers subjectivate these students as particular raced–nationed–religioned subjects, with the possibilities for discursive agency and the constraints of the discursive terms of subjection that this entails. While the pronouncement 'Lebs/Turks Rule' might be a performative constitution of self as Arab not normally permitted in school, practicing these technologies of self simultaneously evokes the very discourses of epidemic difference and threat through which a school and wider society infused by Whiteness subjectivates the Arab Other. As Butler's work suggests they will, these students act their place in this web of discourses. And the school subjectivates these (no longer good) students in these terms and 'responds' accordingly—by keeping vigilant watch at the Multicultural Days most popular stall (and no doubt biggest fund-raiser) and by ejecting from the premises any Leb/Turk/Arab youth who fails to fulfil the schools requirements of the 'good ethnic'. Indeed, the Arab as a good-student-subject might be outside prevailing intelligibility after all.

The notion of subjectivation also allows us to see how these teachers (and potentially their colleagues inside and beyond this school) are constituted by prevailing discourses of education, professionalism, the teacher and teacher authority (perhaps no longer the good teacher) as well as wider discourses—particularly pressing here, hetero-masculinity and Whiteness. And, within this discursive frame, they are also constituted by their own practices of self: White supremacy-masculine authority/entitlement is inscribed through their surveillant practices even as it also subjectivates these men racist and vulnerable (and so perhaps not masculine at all). The cost of being made subject here is not borne by the Lebanese/Turkish/Arabic subject alone. Indeed, by understanding these discursive practices as subjectivating we can begin to consider how these constitutions and their framing discourses might effect other students and subjects more broadly.

A series of tensions seem to endure through these subjectivations. First, the students are good students who contribute (very well) to the school's fund-raising effort. They are also good 'ethnic' students who participate in Multicultural Day by displaying their 'difference'. But at the same time they are 'bad' students, or bad subjects: their ethnic(ized) subcultural display—Islamic crescents, Lebs/Turks Rule proclamations and BMX bikes—are all well outside the good student-subject. Second, this ethnic(ized) subculture is entangled with a further axis of tension in the subjectivation of these students—the discourse of the Islamic threat presses here and overwhelms the possibility of the good student—in this discursive frame the Arab/Islamist is a bad subject. Finally, multicultural pluralism (as enacted by Multicultural Day) also sits in tension with the Islamist threat and the policing of this. And yet, in post-9/11 western contexts, perhaps this pluralism and policing are reconciled in the subjectivation of the good teacher and good citizen who celebrates diversity as long as it remains minoritized, marginalized and willing to be (impossibly) Westernized.

Performative politics, or politics in subjectivation

Butler uses the notion of the performative, the notion of discourse and the notion of subjectivation to think about the constitution, constraint and political possibility of the subject. This paper has demonstrated the deployment of these notions for understanding practices inside schools and begun to show how performative politics might begin to destabilize both the explicit and silent discursive ties between biographies and studenthood, ties that make possible, and normal, the continued subjectivation of differentiated student-subjects.

Yet the relationships between the performative, discourse and subjectivation, and the significance of these relationships for thinking about a post-structural politics, merit further consideration.

The performative, Butler tells us, enacts what it names—it names and makes. In this sense, all categorical names and claims to action are potentially performatively constitutive of the subjects to whom they refer. But it is not only utterances that have the potential to act performatively. Butler (1997a, b) also notes the possibility of bodily practices being performative, and examines this possibility through her consideration of Bourdieu's (1991) bodily *habitus*. I have not pursued this here, but if we reflect on the bodies of the teachers and students in the earlier episode, we can begin to see how, for instance, the *particular way* that the boy sat on his BMX bike, unlit cigarette cupped in his hand, and the *particular way* that the Deputy Principal stood legs apart, shoulders square, walkie-talkie in hand, are bodily practices that simultaneously enact particular sorts of subjects.

In the move from the performativity of names to wider utterances, and from utterances to practices, the performative can be seen as a function within discourse. Indeed, it might be helpful to think of the performative as a particular element of discourse *and* as a nuance within the discursive processes through which discourses come to have productive effects. Discourse itself might be as performative. This suggests that the performative might be understood very specifically, after Butler's earlier engagements with the idea, and that the specific performative *and* the wider discursive field in which it is located can be understood as discursively constitutive.

Subjectivation understands the constitutive effect of discourses in this way, but the notion of subjectivation underscores how this constitution *is simultaneously and unavoidably entangled in the production of discursive relations of power.* Constitution within constraint is always present within the notions of the performative and discursive constitution, but when we take up a notion of subjectivation this simultaneous constitution within constraint—made subject *and* subjected to/by—becomes wholly explicit. Indeed, that discursive relations of power are integral to being a recognizable subject is central to the notion of subjectivation.

Subjectivation is effected through discursive practices, and understanding the performative is an important tool for understanding the constitutive effects of these discursive practices. But it is the more explicit sense of the way that power is implicated in subjectivation that I find particularly helpful. And this has led me to think, alongside Butler's (1997a) notions of performative politics and politics of hegemony, about a *politics in subjectivation* in which discursively constituted and constrained subjects deploy discursive agency and act within and at the borders of the constraint of their subjectivation. By interrogating and rendering visible the subjectivating practices that constitute particular sorts of students tied to particular subjectivities and, by extension, particular educational (and wider) trajectories, we begin to uncover the potential of Butler's performative politics or a politics in subjectivation. Whether challenging the effects of, for instance, discourses of poverty, heredity, intelligence, heteronormativity, or, like here, racism and Whiteness, understanding these processes helps us to see where discursive interventions might enable new discourses to be rendered intelligible or enduring discourse to be unsettled within school contexts.

In mapping the subjectivating practices of a school and its teachers, and the practices of self of teachers and students, this paper demonstrates the importance of engaging these ideas for making sense of the practices and effects of schooling. The particular analysis offered here adds another layer of understanding to existing analyses of enduring patterns of raced educational inequality and exclusion. Yet it is not a pessimistic analysis—these theoretical tools insist that the potential to act with intent and, therefore, shift meaning is inherent to the contingent nature of discourse and the discursive agency inherent to subjectivating processes. The teachers' and students' practices that I have interrogated here are performative politics that both reinscribe and unsettle hegemonic meaning. These teachers are involved in practices of Whiteness that subjectivate raced–nationed–religioned students, and these students are involved in practices of insurrection as they are subjectivated. The teachers' performative politics constitute themselves and Arabic students in their respective places in enduring discourse. The students' performative politics are the skirmishes that these subjectivated subjects engage in when their discursive agency is worked against the prevailing discourses through which they are subjectivated. Or when these subjects deploy subjugated discourses through their practices of self, even if these discourses, and the subjectivities they constitute, are rapidly recuperated. Performative politics does not entreat us to identify the subjectivation and then move on to design a corresponding performative insurrection (although at the level of collective action activists/academics might want to do this). Rather, these are *politics in subjectivation*, enacted at any (every?) moment of constitution.

Notes

1 In 'The Subject and Power', Foucault suggests that we might recognize three forms of struggle that exist in 'complex and circular relations' (1982, p. 213): struggles against domination, against exploitation and against subjection. These struggles against subjection, for Foucault, are increasingly significant both to the subjects who struggle against their own subjection and to the enquirer into the present. At the centre of Foucault's work, then, is a concern with struggles for change. This is not a struggle for the liberation, or self-determination, of the subject; but struggles played out through the persistent potential for resistances in the circulation of counter- and subjugated discourses (vol. 1) and the freedom suggested by the possibility of transformation (Foucault, 1988a).
2 In this setting, as many in multi-ethnic, urban Sydney, 'ethnic' is commonly used on its own to name minority ethnic individuals and communities. Indeed, it has become the object of ironic recuperation.

References

Althusser, L. (1971) Ideology and ideological state apparatuses, in: *Lenin and Philosophy* (B. Brewster, Trans.) (London, Monthly Review Press), 170–186.

Alvesson, M (2002) *Postmodernism and social research* (Buckingham, Open University Press).

Austin, J. L. (1962) *How to do things with words* (Oxford: Clarendon Press).

Ball, S.J. (2003) 'The teachers' soul and the terrors of performativity, *Journal of Education Policy*, 18(2), 215–228.

Baudrillard, J. (1994) *Simulacra and simulation* (Ann Arbor, University of Michigan Press).

Bourdieu, P. (1991) *Language and symbolic power* (Cambridge, MA, Harvard University Press).

Britzman, D. (2000) 'The question of belief': writing poststructural ethnography, in: A. St Pierre & W.S. Pillow (Eds) *Working the ruins: feminist poststructural theory and methods in education* (London, Routledge), 27–40.

Butler, J. (1990) *Gender trouble: feminism and the subversion of identity* (London, Routledge).

Butler, J. (1993) *Bodies that matter: on the discursive limits of 'sex'* (London, Routledge).

Butler, J. (1997a) *Excitable speech: a politics of the performative* (London, Routledge).

Butler, J. (1997b) *The psychic life of power: theories in subjection* (Stanford, Stanford University Press).

Butler, J. (2004) *Undoing gender* (London, Routledge).

Carr, W. & Kemmis, S. (1986) *Becoming critical: education knowledge and action research* (London, Falmer).

Delamont, S. & Atkinson, P. (1995) *Fighting familiarity: essays on education and ethnography* (Cresskill, NJ, Hampton Press).

Derrida, J. (1988) Signature event context, in: J. Derrida (Ed.) *Limited Inc.* (Elvanston, IL, North-western University Press), 1–23.

Foucault, M. (1982) The subject and power, in: H. L. Dreyfus & P. Rabinow (Eds) *Michel Foucault: beyond hermenutics and structuralism* (Brighton, Harvester), 208–226.

Foucault, M. (1988a) Critical theory/intellectual history, in: L. Kritzman (Ed.) *Michel Foucault—politics, philosophy, culture: interviews and other writings 1977–1984* (London, Routledge), 17–46.

Foucault, M. (1988b) An aesthetics of existence, in: L. Kritzman (Ed.) *Michel Foucault—politics, philosophy, culture: interviews and other writings 1977–1984* (London, Routledge), 47–56.

Foucault, M. (1988c) The return of morality, in: L. Kritzman (Ed.) *Michel Foucault—politics, philosophy, culture: interviews and other writings 1977–1984* (London, Routledge), 242–254.

Foucault, M. (1990a) *The history of sexuality volume 1: an introduction* (London, Penguin).

Foucault, M. (1990b) *The care of the self: the history of sexuality* (vol. 3) (London, Penguin).

Foucault, M. (1991) *Discipline and punish: the birth of the prison* (London, Penguin).

Foucault, M. (1992) *The uses of pleasure: the history of sexuality* (vol. 2) (London, Penguin).

Gillborn, D. (2004) Anti-racism: from policy to praxis, in: G. Ladson-Billings & D. Gillborn (Eds) *The Routledge Falmer reader in multicultural education: critical perspectives on race, racism and education* (London, Routledge Falmer), 35–48.

Gillborn, D. (2005) Education policy as an act of white supremacy, *Journal of Education Policy*, 20(4), 485–505.

Gilroy, P. (1986) *There ain't no black in the Union Jack* (London, Routledge).

Hammersley, M. & Atkinson, P. (1995) *Ethnography: principles in practice* (2nd edn) (London, Tavistock Publications).

Harwood, V. (2001) Foucault, narrative and the subjugated subject: doing research with a grid of sensibility, *Australian Educational Researcher*, 28(3), 141–166.

Jacobson, M. F. (1998). *Whiteness of a different color: European immigrants and the alchemy of race* (Cambridge MA, Harvard University Press).

Ladson-Billings, G. (2004) Just what is critical race theory and what's it doing in a nice field like education?, in: G. Ladson-Billings & D. Gillborn (Eds) *The Routledge Falmer reader in multicultural education: critical perspectives on race, racism and education* (London, Routledge Falmer), 49–68.

Lather, P. (1991) *Getting smart: feminist research and pedagogy with/in the postmodern* (New York, Routledge).

Lather, P. (2000) Drawing the line at angels: working the ruins of feminist methodology, in: A. St Pierre & W. S. Pillow (Eds) *Working the ruins: feminist poststructural theory and methods in education* (London, Routledge), 258–312.

Leonardo, Z. (2004) The souls of white folk: critical pedagogy, whiteness studies, and globalization discourse, in: G. Ladson-Billings & D. Gillborn (Eds) *The Routledge Falmer reader in multicultural education: critical perspectives on race, racism and education* (London, Routledge Falmer), 117–136.

Lipman, P. (2004) Education accountability and repression of democracy post 9/11, paper presented at *American Educational Research Association Annual Conference*, San Diego, April.

MacLure, M. (2003) *Discourse in educational and social research* (Buckingham, Open University Press).

McCoy, K. (2000) White noise—the sound of epidemic: reading/writing a climate of intelligibility around a 'crisis' of difference, in: A. St Pierre & W. S. Pillow (Eds) *Working the ruins: feminist poststructural theory and methods in education* (London, Routledge), 237–257.

Miller, G. (1997) Building bridges: the possibility of analytic dialogue between ethnography, conversation analysis and Foucault, in: D. Silverman (Ed.) *Qualitative research: theory, method and practice* (London, Sage), 24–44.

Prior, L. (1997) Following in Foucault's footsteps: text and content in qualitative research, in: D. Silverman (Ed.) *Qualitative research: theory, method and practice* (London, Sage), 63–79.

Rizvi, F. (1997) Educational leadership and the politics or difference, *Melbourne Studies in Education*, 38(1), 90–102.

St Pierre, E. (2000) Nomadic enquiry in the smooth spaces of the field: a preface, in A. St Pierre & W. S. Pillow (Eds) *Working the ruins: feminist poststructural theory and methods in education* (London, Routledge), 258–283.

Said, E. (2003) *Orientalism* (London, Penguin).

Said, E. (1992) *Representing Islam* (London, Penguin).

Seshedri-Crooks, K. (2000) *Desiring whiteness: a Lacanian analysis of whiteness* (London, Routledge).

Silverman, D. (1997) Towards an aesthetics of research, in: D. Silverman (Ed.) *Qualitative research: theory, method and practice* (London, Sage), 239–253.

Skeggs, B. (1994) Situating the production of feminist ethnography, in: M. Maynard & J. Purvis (Eds) *Researching women's lives from a feminist persepective* (London, Taylor & Francis).

Solomos J. & Back, L. (1996) *Racism and society* (Basingstoke, Macmillan).

Stanley, L. & Wise, S. (1993) *Breaking out again: feminist ontology and epistemology* (London, Routledge).

Stronach, I. & Maclure, M. (1997) *Educational research undone: the postmodern embrace* (Buckingham, Open University Press).

Youdell, D. (2003) Identity traps, or how Black students fail: the interactions between biographical, sub-cultural, and learner identities, *British Journal of Sociology of Education*, 24(1), 3–20.

Youdell, D. (2005) Sex–gender–sexuality: how sex, gender and sexuality constellations are constituted in secondary school, *Gender and Education*, 17(3), 247–270.

26

THE INVISIBILITY OF RACE

Intersectional reflections on the liminal space of alterity

Nicola Rollock

Source: *Race Ethnicity and Education*, 15, 1, 2012, 65–84.

It has been argued that racialised Others occupy a liminal space of alterity; a position at the edges of society from which their identities and experiences are constructed. Rather than being regarded as a place of disadvantage and degradation, it has been posited that those excluded from the centre can experience a 'perspective advantage' as their experiences and analyses become informed by a panoramic dialectic offering a wider lens than the white majority located in the privileged spaces of the centre are able to deploy. In this article, I invite the reader to glimpse the world from this liminal positioning as I reflect critically on how the intersections between social class, race and gender variously advantage or disadvantage, depending on the context, the ways in which Black middle classes are able to engage with the education system. While I make reference to findings from a recent school-focused ESRC project 'The Educational Strategies of the Black Middle Classes'[1] the article takes a wider perspective of the education system, also incorporating an autobiographical analysis of the academy as a site of tension, negotiation and challenge for the few Black middle classes therein. I make use of the Critical Race Theory tool of chronicling (counter-narrative) to help demonstrate the complex, multifaceted and often contradictory ways in which ambitions for race equality often represent lofty organisational ideals within which genuine understanding of racism is lacking.

I am invisible, understand, simply because people refuse to see me. (. . .) When they approach me they see only my surroundings, themselves, or figments of their imagination – indeed, everything and anything except me. (. . .) Nor is my invisibility exactly a matter of bio-chemical accident to my epidermis. That invisibility to which I refer occurs because of a peculiar disposition of the eyes of those with whom I come in contact. A matter of the construction of their inner eyes, those eyes with which they look through their physical eyes upon reality. (. . .) It is sometimes advantageous to be unseen, although it is most often rather wearing on the nerves. Then too, you're constantly being bumped against by those of poor vision (. . .) You ache with the need to convince yourself that you do exist in the real world, that you're a part of all the sound and anguish, and you strike out with your fists, you curse and you swear to make them recognize you. And, alas, it's seldom successful.

Ralph Ellison (1965, 7)

Introduction

Drawing on Wynter's (1992) theorisation of the concept of marginality, Ladson-Billings and Donnor 2008, 373) posit that racialised others occupy a 'liminal space of alterity' that is, a position at the edges of society from which their identities and experiences are constructed. They remain at the margins through acts and frequent reminders from dominant groups that regardless of achievement, qualification or status they are locked in 'the power dynamic and hierarchical racial structures' that serve to maintain unequal order in society (Ladson-Billings and Donnor 2008, 372).

Yet Wynter (1992) insists that rather than regarding this space as a site of dismal subjugation, those excluded from the centre can experience a certain profound analytical insight that is 'beyond the normative boundary of the conception of Self/Other' (Ladson-Billings and Donnor 2008, 373). In other words, it is precisely from this position in the margins that racialised others are able to acquire not simply an 'oppositional world-view' (hooks 1990, 149) but what might be understood as a unique *surround vision* that is able to recognise and deconstruct the multifaceted contours of Whiteness and therefore advance the broader objectives of the racial justice project. Such an all-encompassing analytic perspective is particularly important to challenge and move beyond the *not seeing* nature of Whiteness that works to perpetuate a racially inequitable status quo:

One of the most powerful and dangerous aspects of whiteness is that many (possibly the majority) of white people have no awareness of whiteness as a construction, let alone their own role in sustaining and playing out the inequities at the heart of whiteness. (Gillborn 2005, 9)

While recognising and fully supporting the centrality of liminality to advancing a 'counter-hegemonic discourse' (hooks 1990, 149), I seek in this article to provide an extension to these debates by arguing that the very notion of what might be framed as *liminality as resistance* is wholly context dependent. That is to say, the field in which racialised others are operating, the tools or resources at their disposal, the support mechanisms available to them and the relative power of other actors present within the social space or field fundamentally impacts and brings into awkward tension the extent to which occupying a site in the margins becomes advantageous. I variously employ Bourdieu and Critical Race Theory (CRT) as theoretical frames of reference. As such, the arguments presented are located in an understanding, informed by CRT, that racism operates as normal[2] in everyday life (Delgado and Stefancic 2001; Tate IV 1997) and can, in part, be understood through the various forms of capital – to borrow from Bourdieu – that are positioned as having status and legitimacy within formally sanctioned spaces of, for the purposes of this article, the education system which I am taking in its broadest sense to include the academy:

> The members of groups based on co-option (. . .) always have something else in common beyond the characteristics explicitly demanded. The common image of the professions, which is no doubt one of the real determinants of 'vocations,' is less abstract and unreal than that presented by statisticians; it takes into account not only the nature of the job and the income, but *those secondary characteristics which are often the basis of their social value (. . .) and which, though absent from the official job description, function as tacit requirements, such as age, sex, social or ethnic origin* . . . (Bourdieu 1984, 102; emphasis added)

As a theory, CRT affords me, as a scholar of colour, the license and power to 'speak back' about racial inequalities in a way that hitherto I have not found entirely possible through many other theoretical tools. Critical Race Theory offers a framework that explicitly recognises and encourages people of colour to name, speak and theorise about their experiences as shaped by racism. The approach I adopt, therefore, is creative what Tate IV (1997, 210) describes as an 'enactment of hybridity.' I use part autobiography, part data analysis and part counter-narrative to critically interrogate the norms and practices of educational spaces of which I have been part, am part and, predominantly due to my racially minoritised status, am not part. As a Black female academic, I am at once located within this article even as I write hence the use, where appropriate, of pronouns such 'we,' 'our,' 'my.' With reference to data analysis, I draw on findings from a two-year ESRC project 'The Educational Strategies of the Black Middle Classes' which examines the educational perspectives, strategies and experiences of Black Caribbean heritage middle class families as they attempt to navigate their children successfully through the school system. Many of the parents' accounts speak directly to the notion of marginality and how they have developed a complex set of resources with which to manage instances of racism and othering. By drawing these strands of analysis together I am seeking to highlight the pervasiveness of the racial power dynamics at play across the education system as a whole.

There is an additional point to be made. In seeking to capture some of the multifaceted, nuanced and quite complex ways which facilitate the continued existence of race inequality and demonstrate how racialised others manage such experiences, this article attempts an ambitious project. It is near impossible to present such complexity in precise conventional terms with a neat beginning, revolutionary middle and an all-encompassing conclusion; the racial justice project is challenging and it is ongoing hence the naming of this article as a set of 'reflections.' There is no tidy conclusion.

Finally, I invite the reader to consider this article an enterprise in seeking to critically 'name, reflect on and dismantle discourses of Whiteness' (Leonardo 2002, 31) and to not only consider what is written here in a mere academic way but to take account of how their own racial positioning (and awareness thereof) informs how they make sense of and react to the arguments presented.

Understanding liminality

In an attempt to deconstruct and give life to some of the theoretical analyses with which I began this article, I begin with a true story and reflect on the notion of marginality as it came to pertain to my own raced and classed positioning and also how aspects of my gender came to have salience to my identity.

Part I – the true story

When I was precisely eight and a half years old my parents moved me from my local state primary school – a place where, in my nostalgic memory, we played kiss chase at break time, lay on our backs in the field daydreaming at the sky in the summer and where all the kids lived in roughly the same size houses and our dads drove the same kinds of cars – and sent me instead to a private girls' school that seemed, to my young mind, to be an eternity away. The only Black teacher at the state school had warned my parents about the pervasiveness of racism, of how it was affecting her and many Black pupils she knew. I had no idea what racism was but I do remember that my (white) teacher refused to allow me to move up to the next set of *Peter and Jane* books because I was racing ahead of the rest of the class. 'Read them again,' I was instructed. When I told my parents my mum looked at my dad but said nothing.

So to my new school. I arrived on a Monday morning. Monday was spelling day; a test of 20 words that had been given to the girls as weekend homework on the Friday. To the utter amazement of the girl with whom I had swapped to mark our work, I got all 20 correct and won myself a shiny gold star next to my name on the chart on the wall behind Mrs Jackson's desk. I also won the instant friendship of Lucy Gladstone-Brown,[3] Ms Popularity herself. I would recall later how on our way home on the bus one day Lucy pointed out her home. It was massive three-storey sand-coloured affair, standing far enough back from the road to allow two or three generous sized cars to lounge comfortably

on the drive. 'Wow,' I said peering through the bus window, 'It's huge!'
'Well, we can't live in a bungalow,' Lucy retorted, her voice frosted with
a disgust, that I hadn't known possible in an eight-year-old, at the mere
thought. I recalled feeling a bit odd about what she had said. Why hadn't
she just agreed that it was a big house? Why had she uttered the words
with such condescension? It occurred to me that maybe Lucy shouldn't
see where I lived.

In that first week I settled down with my new best friend and enjoyed
school with the rest of the girls. On the Thursday, after break or lunch,
I forget which, we sat in our classroom at the top of the rambling old
Victorian building in which the school was situated, messing around,
giggling and chatting until our teacher Mrs Jackson arrived to take the
afternoon register. Whoever I was messing around with tickled me and
being horrendously ticklish I let out a shriek accompanied by tumbling
notes of carefree laughter. It was at that precise moment that Mrs Jackson
walked through the door. Even now I remember the sound of her high
heels on the tiled lino. 'Who. . .?' she boomed in a tones swelled with
harshness, '. . .screamed?' Hush fell upon the class, all earlier tomfoolery
and laugher dying without trace, without fulfilment into the now stilled
air. We froze, alert to the possibility of something awful that had yet to
occur. I swallowed. I would say that someone had tickled me. She would
understand. After all, she'd seemed nice enough on Monday when she
was awarding me my star. No, I couldn't do that. She would want to
know who had tickled me and I wasn't a grass. 'Well?' she boomed. We
sat meekly peering up at her wanting to appear attentive yet striving to
avoid her inquisitional gaze. Silence. 'It was me,' I finally offered in a
small fragile voice, thinking that perhaps I might receive some reprieve
being the new girl. She glared at me, 'Well, I don't know where *you*
come from but *we* certainly don't do that sort of thing here!' she barked
and clonked in her high heels to her desk.

In making this powerful statement, which I will continue shortly to discuss
through the eyes of my eight-year-old self, the teacher is in a very Bourdieuian
sense letting me know that my act has no place within the 'legitimate culture' of
the school:

> . . . the educational institution succeeds in imposing cultural practices
> that it does not teach and does not even explicitly demand, but which
> belong to the attributes attached by status to the position it assigns, the
> qualifications it awards and the social positions to which the latter give
> access. (Bourdieu 1984, 26)

There is a further complex playing out of power here as I unwittingly become
positioned as having contributed to my own exclusion by not adhering to the rules,

albeit unwritten and unnamed, of the school. Mrs Jackson lets me know that I can – *potentially* – gain 'inclusion,' however, I definitely am not yet on the inside.

The shiny gloss of my newness was ripped from my being as I struggled to make sense of the reprimand. 'Where I come from?' I puzzled and puzzled over this phrase. 'I came from . . . well I live in Tooting, just near the common, very pretty,' I considered. Why would people in Tooting be more likely to scream than. . .? No, that didn't make sense. 'We?' Which we? Who were 'we'? Wasn't I 'we' since I was sat in the same classroom, wearing the same khaki green uniform as everyone else? I felt myself shrink behind a veil of confusion, of hurt. I vowed not to speak for the rest of the afternoon and proceeded to study Mrs Jackson carefully, watching her every move, listening to her language, making note of with whom she smiled, taking note of with whom she did not. I studied the rest of the girls in my class, watched how they interacted with Mrs Jackson, with each other. I was determined to make sense of this 'we' of which I apparently was not part. And it was through my observations that I learnt to see this 'we.' I saw how the class was made up mainly of white girls (living in big houses like Lucy's) who had 'Pops Club' pencil cases that you could only buy from a single shop in Wandsworth Common,[4] somewhere I had never ventured; they had scented erasers and Caron d'Ache[5] pencils, which were terribly expensive. My stationery came from Woolworths. I heard how they 'popped over' to their holiday homes in the south of France during half term. I went (with much excitement because I loved books) to Tooting library loosing myself in fictional tales while gorging on penny sweets from the local newsagent. I watched as their 'mummies' came to collect them in green wellies, Burberry jackets or body-warmers making promises of afternoon tea to other mummies. And they were accompanied by small rosy-cheeked boys wearing blond bowl-shaped tussled hair and the blazers of prep[6] schools of which I had (then) never heard. And golden Labradors wagged excited tails in the back of Land Rovers and cars whose identities I could not place.

I begin to hate my dad's car.

This was the 'we' of which I was not part.

I tell this story, occurring as it does over 30 years ago, as a reflection of how I came to class awareness and the beginnings of my understanding of the power and taken-for-granted privileges embedded in Whiteness. As has been argued at length elsewhere (McIntosh 1997; Wildman and Davis 1997; Leonardo 2002), Whiteness tends to benefit and advantage whites in ways that they seldom see or care to acknowledge. However, my schooling enabled me to not only see Whiteness but understand and develop a level of perception and analyses of how middle class whites engage with one another, the language they use, the pastimes and activities they pursue, their tastes and preferences (Bourdieu 1984) and, significantly, how they treated people who were not like them. It was only much later, despite incessant warnings from the handful of Black girls advising me of which teachers I should remain vigilant and hearing various accounts of racist incidents, that I began to explicitly recognise myself as racialised and, consequently, comprehend how race and class came together in quite complex ways with varying and uneven outcomes depending on your racialised status.

Transferring from a co-educational state school to an independent girls' school enabled me to forge a comprehension of intersectionality[7] and acts of class distinction, shaped as they are by race, long before I learnt and deployed, with some discomfort and resistance, the formally 'sanctioned' theoretical language of the academy without which my racialised experiences apparently had little legitimacy. The African American scholar bell hooks speaks to similar discomforts when she observes 'this language that enabled me to attend graduate school, to write a dissertation, to speak at job interviews, carries the scent of oppression' (hooks 1990, 146).

However, there was a further aspect of my identity to which, at the time, I paid scant attention; that of femininity. Attending an independent girls' school meant I became embedded in discourses of femininity that were predominantly white and middle class. I was teased to the point of anxious self-consciousness about the shape and size of my bottom; my skirt not so much as A-line as awkward pencil-cut thanks to my derriere. Hair was also a subject of white curiosity. How often did I wash it? How long did it take to style and in moments that struck an as yet unanalysed peril in my heart, could they touch it? While white girls flicked their hair or dried it in seconds under the dryer when we went swimming, I and the other Black girls attempted to restore ours to some natural order before, the job yet incomplete, being barked back into hurried lines by impatient gym teachers. These experiences, regardless of school type, location or gender intake, mirror those recounted during interviews with many of the Black middle class parents in the project 'The Educational Strategies of the Black Middle Classes':

> I remember children coming up to me to find out if my bottom was white or Black because they just had no idea at all (. . .) I always remember that (. . .) I couldn't believe that anyone could be so ignorant as to not know (. . .) they were shocked about my hair not being the same as theirs. (. . .) they were just intrigued about me as a person and in turn I was intrigued that they didn't know . . . (Vanessa, Community Development Officer)

Like the parents in the project, these daily moments of othering were not limited to the relatively unmonitored spaces of the playground but were also evident within the classroom. I remember how the musical tastes (classical) of the parents' of a handful of über-trendy, pretty, blond-haired, clique-y girls served to imbue them with a set of unspoken 'secondary characteristics' (Bourdieu 1984, 102) that amounted to boundless status and privilege in our music lessons; they were seldom told off and given countless opportunities to talk ad infinitem about music and skiing holidays while the rest of us sat restlessly in the dull greyness of the shadows. My parents clearly did not have the 'right' taste in music for the fact that neither Bobby Darin (my mother) nor John Holt (my father) were ever mentioned, served to betray the illegitimacy of their musical preferences as much as my hair, bottom and skin represented markers of an undesirable embodied capital within that school (Bourdieu 1986). Like the parents in the Black Middle Classes project, school became a 'site of constant battle for survival in terms of gaining recognition of one's racial identity as legitimate, let alone . . . a place to learn' (Rollock et al. 2011). In becoming racialised within this very specific classed and gendered context, I was beginning to see the world through a different space that I would later understand as 'the margins.'

Yet interestingly during my adult years, I would come to be perversely appreciative of my femininity recognising it as a considerable advantage relative, for example, to the emasculating experiences of my Black male counterparts. Yet there seems to be no place within the academy for my *Black femininity*. I have come to recognise that when white colleagues speak about feminism they do so placing an unspoken Whiteness at the normative centre of their analyses. No mention is made of race or racism. I am continually made invisible. And I would come to recognise that while my transition to middle classness facilitated access to the many spaces dominated by the white middle classes, when white colleagues speak about their class identification there remains scant acknowledgement of how their raced identity shapes a reading of a class identity that, depending on context, is informed differently from the middle classed experiences of other ethnic groups and remains supported by uninterrogated and presumptuous discourses of privilege and power.

I offer these reflections as a way of attending to the various ways in which I came to be and remain at the margins of educational spaces that are marked by intersecting forms of class and race discrimination (as well as inequalities of gender). I came to understand during my (private) schooling that I was an *inside outsider*, 'part of the whole but outside the main body' (hooks 1990, 149). This positioning has remained throughout my career in the academy. For all my class advantage, it is the colour of my skin to which others continue to react with fear, hesitation and intrigue requiring me, therefore, to constantly develop complex forms of *strategising for survival*; acts to which much of WhiteWorld (Gillborn 2008, 162) is completely oblivious.

Survival within the liminal space of alterity

In the section that follows I make use of one of the central tools of Critical Race Theory, story-telling (or counter-narrative) to highlight instances of marginality, resistance and agency within the racial justice project as played out within the academy. Counter-narrative can be semi-autobiographical or fictional in nature and acts as a powerful way for minoritised groups to creatively introduce concepts and arguments aimed at subverting and challenging the normative narratives of the dominant group (Delgado 2000; Delgado and Stefancic 2001). As with *The True Story* described above, I both tell the narrative and, simultaneously, speak back to the reader by interweaving an ongoing analysis and critical reflection of the events as they unfold.

In *The Counter-narrative*, I continue the story of Jonathan, a fictional Black academic working at a prestigious UK university, and chart his experiences as he attempts to successfully navigate his way through a higher education system in which he witnesses few Black academic staff in senior positions (ECU 2009; HEFCE 2008) and an ever increasing number taking their employer to tribunal. I first introduced Jonathan, and his partner Soray, in a paper discussing the concept of racial microaggressions (Rollock forth-coming). Both are composite characters in that they reflect actions and experiences from multiple sources. Both are Black and possess a critical awareness of the various ways in which their racialised identities are (mis)used by dominant others.

Part II – the counter-narrative

The wind howls miserably, shaking the fragile windows of the office. The building is deserted, bar a few security personnel and doctoral students committed to working late into the cold, dark night. Jonathan looks at his watch and sighs, promising himself that he will answer just one more email before heading home. He glances back at his inbox and notices that a new email has arrived. It's from the journal to which, at Soray's insistence, he had eventually submitted his most recent article. His eyes scan the email, voraciously searching for the key sentence that will let him know whether or not he had worked in vain:

'I am pleased to accept your paper for publication subject to your addressing the revisions detailed by the three reviewers. Their comments are attached.'

He relaxes momentarily, not realising how intensely he has been peering at the screen and then double clicks on the attachment. He muses how hesitant he had been about naming so explicitly microaggressions as an issue with which the academy had to contend. 'Outstanding contribution to the field . . .'[8] states the first reviewer. Jonathan smiles and nods to himself, satisfied. His eyes flit over the rest of the glowing review before he turns to the remarks of the second reviewer: 'The author offers an insightful and important theoretical analysis . . . .' Jonathan exhales with relief, his smile broadening. He just didn't think the paper for all its theoretical sensitivities would be readily embraced. Soray had, in retrospect been correct about writing about his experiences, he reflects. He scans the comments of the final reviewer:

'The first thing I should say is that even though I am a white male those who know me will testify to my commitment to the types of diversity

issues described in this paper. . . . While the paper has the potential to make an important contribution to the journal, the use of story-telling is simplistic and anecdotal. . . . I recommend that the author resubmits the paper using a more conventional methodology . . .'

Jonathan reads the comments again, more slowly this time and then, for reasons he cannot immediately articulate, he starts to laugh.

And he is still laughing when he switches off the light to his office, locks the door and begins the cold, long journey home.

Jonathan studied the young Black woman perched eagerly before him on the edge of his spare office chair. He saw it as part of his duty to 'give back' to his community by taking the time to share his experiences and give advice especially to any serious-minded Black person who was interested in becoming an academic or doing a further degree. He sighed inwardly knowing that such time and contributions were precisely the type of activity that wouldn't be acknowledged through any of the internal workload assessment procedures nor through the forthcoming REF[9] even though he was supporting the professional development of the next generation of Black and minority ethnic academics. And heavens knew the academy's record on progressing and retaining Black academics was far from impressive.

This particular woman Sandra (28-years-old, married with a young child) was considering registering to read for a PhD. A white colleague who had supervised Sandra through her Master's programme, had directed her to him adding in the email that Sandra 'might benefit from your particular knowledge and experience.' Having read a copy of her dissertation, Jonathan had been sufficiently impressed by her level of critical engagement with the literature on race theory to agree to an initial meeting.

'I'm sorry,' Sandra repeated, 'I know you're extremely busy. It's just I could really do with your advice. I have no idea of what doing a PhD entails. I would have spoken with Diana but . . . well . . . . I didn't find her very supportive when I was doing my MA. I don't feel she really knows anything about the subject area or understood the issues I was trying to examine. And I'd really appreciate your help about how best to become an academic.'

Sighing inwardly for a second time, Jonathan removed his glasses and uncrossed his legs. He looked at her and sighed again before finally asking: 'Tell me why you want a career in the academy.'

'I want to challenge some of the rubbish that is being published about us, about Black people and I think I can make a real difference through doing research and teaching and . . .'

'You need to write,' he interrupted, now only half-listening to her. 'You need to make sure your work is out there in the best journals. . . . He trailed off dismayed by his own simplicity as he remembered the feedback about his paper that he'd read just the night before. The reviewer's need to clumsily name his acceptance and understanding of 'diversity' (although Jonathan had himself never used that word in the paper) had been made all the more facile by the recommendation that he abandon his theoretical approach, steeped as it was in Critical Race Theory, and adopt a more 'conventional' model. Thank goodness that the other two reviewers had been unequivocal in their praise otherwise the paper would have been rejected altogether leaving him with the option of submitting elsewhere or, quite possibly and horrifically, accepting the reviewer's advice. He shuddered at the thought.

A career in the academy? He recalled his first UK conferences. Soul-destroying spaces of isolation with barely a visible Black face. He noticed how papers that covered race and racism tended to elicit the same steady set of unsophisticated, poorly thought-out questions about the role of absent (read: 'deficient') fathers, about social class, about the influence of peers on Black children's educational attainment, about the perceived lack of parental involvement. Following his first presentation about the Black middle classes and the racism that affected their lives despite their class position, an internationally renowned white Professor had put up his hand and, smiling with apparent conviviality, remarked how similar Jonathan's findings were to his own work on the white working classes, 'Surely this is just about difference and issues of belonging' he'd said, presenting his words as more of a statement than a question. Others in the audience had murmured and nodded in relieved consent at these words that offered welcome and easy escape from their own complicity in the various acts of racism that Jonathan had presented to them.

Such reactions to ignore the role of Whiteness and trivialise or altogether obliterate the possibility of racism can be understood as one of the many tools of Whiteness. Picower's (2009, 205) analyses of the ways in which her white students use such tools to maintain their hegemonic understanding of their racialised normalities is particularly apt here:

> . . . [the] tools of Whiteness facilitate in the job of maintaining and supporting hegemonic stories and dominant ideologies of race, which in turn, uphold structures of White Supremacy. In an attempt to preserve their hegemonic understandings, participants [i.e. her students] used these tools to deny, evade, subvert, or avoid the issues raised. (emphasis added)

Within the context of higher education these acts of Whiteness, exemplified in the dismissive words of the renowned Professor, work to create and maintain what

Delgado Bernal and Villalpando (2002, 169) call an 'apartheid of knowledge' that serves to 'marginalise, discredit and devalue the scholarship, epistemologies and other cultural resources of faculty of color.' We can understand, therefore, the challenge facing Jonathan. Even though he is presenting information gleaned from a serious qualitative study of the Black middle classes, the findings pertaining to racism and their racially minoritised status are alien and uncomfortable to his white colleagues. Committed to seeing the world through the lens of Whiteness they, like Picower's students find ways, albeit steeped in what appears to be civilised academic discourse, to deny the validity of his work and thus maintain this epistemological apartheid. Jonathan is presented with a challenge: how should he respond to such persistent acts of denial and still remain truthful to the data and his own experiences?

> Back then, he hadn't known how to react. Now he understood this as part of the complexity of Whiteness as white colleagues worked to protect their positions of privilege, worked to deny the presence of racism and trivialised his research findings and, by implication, his experience and those of his research participants. 'Everyone is implicated in denial,' a white male colleague who he had thought understood the issues had stated during a discussion about the subject over lunch one afternoon, 'everyone is complicit. Even you,' he chuckled seemingly bemused by his own cleverness, 'are complicit by working in the academy as a Black male.' Jonathan had said nothing, pretending to give the statement serious consideration while chewing slowly on the remnants of his sandwich. In reality, he had been incensed at the way in which his colleague had sought to position as similar their experiences of the academy and, through wilful colour-blindness, disregard (his) white privilege and render Jonathan's racially minoritised experiences insignificant.

Sara Ahmed's (2009, 41) statement, about the complexities of embodying diversity when in a mainly white organisation, is apt here. She astutely reflects: 'if only we had the power we are imagined to possess, if only our proximity could be such a force. If only our arrival was their undoing (. . .). The argument is too much to sustain when your body is so exposed.' I want to situate these various forms of Whiteness, as demonstrated by the fictional white male Professor, the white others at the conference and Jonathan's lunch colleague, and the consequences they impose on our bodies as a *faux niceness* or *violence as niceness*. In the academy, such acts are often presented under the guise of 'polite' collegiality and theoretical debate while the 'violence' they impose on academics of colour, denying and subjugating their experience, remains unnoticed. It is precisely this white investment in niceness that contributes to what Leonardo and Porter (2010) describe as the myth of 'safe racial dialogue.' In other words, those conversations about race that feel comfortable and safe for whites are, in fact, fraught with tension and difficulty for racially minoritised groups who attempt genuine race dialogue but are consistently confronted by what might be described as a *Whiteness as default* positioning. Leonardo and Porter contend that while 'violence' in this context might be conceptualised as 'euphemized,' it is nonetheless damaging, serving to maintain 'links between material distributions of power and a politics of recognition, and lowers standards of humanity' (2010, 140). It is the complex *nano*-politics of these very issues that trouble Jonathan as he considers what advice he might be able to give to a student of colour interested in pursuing a career in the academy:

Should he really tell this young woman sat before him to drop everything to become an academic? What should he tell her: that she could change it from within? Hadn't he learnt the hard way how embedded the systems of Whiteness were? Wouldn't she be better off working in the private sector where although they weren't bound by race equalities legislation she could ultimately earn enough money to enable her to make the choices she needed regarding the schooling of her young child?

'Er . . . yes, I need to write. Is there anything else?' the young woman asked, looking slightly concerned at Jonathan's apparent lapse in concentration. 'Is there anything else I need to do?'

Jonathan's sigh was audible this time. Rising to his feet, he clasped his hands behind his back and paced, deep in thought, to the window that overlooked the university car park below. 'Was she ready?' he wondered, 'Could he trust that she would understand?'

'Yes, there is something else you need to do but . . .' he turned, ready to study her reaction, 'it won't be easy.'

Sandra looked at him expectantly but without the bafflement he had anticipated. Moderately reassured he returned to his desk and identified the folder saved on his computer as 'In Progress.' His eyes scanned the various documents he had saved within it until he found what he was looking for. He paused momentarily, fingers hovering over the keyboard, before entering the password that he had set up to protect the file from any prying eyes and printed the document that finally presented itself to him.

Retrieving the article from the printer he looked down at it, feeling slightly protective of the words that he had written there.

'Here, take this,' he shoved the sheet awkwardly in her direction, keen to have her take it before he changed his mind, 'go away, have a read and if you still want to pursue an academic career get back in touch with me. We can talk then . . . but you must keep this to yourself. Keep what's written there confidential . . .'

Sandra nodded and stood, conscious that the meeting was being brought to a close. Slightly confused by the entire exchange, she accepted the paper from Jonathan's outstretched hand, only able to glance briefly at it as she gathered her coat and bag.

'Oh and it's not quite finished,' Jonathan added, as she made to leave the room.

'Um . . . that's okay. Thank you so much for your time.' As she closed the door behind her, Sandra paused and read the heading on the paper she had been handed. In bold, black text at the top of the page stood the words: *Rules of Racial Engagement for (Possible) Survival in WhiteWorld.*

The rules that follow can be understood as part of what I am defining as the racially minoritised habitus. Although I do not attempt to suggest that every person who is racially minoritised considers their experiences or strategizes in precisely this way it should be borne in mind that the kind of micro-analysis and strategizing that will be revealed shortly in the rules was also reflected in the experiences of many of the Black middle class parents in the ESRC project mentioned earlier. Clearly such thinking is not unusual to those within this group. For example, in the following extract Ella (Senior Management, Health Sector) discusses the tactics she employs to manage incidents where she has been racially othered:

I think it is very very difficult (. . .) you are going to drop the voice, (. . .); you are going to try to talk round it. You try and say look this is why and give an explanation. You have to try not to be angry, you know, it is very difficult but you have to. . .the worst thing you can show is anger right, because then it is all gone, because then you are so obviously the aggressor [in their eyes]. If you try to be calm in dealing with the situation, 'problem-solve' [says this slowly and deliberately, slightly scornful, using her fingers to denote that problem-solving is in quotes]. I am going to work it out with you. We are professionals. I am not going to be emotive about it even though it is a painfully emotive experience. I have got to lose that and I have got to deal with this situation as a problem-solving thing. It means I think that it affects your personality because it means in other situations you tend not to be overly assertive, so that you are not seen in other situations as an aggressor, therefore when you deal with things like this they can look at the rest of your personality, and although they want to label you as an aggressor now it doesn't quite fit the rest. So [it's] almost as if you mould yourself into a certain 'placid' individual (. . .)

What is difficult to reflect here is the tone with which Ella conveyed the above. Her pace was steady, careful, precise. She is clearly recounting experiences and strategies with which she is extremely familiar. She was calm but also sounded both bemused and weary as she detailed the amount of extra work and energy required to defend one's identity from insult while simultaneously remaining alert to white sensitivities about race. And I would go further to suggest that she is also disappointed by continued white denial. Fatigue, bemusement and disappointment are interwoven with undercurrents of condescension as she details the ways in which she is obliged to navigate and manage whites who remain oblivious to, yet complicit in, the complexities of the entire racialised situation. Ahmed (2009, 48) speaks to the personal consequences and challenges of this kind of nano-politicking when she acknowledges how being an outspoken Black feminist who highlights instances of racism or sexism can lead to her being positioned as a 'kill-joy,' as a bringer of bad feeling to an otherwise (perceived) racially and sexually equitable and harmonious discussion. In presenting the 'Rules of Racial Engagement' I am seeking to summarise and name elements of this strategising and, in so doing, reveal the multilayered and nuanced analysis required for survival by those in the margins.

Rules of racial engagement for (possible) survival in WhiteWorld[10]

1 Avoid directly or even in passing accusing whites of racism, even if you believe their words or actions to be horrendously racist or racially Othering. This sends whites in a frenzy of guilt; denial; anger so that they are no longer able to engage in conversation and rather than hearing or understanding the point you are making, you will become positioned as the aggressor or killjoy.

2 On matters concerning race be prepared to 'problem-solve,' engage, negotiate. *In other words act as though you are simply exploring some abstract idea or a suggestion in a professionally engaging manner. This presents you as non-challenging and reasonable and keeps whites 'safe' in feeling that the issues of race inequity being discussed have absolutely nothing to do with them – even though they do. This is a challenging rule for those committed to the racial justice project. The aim is to encourage change, disrupt the status quo, which requires some level of white discomfort. Yet when is it safe for us to make whites uncomfortable?*
Be careful with this rule – you need to maintain the pseudo-safety of the dialogue but also challenge restrictive thinking while keeping your sanity intact. Support mechanisms are crucial. [see #10]

3 Maintain a lowered tone of voice in debates on race, especially where there is a difference of opinion. *The aim is to always seem reasonable and friendly. Use a raised tone with care even if you have been deeply insulted.*

4 Be prepared. *Whites will trivialise and position as anecdotal accounts of racism. Be prepared for this by knowing your subject area. Have countless sources of evidence and supporting examples. Statistics are always helpful. [Note: Qualitative evidence is likely to be refuted and closely questioned]. When*

writing for publication rigorously ground your analysis in theory. Good use of theory can provide a pathway to some form of academic legitimacy, albeit tenuous.

5   Don't show emotion or keep to a 'safe' minimum. Definitely don't show anger.

This is especially important for Black men but applies equally to Black women. Like the raised voice [see #3] use emotion strategically and with care.

Sometimes well-placed emotion, supported by a number of sources of evidence, can be highly effective. Do not overuse this strategy; emotion (irrespective of its appropriateness to the context) is not a license readily available to persons of colour.

6   Work at all times at presenting a friendly and reasonable persona.

This is a central tactic. If you work to present an image as friendly and approachable this will give you some degree of license, since it will seem out of character, to deploy a raised voice and emotion to your advantage should the circumstance warrant it.

7   Employ the 'language of Whiteness' to make your case.

Understand the strength of language as a unifying tactic. Begin discussions and debates with words, phrases, examples and points of reference that whites will understand and relate to. Only then attempt to demonstrate differences that are to do with race and racism. Never be complacent or underestimate the power of Whiteness as default positioning. Always be prepared for the fact that they may never understand the full extent of issues pertaining to racism.

8   Dress and carry yourself in a 'non-threatening' manner.

In your professional capacity never risk wearing clothes or items that whites might use to misread or confuse your class position and subjugate you even more. Your class position can be used as some minimal yet fragile protection against certain forms of racism.[11]

9   Be on your guard.

Acts of Othering and microaggression surface in the most unexpected ways, at unexpected times and are not restricted simply to those conversations that centre explicitly on race.[12]

10 Develop and nurture sacred spaces and protected narratives.

Work to ensure a strong support network comprising of white allies, Black colleagues and friends. This network will act as your sacred space of sanctity where there is minimal or no need for the Rules of Racial Engagement. Such spaces provide an opportunity to engage in forms of narrative protected from the dehumanizing violence of WhiteWorld. These are narratives with which to theorise, decode, de-stress in relative safety and to reaffirm one's humanity.

These rules can be considered as a template for survival or possible survival within mainly white spaces. I do not suggest the list is complete. Indeed Jonathan notes that it is a work in progress yet there is much within them that speaks to the tensions and apparent contradictions of attempting to survive in that space at the margins. I explore these issues further in the following section.

Dismantling discourses of Whiteness

Black folks coming from poor, underclass [sic] communities, who enter universities or privileged community settings unwilling to surrender every vestige of who we were before we were there, all 'sign' of our class and cultural 'difference,' who are willing to play the role of 'exotic Other,' must create spaces within that culture of domination if we are to survive whole, our souls intact (hooks 1990, 148).

In devising a set of strategies for survival, my fictional character Jonathan is both recognising and naming the contours of his own existence as racially marginalised and simultaneously revealing the ways in which Whiteness operates, in quite violent ways, to remain at the normative centre. Even while he comprehends this, his broader commitment to race equality and a personal need for a humanizing existence, necessitates that he finds ways to disrupt the white status quo while at the same time endeavouring to remain vigilant of the ever-ready sensitivities of whites who refuse to name and critically reflect on their place in the manifestation of White Supremacy. There are risks involved in 'outing' not seeing whites, in naming the contours of Whiteness, that could make the difference between a paper being accepted or not accepted by a journal, that could affect the ways in which others engage with his research and thus his capacity to advance his career. This reflects just one aspect of the awkward oscillating tension between liminality as advantageous and liminality as disadvantageous. To what extent does employing the 'language of Whiteness,' a phrase borrowed from a parent in the Black Middle Classes project, while a clever unifying strategy to gain the ear of whites in fact obfuscate the objectives of the racial justice project? What are the conditions under which one is able to make more explicit the goals of the project and reduce or ultimately discard such strategising?

Leonardo and Porter (2010) argue that in order to move towards racial justice there will invariably be some discomfort for those at the centre as they edge with resistance towards the recognition of their own investment in and endorsement of racism. I want further to argue that while such discomfort may be a necessary part of the move towards racial equity, it also represents a point of instability and danger for those of colour if whites fear that their positions of privilege and power are under threat or even merely being called into question. This, indisputably, is a serious consideration within the many spaces where whites are the gatekeepers or hold power in terms of decision-making (Collins 1991; Leonardo 2002). There are also countless additional matters to consider. Steer too far in the direction of disrupting Whiteness and Jonathan is likely to be construed as an aggressor or killjoy. Any future arguments or standpoints he presents will be deemed irrational, overly emotive and ultimately thwart his attempts to advance racial justice. Maintain too closely the 'nice safety' of the racial dialogue and he becomes one of the not seeing, complicit in the very practices he seeks to disrupt. He becomes further dehumanized seemingly unable to escape from what Fanon (1967, 88) evocatively describes as a kind of 'infernal circle.'

In drawing together different strands of analyses – counter-narrative, autobiography, data analysis – I have sought to reveal precisely the extent of the highly strategic and careful analyses required by those in the margins who are able to see. These tensions and negotiations demonstrate the extra work required for the person of colour within white society. Such work can, without contradiction, be conceptualised both as an implicit requirement to survive Whiteness and as an agentic critical response to it. I have demonstrated that power, status, gender and context interact in multiple sometimes opposing ways to lend a complexity to the experiences and very being of those persons of colour who work to advance the racial justice project even while race is becoming more embedded, more nuanced, thus necessitating increasingly sophisticated strategies for survival (Ladson-Billings 1998).

Earlier I described, borrowing from Zeus Leonardo, the need within the racial justice project to name, reflect on and dismantle discourses of Whiteness. In presenting the arguments in this article I have sought to add my voice from the 'radical space of my marginality' (hooks 1990, 151) to the numerous others engaged in the same fight towards racial justice (e.g. Crenshaw 1989; hooks 1990; Bell 1992; Ladson-Billings 1998; Delgado 2000).

I am talking back and working towards disrupting Whiteness.

Afterword

Extract from Jonathan's diary – Sacred Spaces and Protected Narratives

It is a barren terrain, the lands stretch for indeterminable distance, tumble weeds scatter in the wind. Sometimes in this dry land you encounter others like you, searching for a place, an island of comfort where we can rest, where we can take off the masks and be at one with the person crying with pain beneath the veil. This is a place where we can nurse the cuts, the grazes, the wounds that run deep . . . . And even when we encounter those others we have to still assess their trustworthiness. Can we really take the mask off with them? If we can, we sit on dry, unyielding land and share stories. We find others who recognise the pain. We create sacred spaces that are for us only us. We throw off the oppressive language and embodiment of WhiteWorld and intersperse our speech with colloquialisms, with the tongues of our mother countries and, for a brief precious moment, we relax. We shake our heads, hold each other's hands, we sigh, deep, deep sighs that only we and our ancestors can hear and engage in our protected narratives . . . narratives we keep protected from WhiteWorld. We laugh at the skill, at the strategising, at the recognition of some WhiteWorld act that we each have come to know only too well but of which WhiteWorld is oblivious . . . or unconcerned – caught up as it is in perpetuating the status quo. And we gain a temporary strength – for 'tis only temporary – as we stand, stretch our limbs, dust off our clothes and continue on our journey, leaving behind promises to meet again in this Sacred Space.

Acknowledgment

I would like to thank Gregg Beratan, Jide Fadipe and David Gillborn for their helpful comments on an earlier draft of this paper.

Notes

1   Economic & Social Research Council (RES-062-23-1880). I am carrying out this project with Professors Carol Vincent, Stephen Ball and David Gillborn.
2   Critical Race Theory recognises that racism is endemic and embedded as a normal part of the way in which society functions.
3   Lucy's name is a pseudonym as are those used in relation to the Black Middle Classes project.
4   A 'well-heeled,' relatively affluent area of south-west London.
5   Caran d'Ache is a Swiss based company specialising in writing instruments. According to their website: 'In that area of emotions where writing and images fuse together, graceful shapes, vigorous lines and deep colours create the passion that Caron d'Ache has for Fine Writing.' Only certain girls (white, middle class) owned these pencils. They were presented in flat, Caron D'Ache presentation box sets of 30 to 40 coloured pencils – 'the first water-soluble colour pencil since 1931' – that when dipped in water produced an effect not dissimilar to water paints. www.carandache.ch/m/les-instruments-d-ecriture-et-accessoires/index.lbl (last accessed 15 November 2010).
6   Preparatory schools are independent schools that prepare young children for continued (usually secondary) education in fee-paying schools.
7   Dill and Zambrana (2009, 4) define Intersectionality as a framework that examines the 'relationships and interactions between multiple axes of identity and multiple dimensions of social organization – at the same time.' Intersectionality is particularly useful as a means of reframing and creating new ways of studying power and inequality and challenging traditional modes of thinking about marginalised groups.
8   All of the reviews are entirely fictional.
9   The Research Excellence Framework is a process through which the quality of the research work of academics and UK higher education institutions is assessed. This is a highly competitive process which sees financial rewards attached to the highest university outcomes. http://www.hefce.ac.uk/research/ref/ (accessed 11 November 2010).
10   I am grateful to and have been inspired by the work of Derrick Bell, one of the key proponents of Critical Race Theory, who in a chapter entitled 'The Rules of Racial Standing' emphasizes some of the contradictions evident when in naming racism as a problem in a society where whites continue to deny its existence (Bell 1992).
11   See Rollock et al. (2011).
12   For example, see Rollock (2011).

References

Ahmed, S. 2009. Embodying diversity: Problems and paradoxes for black feminists. *Race Ethnicity and Education* 12, no. 1: 41–52.

Bell, D. 1992. *Faces at the bottom of the well: The permanence of racism.* New York: Basic Books.

Bourdieu, P. 1984. *Distinction: A social critique of the judgement of taste.* New York and London: Routledge.

Bourdicu, P. 1986. Thc forms of capital. In *Handbook of theory of research for the sociology of education,* ed. J.E. Richardson, 241–58. New York: Greenwood Press.

Collins, P. 1991. *Black feminist thought: Knowledge, consciousness, and the politics of empowerment.* 2nd ed. New York and London: Routledge.

Crenshaw, K. 1989. Mapping the margins: Intersectionality, identity politics and violence against women of color. In *Critical race theory: The key writings that formed the movement*, ed. K. Crenshaw, N. Gotanda, G. Peller, and K. Thomas, 357–84. New York: The New Press.

Delgado, R., 2000. Storytelling for oppositionists and others: A plea for narrative. In *Critical race theory: The cutting edge*, 2nd ed., ed. R. Delgado and J. Stefancic, 60–70. Philadelphia, PA: Temple University Press.

Delgado, R., and J. Stefancic. 2001. *Critical race theory: An introduction.* New York and London: New York University Press.

Delgado, B.D., and O. Villalpando. 2002. An apartheid of knowledge in academia: The struggle over the "legitimate" knowledge of faculty of color. *Equity & Excellence in Education* 35, no. 2: 169–80.

Dill, B.T., and R.E. Zambrana. 2009. *Emerging intersections: Race, class and gender in theory, policy and practice.* New Brunswick, NJ: Rutgers University Press.

Ellison, R. 1965. *The invisible man.* London: Penguin Books.

Equality Challenge Unit. 2009. *Equality in higher education: Statistical report 2009.* London: ECU.

Fanon, F 1967 [2008]. *Black skin white masks.* Exeter: Pluto Press.

Gillborn, D. 2005. Education policy as an act of white supremacy: Whiteness, critical race theory and education reform. *Journal of Educational Policy* 20: 485–505.

Gillborn, D. 2008. *Racism and education: Coincidence or conspiracy?* London: Routledge.

Higher Education Funding Council for England. 2008. *Staff employed at HEFCE-funded HEIs: Update.* Bristol: HEFCE.

hooks, b. 1990. *Yearning: Race, gender and cultural politics.* Toronto, Ontario: Between the Lines.

Ladson-Billings, G. 1998. Just what is critical race theory and what's it doing in a nice field like education? *International Journal of Qualitative Studies in Education* 11, no. 1: 7–24.

Ladson-Billings, G., and J. Donnor. 2008. The moral activist role of critical race theory scholarship. In *The landscape of qualitative research*, ed. N.K. Denzin and Y.S. Lincoln, 279–301. Los Angeles, CA: Sage Publications.

Leonardo, Z. 2002. The souls of white folk: Critical pedagogy, whiteness studies, and globalization discourse. *Race Ethnicity and Education* 5, no. 1: 29–50.

Leonardo, Z., and R.K. Porter. 2010. Pedagogy of fear: Toward a Fanonian theory of 'safety' in race dialogue. *Race Ethnicity and Education* 13, no. 2: 139–58.

McIntosh, P. 1997. White privilege and male privilege: A personal account of coming to see correspondences through work in women's studies. In *Critical white studies: Looking behind the mirror*, ed. R. Delgado and J. Stefancic, 291–9. Philadelphia, PA: Temple University Press.

Picower, B. 2009. The unexamined whiteness of teaching: How white teachers maintain and enact dominant racial ideologies. *Race Ethnicity and Education* 12, no. 2: 197–215.

Rollock, N. 2011. Unspoken rules of engagement: Navigating racial microaggressions in the academic terrain. *International Journal of Qualitative Studies in Education* February. DOI:10.1080/09518398.2010.543433.

Rollock, N., D. Gillborn, C. Vincent, and S. Ball. 2011. The public identities of the black middle classes: Managing race in public spaces. *Sociology* 45, no. 6: 1078–93.

Tate IV, W.F. 1997. Critical race theory and education: History, theory, and implications. *Review of Research in Education* 22: 195–247.

Wildman, S.M., with A.D. Davis. 1997. Making systems of privilege visible. In *Critical white studies: Looking behind the mirror*, ed. R. Delgado and J. Stefancic, 314–19. Philadelphia, PA: Temple University Press.

Wynter, S. 1992. *Do not call us Negros: How 'multicultural' textbooks perpetuate racism.* San Francisco, CA: Aspire Books.

Part 7

RACE, CLASS AND POVERTY

27

"WHAT ABOUT POOR WHITE PEOPLE?"

Ricky Lee Allen

Source: W. Ayers, T. Quinn and D. Stovall (eds), *Handbook of Social Justice in Education*, New York: Routledge, 2009, pp. 209–230.

I have been teaching about Whiteness at the university level since 1997. As a veteran of antiracist[1] education, I have become quite familiar with the highly predictable White responses to my (and others') critique of White privilege. White responses typically contain racialized sayings or phrases that are common to White subjectivity. For example, when I talk with nonpoor Whites[2] about White racism as a structural phenomenon that gives all Whites psychological and material advantages, their common refrain is "What about poor White people?" The first time I heard this from a nonpoor White person I was surprised. Growing up around poor Whites (see note 1), I had heard *them* raise this question with one another in discussions about race. But I did not expect *nonpoor* Whites to do the same, especially in a way that seemed to express concern for poor Whites. I was skeptical about their concern because in my own experience I had never known nonpoor Whites to show any serious commitment to ending poverty for poor Whites. Instead, experience told me that nonpoor Whites look down on poor Whites. So this sudden outpouring of concern for poor Whites was perplexing to me.

Out of all the different tactics that nonpoor Whites use to avoid responsibility for their White privilege, "What about poor White people?" is the one that I think about the most, maybe because I grew up as a poor White person, or maybe because I have long thought that it says more about the workings of race in the United States than most people realize. Time after time, nonpoor White education students interject "What about poor White people?" into the conversation when the subject of White privilege is on the table. Yet, they are otherwise curiously silent about the plight of poor Whites both before and after uttering this phrase. It is as though nonpoor Whites think that there is no need to talk about poor Whites unless Whiteness is the main topic of discussion. What this suggests to me is that nonpoor Whites' evocation of poor Whites through the phrase "What about poor White people?" warrants further examination because it appears to be a type of self-interested racial tactic.

In my earlier years of antiracist teaching, I reacted to "What about poor White people?" as if it was just one more of those sayings, or "semantic moves"[3] (Bonilla-Silva, 2003; Bonilla-Silva & Embrick, 2006), that we White people use to avoid the spotlight of racial criticism. Even though the phrase really bothered me, I minimized my gut feeling and considered "What about poor White people?" to be functionally similar to other problematic racial sayings like "I don't see color" or "Everyone gets an equal chance in America." To me, they were all semantic moves that prevented Whites from having to deal with the realities of racial injustice in a system of White supremacy.

However, in more recent years I have come to believe that this one particular semantic move is categorically different from the others that nonpoor Whites employ in that its rhetoric is as much *intraracial*[4] as interracial. In fact, it is one of the few semantic moves nonpoor Whites use that contains overtly intraracial language. It enters into the conversation the notion of a different kind of Whiteness (i.e., poor Whites) in order to make a point about the alleged inadequacy of critical race analyses for identifying and understanding the social and economic differences between Whites and people of color. The implication is that privilege cannot be assigned to all members of a particular group because some members of that group, in this case poor Whites, are not privileged. Therefore, privilege must be considered at the level of the individual, not the group. Since non-poor Whites are usually not really concerned about poor Whites, most nonpoor Whites who use this phrase are actually suggesting that they should be treated as individuals and not assigned White privilege simply because they are White. If these nonpoor Whites were more direct, they would ask instead, "How do you know me well enough to know that I am privileged?"

But they are not more direct because "What about poor White people?" does more than express a desire for an individualistic notion of racism. It also signifies that poor and nonpoor Whites share a close bond; nonpoor Whites stand up for poor Whites when poor Whites are not around to represent themselves. But do poor and nonpoor Whites actually interact with one another in a positive and unified way? Are nonpoor Whites really acting in the interest of poor Whites when they use "What about poor White people?" Do poor and nonpoor Whites share a hidden or normalized social bond that prevents us from better understanding the significance and ramifications of "What about poor White people?"

As I argue in this chapter, the signification of poor Whites by nonpoor Whites provides a window into the internal political organization[5] of the White race, which has yet to be adequately theorized in race-based terms. Toward this end, my hope is to shed light on the internal machinations of the White race by looking at the hegemonic[6] alliance that exists between poor and nonpoor Whites. Although this alliance has tremendous strength and is arguably the primary mortar holding together White supremacist structure, it has a number of cracks and crevices that need to be exposed and widened in the hope of bringing the whole structure crashing down. In other words, political alliances, such as the alliance that holds together what we know as the White race, can be undone in ways that work towards real social justice.[7] Garvey and Ignatiev (1997) make an important critique when they say,

> The "social construction of race" has become something of a catchphrase in the academy, although few have taken the next step. Indeed, we might say that until now, philosophers have merely interpreted the white race; the point is to abolish it. (p. 346)

If a race can be made, then it can also be unmade. Understanding how the White race is held together is the first step toward the ultimate goal of breaking it apart so as to disassemble the political alliances that keep White supremacy in place. Thus, it is my belief that a critical examination of "What about poor White people?" can add a new dimension to the ongoing debate around the most accurate and strategic way to theorize the intersection between race and class in the United States.

I teach in the field of education. Most of my students are (future) teachers or aspiring education scholars. The majority of these students are White, much like the U.S. teacher workforce. Data gathered in 2001 by the National Center for Educational Statistics shows that 90% of all public school teachers in the United States are White (National Collaborative on Diversity in the Teaching Force, 2004). While I am most disturbed by and focused on the problematic beliefs that my White students hold about students of color, I am also highly troubled by the problematic beliefs that my nonpoor White students hold about poor Whites, which they will take with them to the classroom or research site. Therefore, another goal of this chapter is to look at the social justice implications of poor and nonpoor White relations for poor White students. For example, how does "What about poor White people?" perpetuate pedagogical approaches that see the poor White student as someone who does not have privilege relative to people of color or as someone who is more racist than nonpoor Whites? How does a lack of attention to the racialization of poor Whites work toward reproducing the racial order that encompasses us all? How does the racialization of poor Whites shape the politics of their schooling? And, how should an antiracist education for poor Whites be conceptualized? Drawing from my critique of what I am calling the *White hegemonic alliance* (which I describe later in this chapter), I will address these questions and outline a social and political context of schooling for poor Whites that takes into account the dynamics of the White hegemonic alliance.

Occasionally in this chapter, I will look at White Appalachians as my example of a poor White subgroup, mainly because as a group member I am more familiar with their history, experiences, and positionality.[8]

The racial politics of "What about poor White people?"

For those of us who see the education of Whites as a vital component of the larger anti-racist project, we need to closely examine what may seem at first glance to be "critical" responses to "What about poor White people?" For example, one could argue from a class-based perspective that race critique has its limitations in that although it can show us the construction of power and difference between racial groups it cannot shed light on the construction of power and difference within racial groups. What we would need, or so the logic goes, are class-based or Marxist analyses to sort out intraracial class hierarchies such as the one between poor and nonpoor Whites. The problem with this approach is that it implies that the racialization of White people is monolithic and there are no political struggles within the White race that could be explained by different yet related racialization processes for poor and nonpoor Whites. It assumes that race-based analyses have little or nothing to contribute to understanding and disrupting intraracial stratification. It also naturalizes and minimizes the racial alliance between poor and nonpoor Whites in that it only pays attention to their class-based public tensions (e.g., the exploitation of coalminers by mining corporations) and not their tacit race-based agreements (e.g., remaining silent about the normativity of White privilege). The inherent, teleological assumption being made is that poor and nonpoor Whites *should* be aligned, and class conflicts divert attention from the racial agreements that hold them together.

In the class-based approach, it is as if somehow those people we know as "White" were not politically and historically constructed; they are allegedly natural biological allies. This perspective wrongly assumes that somehow the amalgamation of the White racial polity out of various groups with different status levels had nothing to do with the construction of the "White race," its rise to power, and its persistence in domination. In other words, we must consider whether the initial and ongoing differences in power between subgroups that we now think of as White were and are essential to the life of the White racial polity. My assertion is that the White race *requires* an internal hierarchy in order for it to exist, meaning that those at the bottom of this hierarchy must be willing to submit to the authority of those on the top. I will come back to this point later in the chapter.

Coming from a Whiteness studies approach, another example of a seemingly critical response to "What about poor White people?" is that one could simply argue that all Whites have more privilege than people of color, regardless of the White person's class status. So, there is no need to waste time distinguishing between poor and nonpoor Whites. This position is also problematic. Recent critical studies of Whiteness have tended to lump all Whites into one group monolithically privileged by Whiteness (e.g., McIntosh, 1997; McIntyre, 1997; Tatum, 2003). I believe that this trend arose—justifiably so—as a reaction to the difficulty of keeping folks, especially White folks, engaged in a sustained, transformative dialogue on Whiteness. I have heard numerous antiracist educators say that Whites often try to shift the conversation away from race and toward class when the focus is on Whiteness. They also say, and I would agree, that it is difficult to prevent the shift to class, especially when semantic moves like "What about poor White people?" are made. So, I do understand why an antiracist educator might simply avoid discussing the differences in structural privilege between poor and nonpoor Whites. But avoiding the reality of poor Whites' lower status relative to nonpoor Whites ultimately weakens the overall effort to create cross-racial solidarity and end White supremacy because an opportunity to expose and disrupt the troubling racial alliance between poor and non-poor Whites is lost.

In the Whiteness studies approach, it is the avoidance of discussing poor Whites, both on the part of the educator and the students, that gives "What about poor White people?" much of its power. Although I agree that relative to people of color all Whites are privileged by a system of White supremacy, clearly White supremacy does not privilege all Whites equally (Heilman, 2004). And while class, culture, and language certainly operate to reproduce the multigenerational poverty of poor Whites, we are missing their racialization, which situates them in a different experiential realm and political position within the White group (Hartigan, 2004). Unless we unpack the racialization of poor Whites, we will fail to recognize that the power of the White group lies in the dominant subgroup's (i.e., nonpoor Whites') ability to maintain a tightly defended and seemingly natural allegiance among all group members. A critical understanding of the role of racialization in the formation of the White racial polity holds the key to opening the door to racial justice because it emphasizes the need to disrupt the unnatural solidarity of the White race so as to disband it.

To move beyond the limited analytical vision of undifferentiated-White-privilege versus Marxist-analysis-to-the-rescue, what I suggest is a critical race exegesis of "What about poor White people?" A critical race exegesis is an interpretation of a text or social phenomenon that is rooted in critical race theory (CRT). CRT is a relatively new way of making sense of the social world in explicitly racial terms (Allen, 2006; Delgado & Stefancic, 2001). While its more recent growth can be traced to legal studies, its roots go back at least to the work of W. E. B. DuBois (1868–1963) and Franz Fanon (1925–1961). As it has grown, it has also branched out into disciplines beyond legal studies. Scholars in various social science disciplines have taken up CRT in ways that take from, add to, and go beyond the theorization of CRT by legal scholars. In education, there are now numerous authors who participate in CRT scholarship (e.g., Delgado Bernal & Villalpando, 2002; Dixson & Rousseau, 2005; Ladson-Billings, 1999; Ladson-Billings & Tate, 1995; Love, 2004; Lynn, 1999; Parker & Stovall, 2004; Solorzano & Yosso, 2002; Tate, 1997; Taylor, 1999).

Limited space prevents me from giving an adequate overview of CRT.[9] However, a brief explanation of two general CRT tenets is important for the inquiry at hand. First and foremost, White supremacy is an endemic and structurally determining social system in which we all live (Allen, 2001, 2006; Bonilla-Silva, 1996, 2001). White supremacy is a system of oppression that both parallels and intersects with other systems of oppression, such as capitalism and patriarchy (Bonilla-Silva, 1996, 2001). This means that White supremacy is not subsumed within capitalism or patriarchy, but rather is a related yet distinct social system.

Second, CRT moves the definition of race beyond the older notion of a biologically defined group and the newer notion of a socially constructed group. Instead, CRT sees races as political constructions as opposed to the more passive, and politically neutral notion of a social construction (Mills, 1997). In this view, races are political groups, or polities, with particular political interests that derive in large part from their situatedness within White supremacist racial hierarchies (Mills, 1997). Race membership is based largely on racialized, and thus political, perceptions of the body, or what Fanon (1952/1967) referred to as "body schema." Racial group members act, consciously or not, as political representatives of their racial polity (Mills, 1997). In other words, races are seen as forms of human organization mired in group conflict over status and power.

At the top of the White supremacist hierarchy, the White racial polity is invested in its dominant status and will only give political concessions to people of color when they are pressured from multiple sides to do so and, most importantly, stand to benefit the most from what appears to many as racial progress for people of color. Bell (1980, 1992) calls this White supremacist phenomenon the "interest convergence principle." His primary example is the *Brown* decision in 1954. He argues that the Cold War with the Soviet Union and Black radicalism in the United States pressured White leaders to support ending formal segregation. On the international front, White America needed the support of "Third World" people of color in the fight against communism, but the U.S. system of racial apartheid scared away potential allies. On the domestic front, White America was feeling threatened by growing Black radical and communist movements (Bell, 1980). Although the *Brown* decision appeared to be a victory for people of color, White America gained a larger victory, ultimately, in achieving global domination and breaking apart the Soviet Union. Also, the *Brown* decision did little, if nothing, to disrupt the U.S. racial hierarchy. And once the Soviet Union broke apart, White America quickly turned against civil rights gains like affirmative action and bilingual education.

An exegesis of "What about poor White people?" that is rooted in CRT assumes that texts created by Whites must be scrutinized for their political race implications. As Leonardo (2002) argues, it is crucial that we "dismantle discourses of whiteness" by "disrupting . . . and unsettling their codes" (p. 31). Does a certain discursive text further the dominant status of Whites? Does it strengthen political alliances that maintain White power? Does it set the agenda, acting as a talking point for the White racial polity? When it comes to "What about poor White people?" I believe that the answer is "Yes" to all of these questions. Let me explain further.

On one level of analysis, it is fair to say that "What about poor Whites?" is less about nonpoor Whites' concern for poor Whites and more about their discomfort with their own Whiteness.[10] To avoid discomfort, they have learned that this semantic move can remove them from the spotlight of critique and accountability by shifting the discussion to a group that most "educated" folks have not spent much time thinking about: poor White people. Consequently, they avoid dealing in more positive ways with their pent up feelings of guilt and defensiveness (which nearly all Whites have, even those of us who think of ourselves as antiracist) emanating from their denial of the unearned privilege and status that a White supremacist social system affords them (Allen, 2004; Helms, 1993). Of course, this semantic move never leads to any serious discussion about why poor White people are poor because the speaker rarely has any serious interest in exploring the social, economic, and political situatedness of poor Whites. The speaker's greater concern seems to be about silencing the conversation on Whiteness. Once that happens, it is as if they see the issue of poor Whites as resolved.

Before moving on, I want to point out that indeed there are nonpoor Whites who appear to express genuine concern for poor Whites. Unfortunately, much of their discourse about poor Whites is scripted by a fundamental lack of understanding of the race-based problem at hand. These folks tend to come from a class-based perspective and do not seem to understand the importance of analyzing in structural terms the racialization of poor Whites. So despite the fact that a few of those who ask "What about poor Whites?" may really be concerned about poor Whites, it is my contention that despite their good intentions they are still guided by, consciously or not, a White supremacist ideology that works to not only maintain White domination over people of color but also, ironically, the domination of nonpoor over poor Whites.[11]

Also, I want to make it clear that examining the poverty of White people, especially the entrenched, generational poverty of certain White subcultures, is critical because poor Whites are *in a relational sense* oppressed people who do face institutional and everyday forms of dehumanization. Ignoring their situation leaves behind many potential antiracist allies who are in a position to disrupt the seemingly natural solidarity between poor and nonpoor Whites. In *Racism Without Racists,* Bonilla-Silva (2003) says that in his study of White people's racial beliefs working class White women were the ones most likely to exhibit signs of being racially progressive. In my experience as an antiracist educator, Whites who have grown up poor or working class have been much more likely than nonpoor Whites to embrace an antiracist agenda that places White supremacy at the center of critique. Though these examples do not qualify as definitive evidence, they do suggest that the commonsense notion that nonpoor Whites are more likely than poor Whites to be racially progressive may be erroneous and needs of further study.

One of the ways that poor Whites are dehumanized is through stereotypes. Many of the prevalent slurs used against them directly communicate their lower status in the White group. Yet, stereotypes of poor Whites are not the same as stereotypes of people of color. As Smith (2004) explains,

> Depictions of "rednecks" and "crackers" demean white (male) workers by endowing them with inherent brutality and ignorance; ironically, their sub-human state is also commonly signified by an irredeemably violent racism. This twisted racial logic does *not* mean, however, that white workers are actually victims of racism. Rather, their derogatory representation may be seen as a product of the disjuncture between their racial privilege and class disadvantage, which it serves to explain and legitimate. As whites degraded by class exploitation, they can never be

quite white enough. As working-class whites, they must not be good enough to be truly white, i.e., self-evidently (by virtue of color) superior and deservedly privileged. (p. 46)

Although I agree that poor Whites are not the victims of racism, I disagree with the notion that their denigration stems primarily from class exploitation. Notions of race and the internal racial politics of the White race are also to blame. The "White but not quite"[12] positionality of poor Whites is perpetuated not just by attitudes toward their economic status or alleged cultural dysfunction but also by beliefs about their biological inferiority. To this day, there are many nonpoor Whites who believe that the generational poverty of White Appalachians is due to the role inbreeding has played in creating their allegedly damaged gene pool[13] (Smith, 2004). Beliefs about genetic inferiority have made their way into the media. Comedic actors on TV often portray White Appalachians who marry or have sex with their siblings or cousins, creating children with exaggerated birth defects.

Moreover, stereotypes of poor Whites are often rooted in racial notions. For example, negative images of poor Southern Whites' racism, backwardness, and biological corruption are often juxtaposed against images of the educated, genteel White Southerner who supposedly embodies civility and protects seemingly defenseless Blacks from the violent racism of poor Whites (Smith, 2004). In the 1996 film *A Time to Kill*, a trio of White lawyers, two Southern males and one Northern female, defend a Black man who killed the working-class Southern White men who raped his daughter. *A Time to Kill* conveys a common message that says educated White Southerners are the friends of people of color whereas uneducated poor White Southerners are their enemies. The film fails to depict any poor Whites in a positive light, as if somehow all poor White Southerners are incapable of antiracist thought and action. Consistent with the film's message, the over-the-top ending shows a huge mob of crazed, racist poor Whites shooting up the courthouse in protest of the defendant's acquittal. Meanwhile, the victorious lawyers are presented as the antiracist heroes, saving the South from poor Whites' racism one court case at a time.

While some poor White Southerners do in fact live out the stereotype of the uneducated, virulent racist, the problem is that portrayals of poor White Southerners by seemingly antiracist filmmakers leave nonpoor White Southerners looking as though they are the only members of the White group who work for racial progress. These images communicate to an audience that "redneck hillbillies" or "White trash" are the racists that people should despise the most, not nonpoor White Southerners, or for that matter, nonpoor Whites in general. The fact that White politicians, business people, educators, and policymakers from mostly nonpoor backgrounds have been the primary perpetrators of institutional and structural racism gets obscured. Poor Whites are hated more, even though they do not have as much institutional and economic power as nonpoor Whites. The point is that nonpoor White Southerners require a distortion of the image of poor White

Southerners in order to distort their own image. In other words, they need a White "Other" in order to justify their sense of superiority. I am suggesting that the same is true for all nonpoor Whites. They necessitate an image of the racist poor White to pass themselves off as nonracist.

Given that nonpoor Whites are the main group that distorts the image of poor Whites, one would think that poor Whites would harbor a lot of animosity toward nonpoor Whites. Such is not the case. It is as if poor Whites do not care if they are depicted as crazed racists. In fact, they may have internalized this image of themselves, believing that it is true. My suspicion is that most poor Whites think that they are more racist than nonpoor Whites. However, I am not sure that they would admit it publicly. In my experience as an antiracist educator, rarely do poor White students make comments that suggest that they think nonpoor Whites are more racist than poor Whites. Yet, they rarely express the belief that they are more racist than nonpoor Whites. This does nor necessarily mean that poor Whites do not believe that they are more racist. They might be embarrassed to admit what they really think. Nonpoor White students do not exhibit any turmoil over expressing who is the most racist. Without hesitation, they usually say that they are less racist than poor Whites. They say it as though it is commonsense. Bur commonsense can often mask reality. In this case, it can mask the truer beliefs of poor Whites, and maybe even nonpoor Whites. It can also mask the objective reality: nonpoor Whites are more racist in the sense that their elevated status means that they are in positions of greater power, which they can use to perpetuate or disrupt White supremacy. Research needs to be conducted that examines poor Whites' dispositions toward nonpoor Whites, and vice versa. In particular, researchers should look at how members of each group perceive their own level of racism as well as the other group's level of racism.

Although nonpoor Whites' depiction of poor Whites as virulent racists does not make poor Whites angry, nonpoor Whites' economic exploitation of poor Whites has created animosity. For example, many White Appalachians have a general distrust of wealthy White people due to centuries of economic exploitation by Northeastern corporations. I know that I was raised to distrust business people, especially if they were strangers or worked for a corporation. I have also seen how coalmining companies have exploited some of my relatives, tossing them aside when they contracted black lung. I internalized this animosity even though I grew up in a small town in northern Indiana. My father's family had moved away from the mountains as part of the Appalachian migration to the Midwest after World War II (see note 2). I can only imagine the level of animosity that exists among White Appalachians that still reside in the mountains. Smith (2004) argues that nonpoor Whites sense White Appalachian's animosity, causing them to fear that White Appalachians might someday retaliate.

What this means is that nonpoor White perceptions of and interactions with poor Whites, particularly with members of subgroups like White Appalachians, are largely guided by a combination of fear (of retaliation) and revulsion (toward their genetic inferiority). Also, poor Whites seem to care about how they have been economically exploited, but their anger does not cause them to want to break free of the White group. Instead, they want to be more respected White people, in the eyes of nonpoor Whites, as opposed to leaving the White group altogether.

Although poor Whites experience systemic dehumanization, they are as much oppressors as they are the oppressed. They are invested in Whiteness and receive the benefits of White privilege, even if their returns on their investments are not as great as the returns for nonpoor Whites. Returning to the example of White Appalachians, it may be a surprise to some, as it was for me, that the field of Appalachian Studies has often depicted Appalachia as a place of racial innocence (Billings, Pendarvis, & Thomas, 2004), which is nearly the complete opposite of the more common image in popular media of Appalachia as a place of extreme racism. Appalachia Studies scholars have studied the region as if only poor Whites and coalmines inhabit it. Rarely is Appalachia discussed as a multiracial place[14] (Hayden, 2004). And even more rarely is the Whiteness of Appalachia considered an important arena of study (Smith, 2004). For example, critical studies of Whiteness in Appalachia are just beginning to systematically reveal why there are not more people of color living in Appalachia. In other words, Appalachia is mostly White for a reason. As Smith (2004) explains,

> If whites are the only people left in many parts of the region, then there are no "race relations," hence no enduring relevance to race. The contemporary predominance of whites in Appalachia becomes a benign demographic fact, rather than a product of active practices characterized in part by persistent white supremacy. Racial innocence is preserved. (p. 43)

The racial innocence narrative erases the fact that slavery existed in the mountain South. And after slavery ended, Kentucky created laws that made it difficult for Blacks to settle there (Smith, 2004). In the Tennessee cities of Knoxville and Chattanooga, laws "prohibited blacks from selling groceries and dry goods" (Smith, 2004, p. 43). These are two examples of the many ways that White supremacy created better opportunities for those raced as White by driving away competition from members of other racial groups, especially Blacks.

What I have discussed thus far is a pretext for understanding "What about poor White people?" Moving to a deeper level of critical race analysis, we need to look at how the racialization of poor Whites is part and parcel of their structural relationship with non-poor Whites. To study racialization is to analyze "the social relations in order to comprehend how [racial] groups of people see other [racial] groups in relation to themselves and to each other" (Hartigan, 2004, p. 61). In the case of poor and nonpoor White relations, we also need to look at how intraracial perceptions, interactions, and identity politics reproduce the larger racial order, that is, the racial hierarchy of the U.S. White supremacist social system (Allen, 2007; Bonilla-Silva, 1996).

To better read "What about the poor Whites?" we need to consider the history of the formation of the U.S. White racial polity. After all, the White race has not always existed and its membership has changed over time. One fundamental question seems to guide much of the study of poor Whites and the making of the White race: Why have poor Whites seemingly gone against their own economic interests by siding with higher-status members of the White race and not people of color?

One answer is that nonpoor Whites wanted assistance in repressing the large numbers of Native and African people, groups that Whites considered to be not just as inferior people but also as political and economic adversaries who must be controlled. In the early 1800s, White leaders saw what happened to French colonialists and slaveholders in the Haitian Revolution (1791–1804) and that drove them to seek out and bring in more Whites from Europe to act as a buffer against a similar slave revolt in the United States (DuBois, 1935). The Whites they brought in by the millions were most often members of lower-status European ethnic groups, such as the Irish, Slavs, Jews, and southern Europeans (DuBois, 1935; Jacobson, 1998). Since the history of White supremacy suggests that the White racial polity operates in a self-interested way, I am curious about why U.S. nonpoor Whites would have brought in groups that they saw as inferior. U.S. nonpoor Whites must have perceived a threat to the normative order of White supremacy, such as the possibility of a slave revolt, and were therefore willing to open up the ranks of the White racial polity in order to preserve White domination.

But what did poor Whites, whether they were new immigrants or historically marginalized subgroups, have to gain from a political organization where they were not the top group within their own race? What was available to them in the United States was a multiracial White supremacist society where they could receive what DuBois (1935) called "the public and psychological wages of whiteness". In Europe, they were on the bottom of the social status ladder. In the United States, they were not. White supremacy created a White opportunity structure where the wages of Whiteness were doled out in both de jure and de facto ways (DuBois, 1935; Roediger, 1999). Nonpoor Whites gave these White immigrants— at least the males—certain voting and property rights not offered to others (Roediger, 1999). Also, poor Whites had the opportunity to rise up the economic and social status ladder in ways not open to people of color (Ignatiev, 1995; Jacobson, 1998; Sacks, 1994). And even though many of these Whites did not achieve the "American Dream" (i.e., middle-class status or higher), more poor Whites than people of color did "succeed," which must have reinforced in poor Whites the value of the White opportunity structure in a multiracial society (DuBois, 1935).

Although many poor Whites were not completely happy with this arrangement, as evidenced by their complaints about the limited permeability of the opportunity structure and what they saw as the privileges (i.e., food and shelter) enslaved Blacks received from their masters (DuBois, 1935), they understood that they occupied a higher social status than people of color (Roediger, 1999). I believe that this White supremacist context taught them that they were superior to people of color. In what had to have been a harsh and dangerous society for Blacks enduring enslavement and Indigenous people suffering land loss and genocide, my assumption is that nonpoor Whites' relative favoritism toward poor Whites must have solidified a hegemonic yet unequal alliance among poor and nonpoor Whites and made the stranglehold of the White racial polity over social and economic life in the United States that much greater. Both now and then, the politically interesting aspect of the hegemonic alliance between poor and nonpoor Whites is that while White privilege extends to all of those perceived as White some reap fewer benefits than others. Yet, the unequal rewards do not seem to deter those who get the least, that is, poor Whites, from being staunch defenders of a pro-White agenda.

In our contemporary context, I see "What about poor White people?" as a coded representation of the long-standing hierarchical and hegemonic alliance within the White racial polity. In this hegemonic alliance, poor Whites agree *not* to become race traitors and disrupt the normativity of a White supremacist system. In other words, they agree to support a skewed, racialized opportunity structure that gives them advantages over people of color (Mills, 1997). And, most importantly for the argument I am making here, they comply, whether actively or passively, with being used as the archetypal image of a racist, thus serving to deflect critical racial scrutiny away from those Whites who benefit the most from a White supremacist system, namely nonpoor Whites. Even those White Appalachians who are openly critical of and work against the consuming image of the "racist redneck" often do so in a way that does not name who the most institutionally powerful racists are, which if we follow this line of logic leaves us with the curious situation of having a racist social order but seemingly no racists. As I suggested earlier, too many poor Whites accept the notion that nonpoor Whites are less racist. In fact, I cannot recall a single time I have heard a poor White person say, "I wish those nonpoor Whites would not depict us as the poster-children of racism. They are the real racists, you know." I am not suggesting that poor Whites are not racist. Poor Whites engage in both individual and systemic acts of racism against people of color and they rarely hold themselves accountable for their complicity with a White supremacist social system that most harms people of color. What I am suggesting is that when we say the phrase "racist" whose face is the first to pop-up in your head? And, why do I suspect that in the minds of most Whites, even poor Whites, it is not the face of a nonpoor White, such as a White soccer mom or White professor?

The benefit that dutiful poor Whites receive for playing the role of decoy is the current manifestation of the public and psychological wages of Whiteness. They receive race-based benefits that people of color do not receive (McIntosh, 1997; Oliver & Shapiro, 1997) for allowing themselves to be the distraction that is necessary for nonpoor Whites to evade a high level of scrutiny. Poor Whites would have to organize and publicly protest their depiction as the stereotype of the ultimate racist in order to change their current situation. They would have to join with people of color in denouncing White supremacy as a social system. In effect, they would have to be willing to commit "race suicide" in order to lose their White benefits and gain their humanity (Allen, 2004). But I do not believe that most poor Whites, at least at this juncture in history, are ready to even consider a commitment to end White supremacy; they are in a Weberian sense "rationally" invested in Whiteness (Bobo, 1983; Lipsitz, 1998). They can see how the game

114

is stacked, and they have decided to play the mediocre hand they have been dealt rather than trying to change the game. Maybe poor Whites actually *are* acting in their economic interest, but selling their soul in the process.

What is the benefit of this hegemonic intraracial arrangement for nonpoor Whites? This question needs to be explored because why would higher-status Whites want to be aligned in any way with people they see as "backwards," "rednecks," "hillbillies," and "trailer trash"? After all, nonpoor Whites have defined Whiteness however they have wanted in order to suit their own political and economic interests (Haney Lopez, 1997). And they have been able to keep those perceived as non-European out of the White group. So why would they not redefine "White" such that those "inferior" Whites are no longer considered White?

I think that the reason nonpoor Whites do not expel poor Whites from the White group is that the benefits of the White hegemonic alliance are even greater for those on the higher-status side. Extending DuBois' (1935) framework for thinking critically about poor Whites and nonpoor Whites, my argument is that they gain a buffer group (i.e., poor Whites), a shield between themselves and people of color, and thus a divide and conquer victory. If we step outside of a monolithic view of the White group, we will see that nonpoor Whites need a political alliance with some large part of the population so as to protect their unearned wealth and status against the political force of those who wish to have a more equitable and humanizing situation (e.g., many people of color). They desperately want to avoid becoming equals, let alone subordinates, to people of color. In short, Whiteness itself, as a form of racialized property with high market value, has been offered to poor Whites throughout the history of the U.S. as a political quid pro quo (Harris, 1995; Roediger, 1999).

If there is one novel point I am making in this chapter it is this: higher-status, nonpoor Whites will never want all Whites to be economically equal because there would be no device left to divert attention away from the racism and White racial privilege of nonpoor Whites. To reiterate, nonpoor Whites need a White other who is at once a stereotype of the ultimate racist and a dutiful ally in the White hegemonic alliance. For poor Whites, "ultimate racist" and "dutiful White ally" have become two sides of the same coin, each side working in dialectical relation with the other side to create poor Whites' social identity and political positionality. Together, the two sides of the coin work to elevate the intraracial status of nonpoor Whites. In other words, nonpoor Whites would no longer be able to say "What about poor White people?" if all Whites were nonpoor and considered equally nonracist; in other words, if there were no poor White people. Nonpoor Whites do not want to lose their White other because their White privilege would be too obvious. Although poor Whites would still be supporters of White supremacy in this scenario, people of color would have a more coherent target to organize against. *Therefore, poor Whites will never achieve social justice as long as they are practicing members of the White racial alliance.* Their investment in a unified White racial polity and unwillingness to meaningfully challenge the ultimate racist stereotype prevents cross-racial solidarity between themselves and people of color against the more absolute dominance of nonpoor Whites. Clearly, non-poor Whites have much to gain by claiming that the situation of poor Whites is about class and not race.

Rather than having people of color do all of the antiracist work, we poor Whites need to be the ones who challenge nonpoor Whites during discussions about race when they ask, "What about poor White people?" I have seen too many poor Whites remain silent and let nonpoor Whites do the dirty work of the White hegemonic alliance, but sometimes we poor Whites join them in this semantic move and support more actively the White racial cause. And we do this because we think our interests are being served and to do otherwise, to speak out against the alliance, would be to commit a type of race treason that we seem to be unwilling to do because we fear losing our unearned and immoral benefits, even though the reward would be a more humanizing way of life. We need to break away from this White hegemonic alliance. In short, we need a divorce! (Not to mention, we need to find a healthier relationship!) I am not naive about how difficult it would be to persuade poor Whites to speak out against the individual and collective racism of nonpoor Whites, take responsibility for their White privilege, and create meaningful, trusting, and powerful antiracist alliances with people of color. But, it is an antiracist strategy that deserves serious consideration.

What about poor White students?

The major educational implication of my critique of "What about poor White people?" is that social justice approaches to teaching and researching poor White students need to pay attention to their racialization within the White racial polity and in relation to other racial groups. Absent a curriculum that provides poor White students with an opportunity to unlearn their submission to nonpoor Whites, investment in Whiteness, and learned superiority relative to people of color, the future of poor Whites will most likely resemble their past since they will not be able to forge meaningful and transformative political alliances with people of color. A social justice approach would intervene in this cycle by empowering poor Whites to more forcefully challenge nonpoor Whites. But more importantly, they would first have to acknowledge and be accountable for their relative White privilege and investment in White supremacy. They would have to become solidary[15] in authentic ways with people of color by taking responsibility for their group privilege and gaining the trust of people of color (Allen, 2002, 2004). With poor Whites in alliance with people of color, the movement against nonpoor Whites' investment in White supremacy would be powerful and unlike anything seen before in the United States.

Unfortunately, we are far from achieving this vision. The White hegemonic alliance overdetermines the educational experiences of poor White students. Likewise, their schooling covertly, and sometimes overtly, teaches poor Whites to be agents in the perpetuation of White dominance. We should expect schooling to play a key role in reproducing the White hegemonic alliance. Since nonpoor

Whites need poor Whites as their racial other, we should not expect most nonpoor Whites to work toward making sure poor Whites get a well funded, transformative, and antiracist education. To keep the alliance alive, poor Whites need to learn political complacency and internalize a sense of inferiority relative to nonpoor Whites. And their schooling facilitates this lesson.

Complacency is taught in a number of ways. Given that nonpoor Whites typically see White Appalachians as culturally corrupt (i.e., "rednecks," "trailer trash," and "hillbillies") or biologically damaged (i.e., "inbred"), we should expect most nonpoor White teachers, as well as poor White teachers who act, consciously or not, as supporters of the White hegemonic alliance, to see White Appalachian students from a deficit model. Referring to her research on White Appalachian students in the Midwest, Heilman (2004) reports,

> One elementary school principal, known for her support for progressive curriculum and multiculturalism quite unselfconsciously reported, "We have a big group of trailer trash in this school," when orienting a new group of preservice teachers. Similarly, an urban Indianapolis teacher insidiously confided, "These city hillbilly kids are the *real* bottom of the barrel, if you know what I mean." (p. 67)

Since stereotypes about poor White Appalachians abound, it is fair to assume that nonpoor White teachers internalize messages that say that the problems of poor White Appalachians are caused by dysfunctional families, violent neighborhoods, alcoholism, child abuse, teen pregnancy, virulent racism, welfare dependency, and so on.

With a deficit view firmly entrenched, it is hard to imagine that nonpoor White educators see White Appalachian students as possessing particular forms of knowledge, experience, and wisdom that are insightful and valuable. Moreover, it is doubtful that nonpoor White teachers see themselves as members of the group most responsible for creating the negative learning conditions for poor Whites and people of color. We should not expect then that nonpoor White teachers are teaching poor Whites ways of gaining a positive sense of self through learning how to challenge the White hegemonic alliance. This would go against the normative role that nonpoor White social actors are taught to play. Instead, we should expect nonpoor Whites to be teaching White Appalachian students as if they are just like all other White people, and we should expect them to chastise White Appalachians for not living up to the model of the "nonpoor White."

Of course, some White Appalachians, such as myself, will be seen as successful exceptions to the rule and used as examples to put down the others. Without a critical discourse to reveal the myth of the achievement ideology, a good many White Appalachians will experience self-hate and blame themselves or others of their group for their predicament. As a relative of mine once told me, "I tell my kids that if they study hard like Ricky then they will be successful." The reality is that I did not study hard in high school, mainly because I did not have to. Additionally, I seriously doubt that the quality and quantity of study habits explains why less than 10% of my nearly all White high school class went on to a four-year college. I think a better explanation is that we were taught relative to the norm of nonpoor Whites as the model of humanity and success. We were never engaged in discussions of what it meant to be poor Whites or Appalachian Whites. We were never taught about White privilege or how systemic racism affected people of color. Consequently I am sure that many of my classmates did not critically understand that they were being educated to fill their prescribed role in the White hegemonic alliance.

Despite the educational woes of poor Whites, it would be a mistake to suggest that poor Whites, such as White Appalachians, are in the same social and educational situation as students of color. This is not the case. Although poor White students are racialized, they are not "racial minorities." Since race operates as a castelike system, White Appalachians can pass into the middle-class, much as I have, in ways that people of color cannot because our bodies are perceived as White. Also, to say that White Appalachians are racial minorities is to grossly underestimate the current horrendous state of systemic and institutional racism in the United States and its consequences for people of color (Smith, 2004). Sometimes White educational scholars use the notion of White Appalachians as a racial minority in order to make the case that their oppression is equal to that of people of color. For example, Heilman (2004) discusses how White Appalachians are prone to joining overt White supremacist organizations. To keep them from joining groups like the KKK, she says that they should learn about processes of marginalization and injustice for various oppressed groups, not just White Appalachians. While I agree that they should learn about other oppressed groups, she goes too far when she says, "This understanding would instead promote solidarity and social action among different marginalized 'races'" (p. 77). The implication is that White Appalachians are one of the "marginalized races." While White Appalachians are surely marginalized, they do not constitute a separate race because they are seen as White regardless of their lower status within the White polity. With the exception of a few melungeons (see note 14), I do not know of any White Appalachians who have been asked, "What is your race?" In other words, actual social practice does not suggest that White Appalachians are seen as a separate race, or even a race within a race.

Sometimes, it seems to me that White scholars think that they have to show that poor Whites experience oppression that is close, if not equal, to that which people of color face in order for others to pay attention to their plight. But painting a false or overstated picture of reality can have the opposite effect by demonstrating a lack of accountability for White privilege, creating doubt about whether poor Whites are trustworthy in the minds of antiracist people of color. Ultimately this distances poor Whites from the antiracist imagination. As Smith (2004) states,

> The argument for hillbillies-as-an-oppressed-minority-whose-disparagement-exceeds-that-of-other-racial-groups pulls up the drawbridge even further, and

guards Appalachian distinctiveness against the possibility that hillbilly stereo-types largely represent the ugly ideology of racism turned against poor and working class whites (p. 51).

The benefits of being White and Appalachian are highly evident when looking at educational attainment. According to the 2000 Census, White Appalachians have significantly higher graduation rates than Appalachians of color. For White Appa-lachians, 77.5% have high school diplomas and 17.9% have college degrees. For Black Appalachians, 69.9% have high school diplomas and 12.2% have college degrees. For Hispanic Appalachians, 51.4% have high school diplomas and 13.0% have college graduation degrees (Shaw, DeYoung, & Rademacher, 2004). Assum-ing U.S. patterns hold for Appalachia, we could further speculate that the economic return for the degrees that Appalachians earn vary by race (and gender), meaning educational attainment disparities have an amplified material effect in the job mar-ket that makes the real benefits of White privilege that much greater (Fine, 1991).

I agree with Heilman's (2004) contention that educational researchers have overlooked the struggles of White Appalachian students. However, we need to be careful about how we explain this omission. Although groups like Blacks and Latinos are now often the object (for better or worse) of educational research, they used to be overlooked, too. The attention given to students of color is a recent historical phenomenon. It is not, as some may believe, a natural state of affairs but rather a contemporary construction that is in large part the result of organized social justice efforts to pressure researchers, educators, and policymakers to pay greater attention to students of color. If the educational struggles of people of color are "noticed" and not "hidden," it is because they have made themselves noticed, risking the wrath of White supremacy in an attempt to better their school-ing experiences. And the risk is real. One could argue that Whites have in fact retaliated against people of color by creating a public discourse that depicts the problems of students of color as the result of their alleged cultural deficits, which in turn leaves White students looking superior.

The point is that if the struggles of poor Whites are hidden then it is due to their situatedness within the White hegemonic alliance. Poor Whites seem unwilling to create an organized social movement to bring to the public's atten-tion the problems that poor White students face. I think that a major reason that they have not organized is that they do not want to anger nonpoor Whites and risk losing White benefits. Given the current racial climate, the only way that they might be willing to organize is if they claim that "reverse racism" is the reason that poor Whites have been overlooked. In other words, educational scholars' inattention to poor White groups such as White Appalachians is seen through a White supremacist ideology as a form of discrimination against White peo-ple. The reverse racism approach would perpetuate a pro-White politics and thus appease nonpoor Whites, but ultimately nonpoor Whites would undermine any gains for poor Whites that may derive from this strategy because they do not want to lose their White other. A more likely scenario is that groups like White

Appalachians will continue with the status quo, meaning that their educational struggles will continue to be overlooked.

Poor Whites' learned sense of inferiority relative to nonpoor Whites is only half of the story. For the other half, we need to think about the benefits that poor Whites receive for not engaging in an antiracist social movement to change the dehumanizing education that they are offered. Through the hidden curriculum of Whiteness, poor Whites are taught a sense of superiority relative to people of color. Yet, they do not receive all of the benefits that nonpoor Whites get. Plus, nonpoor Whites often interact negatively with poor Whites. One would think that this would be enough to cause poor Whites to protest. But this has not happened on a broad, organized level. I do not believe that it is a natural characteristic of any group to silently accept mistreatment. There has to be coercion, persuasion, or some combination of the two to create a condition of complicity and complacency. My argument is that nonpoor Whites offer poor Whites an educational concession in order to keep the peace and maintain the White hegemonic alliance. While the education of poor Whites is denigrating, it cannot be so denigrating as to make poor Whites think that they would be better off if they were students of color. Currently, poor Whites do not believe that they are worse off than people of color. Sure, there are poor Whites who will say that they think affirmative action gives people of color an unfair advantage. But my sense is that these same folks do not really believe that they, as a group, are worse off than people of color, as a group. Just try asking a group of poor Whites if they would want to trade places *as a racial group* (not as individuals) with any other racial group, that is, White people would take on the racial situation of, say, Blacks. I doubt there would be any takers. I have never found any when I ask them this question. To be educated into the White hegemonic alliance, poor White students need to exit schooling believing that although they may have had it bad at least they have had it better than most Blacks and Latinos. And, my guess is that schooling is "successful" at instilling this belief in poor Whites, although an empirical study of this hypothesis is necessary and would be quite interesting.

It is also important for the maintenance of White supremacy that poor Whites leave school believing that their worldviews and knowledge systems are superior to those of people of color (Mills, 1997). Indeed, they must leave believing, at some level of consciousness, that they *are better people* than people of color. Although, as mentioned above, some White Appalachians feel victimized by affirmative action programs and other forms of so-called "reverse racism,"[16] it would be a mistake to think that their feelings of victimization have a positive correlation to feelings of inferiority relative to people of color. If there were a positive correlation, they would not feel so angry about "reverse racism" because they would have internalized that they belong in a lower status than people of color and taken a more complacent role, as they have relative to nonpoor Whites. Instead, what they are more likely to feel is that they are being cheated out of opportunities that should be rightfully theirs as faithful, superior White people. Anger is more likely to result from this psychosocial condition. Thus, poor Whites are more likely to blame people of color because they perceive people of color as inferior people who will allegedly squander scarce opportunities. Also, poor Whites are less likely to blame nonpoor Whites because they are perceived as a natural ally, even though poor Whites harbor conflicted feelings about nonpoor Whites' deceptiveness and superiority.

Although White Appalachians and other poor Whites are taught to feel superior to people of color through the hidden curriculum of Whiteness, educating against the White hegemonic alliance means that we need to stop seeing poor Whites as little more than racists in the making. Rather, they need to be seen as racialized subjects situated within both intraracial and interracial hierarchies. It is important to understand and create pedagogy around their racialization so as to maximize their social justice potential. They need to be seen as possible antiracist allies who, with the proper education, can transform their complicity with the White hegemonic alliance so as to not only better their own lot but also to better the lot of those who have even less social power.

We also need to avoid class-based approaches that see race as an empty ideology (Leonardo, 2005) and stop imagining poor Whites primarily, if not solely, as victims of capitalist exploitation. These class-based approaches do not take into account that White supremacy itself is an opportunity structure that Whites are invested in and are not going to give up easily because there are serious psychological and material benefits to being White, even to being a poor White. Class-based approaches say nothing about how the White hegemonic alliance operates through social institutions, such as schools, to maintain the U.S. racial order.

In "Walking the Dance: Teaching and Cross-Cultural Encounter," Gilbert Valadez (2004), a self-identified gay Latino, offers a powerful narrative about how he taught White Appalachians in a teacher education course. He writes candidly about how he had internalized the stereotype of the "racist hillbilly." The positive interactions he had with the students, which were partly fostered through the transformative pedagogy he brought to the classroom, changed his perception of White Appalachians. Reflecting upon the course, he says,

> I gained many insights into the lives of White Appalachians. Indeed, many of them live with injustice, prejudice, poverty, and pain. As time passed, the differences between us mattered less than did the process of coming to mutual understandings. Mostly, my students were able to conceptualize the notions of white identity and white privilege. They also were more able to articulate central issues surrounding inequity and inequality in education. (p. 163)

Valadez taught these students as people who occupy an in-between social status, that is, as both oppressor and oppressed. As White Appalachians, they occupied a lower social status than nonpoor Whites. Many had experienced material hardship and psychological trauma that needed to be shared, contextualized, and debated. They also occupied a higher social status than people of color. Valadez engaged them in critical dialogues about their White privilege and asked them to think about ways in which they contributed to a system of White racism. In other words, he did not see them solely as racist oppressors or solely as economic victims. Instead, what he offered was a humanizing pedagogy that reflected some of the complex realities of their social location.

That said, I do have a criticism of his approach. It can leave poor Whites with the misunderstanding that their oppressor position as Whites and their oppressed position as poor Whites are unrelated, or at least, vaguely related. If they are taught to believe that their oppression as poor Whites is due to their class status, as seemed to be the case in Valadez's classroom, then they have a less likely chance of understanding how their alliance with nonpoor Whites oppresses and dehumanizes not only people of color but also themselves. They may still believe that their membership in the White race is a natural and permanent condition. Poor White students need to learn about how the White hegemonic alliance functions, what their role in it has been, and what they can do to end it.

A critical race pedagogy of the White hegemonic alliance must be directly and explicitly taught. Indirect attempts to teach about it are likely to fail. Poor Whites need to see how nonpoor Whites are not just the main beneficiaries of a capitalist system but also of a White supremacist system. Although they certainly need to learn how to unlearn their investment in White domination, they also need to be able to differentiate between how they participate in a White supremacist system versus how nonpoor Whites participate in a White supremacist system. They need to talk with one another about how to break away from nonpoor Whites and how to form solidary relations with people of color. They need to figure out how to muster the courage to confront both the racism and classism of nonpoor Whites. Their loyalty to Whiteness is a dehumanizing condition that requires intervention. As Garvey and Ignatiev (1997) say, "Treason to whiteness is loyalty to humanity." A critical race pedagogy of the White hegemonic alliance should help poor Whites gain their humanity by learning how to be disloyal to the White race and loyal to the antiracist project, and thus, to humanity itself. In short, I am saying that poor Whites should be taught to be effective race traitors.

Conclusion

Nowadays, I react differently when a nonpoor White person asks, "What about poor White people?" I spend a lot of time talking about the workings of the White hegemonic alliance, and I believe that I have become a more effective antiracist educator as a result. I am now able to disarm "What about poor White people?" and turn it into a teachable moment. My hope is that the unveiling of the White hegemonic alliance becomes a focus of the field of social justice education. For social justice education to play an effective role in abolishing White supremacy, it needs to be able to transform poor Whites into race traitors. It needs to be bold enough to seek to dismantle the White race. Some may argue that we can retain the races so long as there are no power differences between them. But as I have argued, races are politically constructed groups. The White race cannot be salvaged because the real problem is how it is constructed. The only real way to abolish White supremacy is to dismantle the coalition of subgroups that comprise the White race. Although Whites' investment in White power and privilege is a serious concern that deserves the attention of social justice educators, the deeper issue is Whites' investment in the White hegemonic alliance.

Acknowledgments

I would like to thank Dr. Annette Henry for her insightful suggestions.

Notes

1 Racism is an ideology that works to perpetuate a social system of racial domination, which in the United States means domination by those raced as White (Bonilla-Silva, 1996). The racialized social system endemic to the United States is White supremacy. Although White people are most responsible for White supremacy, people of color may also support White supremacy through internalized racism (i.e., a learned sense of inferiority about one's own racial identity or racial group) and interethnic racism (i.e., a learned sense of superiority relative to another non-White race). The term *antiracist* refers to those efforts that seek to undo White supremacy by transforming White racism, internalized racism, and interethnic racism.

2 It would take a whole chapter to sort through the debates around how to define "poor" and "nonpoor" Whites, not to mention my reasons for using "poor" and "nonpoor" versus "working class," "middle class," and "upper class." Instead, I offer here a brief description of my position. By using "nonpoor" in a U.S. context, I am primarily referring to upper-, middle-, and even some working class Whites who were raised in nonpoor families. A key point is that not all working class Whites are poor, or are imagined as poor. One reason that I am using the term *poor* is that it is the word contained in the phrase that I am critiquing. I think that the use of the term *poor* is purposeful. My assumption is that when people use the phrase "What about poor White people?" they are referring to all of those Whites who are poor and not necessarily all of those who are working class. So, the term *poor* for me is more contextually precise, even though it may be difficult, if not impossible, to define an exact dividing line between who is or is not poor. That said, it is important not to be paralyzed by debates over the imprecision of the term. My preference is to proceed with a definition that may in fact be dichotomous and incomplete, but it at least provides a starting point to begin the larger discussion of the relations between poor and nonpoor Whites that perpetuate White supremacy. Moving to a working definition, nonpoor White families have little or no experience with multigenerational poverty. They or their families have wealth levels closer to the norm for most Whites. The more difficult subgroups to categorize are White immigrant families, such as those from the former Soviet Union, who might experience a lack of wealth and income for the first generation or two, but ultimately they may become mostly nonpoor as they assimilate into a U.S. construct of Whiteness, as was the case previously for many Jews, Irish, and Slavs. In other words, for some White immigrants we do not yet have any evidence that their condition persists over time, meaning that they may or may not experience *on a group level* a condition of multigenerational poverty, making it unclear whether they fit the definition of nonpoor. Conversely, "poor" Whites are those people who come from families and communities that have experienced entrenched, multigenerational poverty, such as that experienced by many White Appalachians.

3 Bonilla-Silva (2003) describes semantic moves as the "linguistic manners and rhetorical strategies," or more simply as the "race talk," of a racial ideology. Semantic moves

are stylistic maneuvers used during dialogical moments of ideological conflict in an attempt to gain legitimacy for the racial ideology supported by the speaker. They are ideological performances that, if considered effective, are repeated time and time again by multiple actors as they are passed from one ideological subscriber to another.

4 "Intraracial" refers to social phenomena that occur between individuals or subgroups within a particular race whereas "interracial" refers to social phenomena that occur between different racial groups or between individuals of different racial groups.

5 "Political organization" refers to the way in which power and status are created within a social identity group, in this case the White race. Through a complex web of conflicts and alliances between subgroups, the whole group achieves cohesion and social power, even as power and status are hierarchically arranged on an internal (or in this case, intraracial) level.

6 "Hegemonic" is an adjective used to describe those phenomena that contribute to a system of hegemony. Allen (2002) defines hegemony as "a social condition in which relationships of domination and subordination are not overtly imposed from above, but are part of consensual cultural and institutional practices of both the dominant and the subordinate" (p. 106). A hegemonic alliance is a political bond formed between dominant and subordinate groups. Consciously or not, the subordinate group participates in the perpetuation of its own lower status by going along with beliefs and behaviors that maintain the hegemonic system and thus the higher status of the dominant group. Hegemony works more on the level of ideological control than repressive force.

7 "Social justice" refers to a societal condition that is egalitarian and humanizing because it is free from oppressive structures such as White supremacy, patriarchy, heterosexism, and capitalism. Also, the term implies that such a society does not currently exist and efforts must be made to work toward a socially just society.

8 I think of myself as both an insider and outsider to the White Appalachian group. I feel like an outsider in that I did not grow up in Appalachia. Instead, I grew up in a small town in northern Indiana called Medaryville. My father is from Appalachia, and like many others his family moved to Indiana during the mid-1900s to look for better job opportunities. I also have come to feel like an insider as I learn more and more about how my Appalachian heritage has shaped my views and experiences. In the town where I am from, there were many families that had moved there from Appalachia. The non-Appalachian kids looked down on us because we spoke differently and did not have much money. They called us the "Grits."

9 See Richard Delgado and Jean Stefancic's (2001) *Critical Race Theory: An Introduction* for a good overview of CRT.

10 Whereas White supremacy is a social *system* that perpetuates White domination, Whiteness is a social *identity* that shapes and is shaped by White supremacy. As a social identity, Whiteness is a form of individual and collective self-presentation. It is the meaning made from the experience of being a White person and a member of a White group as well as a particular way of being in the world. Like Blackness or Asianness, Whiteness is not a monolithic form of expression and being, though definite patterns of subjectivity and behavior exist. Many Whites are ashamed of their Whiteness because they have learned to be defensive or guilty about White privilege. They have not yet learned how to model their Whiteness after antiracist Whites who offer a more socially and politically positive way of being White in a White supremacist system (Helms, 1993; Tatum, 2003), though this is an intermediate stage since, as I argue in this chapter, the ultimate goal is to disband the White race altogether.

11 From recent work in sociology we know that race is critical for understanding wealth and class in the United States since the average White household has nearly ten times the net financial assets as the average Black household (Oliver & Shapiro, 1997). In fact, even working-class Whites have, on average, more accumulated wealth than middle-class Blacks (Oliver & Shapiro, 1997). In other words, terms like *working class*

are deceptive in that they more accurately signify income, job status, and educational attainment rather than the more crucial aspect of wealth. Thus, there are large wealth gaps between, say, the White working class and the Black working class that get erased when the two are referred to as being of the same "class."

12 I think phrases like "never be White enough," "not quite White," "not fully White," or "not truly White" are problematic in that they do not make it clear that poor Whites are in fact Whites who receive White benefits. Using phrases that depict their White status as only partial can create a slippery slope to where they are constructed by some as non-White since they are "not fully White." But by saying "White but not quite," as I am suggesting, their status as Whites is indexed from the beginning because "White" is the first word. Then "but not quite" references their lower social status within the White group. There is also the problem of confusion with terminology used to describe individuals or groups of color who really do lie on the borderline between being seen as White or as a person of color (e.g., light-skinned Latinos or some multiracials with White heritage). Some may refer to these folks as "not quite White" or "not fully White" because they are perceived as having non-European heritage or features that negate their claim to Whiteness.

13 Alleged genetic inferiority is depicted differently for poor Whites and people of color. For poor Whites, their genetic inferiority is depicted as the result of "good genes gone bad" due to inbreeding and isolation in the mountains. In other words, this type of racist logic assumes that their genetic stock was originally good because it was European but dysfunction and corruption ruined it. For people of color, their genetic makeup is depicted as inherently inferior because they have been perceived historically by Whites as less evolved subpersons. In other words, their genetic makeup was never good, or so the racist "logic" goes.

14 Blacks, Indigenous peoples, Hispanics/Latinos, and mixed-race or "melungeon" folks also inhabit Appalachia. Overall, people of color makeup 11.2% of the Appalachian population (Hayden, 2004). Although race relations in Appalachia have not received enough academic attention, the recent interest in interracialism promises to make race relations a more vital area of interest in Appalachian Studies. The history of race mixture in Appalachia is not widely known. The mixed-race people of Appalachia are often referred to as "melungeons." Melungeons typically have Black, Indigenous, and European ancestry. Many melungeons are accepted as White, although those with darker pigmentation are more likely to be subject to racist ridicule and seen as having a lower status. My own family, on my father's side, is melungeon. Our ancestry includes people who were African, Indigenous, and European. With a couple of exceptions, most of us look White, identify as White, and are treated as White. The existence of melungeons calls into question notions of White racial purity in Appalachia. Also, it would be interesting to look into how Whiteness became constructed in Appalachia given the historical presence of race mixture.

15 "Solidary" is a state of being in solidarity with others. Those who are solidary share common political interests and goals and take part in communal responsibilities.

16 The concept of "reverse racism" against Whites is highly problematic since it is not supported by data (James, 1995).

References

Allen, R. L. (2001). The globalization of white supremacy: Toward a critical discourse on the racialization of the world. *Educational Theory, 51*(4), 467–485.

Allen, R. L. (2002). Wake up, Neo: White consciousness, hegemony, and identity in *The Matrix*. In J. Slater, S. Fain, & C. Rossatto (Eds.), *The Freirean legacy: Educating for social justice* (pp. 104–125). New York: Peter Lang.

Allen, R. L. (2004). Whiteness and critical pedagogy. *Educational Philosophy and Theory, 36*(2), 121–136.

Allen, R. L. (2006). The race problem in the critical pedagogy community. In C. Rossatto, R. L. Allen, & M. Pruyn (Eds.), *Reinventing critical pedagogy: Widening the circle of anti-oppression education* (pp. 3–20). Lanham, MD: Rowman & Littlefield.

Allen, R. L. (2007, April). *Schooling in white supremacist America: How schooling reproduces the racialized social system*. Paper presented at the annual meeting of the American Education Research Association, Chicago, Illinois.

Bell, D. (1980). *Brown v. Board of Education* and the interest-convergence dilemma. *Harvard Law Review, 93*(3), 518–533.

Bell, D. (1992). *Faces at the bottom of the well: The permanence of racism*. New York: Basic Books.

Billings, D., Pendarvis, E., & Thomas, M. K. (2004). From the editors. *Journal of Appalachian Studies, 10*(1–2), 3–6.

Bobo, L. (1983). Whites' opposition to busing: Symbolic racism or realistic group conflict? *Journal of Personality and Social Psychology, 45*(6), 1196–1210.

Bonilla-Silva, E. (1996, June). Rethinking racism: Toward a structural interpretation. *American Sociological Review, 62*, 465–480.

Bonilla-Silva, E. (2001). *White supremacy and racism in the post-civil rights era*. Boulder, CO: Lynne Rienner.

Bonilla-Silva, E. (2003). *Racism without racists*. Lanham, MD: Rowman & Littlefield.

Bonilla-Silva, E., & Embrick, D. (2006). Racism without racists: "Killing me softly" with color blindness. In C. Rossatto, R. L. Allen, & M. Pruyn (Eds.), *Reinventing critical pedagogy: Widening the circle of anti-oppression education* (pp. 21–34). Lanham, MD: Rowman & Littlefield.

Brown v. Board of Education, 3247 U.S. 483 (1954).

Delgado, R., & Stefancic, J. (2001). *Critical race theory: An introduction*. New York: New York University Press.

Delgado Bernal, D., & Villalpando, O. (2002). An apartheid of knowledge in academia: The struggle over the "legitimate" knowledge of faculty of color. *Equity & Excellence in Education, 35*(2), 169–180.

Dixson, A., & Rousseau, C. (2005). And we are still not saved: Critical race theory in education ten years later. *Race, Ethnicity and Education, 8*(1), 7–27.

DuBois, W. E. B. (1935). *Black Reconstruction in America (1860–1880)*. New York: Simon & Schuster.

Fanon, F. (1967). *Black skin, white masks* (C. L. Markmann, Trans.). New York: Grove Press. (Original work published 1952)

Fine, M. (1991). *Framing dropouts: Notes on the politics of an urban high school*. Albany, NY: SUNY Press.

Garvey, J., & Ignatiev, N. (1997). Toward a new abolitionism: A race traitor manifesto. In M. Hill (Ed.), *Whiteness: A critical reader* (pp. 346–349). New York: New York University Press.

Haney Lopez, I. (1997). *White by law: The legal construction of race* (rev. ed.). New York: New York University Press.

Harris, C. (1995). Whiteness as property. In K. Crenshaw, N. Gotanda, G. Peller, & K. Thomas (Eds.), *Critical race theory: The key writings that formed the movement* (pp. 276–291). New York: New Press.

"WHAT ABOUT POOR WHITE PEOPLE?"

Hartigan, J. (2004). Whiteness and Appalachian studies: What's the connection? *Journal of Appalachian Studies, 10*(1–2), 58–72.

Hayden, W., Jr. (2004). Appalachian diversity: African-American, Hispanic/Latino, and other populations. *Journal of Appalachian Studies, 10*(3), 293–306.

Heilman, E. (2004). Hoosiers, hicks, and hayseeds: The controversial place of marginalized ethnic whites in multicultural education. *Equity & Excellence in Education, 37*(1), 67–79.

Helms, J. (1993). *Black and white racial identity*. Westport, CT: Praeger.

Ignatiev, N. (1995). *How the Irish became white*. New York: Routledge.

Jacobson, M. (1998). *Whiteness of a different color: European immigrants and the alchemy of race*. Cambridge, MA: Harvard University Press.

James, C. E. (1995). "Reverse racism": Students' response to equity programs. *Journal of Professional Studies, 3*(1), 48–54.

Ladson-Billings, G. (1999). Preparing teachers for diverse student populations: A critical race theory perspective. *Review of Research in Education, 24*, 211–247.

Ladson-Billings, G., & Tate, W. (1995). Toward a critical race theory of education. *Teachers College Record, 97*(1), 47–68.

Leonardo, Z. (2002). The souls of white folk: Critical pedagogy, whiteness studies, and globalization discourse. *Race, Ethnicity and Education, 5*(1), 29–50.

Leonardo, Z. (2005). Through the multicultural glass: Althusser, ideology and race relations in post-civil rights America. *Policy Futures in Education, 3*(4), 400–412.

Lipsitz, G. (1998). *The possessive investment in whiteness: How white people profit from identity politics*. Philadelphia: Temple University Press.

Love, B. (2004). *Brown* plus 50 counter-storytelling: A critical race theory analysis of the "majoritarian achievement gap" story. *Equity & Excellence in Education, 37*, 227–246.

Lynn, M. (1999). Toward a critical race pedagogy: A research note. *Urban Education, 33*(5), 606–626.

McIntosh, P. (1997). White privilege and male privilege. In R. Delgado & J. Stefancic (Eds.), *Critical white studies: Looking behind the mirror* (pp. 291–299). Philadelphia: Temple University Press.

McIntyre, A. (1997). Constructing an image of a white teacher. *Teachers College Record, 98*(4), 653–681.

Mills, C. (1997). *The racial contract*. Ithaca, NY: Cornell University Press.

National Collaborative on Diversity in the Teaching Force. (2004, October). *Assessment of diversity in America's teaching force: A call to action*. Washington, D.C.: Author.

Oliver, M., & Shapiro, T. (1997). *Black wealth/white wealth: A new perspective on racial inequality*. New York: Routledge.

Parker, L., & Stovall, D. (2004). Actions following words: Critical race theory connects to critical pedagogy. *Educational Philosophy and Theory, 36*(2), 167–182.

Roediger, D. (1999). *Wages of whiteness: Race and the making of the American working class* (Rev. ed.). New York: Verso.

Sacks, K. B. (1994). How did Jews become white folks? In S. Gregory & R. Sanjeck (Eds.), *Race* (pp. 78–102). New Brunswick, NJ: Rutgers University Press.

Shaw, T. C., DeYoung, A. J., & Rademacher, E. W. (2004). Educational attainment in Appalachia: Growing with the nation, but challenges remain. *Journal of Appalachian Studies, 10*(3), 307–329.

Smith, B. E. (2004). De-gradations of whiteness: Appalachia and the complexities of race. *Journal of Appalachian Studies, 10*(1–2), 38–57.

Solorzano, D., & Yosso, T. (2002). A critical race counterstory of race, racism, and affirmative action. *Equity & Excellence in Education, 35*(2), 155–168.

Tate, W. F. (1997). Critical race theory in education: History, theory, and implications. *Review of Research in Education, 22*, 195–250.

Tatum, B. D. (2003). *"Why are all the Black kids sitting together in the cafeteria?" and other conversations about race* (5th ed.). New York: Basic Books.

Taylor, E. (1999). Critical race theory and interest convergence in the desegregation of higher education. In L. Parker, D. Deyhle, & S. Villenas (Eds.), *Race is . . . race isn't: Critical race theory and qualitative studies in education* (pp. 181–204). Boulder, CO: Westview Press.

Valadez, G. (2004). Walking the dance: Teaching and cross-cultural encounter. *Journal of Appalachian Studies, 10*(1–2), 152–166.

28

MOMENTS OF SOCIAL INCLUSION AND EXCLUSION

Race, class, and cultural capital in family-school relationships

Annette Lareau and Erin McNamara Horvat

Source: *Sociology of Education*, 72, 1, 1999, 37–53.

This article presents a case study of parents' involvement with their third-grade children. Using interviews and classroom observations, the research revealed how some black parents, deeply concerned about the historical legacy of discrimination against blacks in schooling, approach the school with open criticisms. Since educators seek a positive and deferential role for parents in schooling, race appears to play an independent role in parents' ability to comply with educators' requests (although social class also mediates the ways in which black parents express their concerns). The results highlight the difference between possession and activation of capital and the value accorded displays of capital in particular settings. Taken together, the findings suggest the importance of focusing on moments of inclusion and exclusion in examining how individuals activate social and cultural capital.

Scholars who are interested in how schools replicate existing social inequalities have found the concept of social reproduction to be useful, especially as articulated in the work of Bourdieu and his associates (Bourdieu 1977a, 1977b, 1984, 1990; Wacquant 1992, 1993). One of Bourdieu's major insights on educational inequality is that students with more valuable social and cultural capital fare better in school than do their otherwise-comparable peers with less valuable social and cultural capital. The social reproduction perspective has proved especially useful in attempts to gain a better understanding of how race and class influence the transmission of educational inequality.

However, a key dilemma that confronts those who seek to understand how the reproduction of inequality occurs in schools has been where to focus the debate.

Exactly how is inequality perpetuated in school settings? Much of the literature has identified important class differences in parents' and students' attitudes or behaviors toward schools and has shown that these class differences affect children's progress in school (Brantlinger 1993; DiMaggio and Mohr 1985; Lareau 1989; McDonough 1997; Useem 1992). As valuable as this line of research has been, these theories do not always attend to individual interactions and interventions that more accurately characterize the students', teachers', and parents' interactions in schools. In other words, these studies have identified cultural and social factors that contribute to educational inequality but have not advanced knowledge of the process whereby social and cultural resources are converted into educational advantages. Thus, the picture that emerges from them is incomplete and overly simplistic.

Despite these difficulties, the overall perspective of social reproduction, with its focus on conflict, change, and systemic inequality, is still worthy of attention. Bourdieu's method allows for a more fluid interplay and better understanding of the relationship between structure and agency than do other theoretical perspectives. Although the theoretical potential of offering an intricate and dynamic model is embedded in Bourdieu's original conceptual work, the empirical research has often been disappointing. The translation of the theoretical model into "variables" has often decontextualized key concepts from the broader theoretical mission (see Wacquant 1992 and 1993 for a discussion of these issues).

Still, Bourdieu has always remained attuned to the strategies and actions that individuals follow in their daily lives. Nevertheless, he has not always been sufficiently aware of variations in the ways in which institutional actors legitimate or rebuff efforts by individuals to activate their resources. Nor has he given sufficient attention to the moments of reproduction and exclusion. Although both these points are clearly implied in Bourdieu's work, we see it as an important clarification.

In sum, the empirical work on social reproduction, despite the original theoretical richness of Bourdieu's writing, has not sufficiently recognized three important points. First, the value of capital depends heavily on the social setting (or field). Second, there is an important difference between the possession and activation of capital or resources. That is, people who have social and cultural capital may choose to activate capital or not, and they vary in the skill with which they activate it. Third, these two points come together to suggest that rather than being an overly deterministic continual process, reproduction is jagged and uneven and is continually negotiated by social actors.

We find it helpful to point to moments of "social inclusion" and "social exclusion" (Lamont and Lareau 1988). To understand the character of these moments, one needs to look at the context in which the capital is situated, the efforts by individuals to activate their capital, the skill with which individuals activate their capital, and the institutional response to the activation. These factors, working together, can produce moments of reproduction or moments of contestation, challenge, and social change.

130

In this article, we highlight three aspects of the reproduction process: the value attached to capital in a particular social context, the process through which individuals activate their social capital, and the legitimacy the institutions accord these displays. In our analysis of these patterns, we explicate specific moments of inclusion and exclusion that have been muffled by the overly global approach to the process of social reproduction.

In exploring these theoretical issues, we investigate the complex topic of the relative influence of race and social class in aspects of children's school experiences. Although previous research (Lareau 1989; Spade, Columba, and Vanfossen 1997; Useem 1992) stressed the importance of social class in shaping family-school relationships, in this article, we show how race acts to mediate the importance of class and has an independent theoretical significance in shaping family-school relationships. We suggest that it is more difficult for black parents than white parents to comply with the institutional standards of schools.[1] In particular, educators are relentless in their demands that parents display positive, supportive approaches to education. The historical legacy of racial discrimination, however, makes it far more difficult for black parents than white parents to comply with such demands. Although social class seems to influence how black and white parents negotiate their relationships with schools, for blacks race plays an important role, independent of social class, in framing the terms of their relationship.

Theoretical tools

In this section, we present a brief overview of the conceptual model developed by Bourdieu and his associates (Bourdieu 1977a, 1977b, 1984, 1990; Wacquant 1992, 1993). Bourdieu himself has stressed the situational fluidity that defies simplistic definitions of key concepts (Brubaker 1993). In addition, as Robbins (1991) noted, he seeks to offer a particularly dynamic model, capturing "a bird in flight." We realize that we flirt with an overly reductionist approach here, but, particularly for the uninitiated reader, believe that a discussion of the core elements of the model is essential (for other secondary discussions, see Buchmann 1989; Calhoun, LiPuma, and Postone 1993; Robbins 1991).

Briefly, the notion of capital exists in Bourdieu's method of viewing the social world. In his approach, all behavior is situated within a field of action, which has its own system of valuation and practice. The habitus can be viewed "as a system of lasting, transposable dispositions which . . . functions at every moment as a matrix of *perceptions, appreciations, and actions*" (Bourdieu 1977b:82–83; italics in the original). However, habitus can be understood only in light of the dominant practices in the broader society. Bourdieu has used the term field to capture the "rules of the game" (Bourdieu and Wacquant 1992).

In addition, individuals have strategies or practice. Practice in the field of interaction is shaped by multiple, interacting forces, including the rules governing the field and the relative position of players in the field. In a given field of interaction, different forms of capital have various values. As Bourdieu showed, the value of these resources can take many forms. Much attention has been paid to the concrete and potentially measurable benefits of social relations to promote advancement (social capital), cultural knowledge or resources (cultural capital), or economic resources (economic capital). But Bourdieu also has clearly highlighted the symbolic value of various displays in the social space (Bourdieu 1977a, 1977b, 1977c, 1984, 1985, 1987a, 1987b; Bourdieu and Passeron 1977; Bourdieu and Wacquant 1992).[2]

Using Bourdieu's theory allowed us to draw two critical distinctions regarding the notion of capital in the process of social reproduction. First, all individuals have social capital to invest or activate in a variety of social settings or fields. However, all social or cultural capital does not have the same value in a given field. In addition, although the difference between possession of forms of capital and activation in specific settings is compatible with Bourdieu's model, Bourdieu (1984) did not draw sufficient attention to it. In this article, we stress that to be of value in a given field, social and cultural capital must be activated. The ability to activate social and cultural capital and the way in which it is activated influence its value in a field of interaction. The analogy of a card game, often used by Bourdieu (see, for example, Bourdieu, 1976), illustrates these two points.

In a card game (the field of interaction), the players (individuals) are all dealt cards (capital). However, each card and each hand have different values. Moreover, the value of each hand shifts according to the explicit rules of the game (the field of interaction) that is being played (as well as the way the game is being enacted). In other words, a good hand for blackjack may be a less valuable hand for gin rummy. In addition to having a different set of cards (capital), each player relies on a different set of skills (habitus) to play the cards (activate the capital). By folding the hand, a player may not activate his or her capital or may play the cards (activate the capital) expertly according to the rules of the given game. In another game, the same player may be dealt the same hand, yet because of a lack of knowledge of the rules of the game play the hand poorly. Thus, in analyzing social settings, researchers must attend to the capital that each individual in a given field has, as well as each individual's ability and skill in activating the capital.

Method

The study was conducted in Lawrence (a fictitious name, as are all the names used here), a small Midwestern town with a population of about 25,000. Located two hours from a metropolitan center, the town's commercial base is dominated by farming, coal mining, light manufacturing, retail stores, state government offices, and a university. At the time of the study, the public school system enrolled approximately 1,500 elementary and junior high school students in six schools. Of these students, 52 percent were white, 44 percent were black, 3 percent were Asian, and 1 percent were Hispanic. Forty percent of the children were classified as low income (eligible for the free-lunch program or receiving public assistance).[3]

132

Of the six schools in the Lawrence school district, one is a school that enrolls only children in kindergarten; four are elementary schools, two for children in Grades 1-3 and two for those in Grades 4-6; and one is a junior high school. Of the four main elementary schools, one is in an all-black section of town, and the other three are in predominantly white areas (although one school is near a black housing area).

Quigley Elementary School, with around 200 students in Grades 1-3, is located in an overwhelmingly white and affluent part of town. Most of the staff members-the superintendent, principal, teachers, and janitors—were white; only one first-grade teacher and the school secretary were black. The first author, a middle-aged white woman, conducted participant-observation in each of two third-grade classrooms twice a week from September to December 1989 and less frequently (for example, three times per month) from January to June 1990. Both teachers, Mrs. Erickson and Mrs. Nelson, were white middle-aged women, each with about 25 years of teaching experience. Each classroom had 30 children. In the spring, the demographic data on each classroom were stratified into groups by race and social class (based on relatively crude and often inaccurate information on the parents' occupations from the children's emergency cards).

A sample of 24 children was chosen for indepth interviews-12 white children (5 girls and 7 boys) and 12 black children (7 girls and 5 boys). Separate two-hour interviews were held in the children's homes with the parents and guardians.[4] The first author conducted most of the interviews, and a black graduate research assistant conducted several interviews with black families. Although there were many informal exchanges between the researchers and the children, the children were not formally interviewed. However, in their interviews, the teachers spoke at length about each of the children in the study.

As Table 1 reveals, social class (see the definition in the table) and racial membership were heavily confounded in the study (as they are in the general population). That is, we essentially compared white middle-class families and black working-class and poor families. About one-quarter of the children lived in single-parent households, a living arrangement that was heavily interwoven with social-class position. That is, all the poor children came from single-parent homes, but only one of the children in the working-class group and none of the middle-class children did.

In all, interviews were conducted with 40 parents and 9 educators (a principal, superintendent, school board member, school secretary, and 5 teachers). Interviews were also conducted with 26 other adults who were working in the community. These adults included civil rights officials (such as the head of the local NAACP chapter and the executive director of a local community center in a black neighborhood) and city officials (such as the city manager and a social worker), who spoke about the broader racial context. In addition, the first author spent one week in the library of the local newspaper reading the newspaper's articles on racial issues, particularly racial tensions in the schools from 1950 to 1990. Although the results of such an intensive case study cannot be generalized to a broader population, they can be used to challenge and modify conceptual models in the field.

Table 1 The distribution of children in the study, by race and social class

Social class	White (n = 12)	Black (n = 12)	Total (N = 24)
Middle class	9	3	12
Working class	3	4	7
Poor	—	5	5

Note: Middle-class families are those in which at least one parent has a college degree and is employed in a professional or managerial position. Working-class families are those in which at least one parent graduated from high school (or is a high school dropout) and is steadily employed in a skilled or semiskilled position, including lower-level white-collar work. Poor families are those in which the parents are on welfare; most of these families are high school dropouts or graduates.

Broader racial context

As a small Midwestern town with a minority population, Lawrence underwent considerable change in the 1950s and 1960s in how blacks were treated. Interviews with civil rights leaders and a review of newspaper articles revealed that many local businesses, including restaurants and movie theaters, practiced racial segregation or exclusion. As a result of demonstrations and pressure to alter these patterns, which began in the 1950s, most businesses altered these racial practices between 1958 and 1964. Discrimination in employment, which was pervasive and generally excluded blacks from all but custodial, domestic, and laborer positions, was slower to be eradicated.

With regard to the schools, Lawrence historically operated a black high school and a white high school. In 1964 the black high school was closed, and the students were sent to the white high school. The parents of the third-grade students, both white and black, remembered the time as turbulent, with open racial hostility among the students. The elementary schools, which drew from neighborhoods, were also racially segregated. In 1968 the district began a controversial busing program that was still in existence at the time of the study.

Since the parents in the study were born between 1941 and 1966, with most born in the 1950s, the majority remembered some of these changes. Many of the black parents began their school careers in segregated schools. Virtually all their parents and grandparents experienced legalized segregation.

At the time the data were collected, there were concerns about the current and past unequal treatment of black children in the Lawrence schools. Frustrated by what they perceived as insensitivity by the school district and angered by the demotion of the only black administrator from principal to teacher, a group of black parents organized a school boycott to protest racial injustice in Lawrence in September 1987. On the first day of the boycott, about 25 percent of the black children did not attend school, and on the second and third (and final) days, about 15 percent were absent.

This boycott and a series of meetings between the district officials and black leaders were prominently featured in the newspaper. There were 20 articles on boycott-related issues in 1987 and 1988 but only a handful from 1989 to 1991. In these articles, officials of civil rights organizations provided biting indictments of the district officials. An article in the summer of 1990, for example, stated that Mr. Gowan, an officer in the NAACP, complained at a district meeting that in the Lawrence schools, black children "sense negative attitudes toward their presence" and often feel like "they are unwelcome participants in the educational process." He also stated that the school district officials "are insensitive to the needs of blacks" and that black parents had no "receptive audience" in the schools. Mr. Gowan then said that the board needed to reestablish lines of communication with the black community and to seek advice from organizations, such as the NAACP, as two other school districts in the region had done. "Why are we having such a problem at Lawrence?" he asked. "A lot of it has to do with attitude."

This brief discussion indicates that until the mid-1960s, racial discrimination was a legalized part of Lawrence institutions and that institutional officials resisted efforts to bring about social change. As young children, the black parents witnessed and experienced this discrimination and the officials' responses to it. Although discrimination was no longer legal at the time of the study, organized protests on racial issues continued, albeit in a radically different form. This climate of racial discrimination severely undermined some parents' trust in dominant institutions, including their children's school.

The value of capital: a stricter test

In *Distinction,* Bourdieu (1984) gave examples of numerous differences in the tastes of the upper middle class and working class in France, ranging from types of foods to home furnishings and music, art, and other forms of leisure pursuits. In the classic formulation, Bourdieu suggested that these class-based differences in dispositions are of unequal value in the broader school setting.

In the area of social and cultural capital, some empirical studies (DiMaggio 1982; DiMaggio and Mohr 1985; Farkas 1996; Farkas, Grobe, Sheehan, and Shaun 1990; Kalmijn and Kraaykamp 1996) have found an effect, but others (DeGraf 1986; Robinson and Garnier 1985) have not. In almost all these studies, however, the presumed value of the capital is based on the patterns of the dominant ideology in the broader culture. For example, attendance at art museums is given a higher status than attendance at baseball games. One problem with this approach is that it is not clear that these cultural patterns are, in fact, highly valued in a specific institutional context. Nor is it clear why these resources should be considered forms of capital, capable of providing advantages in the social world.

In this article, we introduce a stricter test of the definition of capital. Instead of determining whether children's homes have cultural resources or display cultural signals, we suggest that researchers should be able to clarify how these resources are valued in the specific context under investigation—in this instance, the school experience (see Farkas 1996 for a similar view). Not all cultural displays are equally valued.

135

According to this line of thought, parents' cultural and social resources become forms of capital when they facilitate parents' compliance with dominant standards in school interactions. In particular, cultural capital includes parents' large vocabularies, sense of entitlement to interact with teachers as equals, time, transportation, and child care arrangements to attend school events during the school day. Social capital includes social networks with other parents in the school community who provide informal information about the teachers.[5]

Lareau and others have suggested that social class provides cultural capital when it increases parents' compliance with these standards (Lareau 1987, 1989; Lareau and Shumar 1996; McDonough 1997). In this article, we suggest that being black, rather than white, also plays a role. Given the historical legacy of racial discrimination, black parents are more likely to begin the process suspicious and critical of the risk of unfair treatment for their children. Although the terminology is somewhat awkward, we see being white as a cultural resource that white parents unwittingly draw on in their school negotiations in this context. Technically speaking, in this field, being white becomes a type of cultural capital.

In contrast, blacks do not have this cultural resource available to them. This is not to say that blackness is, in itself, a disadvantage per se, as it is in the culture of poverty's conception of disadvantage. Rather, we argue that in this field of interaction, the rules of the game are built on race-specific interactions. Many black parents, given the historical legacy of racial discrimination in schools, cannot presume or trust that their children will be treated fairly in school. Yet, they encounter rules of the game in which educators define desirable family-school relationships as based on trust, partnership, cooperation, and deference. These rules are more difficult for black than white parents to comply with. Furthermore, although race has an independent role, class also makes a difference. Thus, middle-class black parents have access to important forms of cultural capital, just as middle-class white parents do.

Results

The educators thought that they enthusiastically welcomed parental involvement and believed that their requests for parental involvement were neutral, technically efficient, and designed to promote higher levels of achievement. In reality, from a range of potential socioemotional styles, they selected a narrow band of acceptable behaviors. They wanted parents not only to be positive and supportive but to trust their judgments and assessments—a pattern noted by other researchers (Epstein 1986, 1987, 1991; Van Galen 1987). One third-grade teacher stressed the importance of parents being "supportive" when asked about the qualities of an ideal parent:

> There are so many parents that automatically say that you are wrong and my child is right. The parents that I enjoyed working with the most were the ones who would listen to how the child is and what they needed to work on and didn't criticize you.

The teachers repeatedly praised parents who had praised them. They liked parents who were deferential, expressed empathy with the difficulty of teachers' work, and had detailed information about their children's school experiences. In addition, the teachers often stressed the importance of parents "understanding" their children's educational situations, by which they meant that the parents should accept the teacher's definitions of their children's educational and social performance.

Compliance with school standards

The expected standard that parents should be positive and supportive was difficult for some black families to meet. One reason for the difficulty was the parents' understanding of the broader context of race relations and the ways in which it pervaded the school. In these cases, black parents' attempts to criticize educators directly were rebuffed. For example, the Mason family had a difficult and unhappy relationship with the school, partly because Mr. and Mrs. Mason criticized and expressed their anger directly to the educators. This display of parental concern and involvement through anger and criticism was deemed unacceptable and "destructive" by the educators.

Mr. Mason, a pastor of a small church, and his wife, a beautician and associate pastor, were troubled by patterns of racial injustice. Mrs. Mason thought that a "wave of prejudice" was sweeping the country and the community:

> Every now and then there is a wave of prejudice. A spirit of intimidation is placed on the children. . . . It's almost like the law in America is now. You find a black man that might commit a crime, and he gets life for it and a white man might get off in a year and a half or he might get off with probation. So that's the state of law in America.

Mrs. Mason complained that these broader patterns could be seen at Quigley, particularly in the ways the school lavished attention on some holidays and then systematically ignored the celebration of black heroes:

> I've been over to the school all year, and there are certain holidays, I mean like Halloween . . . [when] witches and skeletons and what have you are hitting you all in the face as you walk down the hall. . . . There is a play on Washington's and Lincoln's birthday. But then Martin Luther King is the only black person that is really kind of recognized in America. And they don't really, most times they're saying that they might [recognize him], . . . but I still don't feel like they're giving as much effort as they should.

The lavish attention to Halloween and little notice of Martin Luther King's birthday were noted in the field observations. Overall, however, the school officials were resistant to Mrs. Mason's arguments that there were patterns of racial injustice in the school. The principal rejected her claims of bias and found her accusations upsetting. As the principal stated:

> I just found her to be very upsetting. . . . I think she is doing so much damage. She will not listen. You try to tell her about the volunteers and what is being done and the positive things and . . . that white children are getting detentions, too. . . .
>
> She's the kind of person who makes me wake up in the middle of the night and I'm thinking, "What can I do, how can I reach this parent, what can be done to change her?"

The teachers also thought that the Masons' claims were undermining their authority by making it more difficult for them to educate their children. As another teacher, who provided supplemental reading instruction to all third-grade children, commented about Mrs. Mason's daughter Faith:

> When I would try to correct [Faith], she would smart back at me. If she got in trouble because of her behavior, she would say it was because I am prejudiced, not because she was running in the hallway or throwing something in the playground.

Mrs. Erickson found the Masons to be among the "most upsetting" parents in her teaching career. She was particularly disturbed by them raising their voices in conversation and "just out and out yelling." Because the Masons seemed always to be angry, Mrs. Erickson tried to avoid interacting with them. As she stated:

> They came in angry in January basically over her health grade. And then because there weren't enough black history pictures in the library. And angry that she had been tested and found to have a language delay, and they refused to sign for the testing. . . . I just thought I should leave well enough alone.[6]

For the most part, the Masons' efforts resulted in moments of exclusion. Faith stayed in her reading group (below grade level), rather than being moved up, and hence was not exposed to the higher-level reading curriculum. Still, there were some changes. At the end of the year, Mrs. Erickson "boosted" Faith's English grade a few points because "I just didn't want to have a scene." Thus, rather than appreciate Mr. and Mrs. Mason's interest and concern for the school, the educators defined it as singularly unhelpful.[7] In this educational setting, open conflict and anger were not considered legitimate.

As we discuss shortly, there were variations in how the black parents activated their concern for race with the school. In addition, both the black and the white parents differed in their levels of concern. A few white parents presented a negative vision of racial interaction at the school; for example, one mother thought that the white children were being treated unfairly, and she "resented" it. Overall, however, the white parents' enthusiasm for busing for racial integration and levels of empathy and concern about the potential racial bias at school differed. But none of the white parents exhibited, in the interviews or observations, the wholesale suspicion, distrust, and hostility toward schools that we found among some of the black parents.

Thus, the white parents were privileged in the sense that they began to construct their relationships with the school with more comfort and trust than did the black parents. This lack of suspicion took on substantially more value (capital) in an institutional framework in which the educators stressed positive, affirmative, supportive family-school encounters. Had the school adopted the norms, for example, of a trial court or of a debating team, then the racial differences might not have been of value. In this setting, in which the educators were extremely hostile to expressions of criticism toward them, the membership of whites in a dominant race, without the risk of historical patterns of discrimination, was an advantage in complying with the school's standards.

Race intertwining with social class

Other black parents also approached the school with a suspicion that the legacy of racial discrimination was continuing. There were, however, important social-class differences in how the black parents managed their concerns. The middle-class parents were much more likely than the poor parents to maneuver and "customize" (Lareau 1989) their children's school experiences. At times, they diffused the risk of racial discrimination without the teachers ever knowing of their concern. These patterns point to the importance of differentiating between the *possession* and *activation* of capital. In addition, they point to variations (often by temperament) in the parents' skill and shrewdness in the activation process that have not always been noted in the empirical literature.

Some black parents were extremely skillful in fostering interactions with educators. For example, Mr. and Mrs. Irving, a middle-class couple, were apprehensive that black children were discriminated against in the school and actively monitored their daughter's schooling. But the teacher never knew the source of their concern because they shielded it from her.

Mr. and Mrs. Irving thought that some of the black children were being treated differently from the white children in the school. As members of an black middle-class church, they were friends with other middle-class blacks, including several teachers, who shared their criticisms with the Irvings of how some white teachers treated black students. As Mr. Irving, a former teacher who now works in management for a manufacturing plant, stated:

> I've heard that some young black boys are maybe singled out more often for discipline than young white males. I've heard that before from the teachers who have seen it firsthand. . . . They'll maybe put one of the

black boys on detention a lot faster than one of the white boys who maybe do the same things. I haven't seen it, but I've heard people talk about it that work there that ought to know.

When asked if he thought black children were being discriminated against, Mr. Irving said:

> It's probably happening. I'm just considering the ratio between black teachers and white teachers, I would say it's happening. . . . I think as long as you have black and whites, there is going to be some kind of discrimination—some kind of problems; I don't think it's as bad as it used to be. . . . You don't come out and see it now; it's more covert.

Indeed, his wife appeared to see her husband's bimonthly visits to the school as an activation of resources to prevent problems from developing:

> I guess all in all, looking at my child, I think she's been treated fairly. If she hadn't been, well, we kind of visit the school.

Mr. and Mrs. Irving kept a close eye on their daughter Neema's schooling. Mrs. Irving monitored Neema's homework closely and insisted that Neema read regularly. Mr. Irving would stop by to bring their daughter Neema her lunch, to volunteer, or just to check on how things were going. As one teacher said:

> Her Dad was . . . at the school a lot. Some days he was just bringing her lunch or something, but he would ask me many questions. Probably every time he was in there, [he] would ask, "How was she doing?" "Had she worked on this or that?" . . . [Both parents] seemed to want to do anything they could to help Neema. She was a very smart student.

Not only did Mr. Irving supervise his daughter's progress, but he would occasionally make requests. When Neema was in the first grade, for example, he asked that she be tested for the academically talented program; Neema was tested and admitted to the program. In this case, Mr. Irving activated knowledge (from his days as a teacher) to improve his daughter's educational experience.

The teachers did not seem to know about the Irvings' apprehensions of racial discrimination. In both the interviews and the day-to-day chatter about parents after school, the teachers had only positive things to say about Mr. and Mrs. Irving and thought they were among the most supportive and helpful parents in the school. Thus, unlike the Masons, the Irvings were able to activate their cultural and social resources to intervene in their daughter's school career in a way the school defined as helpful and supportive. The Irvings' efforts to customize Neema's school career were partially motivated by their concern about the broader context of racial treatment in the schools. The Irvings were particularly masterful in gaining advantages for their daughter (for example, enrollment in the academically gifted program) and managing her schooling so they could be reassured that she was not subjected to unfair treatment without revealing their concern to the educators. The interventions provide a portrait of a series of moments of social inclusion in which parent-teacher contacts facilitated Neema's inclusion in high-status educational programs and her continuing success in school.

In contrast, some poor black parents who were concerned about racial discrimination handled the matter differently. Some saw a separation between home and school (Lareau 1989) and did not seek to intervene in the school process. For example, Ms. Caldron had been an alcoholic and cocaine drug addict for most of her children's lives but had been sober for two months. She lived in a government-financed housing project with her children; on her welfare subsidy, she could not afford to have a telephone. Ms. Caldron was concerned that the school was treating the black children, especially those who lived in the housing project, unfairly:

> I don't know, it seems like every black kid out there is getting in trouble one way or the other, and it's mostly black project kids. She [the principal] is just hard on them. It seemed like every time I turn around, Doug [her son] is on detention for something or other. . . . Pauley [another school in the district] was mixed. Now . . . they are in a predominantly white area where, you know, black kids aren't supposed to be. And I don't think that's right.

Ms. Caldron objected to children attending a school in the white part of town and thought it contributed to the racial discrimination at the school. When asked if she thought that the black children were being treated differently from the white children, she replied:

> I just feel that they do. They are being treated differently. For one thing they just got out there. They hadn't been there when the rest of that school was all white. . . . So the kids that are still there get more seniority than these kids who are just coming in there. But it shouldn't be like that.

Ms. Caldron had little contact with the school during the academic year. Although Ms. Caldron requested spelling lists a few times, Mrs. Erickson complained that she did not return forms that required her signature or respond to notes that were sent home. Although Ms. Caldron had negative and hostile feelings toward the school, she did not discuss these concerns with other parents because she did not know any of the mothers of the other children in her children's classrooms. The only person she shared her concerns with was her friend Hope, whose child also attended the school:

> Me and this lady Hope we talked about it [sometimes], but just us two. . . .
> She feels the same way I do, and I feel the same way that she do. I feel that

Mrs. Hertman [the principal] is semiprejudiced. I don't know about the rest of the teachers. I think Mrs. Erickson, she's semiprejudiced, too. Really, the only one I really liked was Mrs. Harrison (a school volunteer), and she's not even a teacher.

Unlike the Irvings, Ms. Caldron was not knowledgeable about her child's schooling (for instance, she did not know the name of his teacher or what reading group he was in), did not monitor and oversee the school experience through volunteer work, and did not attempt to intervene and change the character of the school experience.

In Bourdieu's terms, Ms. Caldron's habitus meant that she approached the educational field with fewer resources to influence her children's schooling successfully. It is also possible that because she was plagued with problems of substance abuse, she "played" her resources (Bourdieu, 1976) less successfully than did other parents with comparable resources. In any case, she felt (and appeared to be) excluded from the educational process. Her son, who had repeated a grade and was at the bottom of the class in educational performance, did not have promising educational prospects. The most important point, however, is that social class appears to mediate how parents with similar types of concern about racial discrimination seek to manage their children's school careers. The results point to the influence of social class on how families manage their concerns about racial injustice at school.

White working-class parents also experienced distance from or conflict with the school. However, they focused exclusively on their own children's experience independent of the political or racial climate at the school. These parents did not talk about "the school" having a particular attitude or stance; rather, they talked about teachers treating their children in a specific manner.

Chad Carson's parents are a case in point. His mother, a manager at a local motel, and his father, a car salesman, never married and do not live together. Ms. Carson had a number of conflicts with Chad's teacher, Mrs. Nelson, which centered on the communication between them. As she put it:

> I got a detention notice in the mail from the principal. This is the first I had heard of anything—two weeks before a report card comes out. So I went in, and she said, "Chad daydreams. He never gets his things done and has a hard time paying attention." Anyway, I talked to Mrs. Nelson, and for the most part we didn't get anything resolved except I just said to her, "I can't do anything unless I know." . . . This is the first time that I had heard of anything that was the matter with Chad. He's bringing home A papers. I didn't understand. And I said, "I can't help if you don't let me know."

This pattern of difficult communication between the teacher and parent appeared in regard to other issues as well. Ms. Carson detailed the problems she had with the school in keeping Chad supplied with paper for school.

142

Chad would call me here at work and say, "I ran out of paper." And I would say, "Chad, could you borrow some from someone, and we'll be sure to get you some for tomorrow." [Chad replied]: "No, Mrs. Nelson won't let me do that. She made me call you." I said, "Chad, I can't leave work to bring you paper." The next day I sent four notebooks with Chad. . . . Well, it happened again. So, the way I handled it the second time was I took two of those big 500-sheet things into the principal's office and said, "Here, if any child comes in here to call their parent for paper, please give them this." I said, "You know, I can't just leave work. . . . If I don't know that Chad is out of paper, I can't do anything about it."

Even though the lack of communication between Mrs. Nelson and Ms. Carson involved a visit to the principal's office to drop off more paper, Ms. Carson remained focused on her and Chad's relationship with the teacher, not with the school in general.

Another white working-class couple, Mr. and Mrs. Jennings, attributed the problems that their daughter Lauren was having in third-grade mathematics to problems that began in the first grade. Mrs. Jennings described when and how Lauren's problems began:

I thought things were goin' fine—and her first-grade teacher was not payin' attention at all. When they got far behind, she wasn't lettin' us know. And all of a sudden, Lauren was comin' home with 10 or 12 pages of math homework in a workbook that she hadn't been doin', that I didn't know she hadn't been doing. 'Cause I thought everything was OK. I mean, I knew she fooled around, but I know a lot of 'em do that. So, it wasn't gettin' remedied.

Despite her daughter's persistent problem in mathematics that was traceable to the first grade, Mrs. Jennings did not hold the school as a whole responsible.

These two families' experiences represent the most difficult conflicts that white working-class parents reported having with teachers or the schools. They clearly did not have the diffuse and pervasive race-based distrust of the school that some of the black parents identified. For them, conflict with the school was limited to and centered on their individual relationships with the teachers.

Variations in parents' perceptions

Black Parents Not all the black parents and guardians had difficult and unhappy relationships with the educators at Quigley school. Some were very positive. One black grandmother, whose daughter died suddenly during the spring, was grateful to Mrs. Erickson. Saying she was "just super," the grandmother could not say enough good things about her. At the end of the year, she gave Mrs. Erickson a necklace as a thank-you gift.

Moreover, not all parents shared the view that black children at the school were subjected to unequal and less favorable treatment compared to the white children. A number of black parents stated that they did not know if there were problems at the school. For example, the grandmother of a child (the drug-addicted mother was unable to provide care) had not heard anything:

Q: Do you know any parents who feel that children are being treated differently at the school because of their race?

A: To tell you the truth, I never really discussed it with any parent, you know, the way they feel their children are being treated. Cause I don't go around and talk to people a lot. We might talk about church or something like that, but as far as racial things, I never really talk about it. . . . I haven't heard anything said.

Other black parents stated that children at Quigley school were not being treated unfairly on the basis of race. Some of these parents, from a range of social-class positions, were openly hostile to the black parents who complained about racial injustice. For example, one poor mother energetically defended the principal, Mrs. Hertman, from accusations of racism that she had heard in the public housing project in which she lived:

The people who call Mrs. Hertman prejudiced are just rebellious. I don't brainwash my kids with that white-folks stuff. It's not that she's prejudiced. It's that a lot of black kids are hard to handle because their parents are on drugs or don't care.

A working-class father who worked as a laborer on the railroad was cautious as well:

Tracking [of black students] is a problem, but I've got different feelings: . . . A lot of parents don't take the time and make their kids do their part. If parents participated more, I don't think you [would] have a problem.

In a different vein, a middle-class father acknowledged that other parents were concerned that blacks were not sufficiently active in the schools but he, too, placed responsibility on the parents. He thought that the parents needed to take an active role in monitoring schooling: "My biggest thing is that a lot of black people just need to get more involved."

White Parents The white parents' assessments of the existence of racial problems in the schools also varied. Some white parents agreed there were problems. As one white mother said:

I think the teachers need to go, a lot of them, for a good semester, not a Friday workshop, . . . and become sensitized to some of the problems these kids have.

This mother also noted that she would never discuss these issues with some parents because "I know that they are prejudiced."

Other white parents said that they did not know what to think about race relations in the schools. For example, one father had read of black parents' concerns in the newspaper, but he was not sure if they were happening in the school. Another mother also expressed confusion:

> I don't know. I can't tell. I mean, I know that there's a disciplinary problem with some of them. And, ah [long pause] Holly has complained about there were certain girls that were picking on 'em. . . . I don't know if the teachers are intimidated by these kids. They probably are, . . . but I think they've pretty much have a handle on it over here, somehow. . . . I mean, it doesn't bother me because they're trying for the right reasons to do the integration.

Discussion

The conceptual model of social reproduction has been rightfully criticized for being overly deterministic. Although ethnographic research has stressed the meaning of daily life, the theoretical models have an "automatic pilot" quality to them. The skills that Bourdieu clearly pointed to in parents "playing their hands" are not brought to bear. The models also substantially underemphasize the crucial role of institutions in accepting or rebuffing the activation of capital by family members.

A more fruitful approach, we believe, is to adopt the conceptual framework of moments of inclusion and moments of exclusion. (One could also use the terms *moments of reproduction* and *moments of contestation*.) We define moments of inclusion as the coming together of various forces to provide an advantage to the child in his or her life trajectory. In the realm of school, these moments may include placement in an academically gifted program or the highest academic track (Oakes 1985), enrollment in a suburban school (Wells and Crain 1997), encouragement and preparation for applying to college (McDonough 1997), attendance at an elite college, and use of networks for job placement. In contrast, moments of exclusion may include placement in a low reading group, retention, placement in remedial courses, and the failure to complete college-preparation requirements.

In this definition, we focus on the "objective" completion of or gaining access to a particular school task, not on the subjective experience attached to this task. Obviously, however, subjective experiences are integral to the entire process leading up to and through these critical moments in a life trajectory.

These moments are important. The social reproduction model has implied that the passing of privilege of family to child is relatively automatic. It is not. Although social class is heavily tied to educational outcomes, a student's performance is a core feature in determining educational access in the United States. Thus, even wealthy parents cannot guarantee admission to an elite university, such as Harvard, if their son or daughter has a combined SAT score of 780 and a grade point average of 2.2. By stressing the objective standards for entrance, this approach highlights more clearly the numerous strategies that parents, especially middle-class parents, take to gain advantages for their children in the educational system. For a strategy to be successful, however, it must be legitimated and accepted by the school officials. When it is, it can be termed a moment of inclusion.

To return to the parents, when Mr. and Mrs. Irving requested that their daughter Neema be tested for the academically gifted program, she was tested and admitted. This was a moment of inclusion, since the program was prestigious and exposed children to a higher level of academic work than in the regular classroom. Generally, teachers recommend that children be tested for the gifted program. In this instance, the Irvings were able to gain an advantage that, in all probability, would not have occurred otherwise.

In contrast, Mr. and Mrs. Mason's involvement was, for the most part, less successful. Mrs. Mason repeatedly asked her daughter Faith's third-grade teacher, Mrs. Erickson, to move Faith up to a reading group at grade level, but Mrs. Erickson, who thought that Faith's vocabulary was inadequate for a higher group, refused. Mrs. Mason also complained that Faith wasn't being called on enough during class. In addition, she was unhappy that the school library did not have enough books that celebrated black heroes and expressed concern about the uneven distribution of detentions by race.

The situation of these girls, is, of course, not strictly comparable, since there were important differences between the girls, especially in reading level. Our point, however, is not the girls' absolute level of performance in the class, but the ability of their parents to intervene in a fashion that the educators defined as appropriate and legitimate.

One can argue that, in Bourdieu's terms, Mr. and Mrs. Mason were drawing on their habitus and seeking to activate cultural capital for their daughter within the educational field. Most of their efforts were rebuffed. For example, the school (with elaborate special decorations, a special program, and a special school assembly) devoted far more time and energy to the celebration of Halloween than to Martin Luther King's birthday, and their daughter's reading group was not changed. These interactions, which further compounded the Masons' feelings of alienation and anger, should be characterized as moments of social exclusion. Although Mrs. Erickson "boosted" Faith's grade on her report card, an action that could theoretically be considered a moment of social inclusion, this action was the exception, and the Masons did not know about it.

Moreover, these moments of social exclusion were heavily (but not entirely) connected to Mr. and Mrs. Mason's membership in a minority group with a history of legal discrimination. The Masons framed the issues with contestation and anger, but the school had a standard that emphasized positive, polite interactions. (The standard was not formally stated or made explicit.) In a setting (field of interaction) in which the educators defined a particular socioemotional style (calm voices, positive affirmations, and few criticisms) as legitimate, the anger and hostility that these black parents brought to bear were not recognized as legitimate.

Thus, we stress the value of particular cultural displays should not be presumed to be general, but should be linked to legitimated standards in specific social settings (fields). In the case of parental involvement in white-dominant schooling, being white is an advantage. Whiteness represents a largely hidden cultural resource that facilitates white parents' compliance with the standard of deferential and positive parental involvement in school. Even when white parents approach the school with suspicion and hostility, they are spared the concern over historically recognized patterns of racial discrimination of black children in schools.

Conclusion

What are the implications of this study for research in sociology of education? On a substantive level, the work points to the independent power of race in shaping key interactions in school settings. Although middle-class black families still benefit from their class position (and interact with schools in different ways than their less-privileged counterparts), they still face an institutional setting that implicitly (and invisibly) privileges white families. We assert that in this instance, the role of race is independent of the power of class. This study echoes, in some respects, other research that has suggested the primacy of race in shaping school experiences (Fordham and Ogbu 1986; Ogbu 1974, 1988). Similar to O'Connor's (1997) and Fordham's (1996) findings, we point to the interplay of the individual and the institution in mediating the complex ways that race shapes school experiences.

At the theoretical level, we suggest the value of using Bourdieu's theory to explore social reproduction. Our study sought to highlight the fluid nature of social interaction and the reproduction of inequality in society in a way hinted at, but often underdeveloped, in the literature on social reproduction. Relying on the theoretical purchase offered by Bourdieu's method, our results suggest three modifications to notions of social reproduction. First, researchers should pay more attention to the field of interaction and the explicit and implicit rules for interaction embodied in a given field. Any form or type of capital derives value only in relation to the specific field of interaction. Particular types of social capital do not have inherent value exclusive of what is accorded in a specific field. Second, individuals must activate capital in social environments, and they vary in the level of skills they have to do so.

Accepting these two points leads to our third and concluding point. The process of social reproduction is not a smooth trajectory based on individual characteristics that are seamlessly transmitted across generations. An individual's class and racial position affect social reproduction, but they do not determine it. Each person (in this instance, a parent), through the skill with which he or she activates capital or plays his or her hand, influences how individual characteristics, such as race and class, will matter in interactions with social institutions and other persons in those institutions.[8] Thus, a closer focus on moments of the activation of capital situated in a field analysis that emphasizes how individual behaviors are recognized and legitimated or marginalized and rebuffed provides a more conceptually accurate picture of how social reproduction occurs.

The process of social reproduction is not a continual, deterministic one. Rather, it is shaped moment by moment in particular social fields. By not abandoning the concept of capital, but showing more forcefully the individual's use of strategies in their displays, as well as the nature of the field, researchers stand to develop more nuanced and accurate models of the continuing nature of social inequality.

Notes

1   We recognize the complex symbolic politics surrounding the naming of racial and ethnic groups and the growing tendency to use the term *African American,* rather than *black.* However, we chose to use the everyday language of the people in the study, who consistently used the term *black.* As a result, throughout the article, we use black to refer to African Americans and white to refer to European Americans.

2   In recent years, multiple interpretations of the definitions of capital have proliferated, particularly for notions of social capital and cultural capital (Portes 1998). We acknowledge the core focus on social relationality and social networks in most definitions of social capital. However, we stress the potential power of these social relationships to provide not intergenerational closure, but access to highly desirable social locations. For cultural capital, we stress the historical and contingent character of the definition of cultural resources. In contrast to Bourdieu, we draw more on the role of gatekeeping institutions in determining the value of various displays of cultural capital. Thus, although there were differences in the home furnishings, fashions, and personal appearances of the families and teachers in our study, our focus was on the cultural resources that facilitate or impede compliance with the school's standards. In the moments of inclusion and exclusion we discuss here, cultural resources include parents' vocabularies, socioemotional styles of discourse, and definitions of the roles that family members can take to be the most helpful in advancing their children's school performance.

3   These proportions differed considerably from the town's racial population, which was 73 percent white, 18 percent black, and 9 percent other. The racial composition of Quigley school was not, however, linked to a heavy private school enrollment. Although there were three private or parochial schools within the city limits, they enrolled only 130 children from kindergarten to the 12th grade.

4   For several families, multiple visits were required to establish contact. One white family refused to participate, and another family moved several times and could not be contacted; both were replaced with other comparable families. In addition, in three families, the mothers, but not the fathers, agreed to be interviewed.

5   These should not be seen as an exhaustive list of forms of capital; children's exposure to, for example, classical music, 19th-century novels, and art museums also may provide advantages in other ways.

6   Mrs. Erickson thought that Mr. and Mrs. Mason would not defer to her assessment of Faith's educational needs and lacked a good understanding of these needs. She also thought that the Masons "put a lot of pressure" on Faith and that Faith was "insecure."

7   We do not want to paint an overly deterministic picture of the relationship between the Masons and Mrs. Erickson. Although they had clear periods of conflict, they also had times when relations were more cordial, as, for example, on Back-to-School Night. There were even rare signs of genuine warmth, as on the last day of school when Faith and Mrs. Mason separately gave Mrs. Erickson hugs in the classroom as they were getting ready to depart. Mrs. Mason told Mrs. Erickson that she "wanted things to be better between us." She also said she would be tutoring some of the children over the

summer in the program organized by her church. In addition, she said that she planned to be back next year to volunteer in the school, a suggestion that Mrs. Erickson warmly responded to by saying that they needed volunteers.

8   Clearly, parents' actions reflect their assessment of their child's needs and temperament. In addition, the child's response to the parents' strategies further mediates the entire process. In this study, we were observing children in the third grade. When children are in high school or college, however, they generally take much more of an independent role in this process. Peer groups also come to play a more central role in children's lives as they grow older.

References

Bourdieu, Pierre. 1976. "Marriage Strategies as Strategies of Social Reproduction." Pp. 117–44 in *Family and Society,* edited by Robert Forster and Orest Ranum. Baltimore: John Hopkins University Press.

———. 1977a. "Cultural Reproduction and Social Reproduction." Pp. 487–511 in *Power and Ideology in Education,* edited by Jerome Karabel and A. H. Halsey. New York: Oxford University Press.

———. 1977b. *Outline of a Theory of Practice* (R. Nice trans.). Cambridge, England: Cambridge University Press.

———. 1984. *Distinction: A Social Critique of the judgment of Taste* (R. Nice trans.). Cambridge, England: Harvard University Press.

———. 1990. *In Other Words: Essays Towards a Reflexive Sociology.* Stanford, CA: Stanford University Press.

Bourdieu, Pierre, and John C. Passeron. 1977. *Reproduction in Education, Society and Culture.* Beverly Hills, CA: Sage.

Bourdieu, Pierre, and Loic J. D. Wacquant. 1992. *An Invitation to Reflexive Sociology.* Chicago: University of Chicago Press.

Brantlinger, Ellen A. 1993. *The Politics of Social Class in Secondary School.* New York: Teachers College Press.

Brubaker, Rogers. 1993. "Social Theory as Habitus." Pp. 212–35 in *Bourdieu: Critical Perspectives*, edited by Craig C. Calhoun, Edward LiPuma, and Moishe Postone. Chicago: University of Chicago Press.

Buchmann, Marliss. 1989. *The Script of Life in Modern American Society.* Chicago: University of Chicago Press.

Calhoun, Craig C., Edward LiPuma, and Moishe Postone, eds. 1993. *Bourdieu: Critical Perspectives.* Chicago: University of Chicago Press.

De Graaf, Paul M. 1986. "The Impact of Financial and Cultural Resources on Educational Attainment in the Netherlands." *Sociology of Education* 59:237–46.

DiMaggio, Paul. 1982. "Cultural Capital and School Success: The Impact of Status Culture Participation on the Grades of U.S. High School Students." *American Sociological Review* 47:189–201.

DiMaggio, Paul, and John Mohr. 1985. "Cultural Capital, Educational Attainment, and Marital Selection." *American journal of Sociology* 90:1231–61.

Epstein, Joyce L. 1986. "Parents' Reactions to Teacher Practices of Parent Involvement." *Elementary School Journal* 86:277–94.

———. 1987. "Toward a Theory of Family-School Connections: Teacher Practices and Parent Involvement." Pp. 121–36 in *Social Interventions: Potential and Constraints*, edited by Klaus Hurrelmann, Franz-Xaver Kaufmann, and Friedrich Losel. New York: Walter de Gruyter.

——. 1991. "Effects on Student Achievement of Teachers' Practices of Parent Involvement." Pp. 261–76 in *Literacy Through Family, Community, and School Interaction,* edited by Steven Silvern. Greenwich, CT: JAI Press.

Farkas, George. 1996. *Human Capital or Cultural Capital? Ethnicity and Poverty Groups in an Urban School District.* New York: Aldine de Gruyter.

Farkas, George R., Robert P. Grobe, Daniel Sheehan, and Yuan Shaun. 1990. "Cultural Resources and School Success: Gender, Ethnicity, and Poverty Groups within an Urban District." *American Sociological Review* 55:127–42.

Fordham, Signithia. 1996. *Blacked Out: Dilemmas of Race, Identity, and Success at Capital High.* Chicago: University of Chicago Press.

Fordham, Signithia, and John U. Ogbu. 1986. "Black Students' School Success: Coping with the Burden of 'Acting White.'" *Urban Review* 18:176–206.

Kalmijn, Matthijs, and Gerbert Kraaykamp. 1996. "Race, Cultural Capital and Schooling: An Analysis of Trends in the United States." *Sociology of Education* 69:22–34.

Lamont, Michelle, and Annette Lareau. 1988. "Cultural Capital: Allusions, Gaps, and Glissandos." *Sociological Theory* 6:153–68.

Lareau, Annette. 1987. "Social Class and Family-School Relationships: The Importance of Cultural Capital." *Sociology of Education* 56:73–85.

——. 1989. *Home Advantage: Social Class and Parental Intervention in Elementary Education.* Philadelphia: Falmer Press.

Lareau, Annette, and Wesley Shumar. 1996. "The Problem of Individualism in Family-School Policies." *Sociology of Education* [Special Issue on Sociology and Educational Policy]:24–39.

McDonough, Patricia M. 1997. *Choosing Colleges: How Social Class and Schools Structure Opportunity.* Albany: State University of New York Press.

Oakes, Jeannie. 1985. *Keeping Track: How Schools Structure Inequality.* New Haven, CT: Yale University Press.

O'Connor, Carla. 1997. "Dispositions Toward (Collective) Struggle and Educational Resilience in the Inner City: A Case Analysis of Six African-American High School Students." *American Educational Research Journal* 34:593–629.

Ogbu, John U. 1974. *The Next Generation: An Ethnography of Education in an Urban Neighborhood.* New York: Academic Press.

——. 1988. "Class Stratification, Race Stratification, and Schooling." Pp. 163–89 in *Class, Race, and Gender in American Education,* edited by Lois Weis. Albany: State University of New York Press.

Portes, Alejandro. 1998. "Social Capital: Its Origins and Applications in Modern Sociology." *Annual Review of Sociology* 24:1–24.

Robbins, Derek. 1991. *The Work of Pierre Bourdieu.* Boulder, CO: Westview Press.

Robinson, Robert V., and Maurice A. Garnier. 1985. "Class Reproduction Among Men and Women in France: Reproduction Theory on Its Home Ground." *American Journal of Sociology* 91:250–80.

Spade, Joan Z., Lynn Columba, and Beth Vanfossen, 1997. "Tracking in Mathematics and Science: Courses and Course-Selection Procedures." *Sociology of Education* 70:108–27.

Useem, Elizabeth. 1992. "Middle School and Math Groups: Parents' Involvement in Children's Placement." *Sociology of Education* 65:263–79.

Van Galen, J. 1987. "Maintaining Control: The Structure of Parent Involvement." Pp. 78–90 in *Schooling in Social Context,* edited by George Noblit and William T. Pink. Norwood NJ: Ablex.

Wacquant, Loic, J. D. 1992. "Toward a Social Paxeology: The Structure and Logic of Bourdieu's Sociology." Pp. 1–59 in *An Invitation to Reflexive Sociology,* edited by Pierre Bourdieu and Loic J. D. Wacquant. Chicago: University of Chicago Press.

Wacquant, Loic, J. D. 1993. "Bourdieu in America: Notes on the Transatlantic Importation of Social Theory." Pp. 235–63 in *Bourdieu: Critical Perspectives,* edited by Craig C. Calhoun, Edward LiPuma, and Moishe Postone. Chicago: University of Chicago Press.

Wells, Amy Stuart, and Robert L. Crain. 1997. *Stepping Over the Color Line: African American Students in White Suburban Schools.* New Haven, CT: Yale University Press.

29

CONSERVATIVE ALLIANCE BUILDING AND AFRICAN AMERICAN SUPPORT OF VOUCHERS

The end of *Brown*'s promise or a new beginning?

Michael W. Apple and Thomas C. Pedroni

Source: *Teachers College Record*, 107, 9, 2005, 2068–2105.

A new kind of conservatism has evolved and has taken center stage in many nations, one that is best seen as "conservative modernization." Although parts of these conservative positions may have originated within the New Right, they are now not limited to what has traditionally been called the Right. They have been taken up by a much larger segment of government and policy makers and have also even been appropriated by groups that one might least expect to do so, such as African American activists in cities like Milwaukee.

In this article, we examine a growing phenomenon: the growth of seemingly conservative sentiments among some of the least powerful groups in this society. Perhaps the most significant organization to emerge has been the Black Alliance for Educational Options (BAEO). It has mobilized around voucher advocacy for urban working-class communities of color. BAEO has attracted significant attention not just for its iconoclastic alignment with conservative educational reform, but also for accepting funding from far-Right foundations. This article analyzes the complexity of the discursive and sociopolitical space that BAEO occupies. The organization's awareness of its critics, allies, and the limited range of educational options within which low-income African American families must act belies the notion, put forward by some, that BAEO is simply a front organization for the educational Right. Nevertheless, BAEO's importance to the larger rightist project in education cannot be overstated.

At the core of our analysis is a concern about what is at stake for all of us if a rightist educational agenda succeeds in redefining what and whose knowledge is of most worth and what our social and educational policies are meant to do. Yet, no matter what one's position is on the wisdom of BAEO's strategic actions, this case provides a crucial example of the politics of how social movements and alliances are formed and reformed out of the material and ideological conditions of daily life.

A critical but sympathetic understanding of groups such as BAEO may enable us to avoid the essentialism and reductionism that enters into critical sociological work on the nature of ongoing struggles over educational reform. It can provide a more nuanced sense of social actors and the possibilities and limits of strategic alliances in a time of major conflicts over educational reform during a period of conservative modernization.

This is both a good and bad time in the world of educational policy. On the one hand, there have been very few periods when education has taken such a central place in public debates about our present and future. On the other hand, an increasingly limited range of discursive resources dominates the ways in which this debate is carried out. Indeed, the ideological playing field is so uneven that what were formerly seen as rightist policies have now become "common sense" (Apple, 2000, 2001). Thus, conservative policies have a different kind of cachet today, seen as both efforts to protect a romantic past and as "radical" but necessary solutions to an educational system that is out of control and is no longer responsive to the needs of "the people."

Hence, a new kind of conservatism has evolved and has taken center stage in many nations, one that is best seen as "conservative modernization" (Apple, 2001; Dale, 1989/1990). Although parts of these positions may have originated within the New Right, they are now not limited to what has traditionally been called the Right. They have been taken up by a much larger segment of government and policy makers and, as we will see in this article, they have even been appropriated by groups that one might least expect to do so, such as African American activists in cities like Milwaukee.

Strange bedfellows?

That we might be surprised by the forging of alliances between African American activists and educational actors and tendencies on the Right is a testament to the ways in which we have underestimated both the power of insurgent conservative educational discourses and the urgency of the ongoing educational and social emergency confronting urban working-class and poor families of color.

Any investigation of African American participation in conservative educational reform—such as the one that we undertake in this article—must radiate from an honest appraisal of the conditions, contemporary and historical, that have characterized African Americans' experiences of schooling in places like Milwaukee—one of the first places where an alliance between conservative market-oriented educational reformers and community leaders of the educationally dispossessed has been formed. The move toward support of vouchers among many African American families and community leaders in cities like Milwaukee has come only after a very long history of struggle for greater responsiveness from public school systems. In many ways, the emergence of considerable African American support for seemingly right-wing market-based educational reforms is itself a legacy of the failure of the *Brown vs. Board of Education* decision to adequately animate the desegregationist policies that were carried out under its banner in places like Milwaukee.

Indeed, we know from research on desegregation that these plans—in Milwaukee and hundreds of other school districts—were often designed and carried out in a manner that systematically maintained White privilege under the banner of an "equity-minded" policy. Thus, Black schools were closed, the burden of busing was placed disproportionately on Black students, students were resegregated across classrooms within their "desegregated" schools with mostly White students in high-level classes, and White students were provided greater access to highly desirable and usually well-funded magnet schools (see Bell, 2004; Shujaa, 1996; Wells, Holme, Revilla, & Atanda, 2004).

This history of school desegregation in the United States is a tribute to the power of White privilege to reassert itself even into policies and programs that were supposedly designed to alter this privilege by helping African Americans gain access to better schools and educational opportunities. Our recognition of this history is not an indictment of the spirit of *Brown*; rather, it is a sober assessment of how difficult it is for educational policies to change a society so deeply rooted in racial inequality and segregation. The racial apartheid that envelopes U.S. public education renders efforts to desegregate it nearly futile; virtually all policies and programs designed to "equalize" opportunities are rooted in the advantages that Whites have and fight to maintain (see Wells, Holme, Atanda, & Revilla, 2005).

It is in this context that a vocal and energized group of African Americans in Milwaukee came to see vouchers and private school choice as the best option, given their frustration with a school desegregation plan that had for so long sent Black students across the city and across urban–suburban lines while many neighborhood schools in the Black community were either closed or converted into sought-after magnet schools that were nearly 50% White. While these African American voucher supporters do not speak for all African Americans in Milwaukee (e.g., thousands enrolled their children in magnet and suburban schools through the desegregation plan),[1] they do speak to the larger issue of Blacks' growing frustration with ongoing White resistance to developing *comprehensive* and *equal* school desegregation policies. They also speak to the ways in which that frustration manifests itself into seemingly odd political alliances with advocates on the political Right—those whose views many have seen as antithetical to an agenda of racial equality and social justice.

The genesis of African American voucher support in the post-*Brown* era

Beginning in the Civil Rights era, African Americans in Milwaukee participated in extensive direct and legal action in order to bring about the desegregation of their school district. Prior to a 1979 consent decree mandating desegregation,

Milwaukee's history of segregation included a very elaborate and intentional system of unequal partitioning of resources, teachers, and students between predominantly White and predominantly Black schools in the urban core. The essential priority of this system was to maximize educational quality for students of European American descent (Carl, 1995; Dougherty, 2004; Fuller, 1985).

Predominantly Black schools, even in times of exceptional overcrowding, were called upon to take responsibility for new Black students, even when predominantly White schools in the area were noticeably undersubscribed. In the most extreme segregation-era cases, a system of "intact busing" was devised in which whole classrooms of Black students from overcrowded Black schools were transported by bus to undersubscribed "White" schools to use separate classroom space there. Until 1971, when the practice was discontinued, the students of "intact busing" would report in the morning to their "home" school, board the bus for the predominantly White school, and return to their "home" school for lunch (at least until 1964) and again at the end of the school day (Carl, 1995; Dougherty, 2004).

The extended struggle for desegregation sought to end practices such as intact busing and bring about a redistribution of educational resources that would guarantee access to quality education for all students regardless of race. The final Milwaukee desegregation plan included both an intracity plan of student reassignments and magnet schools of choice and an uncommon urban–suburban student transfer program, known as Chapter 220, which allowed Black students from the city to choose to transfer to predominantly White suburban schools.[2] (The state pays for Black students' transportation to their suburban schools so that they are not dependent on a parent to get them to and from a suburban school every day.) In the late 1980s and early 1990s, when the critics of desegregation were most vocal, nearly 6,000 African American students were attending predominantly White suburban schools through this program (Schmidt, 1993).

Yet the legacy of desegregation in Milwaukee is a highly tainted one (e.g., Carl, 1996; Dougherty, 2004; Fuller, 1985). In the hands of White politicians and school officials, the primary aim of Milwaukee's desegregation efforts eroded from guaranteeing educational opportunity to African American students into a superficial compliance with the desegregation decree, one that typically maximized the benefits of the desegregation system for White students.[3] Funding formulas rewarded "White" schools both in the city and in the suburbs (through Chapter 220 programs) when they enrolled Black students, who typically took long bus rides to school only to be separated from many of the White students through tracking systems. At the same time, many of the public schools in historically Black inner-city neighborhoods were closed down in order to make way for specialty magnet schools (Metz, 2003), which were required by a court order to engage in admissions practices that made them disproportionately White (Dougherty, 2004). We should note that under the final settlement agreement in the 1980s, Milwaukee Public Schools also received extra funding targeted toward the remaining all-Black inner-city schools. This money was used to reduce large class sizes in the Black schools—as high as 35 students in elementary classes—and to implement all-day kindergarten programs (see Olson, 1990).

Still, as in most school districts forced by the courts to deal with racial segregation and inequality, desegregation in Milwaukee meant that much of the burden of busing was placed on the shoulders of African American students. Like many school desegregation programs, the Milwaukee plan began by closing several schools in the Black community and reopening those schools as magnet schools that would attract White and Black students alike. (Thus, it should be pointed out, "racial balance" was often achieved by decreasing the number of Black children attending their neighborhood schools.) A substantial number of Black children were reassigned to, or provided choices of, predominantly White schools in the city or the suburbs (Olson, 1990). The plan never involved the mandatory reassignment of White students into predominantly Black non-magnet schools in the inner city (Carl, 1995; Dougherty, 2004; Fuller, 1985). As a result, when the voucher program began in 1990, Black students were bused twice as often as White children (Olson, 1990).

Not only did this student assignment policy place a far greater burden on Black students, but it also resulted in a tremendously costly and baroque transportation system. In perhaps the most extreme example, Black children from what was previously a single neighborhood school's catchment area attended 97 separate schools throughout the Milwaukee metro area (Carl, 1995; Fuller, 1985).

Not only has this program been criticized for its tremendous inefficiency in using educational resources for educational benefits, but it has also been decried by voucher supporters and others in the African American community for the enormously destructive effects they say it has had on Black students, their families, and their communities in general (Fuller, 1985). For instance, one of the most prominent critics of the Milwaukee desegregation program, Howard Fuller (1985), has documented how Black students participating in various mandatory and voluntary busing programs frequently endured long bus rides twice a day to and from their home neighborhoods, sometimes as long as an hour or more each way. As a result of these long bus rides, Fuller noted, Black students often arrived exhausted in the morning and lost significant time for homework in the afternoon.

For the same reasons, critics argued that school desegregation often made involvement in their children's schools an insurmountable challenge for many Black parents and families because visiting these schools required an often lengthy journey into an unfamiliar and unwelcoming neighborhood. This proved to be particularly difficult for African American families with no car and with adults who worked away from home (Dougherty, 2004; Fuller, 1985). Researchers studying a desegregation plan in St. Louis, Missouri, which was partly modeled after the Milwaukee program, found similar problems facing Black parents in the city who chose to enroll their children in predominantly suburban schools (see Wells & Crain, 1997).

Furthermore, in the case of Milwaukee, the critics of desegregation policies contend that the all-Black neighborhood schools during segregation, although underfunded, underresourced, and extremely overcrowded, had served as centers of the community. They wrote that the public schools that many African American students attended under desegregation often seemed alien and uninviting. Similarly, although we must not romanticize the conditions found in such segregated schools, the critics of desegregation in Milwaukee claim that these segregated "Black" schools usually featured a larger proportion of Black teachers and sometimes offered a curriculum more rooted in students' everyday lives. They noted that such community-based schools were largely replaced by nominally desegregated schools that offered curricula and teaching methods foreign to many Black students' experiences (Dougherty, 2004; Fuller, 1985).

It would be a mistake to overlook the actual but uneven gains of school desegregation in Milwaukee or to deny the experiences of thousands of Black students and parents who argue that the desegregation plan was a valuable, if far from perfect, policy (see Carr, 2004; Schmidt, 1993; Wells & Crain, 1997). Still, general failure of the plan to adequately and comprehensively address issues of educational quality for Black students, coupled with the closing of many predominantly African American neighborhood schools, resulted in the creation of a movement for schools controlled by Milwaukee's communities of color. The decade after the Civil Rights era saw the birth of a number of Black-controlled independent private schools (many of which still exist today as part of the voucher program) that have historically sought public funding (Carl, 1995; Dougherty, 2004). Beginning in the mid 1980s, a group of African American community leaders and representatives participated in a narrowly defeated effort to create a separate predominantly Black public school district out of 11 mostly Black public schools—9 elementary schools, 1 middle school, and North Division High School on Milwaukee's north side (Carl, 1995; Dougherty; Snider, 1987).

Coupled with the reality of a political climate of insurgent conservatism in Wisconsin, as well as a relative increase in Black political representation in Milwaukee, the continued frustration of communities of color with the public school system's intransigence paved the way for Milwaukee in the late 1980s to become, with the assistance of conservative grant makers such as the Bradley Foundation, the staging ground for the first publicly funded voucher experiment in a large urban area in the United States (Carl, 1995).

It is within this post-*Brown* context of persistent and grave educational inequality that the suturing of African American activists with elements of conservative modernization needs to be understood. The fact that the neoliberal and neoconservative school choice agenda is often couched as a critique of school desegregation policy—albeit from a very different perspective—needs to be noted here as well. Yet if the formation of groups of African American voucher advocates is a response to the failure of the post-*Brown* era to sufficiently deliver upon *Brown's* promise of democratic educational access and control, the question still remains as to whether it is an effective response.

Mapping conservative modernization

Answering the question of effectiveness depends both on what kind of conceptual and political apparatus is employed and the values applied to such concepts. In this section, we discuss the conceptual and political apparatus that helped to frame the Milwaukee voucher plan as a solution to the educational inequalities and injustices experienced on a daily basis in the African American community. By placing this story of many of Milwaukee's African American leaders and the voucher program they came to embrace in the larger context of an era of conservative modernization in education, we can see how vouchers began to symbolize the hope that *Brown* and the school desegregation policies it fostered did not deliver. We begin this journey by examining the language and subsequent power of the supporters of vouchers and many other recent educational reforms.

It is somewhat commonplace to say that the concepts we use to try to understand, evaluate, and act on the world in which we live do not by themselves determine the answers that we may find. Answers are not determined by words, but by the power relations that impose their interpretations of these concepts. There are key words that continually surface in the current debates over education and that are caught up in crucial power relations. These key words have complicated histories, histories that are connected to the social movements out of which they arose and in which they are struggled over today. These words have their own histories, but they are increasingly interrelated. The concepts are simple to list: markets, standards, accountability, tradition, God, and a number of others. Behind each of these topics is an assemblage of other, broader concepts that have an emotional valence and that provide support for the ways in which differential power works in our daily lives. These include democracy, freedom, choice, morality, family, culture, and a number of other key concepts. And each of these, in turn, is intertextual, connected to an entire set of assumptions about "appropriate" institutions, values, social relationships, and policies.

Think of this web of words as something of a road map. Using one key word—for example, *markets*—sends you onto a highway that is going in one direction and that has exits in some places but not others. If you are on the highway labeled *market,* your general direction is toward a section of the country named *the economy.* You take the exit named individualism that leads you to another road called *consumer choice.* Exits with words such as *unions, collective freedom, the common good, politics* and similar destinations are to be avoided if they are on the map at all.

The popular "market" highway is a simple route with one goal: namely, deciding where one wants to go without a lot of time-wasting discussion and getting there by the fastest and cheapest method possible. There is a second route, however, labeled *social democracy,* and this one involves a good deal of collective deliberation about where we might want to go. It assumes that there may be some continuing deliberation about not only the goal, but also even the route itself. Its exits are the ones that were avoided on the first route.

There are powerful interests that have made the road map and the roads, limiting the options that policy makers, educators and families have in the field of education. Currently, the market road is one of the most popular, albeit for different reasons, for different groups of people who are the key architects of what we refer to as conservative modernization. Some want the road "market," because this supposedly leads to the exit of individualism and consumer choice. Others will go down the market road, but only if the exits are those that have a long history of "real culture" and "real knowledge." Still others will take the market road because for them, God has said that this is "His" road. And finally, another group will sign on to this market tour because they have skills in map making and in determining how far we are from our goal. There's some discussion and some compromise—and likely even some lingering tension—among these various groups about which exits they will ultimately stop at, but by and large, they all head off in that direction.

This exercise in storytelling maps on to reality in important ways because it describes the preferred pathways of these main ideological groups participating in and furthering what we call the project of conservative modernization. The first group is what is appropriately called *neoliberals*. They are deeply committed to markets and to freedom as "individual choice." The second group, *neoconservatives*, has a vision of an Edenic past and wants a return to discipline and traditional knowledge. The third, one that is increasingly powerful in the United States and elsewhere is what one of us has called *authoritarian populists*—religious fundamentalists and conservative evangelicals who want a return to (their) God in all our institutions (Apple, 2001; see also Hall, 1980). And finally, the map makers and experts on whether we got there are members of a particular fraction of the managerial and professional *new middle class*.[4]

In analyzing this complex configuration of interests around conservative modernization, we need to act in a way similar to what Eric Hobsbawm (1994) described as the historian's and social critic's duty. For Hobsbawm, the task is to be the "professional remembrancers of what [our] fellow citizens wish to forget" (p. 3). That is, it requires us to detail the absent presences, the there that is not there, in most rightist policies in education. How does the language work to highlight certain things as "real" problems while marginalizing others? What are the effects of the policies that they have promoted? How do the seemingly contradictory policies that have emerged from the various fractions of the Right, aspects of which have now taken on a life of their own at times—such as the marketization of education through voucher plans, the pressure to "return" to the Western tradition and to a supposedly common culture, the commitment to get God back into the schools and classrooms of America, and the growth of national and state curricula and reductive national and state (and often high-stakes) testing—actually get put together in creative ways to push many of the aspects of these rightist agendas forward? In our discussion of these questions, we will focus most of our attention on the first two of these elements of the alliance: neoliberals and neoconservatives. In the process, we will make our mapping less taxanomic and more subtle.

In a number of recent books, one of us (Michael) has critically analyzed why and how the policies emerging from the politics of conservative modernization have been embraced by so many policy makers as the right way to reform education. The resulting range of proposals for educational "reform"—such as marketization via vouchers and private school management companies, national mandates for statewide curricula standards, and testing—has been critically examined (see, e.g., Apple, 2001; Apple et al., 2003; see also Gillborn & Youdell, 2000; Whitty, Power, & Halpin, 1998). This critical examination has demonstrated that, irrespective of the often good intentions of the proponents of many of these kinds of proposals, in the long run, they may actually exacerbate inequalities, especially around class and race. Furthermore, they may paradoxically cause us both to misrecognize what actually produces difficult social and educational problems and to miss some important democratic alternatives that may offer more hope in the long run (see, e.g., Apple et al.; Apple, 2000; Apple, 2001; Apple & Beane, 1999).

How is it, then, that so many voters and policy makers have come to see these neoliberal views as common sense? It is helpful to think of this as having been accomplished through the use of a vast socio/pedagogic project, a project that has actively—and in large part successfully—sought to transform our very ideas about democracy. Within this neoliberal paradigm, democracy is no longer a political concept; rather, it is wholly an economic concept in which unattached individuals making supposed "rational" choices in an unfettered market will ultimately create a better society; they will lift the tide that is supposed to raise all boats.[5] Democracy in this instance is defined as the freedom to consume as one chooses, and the result of thousands of these individualized choices will, in theory, add up to be the greater good. As Foner (1998) reminded us, it has taken decades of creative ideological work to change our commonsense ideas about democracy into ideas of consumption. Not only does this change fly in the face of a very long tradition of collective understandings of democracy in the United States, but it has also led to the destruction of communities, jobs, health care, and so many other institutions not only in the United States, but also throughout the world (Greider, 1997; Katz, 2001). Hidden assumptions about class (that we are not a society that is deeply and increasingly divided by class and that marketizing logics do not consistently privilege those who already have economic and cultural capital) and a goodly portion of the politics of Whiteness (that there are not consistent structural benefits to being White in this society) may make it hard for us to face this honestly (see Fine, Weis, Powell, & Wong, 1997).

Given the subject of this article, however, we should have put two words in the last sentences of the preceding paragraph—*us* and *we*—in quotation marks. Who is the "we"? Does it include all those who have been hurt by that combination of neoliberal and neoconservative polices that now play such an important role in our discourse in education? If these policies have a disproportionate and negative effect on, say, working class people of color, as they seem to do (see Apple, 2001; Valenzuela, 2005)—should we assume that, for example, all persons of color will reject both the policies and their underlying ideologies? For the reasons we enumerated earlier, this is not necessarily the case, as the example of support for vouchers among a number of Black activists in Milwaukee demonstrates.

Facing the complexity of "strange bedfellows"

Given the history of their struggles both for redistribution and recognition, it would be very difficult to integrate historically disenfranchised social groups, especially people of color, under the ideological umbrella of conservative modernization (Apple, 2000; Fraser, 1997). However, this does not make it impossible. One of the ways in which hegemonic alliances are built is through a process in which dominant groups—in this case, the conservative alliance—creatively but partially appropriate the elements of "good sense" that disenfranchised groups possess into their neoliberal and neoconservative agendas (Apple, 2001). Unfortunately, the partial success of such a strategy on the part of the conservative alliance among those groups who are often counted as "despised others" (Fraser) in our societies is a subject that some progressives would like to forget. Yet, well beyond both Milwaukee and the field of education, there is increasing evidence of growing numbers of racial/ethnic "minority" group members, women, and gays and lesbians who are activists in neoliberal and neoconservative movements, and to a lesser extent in authoritarian populist religious movements. Let us place these points in their larger context within Milwaukee.

The 1990 Milwaukee Parental Choice Program (MPCP), at the time of its inception, represented one of the most important interventions by elements of conservative modernization in their larger drive to destabilize public schooling "as we know it" as a key element of the (relatively anemic) American welfare state (Apple, 2001). Through a complex amalgamation of forces and actors, Milwaukee became a center stage on which larger ideological battles over the character, form, and funding of education in the United States and elsewhere were to be fought.

In his own historical analysis of Milwaukee's choice plan, Carl (1995, 1996) pointed to complexities that seem to fit less comfortably within the initial theorization of the key ideological tendencies within conservative modernization that we have delineated.

As we did, Carl began his analysis of factors leading to the rise of the "parental choice" debate in Milwaukee by describing the emergence nationally of the hegemonic alliance within conservative modernization in the early 1980s. Within this alliance, Carl depicted the tensely intersecting agendas of two dominant groups—neoliberals and neoconservatives—in relation to the Milwaukee voucher program. According to Carl, local neoliberal education reformers, on the one hand, believed that the extension of private markets into the state's education systems would bring improvement in educational attainment and profitability. On the other hand, local neoconservative educational reformers privileged private schools for their supposed traditional academic curriculum, religious training, and strict discipline (Carl, 1996).

However, Carl (1996) also acknowledged that "not all proponents of vouchers in Milwaukee can be described as agents of the conservative restoration"

161

(p. 268). Rather, Carl outlined a "conditional alliance" between state-level neoliberal reformers and Milwaukee-based supporters of a handful of independent community schools:

> Five factors generated this conditional alliance: dissatisfaction among many black Milwaukeeans with a school system that failed to deliver acceptable educational outcomes for disproportionately high numbers of black students; the existence of community schools whose multicultural supporters had sought public funding for two decades; the growth of black political representation in Milwaukee during an era when government policies tilted rightward, as personified by state representative Polly Williams; the efforts of Governor Tommy Thompson's administration to craft neoliberal and neoconservative social policy; and the rise of Milwaukee's Bradley Foundation as the nation's premier conservative grantmaker. (p. 268)

Carl is correct about these factors. But even if they exist, it takes hard work to put them all together and to engage in the creative process of disarticulation and rearticulation so that key groups, especially members of dispossessed groups, support policies that come from ideological positions for which they have historically not had a strong affinity. How are we to understand both how this went on and the complex nexus of power relations on all sides that connected African American activists and neoliberal and neoconservative policies? There has been a relative lack of writing and theorizing about articulations among conservatives and the dispossessed.

Recently, however, there have been exceptions to this relative neglect. In a recent book, Dillard (2001), for example, critically examined a number of the key actors within conservative circles who themselves are members of historically oppressed groups, but who, for a variety of personal and political reasons, give vocal support to neoliberal and neoconservative causes. Aggressively "free" market policies, such as a rejection of affirmative action and the use of race or gender as a category in public decisions; public funding for religiously based schooling; welfare "reform"; and a host of similar issues provide the centers of gravity for these individuals. Many of the figures on which Dillard focused are familiar names: Dinesh D'Sousa, Thomas Sowell, Clarence Thomas, Linda Chavez, Glenn Loury, Richard Rodriguez, and similar national spokespersons of conservative causes. Each of these figures is a person of color, and they include academics, journalists, government officials, and a justice of the Supreme Court. Other figures may be familiar only to those readers who have closely followed the cultural and political debates on the Right in the United States over such things as educational policy, sexuality, affirmative action, and welfare reform, but they have played important roles as well: Star Parker, George Schuyler, Andrew Sullivan, Elizabeth Wright, Bruce Bawer, and Susan Au Allen, among others.[6]

There is, of course, a history of dominant groups using, or at least giving visibility to, "minority" voices to "say the unsayable" in the United States and elsewhere

(Lewis, 1993, 2000). Thus, for example, Ward Connerly, a prominent conservative African American businessman and a vocal member of the board of regents of the University of California, has taken a very visible stand against affirmative action. In his view, government involvement in helping Blacks gain access to higher education and jobs is actually harmful to Black Americans. According to Connerly, "While others are assimilating, blacks are getting further and further away from one nation indivisible" (Dillard, 2001, p. 50). His insistence that "individual merit" as opposed to state intervention is the means of greater equality has clearly been employed by the larger, and mostly White, conservative movement to legitimate its own policies. As a prominent conservative spokeswoman put it, "You can't have white guys saying you don't need affirmative action" (p. 15).

Hence, powerful neoliberal and neoconservative movements both inside and outside government circles can steadily expand the realm of what is in fact sayable by prefacing what would otherwise be seen as consistently racist positions with a quote from a well-known Black spokesperson. Dillard (2001), one of the most articulate critics of such moves, stated that this enables dominant economic, cultural, and racial groups "to cannibalize the moral authority of minority voices by skirting responsibility" (p. 20).

Because of this very history of dominant groups employing the selective voice of "the other" to legitimize their actions, there has been a concomitant history of regarding those members of minority communities who openly affiliate with conservative movements as "pariahs." They have been dismissed as either traitors or sellouts, and have even been seen as "self-loathing reactionaries who are little more than dupes of powerful white . . . conservatives" (Dillard, 2001, p. 4). Although these labels are powerful indeed, many conservative persons of color see themselves very differently. In their self-perception, they are "crusading rebels" against a state and a liberal elite within the ranks of their own communities; their self-understanding of "helping the people" challenges policies that, in their eyes, work to destroy the very moral and social foundations of their communities. Here they can also turn to a rich history of nationalist, self-help, and conservative moral principles within these communities as a source of "authenticity" and legitimacy (Dillard, 2001, p. 13).

Of course, there *are* internally developed conservative traditions within, say, communities of color, many of which have made lasting contributions to the very existence and continuity of the cultures within these communities (see, e.g., Lewis, 1993, 2000). However, that so much of the conservative tradition in the United States was explicitly shaped by racist and racializing discourses and practices, and by a strongly anti-immigrant heritage as well, and given that many of the current neoliberal and neoconservative attacks on the public sphere have had disproportionately negative effects on the gains of poor communities and on communities of color (Katz, 2001), the current existence and growth of such movement among dispossessed groups is more than a little striking.[8] This makes their current iterations all the more interesting.[9] As we will see, neoliberal and neoconservative economic, political, and cultural movements *and* some of the African American groups that have been connected to them are both seeking to redefine the relations of power in particular social fields, with education being a prime site where these relations of power are being worked through (Bourdieu, 1984).

A complex process of discursive and positional disarticulation and rearticulation is going on here as dominant groups attempt to pull dispossessed collectivities under their own leadership and dispossessed groups themselves attempt to employ the social, economic, and cultural capital usually possessed by dominant groups to gain collective power for themselves. As we will demonstrate through our analysis of interviews with African American parents using vouchers in Milwaukee, in the debates over vouchers in the United States, the label *conservative* cannot be employed easily in understanding the actions and characterizing the identifications of all the dispossessed groups that ally themselves with conservative causes without, at the same time, reducing the complexity of the particular social fields of power on which they operate.

The story of the Milwaukee alliance between African Americans and conservative reformers is a powerful illustration of this point. This is so because one of the most interesting examples of the processes of discursive and social disarticulation and rearticulation today is the growing African American support for neoliberal policies, especially voucher plans (see, for e.g., Moe, 2001). The most influential symbol of this support is the increasingly powerful Black Alliance for Educational Options (BAEO), a group of African American parents and activists that is chaired by Howard Fuller, the vocal critic of the Milwaukee school desegregation plan that we cited above. Fuller, the former superintendent of Milwaukee Public Schools, is one of the most vocal supporters of the Milwaukee voucher plan and one of the most vocal critics of Milwaukee Public Schools.

BAEO provides vocal support for voucher plans, school "choice" (a sliding signifier whose meaning has increasingly become fixed around issues of vouchers in the United States when it is used in political discourse), and similar conservative proposals. BAEO has generated considerable support within Black communities throughout the nation, particularly in poor inner-city areas, and has an identifiable presence in at least 27 cities within the United States.[10] That the Supreme Court of Wisconsin has ruled that the Milwaukee voucher plan is constitutional and the United States Supreme Court recently ruled that the Cleveland voucher plan is also constitutional gives more legal and political legitimacy to BAEO's efforts because both plans were officially aimed at providing the "right to exit" for inner-city and largely "minority" residents. BAEO's language and mission are clear: "The Black Alliance for Educational Options is a national nonpartisan member organization whose mission is to actively support parental choice to empower families and increase educational options for Black children" (BAEO, 2005). Its position is even clearer in its Manifesto:

BAEO Manifesto

Current systems of K–12 education work well for many of America's children. But, for far too many children, the current systems do not work well at all. A high percentage of these children are poor children of color living in urban areas. For these children, the old educational strategies and institutional arrangements are not preparing them to be productive and socially responsible citizens. This requires that we dramatically change our teaching and learning strategies and create new governance and financial structures.

BAEO believes we must develop new systems of learning opportunities to complement and expand existing systems. We need systems that truly empower parents, that allow dollars to follow students, that hold adults as well as students accountable for academic achievement, and that alter the power arrangements that are the foundation for existing systems.

BAEO understands that there are no "silver bullets" or "magic wands" which will instantly make things better for our children. BAEO is also not anti-public school. However, we do believe that parent choice must be the centerpiece of strategies and tactics aimed at improving education for our children. We must empower parents, particularly low-income parents, to make the best choices for their children's education.

Consider the potential impact of this power in the hands of families who previously have had little or no control over the flow and distribution of the money that drives the policies and procedures of the educational systems of this country. Consider how the absence of this power means that their children will remain trapped in schools that more affluent parents, some of whom oppose parental choice, would never tolerate for their own children. Consider how this power shift may change the shape of the future for their children.

BAEO will bring together the ideas, aspirations, energies, and experiences of all generations in this struggle.

The use of language here is striking. The language of neoliberalism (choice, parental empowerment, accountability, individual freedom) is reappropriated and sutured together with ideas of collective Black freedom and a deep concern for African American children. This creates something of a hybrid discourse that blends meanings from multiple political sources and agendas.[11] For instance, amid the Manifesto's market language of allowing "dollars to follow students," we also discern the language of redistribution (Fraser, 1997): "Consider the potential impact of this power in the hands of families who previously have had little or no control over the flow and distribution of the money that drives the policies."

This language of redistribution both resonates with and goes beyond the language of "Black Freedom," further complexifying this discursive hybridity with social democratic undertones. After all, the Milwaukee Parental Choice Program, however flawed, does put material and symbolic resources into the hands of a small number of the people who we feel should have more of these things.

Meanwhile, it is essential to recognize something that makes the creative bricolage in which BAEO is engaged somewhat more problematic: A very large portion of the group's funding comes directly from conservative sources such as the Bradley Foundation. The Bradley Foundation, a well-known sponsor of conservative causes, has not only been in the forefront of providing support for vouchers and privatization initiatives, but it is also one of the groups that provided significant support for Herrnstein and Murray's book, *The Bell Curve* (1994), which argued that African Americans were, on average, genetically less intelligent than Whites. Thus, it would be important to ask about the nature and effects of the connections being made between rightist ideological and financial sources and BAEO itself. It is not inconsequential that neoliberal and neoconservative foundations provide not only funding, but also media visibility for "minority" groups that support, even critically, their agendas.

Many of the strongest proponents of vouchers and similar plans may claim that their positions are based on a belief in the efficiency of markets, on the fear of a secularization of the sacred, or on the dangers of losing the values and beliefs that give meaning to their lives. However, historically, neither the economic nor the moral elements of this provoucher argument can be totally set apart from their partial genesis in the struggles over racial segregation and busing to achieve integration and in the loss of a federal tax exemption by conservative, and usually White-only, religious academies. In short, the fear of the "racial other" has played a significant role in this discursive construction of the "problem of the public school" and in the political backlash against many of the public policies of the Civil Rights era, including school desegregation (Apple, 2001; see also Edsall & Edsall, 1991). Does this mean that groups such as BAEO are simply being manipulated by neoliberal and neoconservative foundations and movements? An answer to this question is not easy, but even with our cautions stated above it is certainly not a simple yes.

Strategic compromises?

It is important not to engage in reductive analyses here—analyses that, for example, assume that simply because a group's funding comes from a specific source, all its own agendas will be fundamentally determined by where it gets its money. This is certainly not always the case. Indeed, in public forums and in discussions that we have had with some of the leaders of BAEO, they have argued that they will use any funding sources available so that they can follow their own specific program of action. They would accept money from more liberal sources, but Bradley and other conservative foundations have come forward much more readily.[12] In the minds of the leaders of BAEO, the African American activists are in control, not the conservative foundations. Thus, although the BAEO leaders admit that they are strategically positioning themselves (by publicly supporting vouchers, for instance) to get funding from conservative sources, once they get the funding, it is up to them. According to these BAEO leaders, the space provided by educational markets can be reoccupied for Black cultural or nationalist politics and can be employed to stop what they consider to be the strikingly ineffective, and even damaging, education of Black children.[13]

However, although we respect many BAEO leaders, it is important to remember that they are not the only ones strategically organizing on this social field of power. Like BAEO, other groups affiliated with, say, the Bradley Foundation also know exactly what they are doing and know very well how to employ the agendas of BAEO for their own purposes—purposes that in the long term often may run directly counter to the interests of the majority of those with less power at both national and regional levels.[14] Is it really in the long-term interests of people of color to be affiliated with the same groups who provided funding and support for books such as *The Bell Curve*? We think not, although once again, we need to recognize the complexities involved here.

We are certain that this kind of question is constantly raised about the conservative stances taken by the people of color who have made alliances with, say, neoliberals and neoconservatives, and by the activists within BAEO itself. When members of groups who are consistently "othered" in this society strategically take on identities that support dominant groups, such questioning is natural and, we believe, essential. However, it is also crucial to remember that members of historically oppressed and marginalized groups have always had to act on a terrain that is not of their choosing and have always had to act strategically and creatively to gain some measure of support from dominant groups to advance their causes (Lewis, 1993, 2000; Omi & Winant, 1994).

It is also the case that more recently, national and local leaders of the Democratic party in the United States have too often assumed that Black support is simply *there*, that it doesn't need to be worked for. Because of this, we may see the further development of "unusual alliances" over specific issues such as educational policies. When this is coupled with the tacit or overt support within some communities of color not only for voucher plans but also for antigay, anti-abortion, pro–school prayer, and similar initiatives, the suturing together of some Black groups with larger conservative movements on particular issues is not totally surprising (see Dillard, 2001).

The growing popularity of movements such as BAEO, though, does point out that we need to be careful about stereotyping groups that publicly support neoliberal and neoconservative policies. Their perspectives need to be examined carefully and taken seriously; they cannot simply be dismissed as totally misguided people who have been duped into unthinking acceptance of a harmful set of ideologies. There are complicated strategic moves being made on an equally complex social field of power. We may (and do) strongly disagree with a number of the positions that groups such as BAEO take. However, to assume that they are simply puppets of conservative forces is not only to be dismissive of their own attempts at social maneuvering, but we believe that it may also be tacitly racist as well.

The politics of strategic identity formation

To avoid such dangers, it will be useful to turn our attention now to the process of what some have called "identity formation" that occurs as various factions of the conservative alliance, African American educational activists, and low-income parents in Milwaukee suture their interests together within tensely maintained and constructed alliances. In so doing, we will have to make some crucial points about issues of "subaltern agency," or agency that is exercised by the marginalized on a discursive and structural terrain that they did not choose (see the work of Apple & Buras, in press; De Certeau, 1984; Pedroni, 2004; Spivak, 1988).

In the earlier years of the MPCP, discourses circulating through the Milwaukee Public School system and through the voucher alliance positioned Black parents and students and offered identities in particular ways. Primary among the "subject positions" (roles, voices, and choices) in circulation among many teachers, administrators, and other professionals in the Milwaukee Public Schools were those predicated on culturally based, racially based, or biologically based deficit models. African American parents fleeing public schools and embracing the proposed voucher system frequently cited instances in which public school educators or officials would blame the supposedly culturally rooted unruly behavior of students of color for the high failure rates in their schools. Similarly, parents complained about the regularity with which their children were pathologized and abandoned to special education programs after being marked with disability labels (Corporation for Educational Radio and Television, 1993).

In contrast with this, school marketization efforts in Milwaukee seemed to offer much more dignified subject positions to disenfranchised parents, perhaps most significantly that of "rational consumer." Rather than pathologizing "Black" cultural forms through racist social scientific normative discourses, neoliberal voucher advocates first and foremost positioned parents as ideal consumers whose sole constraint consisted of artificially limited, market-defined choice.

An analysis predicated on questions of identify formation is crucial here. It allows for the possibility of a microlevel examination of the tactical choices that parents make in negotiating their sets of perceived educational options. Rather than focusing only on the structural dynamics around educational marketization, which will likely further marginalize low-income urban communities of color, we wish to take seriously the everyday dilemmas, consciousness, and agency of parents as they attempt to negotiate educational structures that have not necessarily been designed with their best interests in mind. Thus, although we are deeply concerned about the likely outcomes of market-oriented educational forms, we also want to take utterly seriously how conservative educational mobilizations succeed by seeming to speak to marginalized people's very real fears and desires. It is only through understanding this articulation as a matter of subject formation that the process of conservative formation will perhaps most effectively be interrupted and supplanted with a more socially democratic (and ultimately more effective) educational vision.

Thus, seen from "below" (from the vantage point of certain low-income parents of color), free-market educational discourses seem to open interesting and contradictory spaces. Although positioning low-income parents of color as rational educational consumers empowered to make the best choices for their children dehistoricizes their agency by largely failing to see it as emerging within unequal material and discursive relations of power, neoliberal discourse allows parents to be seen, heard, and understood—and perhaps most important, to act in ways that are often simply not possible within the pathologizing frames that often dominate the reality of urban public schools.

To approach this question of how offered subject positions are tactically "taken up" by and "inhabited" by parents, we are aided by critical cultural theorists such as Michel de Certeau (1984), who argued that "users" such as the parents in question are never passive or without agency within this process of subject formation. They, to use one of his phrases, "make do" within the very limited identity options that are made available to them, turning these options, as much as they are able, to purposes that they feel will best serve their perceived educational and social needs (Apple, 1996; De Certeau, 1984). According to research on African Americans' often difficult choices to participate in voluntary school desegregation plans (particularly those that take them from urban to suburban schools far from home) and in other school choice programs, "making do" is part of a longer historical struggle for social justice (see Carr, 2004; Cooper, 2001; Wells & Crain, 1997).

We believe that such a focus on identity formation allows us to discern that the articulations and alliances formed around vouchers in Milwaukee are much more transient, ephemeral, opportunistic, and unstable than current literature implies (see also Cooper, 2001). Nevertheless, despite the often transient nature of such alliances, crucial and lasting gains are in fact won by educational conservatives as a result of the reforms that fleeting alliances are able to engender. The effect of voucher mobilizations on legislation and on the global currency of private vouchers is not nearly as ephemeral as the alliances that undergird and enable their initial success.

A more nuanced theorization of groups such as the grassroots followers of BAEO—which cannot be adequately posited either as dominant elements within a hegemonic alliance or as relatively ideologically unformed and "ordinary" individuals articulated into the Right as a result of the state's intransigence—is crucial to a fuller understanding of the Right's continued success in dismantling key vestiges of the American welfare state. In fact, a retheorization of the subaltern agency constituted in such tactical alliances will also underscore the importance of "strange bedfellows" in other successful rightist projects. Even a cursory consideration of other parallel debates within and around the preservation or dismantling of key elements of the social democratic accord in the United States seems to indicate the pivotal importance of such ephemeral and tactical alliances in hegemonic successes, and therefore warrants further study and conceptualization. For example, we should ask ourselves how much the call for Black male redemption and responsibility by Minister Louis Farrakhan in the mid-1990s discursively supported the cause of conservative welfare reform. This normative recasting of Black masculinity by Farrakhan may have been a key element in significant Black acquiescence to such reforms, which have consequently had a disproportionate and considerable impact on African American families (Brown, 2003).

The current underemphasis on the importance of subaltern agency in hegemonic successes might result from our inclination to theorize powerful elements within conservative modernization as "groups" unproblematically embodying "ideal types" rather than as "discursive tendencies." While some individuals and organizations can be more or less correctly categorized into one of the four elements of conservative modernization that we described earlier, there are also almost always contradictory tendencies within these groups and individuals. That these tendencies are not embodied as ideal types, but rather are mediated in contradictory ways, actually expands conceptually the spaces for progressive rearticulation within the formation of these subjectivities.

Because we still want to foreground the ways in which these discourses construct and are constructed by real social actors, thus sidestepping the disposition of some poststructural theorists to see the world as made up only of competing discourses that somehow exist beyond history and human agency (Pedroni, 2005), we may want to refer to the four elements of conservative modernization as "embodied tendencies." To not do so restricts our likelihood of apprehending the importance of subaltern groups in hegemonic successes because subaltern groups often act tactically. That is, their action is often *not* through the deployment of largely internally cohesive discourses that seek to (re)narrate a set of relationships between elements such as the state, the economy, individuals, and the social formation (De Certeau, 1984). The ability to materialize such elaborate and cohesive intellectual discursive production is more typically a privilege of the powerful, who, as de Certeau suggested, shape and control the terrain upon which ideological and material battles over such things as access to education are fought. Rather, subaltern yet politically savvy groups, such as the African American and Latino supporters of private school vouchers in Milwaukee, quite often operate in a tactical relationship to power, sensing the need to act within the spaces that the powerful provide. At times, they do this in ways that creatively turn the strategic deployments of the powerful back against the powerful, and other times in ways that are ultimately self-defeating for subaltern groups. This is a crucial point. Powerful groups often accomplish their objectives precisely because of tactical "poaching" by subaltern groups. This latter scenario, we would argue, is the far more likely long-term outcome of African American support of private school vouchers in Milwaukee.

In fact, a 2-year study that one of us (Tom) has conducted with parents and other African American voucher advocates in Milwaukee provides significant evidence that African American articulation to neoliberal interventions including voucher programs seems to be largely tactical and opportunistic, rather than strategic and ideologically disciplined (Pedroni, 2004). African American voucher advocates rarely offer "intact" neoliberal or neoconservative discourses as underpinning their investment in vouchers. Although their discourses include occasional neoliberal and neoconservative elements, they also contain other elements that run significantly counter to each of these discourses. Because of the tactical nature of their relationship to conservative alliances and because of their investment in other mobilizations that are clearly well outside the parameters of conservative modernization, most African American supporters of vouchers in Milwaukee do not "become Right" as far as identity formation is concerned, despite their tactical investment in neoconservative and neoliberal subject positions (Apple, 1996; Apple et al., 2003; Pedroni, 2004).[15] We will further illustrate this point with a brief analysis of two interviews that a Bradley-supported conservative videographer based in Milwaukee conducted with two African American voucher activists.

Living tactical identities

Cherise Robinson and Laura Fordham[16] are African American parents and guardians of children using vouchers provided through the Milwaukee Parental Choice Program to attend participating parochial and nonsectarian private schools. The interviews from which we draw this brief analysis were recorded in 1998 shortly before the Wisconsin Supreme Court upheld the constitutionality of the MPCP, including the participation of religious private schools, thus lifting an Appeals Court injunction predicated on issues of separation of church and state. The two interviews, conducted by a Bradley Foundation-supported European American professional videographer closely affiliated with neoconservative Catholic educational organizations in Milwaukee, took place in Madison, Wisconsin, shortly after a well-publicized speak-out and rally among voucher proponents protesting the injunction (personal communication [phone interview] with videographer, November 22, 2000).

Cherise Robinson is the grandmother of a 5-year-old child who began the school year in a private nonsectarian school participating in the Milwaukee voucher program. Her granddaughter was soon relocated to a public daycare facility after the voucher school in which she was enrolled "had to close before the year was up." Despite this disruption, Ms. Robinson is stridently positive about her granddaughter's advances in her initial months of private school attendance. "If you were to talk to her, you would think that she's about 7 or 8 years old. And judging from the other children that are in Milwaukee Public Schools, she's at a level now of at least a second-or third-grader. And I know that this is because of her beginnings."

Ms. Robinson attributes this success to the existence of small class sizes and greater individual attention—something that she identifies as lacking in many of Milwaukee's urban public schools. "I think it's because of the individual attention that she's able to get in the private schools. And not so much individual, but not so many students. That the teacher has more time for her in whatever her little situation may be."

Implicit in Ms. Robinson's assessment is a juxtaposition of the attentive private school teacher with the less attentive public school teacher. That which facilitates the better attention of the private school teacher, however, is that she has "not so many students." She does not face the same overcrowded classroom conditions as her public school counterpart. This implicit characterization of the public school teacher beset by overcrowding contrasts markedly with the figure of the public teacher in the interviewer's own (in this instance, largely neoliberal) narrative in which public schools are seen as failing not because of overcrowded classrooms, but because of their monopolization by teachers' unions that protect unworthy teachers while sheltering grossly bloated and inefficient school bureaucracies from market discipline (Creative Media Services, 1998).

An indictment of overcrowded classrooms, rather than union monopolies and a lack of competitive educational markets, then, points to a diagnosis and prescription for public schools that can only sit awkwardly within the neoliberal frame of market efficiency/inefficiency. We can begin to imagine other less awkward articulations with Ms. Robinson's concerns.

But this is not the only juncture at which Ms. Robinson's frame exists in tense relationship with that of the interviewer and the various fragments of the neoliberal and neoconservative voucher alliance with which he is allied. Ms. Robinson describes her active defense of the voucher program as follows: "It seems as if there are some who say that certain children shouldn't have a certain type of education. And it seems to me that choice is saying every child should have the best education that they can get."

Ms. Robinson understands choice as a mechanism that provides every child, regardless of socioeconomic or other circumstances, the ability to obtain high-quality education. This sense of choice as the ability of all families to choose a high-quality, adequately funded education is articulated with models of market-based consumer choice in which parents are limited to the best that they can afford, only as the result of considerable work.

Laura Fordham, the second parent interviewed by the videographer, has a daughter who attends a private nonsectarian elementary school. For Ms. Fordham, who also works as the school's admissions chairperson, the overriding factor in using a voucher to choose this particular school was its proximity to the family's home. In Milwaukee, this is not an inconsequential issue. With the advent of desegregation, many public neighborhood schools in the urban core were closed. This has presented significant difficulties related not just to the daily transportation of children; distance has also formed a significant obstacle to parental involvement in the public schools, particularly when many families do not own cars. This in turn has exacerbated the sense that public schools are frequently out of touch with the communities they serve. (Naturally, this issue also impacts families' relationships to various voucher school options, particularly when such schools are far from their homes and do not provide adequate transportation.)

As Ms. Fordham explains, "If she has to go back to the public schools, then she would be bused possibly across town. Well, I would not allow for her to be bused across town. First thing's, she's a chronic asthmatic kid. And for her to be bused, it would be impossible." Ms. Fordham's decision to relocate her child to a neighborhood private school came only after considerable effort to make the public school option work. "I could not transport her to school back and forward every day. I did that for her first year . . . that was 17 and a half miles away. So when she become more chronically ill, and my husband becomes ill, she had to stop going to school there because I couldn't take her to school. Plus, we couldn't afford it."

Ms. Fordham is nostalgic for a time "when the schools were so much better than they are now, the public schools at least. . . . You could go to school down the street and meet your neighbors." That is, public schools were also important centers of life within the community. "Now, the way the [public] schools are going, they tell you where your kid can go. Where with the Choice program, you're able to put your kid . . . where you want them to go. . . . And you're able to afford it."

Today in Milwaukee, private voucher-accepting schools are typically located in low-income neighborhoods and are legally restricted from engaging in selective admissions practices. (Still, we know from much research on deregulated school choice policies that "choice schools" can shape who attends them via selective recruitment strategies and the expulsion of students who pose behavioral problems among other strategies; see Lopez, Wells, & Holme, 2002.) Nevertheless, these schools, according to many in the Black community, often fulfill the community role that the neighborhood public schools once played. According to Ms. Fordham, "that's important, because we find that for our private schools are closer around in the circle than public schools are."

Beyond the absence of public schools within some Milwaukee urban neighborhoods, Ms. Fordham also characterizes the experiences of some public school children in the following way: "They are in the classroom, and they're crowded. And if a kid is a little slower learning he [doesn't] have the time to take . . . so after a while he'll just stop going to school, or he'll miss school because he didn't know his lesson, or he had nobody to pay attention to him."

Ms. Fordham's description of public school classrooms as overcrowded and underresourced resonates with earlier criticisms by Ms. Robinson. Like Ms. Robinson, Ms. Fordham's assumptions concerning the troubles of some urban public schools differ sharply from those of the interviewer and the neoliberal and neoconservative constituencies he represents.

This divergence of assumptions between Ms. Fordham and the interviewer is further evident as they negotiate the content of the interview. For example, in relation to the issue of consumer choice within educational markets, he asks, "Why should that be your choice? As a parent, or as a grandparent, or as a family member, why should you have the right to [choose] that?" While the interviewer positions Ms. Fordham as a consumer within an educational marketplace, she answers from a very different subject position—that of a member within a community and society: "One of the things I feel is going to improve our society is if we can educate our kids better." Again, Ms. Fordham's "parent as community member" sits awkwardly with the interviewer's own "parent as consumer."

These brief excerpts represent, at the microlevel, an important instantiation of the tense, contradictory, and often successful process of articulation and alliance building within the movement for vouchers. While the tensions and contradictions in such articulations are clearly evidenced in the differing purposes, resources, and identities that the interviewer and the two interview participants bring to the interviews, clearly they also share a limited common purpose that allows them to stand together "in the same room," however awkwardly and momentarily. Both the interviewer (as a neoliberal and neoconservative advocate of educational marketization and Catholic schools) and the interview subjects (as parents and guardians concerned about their children's education) are interested in furthering at least a specific, limited version of "parental choice" in Milwaukee. One can imagine that these parents and guardians, in contrast to the interviewer, are unlikely to favor "choice" beyond the low-income parameters within which it was initially established.

In significant ways, then, the subaltern and tactical agency that Ms. Robinson, Ms. Fordham, and other African American parents and guardians have demonstrated within the contested terrain over vouchers is a testament to the strength of their potential political agency, rather than, as is sometimes suggested, an indication of naïve submission to hegemonic conservative educational and economic discourses. This remains true even if these parents ultimately are proved wrong, as we believe they will be, in their assertions that their actions will be of maximum benefit in the long run not just for their children, but also for other children left behind in newly market-disciplined urban public schools. And we believe that this tactical agency will in all likelihood be further instantiated in future mobilizations, quite possibly around other traditionally conservative themes. Many of these themes have long been issues of concern for large numbers of African American parents, including support for school prayer and "religious freedom," as well as antipathy toward abortion and the interests of sexual minorities. African Americans and other subaltern groups are not essential Democrats, although in recent history, many have tactically aligned themselves with this party.

We feel that this last point bears repeating. Critical theorists and others on the educational left should recognize that African American articulation to the Democratic party and other powerful and sometimes liberal, progressive, and centrist groups has almost always been based on the carefully debated strategic value of such alliances. When social movements rooted in broader African American struggles for racial uplift encounter the limitations that previously articulated alliances now present, political alignments are potentially subject to considerable flux. To theorize African Americans as "intelligent" when they show unquestioning loyalty to the Democratic party and other liberal causes (even when the Democratic party takes their support for granted as it drifts to the Right on significant socioeconomic issues) and "foolish" when they tactically participate in other, sometimes more conservative, alliances grossly misrepresents African American agency and betrays what we feel is a racist essentialization of Black intelligence. Subaltern, relatively powerless groups have always needed to tactically associate in seemingly contradictory ways with powerful groups and individuals, such as the Heritage Foundation, the Bradley Foundation, and the Democratic Leadership Council, in order to seek to protect their interests.

Reflecting on the pivotal role played by subaltern groups, we want to suggest that the conservative hegemonic alliance in the late 1980s recognized that it *almost* wielded the power to get vouchers through. Although by itself the hegemonic alliance was not able (yet) to successfully realize its marketization agenda concerning education and vouchers, the Right could stretch its power by bringing parts of a traditional liberal constituency—a portion of African American parents—on board. Articulating the privatization agenda in education to these parents' "good sense" and perceived interests would enable the Right to tip the scales of educational power away from an alliance of liberal groups—including unions, civil liberties organizations, antiracist groups, and feminist and environmental organizations— and toward the amalgamation of groups pursuing conservative modernization in education. Given the Wisconsin political climate of the late 1980s—in which progressives wielded very little power—coupled with a long and historic movement among African American parents in Milwaukee for community-controlled schools that would protect their children from the sometimes reprehensible racial practices of Milwaukee Public Schools, Milwaukee presented itself as an ideal battleground upon which the conservative alliance might win crucial ideological battles over the character, form, and funding of education in the United States (Carl, 1996). Such a victory would also have promising implications for further-reaching conservative goals involving the broad privatization of the public sphere and the "deresponsibilization" of the state (Leys, 2002).

In the process, the immediate and long-term conservative agendas around privatization in education and elsewhere would not be the only part of the hegemonic project that would be served. It will be useful here to reinvoke the conceptualization that one of us has proposed of the conservative hegemonic alliance as constituted through a series of tensely negotiated and maintained compromises among disparate but overlapping discursive tendencies (Apple, 1996, 2000, 2001). With regard to the contestation of such a tense alliance, critical theorists in education and elsewhere have correctly argued that one strategy to forward the agenda of a radically democratic social and educational project might be to carefully discern these fault lines within the hegemonic alliance so that potential differences among the different positions might be exacerbated, thereby pushing the project of conservative modernization in the direction of crisis. Just as the American Left hopes to strategically promote its interests through capitalizing on these points of suture on the Right, so too does the Right have an interest in continuing to capitalize on, and subvert tensions among, real and potential progressive allies.

One of the fault lines that the Right seems to have successfully discerned and targeted is the articulation within what we might call the traditional progressive alliance between African American groups and teachers' unions such as the NEA and the AFT. By infusing the common sense of the United States' social formation with narrativized images of self-interested teachers' unions protecting their own jobs and "enriching" themselves with little concern for the students of color who increasingly make up our public school populations, the Right may be succeeding in destroying residual elements of a progressive alliance at the same time that it strengthens its own ascendancy (Holt, 2000). Calls by national teachers' unions for the improvement of teachers' working conditions through "zero tolerance" in student discipline, although in some ways justifiable, has likely only contributed to these tensions. (However, it should be noted that nothing prevents voucher schools from adopting "zero tolerance"-type policies.) Regarding this disarticulation between teachers' unions and African American parents, we want to assert that a careful appraisal of such educational dynamics in contexts such as Milwaukee will be quite instructive in both the theorization and the contestation of this process of disarticulation among potential and actual progressive allies (see Apple et al., 2003).

This situation is exacerbated by the following. For many African American urban leaders who have, sometimes even tepidly, supported vouchers, the reaction of some progressive Whites has been quite illuminating. It is characteristically a reaction of progressives who were previously content to see Blacks as "wisely" coalescing with predominantly White progressive initiatives and now see these same Blacks as foolishly allying themselves with dangerous forces. A tacit message here appears to be that Blacks do not know the real dangers of allying with "reprehensible" conservative people; only White liberals know that. It smacks of a feeling of the "White man's burden," where liberal White educators are now angry at the "Black children" whom they had gathered under their umbrella because those children are showing independence of mind (see Fanon, 1967).

Social movements and redefining democracy

Our analysis of contradictory tensions and alliances does not mean that we need to weaken our arguments against marketization and privatization of schooling. Voucher and tax credit plans (the latter ultimately may actually be more dangerous) are still regressive policies that will most likely have some extremely problematic effects in the long term. One of the most important effects could be a *demobilization* of social movements within communities of color. Schools have played central roles in the creation of movements for justice. In essence, rather than being peripheral reflections of larger battles and dynamics, struggles over schooling—over what should be taught, over the relationship between schools and local communities, over the very ends and means of the institution itself— have provided a crucible for the *formation* of larger social movements toward equality (Apple et al., 2003; Hogan, 1982). These collective movements have transformed our definitions of rights, of who should have them, and of the role of the government in guaranteeing these rights. Absent organized, community-wide mobilizations, these transformations would not have occurred (Fraser, 1997; Giugni, McAdam, & Tilly, 1999).

This is under threat currently. Definitions of democracy based on possessive individualism, on the citizen as only a "consumer," are inherently grounded in a process of deracing, declassing, and degendering (Ball, 1994). Yet, less advantaged raced, classed, and gendered people constitute the very groups that have employed struggles over educational access and outcomes to form themselves as self-conscious actors. If it is the case—as we strongly believe it is—that the organized efforts of social movements ultimately have led to the transformation of our educational system in more democratic directions (Apple, 2000; Hogan, 1982), the long-term

176

effects of neoliberal definitions of democracy may be truly tragic for communities of color, not "only" in increasing inequalities in schools (see, e.g., Apple, 2001; Gillborn & Youdell, 2000; Lipman, 2004; McNeil, 2000), but also in leading to a very real loss of the impetus for *collective* solutions to pressing social problems.

If all problems are simply "solved" by individual choices within a market, then collective mobilizations tend to wither and perhaps even disappear.[17] Thus, although short-term support for neoliberal and neoconservative policies may seem strategically wise to some members of less powerful groups, and may in fact generate short-term mobilizations, we remain deeply worried about what will happen over time.[18] It is the long-term implications of individuating processes and ideologies, and their effects on the necessity of larger and constantly growing social mobilizations that aim toward substantive transformations within the public sphere, that need to be of concern as well.

A concern over the effects of individuation that such "choice" programs may ultimately bring is unfortunately actually mirrored in the (already limited) literature on Black support for neoliberal and neoconservative policies. All too much of the critical literature on such "strategic alliances," even such work as Dillard's compelling book (2001), tends to focus on individuals rather than on larger social movements. As we noted above, it is social movements that historically have had the power to transform social and educational policy and practice. An emphasis on individuals does humanize the issues that are in contention and allows us to see the people behind the rightist presence within marginalized communities. However, this very focus causes us to miss the dynamics that have led to the growth of groups such as BAEO and to the strategic moves that are being selfconsciously made on the unequal social fields of power in which educational policy operates.

This doesn't vitiate the strength of what such analyses of the growing conservative tendencies among some "othered" communities have given us. However, the question is not whether it is possible to build a rightist-led coalition that will include elements of "multiculturalism." Indeed, as we have shown in this article, such a process is in part already being successfully attempted. Instead, the questions we must constantly ask are the following: At what cost? At whose expense? Whose interests are served?

We do know, for example, that the integration of some elements of communities that have historically been seen as "the other" has occurred and that certain elements have been brought under the umbrella of conservative modernization. For instance, some Latin Americans, Asian Americans, gays, lesbians, and others have given their support to what are surprisingly conservative causes. Although perhaps overstating her arguments for political reasons, Dillard, for example, is at her most perceptive when she sees that the roots of the support of conservative positions among some members of oppressed groups may often be based on not wanting to "be Black." It is worth quoting her at length here.

> [One] point on which Latino, Asian-American, women, and homosexual conservatives seem to agree is the desire, to restate the matter bluntly,

not to be like blacks—members of a group that persists in pressing for collective redress from the government rather than pursuing the path of individualism, upward mobility, and assimilation. That some Latino and Asian-American conservatives have engaged in this narrative is troubling. If Toni Morrison is even partially correct in asserting that previous waves of immigrants have embraced (white, middle class) American identity "on the back of blacks," then there is reason to fear that new immigrants will seek to replicate this pattern. In the process, the already tense relationships among African Americans, Latinos, and Asian-Americans could degenerate. That some African American conservatives, a contingent that remains predominantly middle and upper-middle class, appear content to follow suit—to assimilate on the backs of the black poor—is doubly disturbing. (Dillard, 2001, p. 182)

Obviously, Dillard's arguments are not as applicable to Black activist groups such as BAEO, which invokes a Black Nationalist sensibility concerning community control of schools. Yet for the many other persons and organizations with which she does deal, Dillard's points need to be taken very seriously, for the implication of such arguments is that the major losers in the shifting discursive terrain surrounding race and identity may very well prove once again to be poor Blacks. Once more, they will be pathologized. Their voices will be silenced. And they will continue to be "everybody's convenient and favorite scapegoat" (Dillard, 2001, p. 182). Given the central place that race has played in the development of the neoconservative movement of "return" and the neoliberal movement of "choice" (Apple, 2001), we should not be surprised if rightist multiculturalism promises more of the same, but covered in a new and seemingly more diverse discourse.

"Not wanting to be Black" does not explain the support of vouchers by groups such as BAEO, of course, given its Black Nationalist sensibilities. Instead, it is the very fact of *being Black*, of recognizing and fighting against their social and cultural positioning as the ultimate "other," that has caused them to seek out strategic—some might say heretical—alliances with some of the main tendencies that, paradoxically, have been in the forefront historically in supporting such positioning. In *Educating the "Right" Way* (Apple, 2001), one of us has called for thinking heretically about possible alliances that might subvert parts of the agendas involved in conservative modernization. Whether BAEO's "heretical actions" actually do subvert such agendas and the racial and social class stratification of schools remains to be seen. We fear that ultimately, their actions may not. But one must also ask what choices Black activists in fact do have given the structures of inequality that currently exist.

Conclusion

In this article, we have examined a growing phenomenon: the growth of seemingly conservative sentiments among "despised others." At the core of our analysis is a concern about what is at stake for all of us if a rightist educational agenda succeeds in redefining what and whose knowledge is of most worth and what our social and educational policies are meant to do. Yet, no matter what one's position is on the wisdom of BAEO's strategic actions, this case provides a crucial example of the politics of disarticulation and rearticulation on the ways in which social movements and alliances are formed and reformed from of the material and ideological conditions of daily life and of the politics of discursive reappropriation (Apple, 2001; Hall, 1996).[19] Thus, an analysis of such movements is important both in terms of the balance of forces and power involved in specific educational reforms and in terms of more general issues concerning the processes of social transformation and agency. A critical but sympathetic understanding of groups such as BAEO may enable us to avoid the essentialism and reductionism that enters into critical sociological work on the role of struggles over the state. It can provide a more nuanced sense of social actors and the possibilities and limits of strategic alliances in a time of conservative modernization (see Pedroni, 2004).

Although we have a good deal of sympathy for BAEO's critique of the current functioning of public schools, we have very real worries about whether they can control the uses to which their support of neoliberal policies will be put. Yet, having said this, there may be some salutary effects of their efforts to mobilize around vouchers.

If the common school loses its legitimacy among significant numbers of people within communities of color, it may force a reexamination of the unequal ways that schools are currently financed in the United States, where a school's funding is dependent on the local tax base and its very real inequalities. It also may create the conditions in which teachers and their unions may have to work much more closely with local communities than is the case now simply in order for teachers to maintain their legitimacy in the eyes of people of color. We say this knowing that, oddly enough, this might provide evidence for parts of the neoliberal case about school markets. Even though the arguments of voucher supporters such as Chubb and Moe (1990) are more than a little simplistic about the nature of what counts as "rational choices" for whom and about the nature of markets themselves, it still may be the case that fear of competition over positions and schools among teachers and other educators may then have hidden effects that also may finally lead to even more support among them for needed changes in schools.

Having said this, however, we predict the opposite. Although these changes may occur, it is unfortunately much more likely that the effects will be ones less positive in their long-term consequences. Less funding will be given to public schools. A politics of blame will evolve in which parents who have no choice but to keep their children in underfunded and highly policed inner-city schools and the teachers who remain in those schools will be seen as the source of the problem of the common school—not the highly stratified and unequal society that supports and sustains a system of highly unequal educational opportunities. Much depends on the balance of forces at the time. Given what has been shown about the often negative results of the combination of neoconservative and neoliberal reforms in schools, we are not sanguine about what will happen (Apple, 2001; Lipman, 2004; McNeil, 2000). At the very least, though, we need to be aware that the complicated politics and strategic maneuvering occurring on the terrain of educational policy will have complicated, contradictory, and unforeseen results. The example of BAEO signifies the beginning, not the end, of this story.

Although we have focused on the growth of strategic alliances between "despised others" and conservative forces in the United States, we predict that such alliances may not be limited to this one nation.[20] Furthermore, we envision that the conceptual modifications that such evidence suggests and that we have sought to develop clearly here concerning the importance of subaltern groups in conservative formation will help researchers in other contexts to discern similar processes and trajectories. We can imagine that tactical investments in fleeting conservative alliances and subject positions among marginalized communities will play an increasingly significant role both here and elsewhere.

This may be disturbing to many progressively inclined educators, and this leads to our final point. Any groups that disagree with BAEO about the wisdom of supporting vouchers and of making tactical alliances with the Right have a task that goes well beyond simply criticizing their position or their strategy. Critics of BAEO's positions and strategies must have a detailed and in-depth understanding of what generates the anger at the lack of responsiveness that all too many school systems have shown to communities of color and the poor and working class for decades. The deplorable school conditions and gross inequities in educational access and control that remain in the post-*Brown* era—and to which groups like BAEO are responding—are real and immensely destructive to real children in real communities (see, for example, Kozol, 1991). Thus, those who worry about BAEO must ask what they themselves are for. They need to redouble their own efforts to end the racial contract that underpins "our" economic and political institutions (Mills, 1997), work even harder to provide the economic and cultural conditions that would make African American parents have faith in their schools, and challenge the ways in which a politics of "Whiteness" underpins so much of the daily life of this society. Simply saying no to BAEO, then, in an era marked by the persistence of many of the massive injustices that the *Brown* decision sought to address, is not enough. Indeed, we would claim that it is a racializing act itself unless it is accompanied by powerful antiracist actions.

We would like to thank David Gillborn, Steven Selden, and especially Amy Stuart Wells for their perceptive comments on the issues raised in this article.

Notes

1 In the late 1980s and early 1990s, when the critics of desegregation were most vocal, nearly 6,000 African American students were attending predominantly White suburban schools through the voluntary transfer (i.e., "choice") Chapter 220 program (Schmidt, 1993).
2 Milwaukee is one of only a handful of desegregation cases that allows students to cross urban–suburban boundaries after 1974 when the U.S. Supreme Court ruled

in the *Milliken v. Bradley* case against metropolitan wide remedies, except when Constitutional violations could be clearly linked to each suburb (see Hankin, 1989).

3 This, of course, was and is not only the case in Milwaukee. As Wells et al. (2004, 2005) and many other scholars have documented, White privilege was constantly reasserted into the context of desegregation policies that, in theory, were intended to remedy years of discrimination against Black and Latino students. For a copy of the Wells et al. (2004) report, see http://www.tc.edu/desegregation.

4 As will be discussed at length later in this article, we must recognize that most members of what are often referred to as minority groups travel the highway labeled *market* in considerably less comfort than the powerful interests at the heart of this story. Quite often, disenfranchised people find themselves on this road only as the equivalent of hitchhikers, subject to the whims of those who navigate this highway with the sense of confidence and ownership that is the hallmark of their power and class habitus (Bourdieu, 1984). Yet for some of the less well-off on the side of the road, the road at least offers the hope that it might pass closer to a vision of community control and opportunity than previous avenues have allowed. Therefore, as we will later argue, for many African American parents choosing market alternatives such as vouchers, "anywhere else" sometimes seems better than where we stand educationally in our urban cores right now.

5 Perhaps this statement oversimplifies things a bit. Notions of "economic democracy" (i.e., free markets) in the current moment have actually become entangled in complicated ways with conceptions of political democracy; the conceptual slippage that this entanglement enables is actually more useful for those who endorse and benefit from this reconceptualization as compared with a complete displacement of the political by the economic.

6 Although her analysis could be more detailed and subtle in certain places, Dillard (2001) does a good job of detailing the "structures of feeling" of conservative affiliations among a number of people who usually are not expected to take such positions. She deals with a wide range of different forms of conservative leanings, from the economy, the legitimacy of activist government, the politics of the body, and the role of religion in public affairs, on the one hand, to questions dealing with what knowledge should and should not be taught as "legitimate" and, say, the place of race in university admissions on the other.

7 "Progressive" traditions in the United States were not free of such racializing and racist logics. See, for example, Selden (1999).

8 That the number of African American groups that are making alliances with distinctly conservative movements is growing says something very important about the fascination with identity politics among many progressive scholars and activists in education and elsewhere. Too often, writing on identity (wrongly) assumes that identity politics is a good thing, that people inexorably move in progressive directions as they pursue what Nancy Fraser would call a politics of recognition (1997). Yet, any serious study of rightist movements demonstrates that identity politics is just as apt to take, say, angry and retrogressive forms—antigay, racist nativism, antiwomen, and so on. For many such people, "we" are the new oppressed, with that "we" not including most people of color, feminists, "sexual deviants," immigrants, and so on (see, e.g., Blee, 2002; Kintz, 1997). Yet, as we noted earlier, even people within these "despised" groups themselves may (strategically) take on such retrogressive stances.

9 We do not mean to imply that the conservative tradition in American politics is the only one that does this. Rather, dominant traditions in American politics, whether liberal or conservative, are generally culpable in this regard.

10 BAEO is a heterogeneous organization. Much, though not all, of BAEO's leadership is from the middle class, but it does have a good deal of grassroots support. Where it specifically meets and intersects with rightist organizations, those who interact with

such organizations tend not to be among the poor and working class. However, a class analysis is not sufficient here. Racial solidarity may come first; race fundamentally mediates class relations. Thus, the issue of the class position of BAEO's leadership needs to be thought about in complex and subtle ways.

11 In some ways, this is similar to the long history of critical cultural analyses that demonstrate that people form bricolages in their daily lives and can employ language and commodities in ways undreamed of by the original producers of the language and products (see, e.g., Willis, 1990).

12 The continuing research on BAEO and similar groups by one of us (Tom) sheds considerable light on this. See Pedroni, 2004.

13 In this regard, the political issue that they are facing is in some ways similar to the debates over "market socialism." Can economic and political forms developed under the auspices of less progressive tendencies and power relations be employed to further goals that are organized around a very different set of ideological sentiments? See, for example, Bardhan and Roemer (1993) and Ollman (1998).

14 We do not want to argue that all these decisions are based on some sort of rational choice model. There are powerful emotional economies at work here. On the ways in which emotional economies work in mobilizations, see Kintz (1997).

15 In an essay entitled "Becoming Right: Education and the Formation of Conservative Movements," the argument was made that relatively ideologically unformed citizens "became Right"—that is, became more fully formed conservative actors within rightist social movements—as the result of a complex set of interactions between individuals' elements of "good sense" and the intransigence of a bureaucratic state (Apple, 1996; Apple et al., 2003). Here we wish to propose a substantive addition to this argument. Our present research points to the possibility and actuality of individuals and groups making tactical investments in conservative subject positions and social movements while still retaining political investments and identities that are anything but conservative. Although such individuals and groups do not "become Right," their tactical investment in rightist social movements does lend significant credibility and legitimacy to rightist forms.

16 The names of the interview participants have been changed to preserve their anonymity. Complete transcripts of the interviews upon which the analysis here is based are available upon request from the authors of this article.

17 However, we do not wish to sound overly deterministic here. Although we maintain that this is in fact the most likely outcome, a model of linear causality, misapplied here, would deny the agency that voucher parents actually possess in the process of conservative formation. Rather than "the collective" withering in Milwaukee, there is significant evidence that much of the movement is about moving resources to more community-controlled (albeit private) schools (Pedroni, 2004). The argument among many parents is precisely that vouchers enable them to choose schools that are more rooted in the community, in Black culture, and even in Black faith. This, however, is only a possibility. Once again, we need to remember that these strategic moves do not take place on a level playing field.

18 Dillard (2001) herself is very fair in her assessment of what the implications of such support may be. She nicely shows the contradictions of the arguments and logic of the people she focuses upon. In doing so, she draws upon some of the more cogent analyses of the relationship between democracy and the maintenance of the public sphere on the one hand, and an expansive and rich understanding of what it means to be a citizen on the other. Readers of her discussion would also be well served to connect her arguments to the historical struggles over the very meanings of our concepts of democracy, freedom, and citizenship, such as that found in Eric Foner's illuminating book, *The Story of American Freedom* (1998), but Dillard's discussion is substantive and useful. It also serves as a reminder of the continuing importance of a number of democratic and critical

writers, such as Hannah Arendt (1973, 1990), whose work, although not perfect by any means, unfortunately is no longer read as often as it should be.

19 An analysis of groups such as BAEO could enable us to extend the range of Basil Bernstein's work on *recontextualization* as well. See Bernstein, 1990.

20 Extensive observations by one of us in New Zealand and England over the past decade confirm that this in fact is a distinct possibility.

References

Apple, M. W. (1996). *Cultural politics and education*. New York: Teachers College Press.

Apple, M. W. (2000). *Official knowledge* (2nd ed.). New York: Routledge.

Apple, M. W. (2001). *Educating the "Right" way: Markets, standards, God, and inequality*. New York: Routledge.

Apple, M. W., Aasen, P., Cho, M. K., Gandin, L. A., Oliver, A., Sung, Y.-K., et al. (2003). *The state and the politics of knowledge*. New York: RoutledgeFalmer.

Apple, M. W., & Beane, J. A. (1999). *Democratic schools: Lessons from the chalk face*. Buckingham, UK: Open University Press.

Apple, M. W., & Buras, K. L. (in press). *The subaltern speak: Curriculum, power, and educational struggle*. New York: RoutledgeFalmer.

Arendt, H. (1973). *The human condition*. Chicago: University of Chicago Press.

Arendt, H. (1990). *On revolution*. New York: Penguin Books.

Ball, S. (1994). *Education reform*. Buckingham, UK: Open University Press.

Bardhan, P., & Roemer, J. (Eds.). (1993). *Market socialism: The current debate*. New York: Oxford University Press.

Bell, D. (2004). *Silent covenants*: Brown v. Board of Education *and the unfulfilled hopes for racial reform*. Oxford: Oxford University Press.

Bernstein, B. (1990). *The structuring of pedagogic discourse*. New York: Routledge.

Black Alliance for Educational Options (BAEO). Retrieved September, 15, 2002, from http://www.baeo.org/

Blee, K. (2002). *Inside organized racism: Women in the hate movement*. Berkeley: University of California Press.

Bourdieu, P. (1984). *Distinction*. Cambridge, MA: Harvard University Press.

Brown, M. K. (2003). Ghettos, fiscal federalism, and welfare reform. In S. F. Schram, J. Soss, & R. C. Fording (Eds.), *Race and the politics of welfare reform* (pp. 47–71). Ann Arbor: University of Michigan Press.

Carl, J. (1995). *The politics of education in a new key: The 1988 Chicago School Reform Act and the 1990 Milwaukee Parental Choice Program*. Unpublished doctoral dissertation, University of Wisconsin, Madison.

Carl, J. (1996). Unusual allies: Elite and grass-roots origins of parental choice in Milwaukee. *Teachers College Record, 98*, 266–285.

Carr, S. (2004, January 11). As program rolls forward, it's slowly losing momentum. *Milwaukee Journal Sentinel*, p. 01 A.

Chubb, J., & Moe, T. (1990). *Politics, markets, and America's schools*. Washington, DC: Brookings Institution.

Corporation for Educational Radio and Television. (1993). *Liberating America's schools* (Video). New York: PBS.

Cooper, C. W. (2001). *School choice reform and the standpoint of African American mothers: The search for power and opportunity in the educational marketplace*. Unpublished doctoral dissertation, UCLA, Los Angeles, CA.

Creative Media Services/CMS. (1998). Interview segments. Milwaukee, WI: Author.

Dale, R. (1989/1990). The Thatcherite project in education. *Critical Social Policy, 9,* 4–19.

De Certeau, M. (1984). *The practice of everyday life.* Berkeley: University of California Press.

Dillard, A. D. (2001). *Guess who's coming to dinner now: Multicultural conservatism in America.* New York: New York University Press.

Dougherty, J. (2004). *More than one struggle: The evolution of Black school reform in Milwaukee.* Chapel Hill: University of North Carolina Press.

Edsall, T., & Edsall, M. (1991). *Chain reaction: The impact of race, rights, and taxes on American politics.* New York: Norton.

Fanon, F. (1967). *Black skin, White masks.* New York: Grove.

Fine, M., Weis, L., Powell, L., & Wong, L. M. (Eds.). (1997). *Off White.* New York: Routledge.

Foner, E. (1998). *The story of American freedom.* New York: Norton.

Fraser, N. (1997). *Justice interruptus.* New York: Routledge.

Fuller, H. (1985). *The impact of the Milwaukee Public School system's desegregation plan on Black students and the Black community (1976–1982).* Unpublished doctoral thesis, Marquette University, Milwaukee, WI.

Gillborn, D., & Youdell, D. (2000). *Rationing education.* Philadelphia: Open University Press.

Giugni, M., McAdam, D., & Tilly, C. (1999). (Eds.). *How social movements matter.* Minneapolis: University of Minnesota Press.

Greider, W. (1997). *One world, ready or not.* New York: Simon & Schuster.

Hall, S. (1980). Popular democratic vs. authoritarian populism. In A. Hunt (Ed.), *Marxism and democracy* (pp. 150–170). London: Lawrence and Wishart.

Hall, S. (1996). On postmodernism and articulation. In D. Morley & K.-H. Chen (Eds.), *Stuart Hall: Critical dialogues in cultural studies* (pp. 131–150). New York: Routledge.

Hankin, G. G. (1989). Like a bridge over troubled waters: New directions and innovative voluntary approaches to interdistrict school desegregation. *The Journal of Negro Education, 58,* 345–356.

Herrnstein, R., & Murray, C. (1994). *The bell curve.* New York: Free Press.

Hobsbawm, E. (1994). *The age of extremes.* New York: Pantheon.

Hogan, D. (1982). Education and class formation. In M. W. Apple (Ed.), *Cultural and economic reproduction in education* (pp. 32–78). Boston: Routledge and Kegan Paul.

Holt, M. (2000). *Not yet "Free at Last": The unfinished business of the civil rights movement: Our battle for school choice.* Oakland, CA: Institute for Contemporary Studies.

Katz, M. B. (2001). *The price of citizenship.* New York: Metropolitan Books.

Kintz, L. (1997). *Between Jesus and the market.* Durham, NC: Duke University Press.

Kozol, J. (1991). *Savage inequalities.* New York: Crown.

Lewis, D. L. (1993). *W.E.B. DuBois: Biography of a race, 1868–1919.* New York: Henry Holt.

Lewis, D. L. (2000). *W.E.B. DuBois: The fight for equality and the American century, 1919–1963.* New York: Henry Holt.

Leys, C. (2002). *Market-driven politics: Neoliberal democracy and the public interest.* New York: Verso.

Lipman, P. (2004). *High-stakes education.* New York: RoutledgeFalmer.

Lopez, A., Wells, A. S., & Holme, J. J. (2002). Creating charter school communities: Identity building, diversity, and selectivity. In A. S. Wells (Ed.), *Where charter school policy fails: The problems of accountability and equity* (pp. 129–158). New York: Teachers College Press.

McNeil, L. (2000). *Contradictions of school reform*. New York: Routledge.

Metz, M. (2003). *Different by design*. New York: Teachers College Press.

Mills, C. (1997). *The racial contract*. Ithaca, NY: Cornell University Press.

Moe, T. (2001). *Schools, vouchers, and the American public*. Washington, DC: Brookings Institution.

Ollman, B. (Ed.). (1998). *Market socialism: The debate among socialists*. New York: Routledge.

Olson, L. (1990, September 12). Milwaukee's choice program enlists 391 volunteers. *Education Week,* Retrieved July 25, 2005, from http://www.edweek.org/ew/articles/1990/09/12/10120061.h10.html?querystring=Olson

Omi, M., & Winant, H. (1994). *Racial formation in the United States* (2nd ed.). New York: Routledge.

Pedroni, T. C. (2004). Strange bedfellows in the Milwaukee "parental choice" debate: Participation among the dispossessed in conservative educational reform. *Dissertation Abstracts International, 64*(11), 3946A. (UMI No. 3113677).

Pedroni, T. C. (2005). *Can post-structuralist and neo-Marxist approaches be joined? Building composite approaches in critical educational theory and research*. Unpublished manuscript, Utah State University, Logan.

Schmidt, P. (1993, May 12). Governor seeks scrutiny of Milwaukee busing plan. *Education Week*, Retrieved July 25, 2005, from http://www.edweek.org/ew/articles/1993/05/12/33wis.h12.html?querystring=Schmidt

Selden, S. (1999). *Inheriting shame*. New York: Teachers College Press.

Shujaa, M. J. (1996). *Beyond desegregation: The politics of quality in African American schooling*. Thousand Oaks, CA: Corwin Press.

Snider, W. (1987, November 4). In Milwaukee, dissatisfied Black leaders draw ire with "mostly Black" district plan. *Education Week*, Retrieved July 25, 2005, from http://www.edweek.org/ew/articles/1987/11/04/07340034.h07.html?querystring=Snider

Spivak, G. C. (1988). *In other worlds: Essays in cultural politics*. New York: Routledge.

Valenzuela, A. (Ed.). (2005). *Leaving children behind*. Albany: State University of New York Press.

Wells, A. S., & Crain, R. L. (1997). *Stepping over the color line; African American students in White suburban schools*. New Haven, CT: Yale University Press.

Wells, A. S., Holme, J. J., Atanda, K. A., & Revilla, A. T. (2005). Tackling racial segregation one policy at a time: Why school desegregation only went so far. *Teachers College Record, 107*, 2141–2177.

Wells, A. S., Holme, J. J., Revilla, A. T., & Atanda, K. A. (2004). *How desegregation changed us: The effects of racially mixed schools on students and society*. Final report from the Understanding Race and Education Study. New York: Teachers College, Columbia University.

Whitty, G., Power, S., & Halpin, D. (1998). *Devolution and choice in education*. Buckingham, UK: Open University Press.

Willis, P. (1990). *Common culture*. Boulder, CO: Westview.

185

30

RACE, CLASS, AND EDUCATION

Lessons for school leaders from Hurricane Katrina and the Gulf Coast

T. Elon Dancy II and M. Christopher Brown II

Source: Linda C. Tillman and James Joseph Scheurich (eds), *Handbook of Research on Educational Leadership for Equity and Diversity*, New York: Routledge, 2013, pp. 517–536.

In an edited volume on the relevance of Hurricane Katrina to education, Brown, Dancy, and Davis (2007) drew upon ancient texts in a prophetic declaration. The authors predicted that—should educators fail to adequately address disparities at the intersection of race and education—the Gulf coast would not be plagued by water but "the fire next time" (p. 69). On April 20, 2010, fire killed 11 platform workers and injured 17 others when a drilling rig operated by British Petroleum (BP) exploded in the Gulf of Mexico just 41 miles off the coast of Louisiana. The result was the most massive oil spill in marine history.

The impact on the Gulf coast region has been devastating in the immediate wake of the oil spill. For instance, many aquatic species like whales and dolphins were greatly endangered by the spill. Additionally, the seafood industry was negatively impacted by the number of oysters, shrimp, and crab that may have been contaminated by the spill. Economically, it is reported that Gulf states like Louisiana and Florida have suffered—and will continue to suffer—the loss of tourism revenue. It is well established in the literature that what affects Americans in general often affects vulnerable populations (e.g., people of color, low socioeconomic status persons) more harshly. Disastrous moments like those in the Gulf serve to amplify social inequalities. Disasters may also serve as haunting metaphors for the realities of racial and/or social inequalities in education. For instance, in the aftermath of the Katrina, primarily poor and African American citizens tragically drowned beneath rising tides of breached levees. The sad and metaphoric irony of this tragedy was that nearly 30 years earlier the National Commission on Excellence in Education (1983) argued that K-12 schools in America were "drowning" underneath a "rising tide of mediocrity." These metaphoric moments thus provide opportunities for critical reflection about American education for the most vulnerable populations.

While the authors acknowledge that the BP oil spill is a relevant context for discussing race, class, and education, this chapter concentrates most closely on

Hurricane Katrina given this event's more established presence in the education literature. More specifically, the chapter follows Gay's (2007) two-pronged model for discussing equity: (a) understanding inequitable trends according to specific manifestations of time circumstance and group and (b) bringing historical analysis to the examination of inequity during contemporary times. In this vein, this chapter first discusses the impact of Hurricane Katrina on the educational experiences of students. Next, perennial challenges of schools and society (which prevailed before and after the storm) are identified to remind readers of the persistent realities of social inequality in education. Then, the contemporary social context of educational settings is reviewed, considering how schools, schooling, and the role of policy and practice have evolved over time. Based on prima facie evidence, meditations on the significance of Hurricane Katrina and emerging opportunities follow. Concluding sections will seek to situate recommendations for education leaders in the large existing knowledge base on race and education (Anyon, 1997; Brown & Bartee, 2007; Brown & Land, 2005; Darling-Hammond, 2010; Delpit, 2006; Howard, 2010; Ladson-Billings, 1994; Moses, 2002; Noguera & Wing, 2006; Rolòn-Dow, 2005; Weis & Fine, 2000).

Hurricane Katrina: the catastrophic bigotry of low expectations

On Monday, August, 29, 2005, at 6:10 a.m. CDT, a fluctuating category 4 hurricane made landfall on the southernmost coast of the Mississippi Delta in Buras, Louisiana. Massive devastation would follow as rising flood waters breached levees, drowning and displacing many. Social inequities were evident in the aftermath of Hurricane Katrina, although, undeniably, social and educational neglect was a lived reality in Louisiana before the storm. When, Ladson-Billings (2007) was questioned about the events surrounding Hurricane Katrina, she replied, "Actually, the only difference between the people you are seeing on television today and their status two weeks ago is now they're wet!" (p. 15). Although Ladson-Billings admits feeling her comments to be somewhat cynical, they were, nonetheless, indicative of the persistent failure of the U.S. government to seriously address the plight of poor and disenfranchised persons.

Over the years, the impact of Hurricane Katrina on education has been studied in the research and scholarly literature. For instance, in the edited volume, The *Children Hurricane Katrina Left Behind: Schooling Context, Professional Preparation, and Community Politics* (Robinson & Brown, 2007), education scholars investigated the impact Hurricane Katrina would have on students across schooling contexts. This book, when paired with recent research on educational inequity in crisis contexts, clearly demonstrates the common plight among under-resourced areas, public schools, and students of color (Brown et al., 2007; Gadsden & Fuhrman, 2007; Morris, 2008).

To be certain, Louisiana was a site of neglect and racial, social, and economic inequity long before Hurricane Katrina (Ladson-Billings, 2007). First, Louisiana is one of the poorest states in the nation (U.S. Census Bureau, 2010). According to the U.S. Census Bureau (2004), New Orleans had a population of 484,674 before the hurricane, and 67% of that population was African American. Nearly 25% of the total population and 35% of the African American population lived below the poverty line. Moreover, prior to Hurricane Katrina, over 40,000 New Orleans residents had less than a ninth-grade education and 56,804 residents had between ninth-and 12th-grade educations without diplomas (Ladson-Billings, 2007). Ladson-Billings also noted a telling statistic: nearly 96.1% of public school population was African American, which meant that most of the White families with school-aged children sent their children to private schools.

Research calls for more study of the more than 327,000 students in the Katrina diaspora—i.e., students displaced to other areas and schools following Hurricane Katrina (Morris, 2008). While it is reported that every state (with the exception of Hawaii) received displaced students, Louisiana, Texas, and Georgia received the largest influx (Freeman, 2007). More specifically, other Louisiana school districts absorbed 47,000 students, Texas absorbed 40,200 students, and Georgia absorbed 10,300 students (Freeman, 2007). Freeman also observed the inequitable way in which African American students were funneled into schools following Katrina. She argues that the following trends were exacerbated: (a) displaced students, largely African American and poor, were relocated to schools that were already seriously under-resourced; (b) many displaced students were educated unequally and often segregated within relocated contexts; and (c) race relations were intensified, as schools and communities adjusted to a sudden influx of non-White students. Freeman also suggests that this context of relocation was highly correlated with student attrition. Freeman notes (citing Dewan, 2006) that of 560 children displaced from a trailer park in Baker, Louisiana, only 190 were still attending when the school year ended.

Moreover, in the aftermath of Hurricane Katrina, students and other evacuees were met with chilly climates of reception in the host schools and communities. Zamani-Gallaher and Polite (2007) recalled headlines in the months following the hurricane disaster. One such headline, from the Associated Press read, "Katrina evacuees wear out stay in Houston" and another in the March 14,2006, issue of *Newsweek* read, "Katrina's latest damage: Houston wants Katrina evacuees to move on" (Zamani-Gallaher & Polite, 2007). Standardized test scores only added to the negative stigma associated with displaced students: Only 46% of fifth-grade evacuees passed the reading portion of the Texas Assessment of Knowledge and Skills in contrast to 80% of all students. In addition, 89% of all third graders passed the reading portion of this same test, compared to 58% of Katrina's evacuated students (Zamani-Gallaher & Polite, 2007). Thus, problematic education in Louisiana suddenly became a "problem" for other states.

At the same time, scholars caution the field not to view appalling educational conditions as unique to Louisiana (Darling-Hammond, 2007; Gay, 2007; Ladson-Billings, 2007). As Gay (2007) noted, "the schools affected by the hurricane are merely extreme cases of more generalized problems of educating students who are racially, ethnically, socially, culturally, and economically different from the middle class Eurocentric mainstream" (p. 56). In effect, despite the significance of Hurricane Katrina and the disasters and hardships that followed, we cannot ignore persistent inequalities and socio-historical inequities in education. Undeniably, educational systems are saturated with perennial challenges and contexts concerning power, privilege, and advantage.

Power, privilege, and schools:
perennial challenges and contexts

Schools in America continue to function as sorting devices. Specifically, economic, cultural, racial, and social differences are still found to result in differential privilege in schools (Alexander, 2004; Anyon, 1981; Apple, 1979/1990; Brown, Dancy, & Norfles, 2006; Coleman et al., 1966; Dancy & Horsford, 2010; Lareau, 2000; Morris, 2009). For instance, resources that contribute to educational success—supplies, books, computers, tutors, etc.—are available to children whose families have greater income and wealth (Alexander, 2004; Coleman et al., 1966; Lareau, 2000). To maintain advantage, persons in positions of power use schooling to preserve vantage points for themselves and their progeny. Privileged parents continually investigate ways to pass on their advantages to their children given America's history of systemic inequality (Alexander, 2004; Anyon, 1981; Coleman et al., 1966; Lareau, 2000; Macleod, 1995).

More specifically, racial pluralism in America presents schools with unique challenges. These challenges are perhaps most serious in data describing disparate academic and social outcomes of students. In response, a large body of research studies the peculiarities of race and education in schools (Asher, 2007; Banks, 2002; Gay, 2000; Grant & Sleeter, 2006; Ladson-Billings, 1994; Nieto, 2004). This literature highlights the perennial challenges of educational access, opportunities, and achievement that are widely correlated with student background factors like family income, parent's education, and family structure.

At a micro-level, race has been defined in the literature as social consciousness of groups based on how people look (Omi & Winant, 1989). Thus, skin becomes "a human invention constructed by groups to differentiate themselves from other groups" (Banks, 1995, p. 22). At a macro-level, however, race categories and meanings are centrally sociohistorical, drawing meaning from the particular social relations and historical context which embed those meanings (Omi & Winant, 1989). Tracing the sociohistorical emergence of racial meaning, Omi and Winant write:

> When European explorers in the New World "discovered" people who looked different than themselves, these "natives" challenged then existing conceptions of the origins of the human species, and raised disturbing questions as to whether all could be considered in the same "family of man" . . . The expropriation of property, the denial of political rights,

the introduction of slavery and other forms of coercive labor, as well as outright extermination, all presupposed a worldview which distinguished Europeans from "others." (p. 58)

Omi and Winant (1989) use the term "racial formation" to embody both the challenges and opportunities of race in society. The authors define racial formation as the process by which social, economic, and political forces determine the content and importance of racial categories and by which these forces are shaped by racial meanings. This definition subsequently frames race as an "unstable complex of social meanings constantly being transformed by political struggle" as opposed to a fixed objective or mere illusion (Omi & Winant, 1989, p. 68).

An analysis of race in education involves understanding the meanings that educators ascribe to students who are members of racially diverse groups (Howard, 2010). With this understanding, we describe the ways in which challenges and contexts divide along racial lines. We specifically focus on how the intersection of race and socioeconomic status reproduce educational privilege, disparate trends among schools and communities, and educational experiences among students of color.

Race and class/race *as* class: exposing hidden agendas of privilege at the intersection

Some have argued that disparities in education and society have little to do with race, and perhaps more to do with individual choice, merit, class and/or socioeconomic status (McWhorter, 2000; Steele, 1990; Thernstrom & Thernstrom, 2003; Wilson, 2009). As a result, arguments that evoke race are dismissed and buried in more abstract categories like class (Wilson, 2009). However, as Leonardo (2004) notes, race relations are clearly products of the objective laws of economic processes. Thus, race is a mode of how class is lived (Leonardo, 2004). Despite the allure of classic Marxist interpretations of class and/or class consciousness, the colorlessness of a "pure" Marxist theory of class remains the subject of critique in the literature (Mills, 1997).

As in other international contexts, race has rapidly become a marker of class and status in the United States. To be certain, this race/class elision is not a new phenomenon or a novel concept since cultural and political power has always historically rested with White, Anglo-Saxon Protestants since the country's founding (Gans, 2010). Gans also argues that those in power have always assumed their kind of Whiteness rests at the top of the class hierarchy. This system of race and class privilege thus became a vehicle for colonized thinking or internalized understanding of power and privilege (Fanon, 1963). DuBois's (1903) theory of double-consciousness frames colonized thinking as follows:

After the Egyptian and Indian, the Greek and Roman, the Teuton and Mongolian, the Negro is a sort of seventh son, born with a veil and gifted with second-sight in this American world,—a world which yields him

190

[or her] no true self-consciousness, but only lets him [or her] see himself [or herself] through the revelation of the other world. It is a peculiar sensation, this double-consciousness, this sense of always looking
at one's self through the eyes of others, of measuring one's soul by the
tape of a world that looks on in amused contempt and pity. One ever feels
his [or her] twoness,—an American, a Negro; two souls, two thoughts,
two unreconciled strivings; two warring ideals in one dark body, whose
dogged strength alone keeps it from being torn asunder. (p. 14)

This idea points to a duality of thinking within African Americans. However,
as Freire (1982) argues, this duality is embedded in the innermost thinking of
oppressed peoples in general: those whose humanity has been stolen over time in
various ways. Accordingly, class is one of the most powerful tools of oppression.
Oliver and Shapiros (1996) seminal work, *Black Wealth, White Wealth* provides
keen insights into the intersections of class and race noting that wealth inequalities were structured over many generations through systemic means: slavery, Jim
Crow, discrimination, and institutionalized racism. Unsurprisingly, this research
found that African Americans accumulated less wealth than other groups in
America as a function of systemic inequality.

Further, Oliver and Shapiro (1996) argue that African Americans and Whites
face different opportunities for wealth as both a historical and contemporaneous
function of race and class. The result is that class is contextual, evolving, and varies in accordance with race definitions. For instance, the authors note that African
Americans' claim to the middle class rest heavily on income and not assets, whereas
the latter "supports the white middle class in its drive for middle-class opportunities
and a middle-class standard of living" (p. 97). In fact, middle-class African Americans only earn 70 cents for every $1 earned by middle-class Whites, and African
Americans only maintain 15 cents for every dollar of wealth possessed by the White
middle class. Yet, when African Americans and Whites are similarly educated and
employed, a glaring difference of $43,143 in home equity and financial assets still
remains (Oliver & Shapiro, 1996).

Thus, the fusion of race and class in schools and society is unambiguous. The
2008 median household income for non-Hispanic Whites was $55,530. For His-
panics, it was $37,913; for Native Americans, it was approximately $34,000; and
for African Americans, it was $34,218 (U.S. Census Bureau, 2010). The poverty
rates for these same groups were 7.8% among Whites, 23.1% among Hispanics, 23.9% among Blacks, and 25.9% among Native Americans. Asians' median
income was $52,600, though it is important to note that this does not bear out
across all Asian subgroups.

In effect, a disproportionate number of those who are poor are people of color
(U.S. Census Bureau, 2009). Despite the fact that more persons of color are earning higher incomes than ever, systemic access to higher quality school remains
racially uneven (Brown & Bartee, 2007; Willie, Garibaldi, & Reed, 1991).
Accordingly, children from these backgrounds are likely to have parents with

low-earning jobs or no employment and are, therefore, likely to move and receive an inconsistent quality of schooling (Howard, 2010). In addition, children whose parents received lower levels of education are disadvantaged in the school system; race only amplifies this trend (Alexander, 2004; Bourdieu & Passeron, 1977; Lareau, 2000). Today, as in the past, higher-SES families are afforded opportunities to choose neighborhoods with high-quality schools in the interest of their children's educational outcomes. Higher quality schools are largely defined in the literature as those which positively impact short-term (i.e., test scores) and long-term (i.e., entry into elite and competitive colleges) outcomes (Brown & Bartee, 2005; Darling-Hammond, 2010).

Families not only participate in perpetuating differential access to education, they are also incubators of racial differences. Racial differences—often perceived in group habits, tastes, attitudes, preferences, and linguistic signifiers—are among the many cultural conditions that make it more difficult for students from disadvantaged families to succeed in school (Alexander, 2004; Weis & Fine; 2000; Willie, Garibaldi, & Reed, 1991). Interrogating this idea further, Mitchell and Edwards (2010) argue that students from oppressed groups are pressured to compromise cultural values in conforming to school values. Accordingly, the existence and type of cultural resources in the home become linked to educational success. Students whose families own more books, subscribe to newspapers and magazines, visit libraries, and engage in other compatible enrichment opportunities perform better on cognitive tests, receive higher grades, and stay in school longer than do students from families who lack these resources (Alexander, 2004; DiMaggio 1982; DiMaggio & Mohr, 1985; Howard, 2010).

Schools also perpetuate privilege among groups of students that cluster along racial lines. In many respects, schools reify White, middle-class values (Alexander, 2004; Anyon, 1981; Bowles & Gintis, 1976; Diamond & Moore, 1995; Gay, 2000; Oakes; 1982). Consequently, the values of middle-class students are congruent with the values of the school. Thus, middle-class students—more likely to be White or Asian—seemingly respond to the requirements of schooling more easily than those who are not middle class (Alexander, 2004; Bowles & Gintis, 1976). Concurrently, economic advantages confer benefits by supporting variation among individual students within schools. In other words, students from higher-SES families locate access to activities and opportunities more than students from lower-SES families.

Differential access to social networks continues the work of systemic privilege by contributing to inequality in educational outcomes (Anyon, 1981; Bowles & Gintis, 1976; Coleman 1988; Coleman & Hoffer, 1987). Middle-class social networks provide individuals with insights and information that help them differentially navigate educational and social opportunities than their working-class counterparts (Alexander, 2004; Anyon, 1981; Lareau, 2000; Useem, 1992). Economic, social, and cultural resources, along with the concomitant capital and knowledge they afford, become a potent combination in ensuring educational attainment and achievement (Alexander, 2004; Bourdieu & Passeron, 1977; Collins, 1971; Macleod, 1995). Despite growing diversity

192

within America's schools, signs of change in economic inequalities are modest at best (Alexander, 2004; Darling-Hammond, 2010). Unfortunately, the extant literature maintains that despite interventions, society can expect social and educational inequality to persist throughout the 21st century.

Race and poverty: trends in communities and schools

Concentrated poverty is quickly spreading across the large cities of America. Between 1970 and 1990, the population living in census tracts with poverty rates of 40% or greater increased from 5.2% to 10.7% in the country's 100 largest cities (Alexander, 2004). This impact has been even worse for African Americans and Hispanics (Alexander, 2004). These trends particularly expose a discouraging picture of African Americans in society. In 1990, a fourth of all African Americans and 41.6% of low-income African Americans resided in extreme poverty tracts in these 100 cities. Meanwhile over 80% of low-income African Americans resided in high-poverty tracts (Alexander, 2004). Increasing concentration of poverty among African Americans implies a parallel increase of crime, violence, welfare dependency, family disruption and educational failure (Alexander, 2004). Accordingly, African American and Hispanic children remain more likely than White children to live in poverty and live in inner cities.

Trends show little signs of improving. In 1990, just over 30% of the total U.S. population lived in central cities, down less than 1% since 1970 (Alexander, 2004). In contrast, over half of African Americans lived in central cities in 1990, down just 1.5% since 1970 (Alexander, 2004). Unfortunately, schools and school districts are also affected by the socioeconomic conditions in inner cities. Students in more poorly developed areas are more likely to attend schools with a high level of poverty which is less conducive to student learning (Alexander, 2004; Howard, 2010; Morris, 2009). Moreover, urban schools, unlike their suburban counterparts, encounter many economic and demographic changes as connected to a critical mass of poor, minority, linguistically and ethnically diverse students (Legters, Balfanz, Jordan, & McPartland, 2004).

Since 1940, middle-class individuals have been attracted to suburban development from urban centers. The closing of manufacturing plants only exacerbated this trend. In fact, the proportion of residents living in central cities within a standard metropolitan statistical area (SMSA) dropped more than 22% from 1940 to 1980 (Legters et al., 2004). In the 1980s, urban students were more than twice as likely to attend high-poverty schools in which more than half the students qualify for free or reduced-price lunch (Legters et al., 2004).

In addition, students at urban high schools are performing significantly worse than students in nonurban schools on most measures including achievement and graduation rates. One-third to less than one-half of students in urban districts score at the basic level or higher in reading, mathematics, and science versus over two-thirds of students in nonurban districts (Legters et al., 2004), Attrition is also an outcome of urban high school experiences. High schools in urban districts, on average, lose over half of their students between freshman and senior year, compared to a nationwide average of less than a third (Legters et al., 2004). The single-year dropout rate for urban districts is nearly twice the national average while some urban districts report annual dropout rates as high as 20% (Legters et al., 2004). Cohort analyses studying the same group of students over 4 years of high school suggest that urban dropout rates in some schools may exceed 50% (Legters et al., 2004).

The challenges of poor and minority student overrepresentation in urban schools are many. Urban school districts enroll half of American minority students, one-third of poor students, and only one-quarter of all American public school students (Legters et al., 2004, Howard, 2010). Urban centers are, therefore, responsible for providing educational and social services to needy populations amid increasing poverty rates and eroding tax bases. Additional challenges include: (a) fewer school resources, (b) insufficient preparation, (c) challenging school climates, (d) racial segregation, and (e) political bureaucracy:

1   *Fewer school resources.* Urban schools often serve an educationally needier population of students and face the challenges of aging facilities that often require expensive maintenance and renovation, competition with wealthier districts for teachers, and a tax base that has dwindled in recent decades as residents have moved out of the city. These conditions arguably make urban education costlier than in other more advantaged settings (Darling-Hammond, 2010). In fact, one study (Ferguson, 1991) finds school expenditure levels matter in increasing student performance and that academic outcomes positively increase as funding is more closely tied to students' direct instruction. Ferguson's study also notes the importance of "buying" high-quality teachers (Darling-Hammond, 2010). When controlling for students' socioeconomic status, Ferguson (1991) found that differences in Black and White student achievement were almost entirely accounted for by differences in teacher quality.

2   *Insufficient preparation.* Most students are entering urban high schools with extremely poor prior preparation. Urban students consistently score below nonurban students in math, science, and reading according to national data obtained from various achievement tests (Legters et al., 2004). In Baltimore, for example, in the 1999–2000 school year, 60% of ninth graders passed the basic Maryland functional test in math and 76% passed the functional writing test, compared with statewide averages of 85% and 92%, respectively (Legters et al., 2004). Even worst performance was reported across eight nonselective urban high schools vis-à-vis suburban selective magnet high schools. Less than half (47%) of ninth graders passed the math test and two-thirds (67%) passed the writing test in the eight urban schools (Maryland State Department of Education, 2001, as cited in Legters et al., 2004).

3   *Challenging School Climates.* High concentrations of poverty among students in urban schools and surrounding neighborhoods have implications for

their health, safety, and early transitions into adulthood as well as for the daily operation of urban high schools (Legters et al., 2004). Physical conflicts are also viable concerns in urban schooling environments. Nearly half of the teachers in urban districts characterize physical conflicts among students as moderate or serious problems versus less than a third in nonurban districts (Legters et al., 2004).

4   *Racial Segregation.* Darling-Hammond (2010) argues that by the year 2000, nearly 72% of African American students attended predominantly minority-impacted schools and that the vast majority of students of color (in some cases reaching over 90%) were enrolled in urban high schools (see also Legters et al., 2004). In these contexts, students are exposed to higher levels of academic, linguistic, and cultural diversity than those enrolled in suburban high schools. Moreover, research suggests that urban learners also require more special or individualized services (Legters et al., 2004), but that oftentimes, such services can lead to classroom segregation and/or over-representation of minority students in special education classrooms (Darling-Hammond, 2010).

5   *Political Bureaucracy.* Many urban city school systems sometimes become susceptible to bureaucratic inertia, complicated politics, and short-term lead-ership as side effects of their large size (Macleod, 1995). In fact, in the largest 51 urban districts, research finds that the vast majority of school superinten-dents are relatively new: two thirds having served between 1 and 5 years, and nearly a third having served for 1 year or less (Legters et al., 2004). In these areas, new superintendents usually feel compelled to introduce new reform initiatives and policy/procedural changes to show constituents that they are effective. But, most of these reform efforts are short-lived because of the rapid turnover of the urban superintendent (Legters et al., 2004). As a result of the constant introduction of new reform initiatives, teachers, stu-dents, parents, community members, and other constituents rapidly become disillusioned and hardened to the idea of change (Apple, 1979/1990).

Clearly, the nation's rapidly changing racial and ethnic mosaic is observable in schools. While the actual number of Whites steadily increases, their percent-age of the total population is declining (U.S. Census, 2007). This is largely due to increasing numbers of Latinos and Asians. Pew Research Center data notes that Latinos will count for most of the population's growth between 2005 and 2050. In addition, Pew Research Center projects that nearly 1 in 5 Americans will be an immigrant by 2050 (Howard, 2010). African Americans also con-tinue to steadily grow in the United States population. In schools, students of color were 20% of the U.S. student population in 1970 (NCES, 2003). In 2007, students of color were 42% of the U.S. student populations (NCES, 2007). It is therefore necessary to analyze achievement data and experiences among stu-dents of color. We focus particularly on African American and Latino students who are lowest performing.

Educational outcomes among selected students of color

Recent access and retention data on African American students in the pipeline are disturbing. The enrollment of African Americans in preschool declined 5.4% between 1991 and 1999. African American students comprise approximately 17.1% of the nation's student population, yet they make up a disproportionate number of students receiving special education and remedial services (Howard, 2010). Overall, the enrollment of African Americans at colleges and universities increased 38.8% from 1990 to 2000. However, African American women earn almost twice the number of bachelor's degree when compared to men.

Latino educational attainment throughout the pipeline is significantly lower than that of other ethnic groups in the United States (Swail, Cabrera, & Lee, 2004). In fact, Latinos are less likely to graduate from high school or receive a GED than any other group (Swail et al., 2004). This trend is particularly alarming in California, where Latino students are the largest ethnic group in California schools, comprising nearly 40% of the total K-12 population in the state (Gandara, Larson, Rumberger, & Mehan, 1998). This educational trend, however, is not solely limited to California. In 1995, nearly 30% of all Latinos in the United States ages 1–24 had not finished high school, compared to 9% for non-Hispanic Whites and 12% for African Americans. Moreover, Latinos are also less likely to attend college even if they do finish high school (Gandara et al., 1998; Swail et al., 2004).

In addition, scholars argue that faculty produce and reproduce hidden curriculum of hegemony in the university setting that affects students of color's experiences negatively (Solorzano & Villalpando, 1998; Solorzano & Yosso, 2000). Hegemony describes how ruling groups normalize patriarchal ideologies and marginalize others' ideologies to maintain power and dominance (Gramsci, 1971). Solorzano and Villalpando (1998), insist that while most colleges endorse the importance of multiculturalism and provide educational opportunities to students of color, colleges still remain racially stratified with differential access, opportunity, and experiences.

The intersections of accountability and equity: educational policy attempts at change

Over the past 100 years, policy analysts and think tanks have increasingly argued that American students are ill-equipped to meet the challenges of an ever-evolving society. For example, the 1966 Coleman Report advocated for racial balance among students, schools, and subsequent changes in government education policy. The report found that poor African American students performed academically better in integrated, middleclass schools. Additionally, the report suggested that minority children and White children performed at disparate levels and that this achievement gap only increased as students progressed in school. It was a landmark report, unlike no other previously produced; it not only suggested that schools were unable to overcome the deficits that children of color brought with them from their home environment, but it concretized the idea that the home context itself was in need of remediation, ignoring larger socioeconomic structures and/or barriers that prevented children of color from being successful in school.

In the decades that followed, other reports also suggested that American students were unprepared to negotiate an increasingly competitive global market. For example, *A Nation at Risk* addressed "the widespread public perception that something [was] seriously remiss in our educational system" (National Commission on Excellence in Education, 1983). The report revealed that other countries threatened to exceed American industrial, commercial, and intellectual performance. In response, the U.S. Department of Education's National Commission on Excellence in Education advanced the following the recommendations:

1   Graduation requirements should be strengthened so that all students establish a foundation in five new basics: English, mathematics, science, social studies, and computer science;
2   Schools and colleges should adopt higher and measurable standards for academic performance;
3   The amount of time students spend engaged in learning should be significantly increased;
4   The teaching profession should be strengthened through higher standards for preparation and professional growth.

Then, after nearly 20 years of accountability-driven reform, influenced by *A Nation At Risk,* President George W. Bush announced No Child Left Behind, the cornerstone of his administration's educational agenda, 3 days after he took office. The NCLB Act reauthorizes the Elementary and Secondary Education Act (ESEA) and incorporates the following principles and strategies (U.S. Department of Education, 2004): (a) increased accountability for states, school districts, and schools; (b) greater choice for parents and schools, particularly those attending low-performing schools; (c) more flexibility for states and local educational agencies in the use of federal education dollars; and (d) a stronger emphasis on reading especially for the nation's youngest children. Because of its emphasis on holding school accountable for the education of all children, many individuals, including civil rights advocates, have supported NCLB for its attention to improving test scores among students of color, new English learners, low-income and disabled students.

Others, however, have criticized NCLB for its technocratic understanding of school accountability via standardized tests and curricula. For instance, Darling-Hammond (2010) writes that "where low-quality tests have driven a narrow curriculum disconnected from the higher-order skills needed in today's world, educational quality has languished, especially for the least affluent students whose education has come increasingly to resemble multiple-choice test prep, instead of the skills students desperately need" (p. 67). She argues that where high-stakes testing has occurred, instead of investing, schools experience higher dropout rates among discouraged students. She therefore reminds education policymakers of the pitfalls and unintended consequences of standards-based reform.

In the same vein, Brown et al. (2006) argue that NCLB misinterprets what disadvantaged students actually need. The authors recall that NCLB is presented as a program that places more talented teachers in schools to increase educational outcomes for all students and to address the needs of disadvantaged students with the goal of increasing student performance measures overall. However, the authors noted that many disadvantaged students will remain in poor learning environments given the large number of poor schools. They observe that instituting national standards and testing for every American high school is important but, ultimately, an inadequate substitute for one-on-one academic support and counseling for our most disadvantaged students. Brown et al. cite intervention programs (e.g., the TRIO programs) as critical links for increasing educational opportunity and college access.

Although NCLB had its fair share of critics, by 2009 there was a new education initiative already underway. At that time, President Barack Obama and U.S. Secretary of Education Arne Duncan announced that states leading the way on school reform would be eligible to compete for $4.35 billion under the Race to the Top programs competitive grants to support education reform and innovation in classrooms. They also noted that more than $10 billion in grant money would be available to states and districts driving reform. The centerpiece of the program is the $4.35 billion fund and the ensuing national competition designed to highlight and replicate effective education reform strategies in four significant areas:

1   Adopting internationally benchmarked standards and assessments that prepare students for success in college and the workplace;
2   Recruiting, developing, rewarding, and retaining effective teachers and principals;
3   Building data systems that measure student success and inform teachers and principals how they can improve their practices; and
4   Turning around the lowest-performing schools.

Tennessee and Delaware were selected as the first recipients of Race to the Top funding. Some authors have expressed surprise that Gulf states (e.g., Louisiana and Florida) were not selected (McNeil, 2010). Notwithstanding, it is reported that proposals from Tennessee and Delaware solidly project plans to impact every single child in the ways researchers have claimed were missing (Darling-Hammond, 2010; Brown et al., 2006). This plan therefore includes not only standards of elementary and secondary educational preparedness but post-secondary preparedness as well.

Postsecondary access policy and pipeline issues

Scholars have argued that The Higher Education Act (HEA; 1965) is perhaps the most important piece of education legislation than any that succeeded it (Brown et al., 2006). The HEA was formed by President Lyndon B. Johnson's 1964 War on Poverty statute with the rationale that greater educational attainment would break the cycle of poverty for low-income students and their families and was created to enable access to postsecondary education for all Americans, regardless of their income or family background. President Johnson (1967) noted during his commemorative address that no high school seniors anywhere in America could be denied access to any college or university because they were from a poor family. Subsequently, the Higher Education Act sought to (a) award scholarships up to $1,000 a year to students from disadvantaged backgrounds, (b) provide part-time jobs for students, and (c) provide interest-free, payment-free loans until graduation to worthy and capable students. Over time, affirmative action also became understood as a deliberate attempt to increase access—particularly among people of color. President Johnson's (1967) words illustrate well the significance of affirmative action policy:

> You do not wipe away the scars of centuries by saying: Now you are free to go where you want, and do as you desire, and choose the leaders you please. You do not take a person who, for years, had been hobbled by chains and liberate him, bring him up to the starting line of a race and then say, 'you are free to compete with all the others,' and still justly believe that you have been completely fair.

Since its inception, the use of affirmative action in college admission programs remained controversial, with recent Michigan cases providing fodder for this conversation. In both *Gratz* v. *Bollinger* (2001) and *Grutter* v. *Bollinger* (2001), plaintiffs contended that University of Michigan admissions programs violated both the Equal Protection Clause of the Fourteenth Amendment and Title VI of the Civil Rights Act of 1964. Respectively, White undergraduates were rejected by the University of Michigan College of Literature, Science, and the Arts and the University of Michigan Law School. In the *Gratz* ruling issued on February 26, 2001, the Southern Division of the Eastern District Court of Michigan found unconstitutional use of race in admissions by the University of Michigan. This same court provided a similar decision a month later in the *Grutter case,* ruling that the University of Michigan Law School's admissions program violated both the Fourteenth Amendment and Title VI of the Civil Rights Act. In addition, the court also issued an injunction barring the Law School from considering race in its admissions process. Although the University is appealing the *Grutter* case, diversity programs at the University of Michigan appear likely to end (Brown & Lane, 2003; Dancy, 2010).

Failed attempts of resolution in policy and practice subsequently mirror oppressive structures in society instead of leading the way in reconstructing realities of race, class, and education. As previous sections outline, the ways in which race, class, and their intersections play out in educational settings is the result of historical inheritance. Given this fact, the aftermath of Hurricane Katrina represented a disaster in which these inequalities became powerfully apparent. In the following section, we draw upon the knowledge in this chapter to outline critical lessons taught by the hurricane.

Learning from Hurricane Katrina: meditations on educational moments in time

Hurricane Katrina not only destroyed physical structures, but it also placed enhanced demands on local and state educational infrastructures in New Orleans. It is no surprise that the glaring majority of children displaced by the hurricane were of color (largely African American) and poor. As Gay (2007) argues, the level of racist victimization increases as socioeconomic status decreases. Thus, inequitable trends followed some of the nation's most vulnerable students.

One of these trends is at the intersection of education and geography. Zamani-Gallaher and Polite (2007) remind us that Hurricane Katrina forced another large migration of African Americans, not unlike the former great "migrations" in which large numbers of Africans Americans moved from their respective homelands in search of a better life. However, the significance of the Katrina-based migration was that the impact was educational in nature: approximately 38,000 students, mostly African American, were displaced. When these students entered new school settings, many met oppressive climates in new schools, which foster maladjustment and poor completion. Zamani-Gallaher and Polite (2007) also highlight emerging data which suggest that early childhood learners displaced by Katrina displayed poor school readiness coupled with instability in their respective living situations. This suggests that many families are still in flux and haven't quite "settled" down despite having lived in a particular area following the hurricane.

Second, the migration of students from Louisiana to other states created a systemic problem in education data collection and analysis. One way in which this problem is apparent is that data on students specifically displaced by Katrina is not disaggregated at the building, local, and state levels—meaning that the data is often reported in the aggregate. Given the limitations in data collection, most of the data of/about displaced students in receiving schools and districts are all but lost (Zamani-Gallaher & Polite, 2007)—making it difficult to track the long term performance of these students.

Zamani-Gallaher and Polite (2007) also report that trends describing African American students' transition to colleges and universities remained relatively unchanged and thus require focused attention on educational attainment of African American students. Notwithstanding, the three historically black colleges and universities (HBCUs) in New Orleans were more disparately affected in comparison to predominantly White institutions (PWIs). Many faculty members went unpaid, were temporarily released, or released without reinstatement. Reportedly, the American Association of University Professors (AAUP) data shows that over 25% of Southern University at New Orleans faculty and roughly 60% of Dillard University's full-time faculty was placed on furlough.

Meanwhile, Xavier University of Louisiana released 73 of 246 faculty members (Zamani-Gallaher & Polite, 2007).

Yet, opportunities in education are also clear in the aftermath of the hurricane. A starting point is to aggressively take steps individually and systemically to reduce the numbers of students of color with low academic achievement, low graduation rates, low employment, low wealth likelihood, and uncertain futures. Along these lines, Ladson-Billings (2007) writes:

> The tragedy of Katrina is not only what happened, but also that it is so quickly fading from our consciousness. We are now consumed with worsening news of the war in Iraq, an escalating gasoline and fuel-oil crisis, and massive job cuts at our major automobile manufacturers. The victims of Katrina have melted into the fabrics of cities like Houston, Atlanta, Los Angeles, and Memphis. We have moved on to new crises . . . The schools that are being reopened are unlikely to be those in the Lower Ninth Ward. (p. 19)

Gadsden and Fuhrman (2007) also point to a systemic reimagining for equity issues in educational districts experiencing recovery along the Gulf coast. More specifically, the authors locate change in the form of increased support from other states and localities, education specialists within and beyond academe, and a compassionate and charitable general public.

Smith and Williams-Boyd (2007) push for use of the hurricane as a moment to transform curriculum and pedagogy. As curriculum must shift and change to reflect societal demands, then disaster may inform curriculum and the teaching environment. Smith and Williams-Boyd argue that teaching needs to embrace a community perspective in the aftermath of the hurricane. This involves speaking directly about the experience, sharing stories, and challenging students to become change agents.

Socially reconstructing American education: implications for school leaders

The aftermath of Hurricane Katrina, and potentially any Gulf coast crisis, represents critical opportunities where we may courageously take firm steps toward socially reconstructing education. School leaders who demonstrate competence and proficiency in leading and serving culturally diverse populations are essential to the successful educational experiences and outcomes of all students. The following actions are required: (a) Studying historical and sociocultural contexts of school and campus communities, (b) Resisting cultural reproduction of educational inequality and inequity, (c) Interrogating systems of oppression, privilege, and entitlement, (d) Valuing experiences and perspectives of students of color, (e) Monitoring and mediating cultural conflict through cross-cultural communication, and (f) Identifying preparing, and supporting culturally proficient educational leaders.

201

Study Historical and Sociocultural Contexts of School and Campus Communities. Education leaders must have a keen awareness and understanding of the historical and sociocultural contexts of their school and campus communities if these leaders are to be successful. They must familiarize themselves with histories of discrimination, systems of oppression, and contemporary manifestations of marginalization, which may contribute to mistrust, skepticism, and cynicism by communities and cultural groups that may have been excluded or devalued by an institution and its leaders. This information can be gained through historical research and artifacts to include newspaper reports, governmental data, school, district, and university performance reports, and informal interviews that capture the experiential knowledge of people who have been marginalized, underserved, or silenced in a particular community. Addressing the challenges of the Gulf coast in the aftermath of Hurricane Katrina involves knowledge of demographic shifts and the myriad of cultural issues cited in this chapter that inform society and education about how groups think, know, act and react.

Resist Cultural Reproduction of Educational Inequality and Inequity. Educational leaders must be able to discern patterns of exclusion and segregation as perpetuated through administrative policies and practices and to analyze policies and practices with the intent of identifying those that continue to grant privilege and a sense of entitlement to one group while only offering disadvantage and limited access and opportunity to others. This work is critical in effectively recognizing and resisting the cultural reproduction of educational inequality and inequity in school organizations and throughout the education pipeline. Inequality and inequity are reproduced when education leaders fail to address diversity issues concerning decision making, allocation of resources, and power distribution (Dancy & Horsford, 2010). Thus, education leaders must be unafraid to speak about what matters. Accordingly, Smith and Boyd-Williams (2007) argue the following about teaching post-Katrina:

> As teacher educators, we do ourselves and our students a grave disservice
> if we sit complacently and acquiesce to the demands of the state while
> ignoring the needs of the greater social whole. It is no longer acceptable,
> nor was it ever for us to deny or silence the validity of the voice of the
> marginalized on the basis of our own privilege, one born out of a guise
> of elevated professional educational expertise. (p. 150)

Interrogate Systems of Oppression, Privilege, and Entitlement. Gay (2007) poignantly describes racism can and does play out in the educational lives of children post-Katrina:

> Operating on the assumption that the same instructional practices are
> equally effective for all students is a form of academic racism . . . No
> one should be surprised when it is revealed that the displaced children of

Katrina performed even lower in their new schools than the old. If that does happen it will not be the fault of students, but educational systems that did not modify curriculum, content, instruction, and support services to accommodate their . . . diversity. (p. 59)

Across colleges and universities, teacher preparation programs require the study of Whiteness as it impacts teacher and learner epistemology and teacher pedagogy, and we believe this practice should be extended to the field of educational leadership. The work of scholars like Giroux (1998), Marx and Pennington (2003), Delgado and Stefancic (1997), and Leonardo (2009) provide excellent starting points for familiarizing future educational leaders to research on White privilege and Whiteness studies.

Value Experiences and Perspectives of Students of Color. Leaders in educational settings must assume a similar understanding of culture as teachers. More specifically, they must understand how culture operates daily in the classroom, foster learning environments that value cultural and ethnic diversity, and understand how these environments inform student achievement. This knowledge is foundational in establishing a school or institutional culture and climate that advances student learning, engagement, and success. In the context of teaching and learning, Gay (2000) explains, "Opportunities must be provided for students from different ethnic backgrounds to have free personal and cultural expression so that their voices and experiences can be incorporated into teaching and learning processes on a regular basis" (p. 43). We agree, and believe that the experiences and perspectives of students of color should also be considered and embrace by educational leaders in their efforts to lead organizations that meaningfully educate and serve all students.

Monitor and Mediate Cultural Conflict through Cross-Cultural Communication. According to Tatum (1997), "we are confronted by the loss of civility in increasingly diverse communities" at the same time we are in desperate need of "balance, integrity, vision; a clear sense of collective responsibility and ethical leadership—in order to prepare our students for wise stewardship of their world and active participation in a democracy" (pp. 105–106). Our commitment to preparing students educationally along the P-20 pipeline requires school, college, and university leaders who can successfully monitor and mediate cultural conflict by modeling cross-cultural communication effectively and proficiently. Therefore, educational leaders and administrators must be trained and experienced in assuming the role of mediators in diverse contexts (Ryan, 2007) and able to navigate and negotiate opposing cultural perspectives and conflict through dialogue and mediation. These lessons can be learned and guided by the research on teachers and faculty as cultural mediators (Diamond & Moore, 1995; Gay, 2000). This work demonstrates how educators must provide opportunities for students to engage in critical dialogue about conflicts among cultures and analyze inconsistencies between mainstream cultural ideals/realities and those across cultures.

Just as teachers and faculty are required to do, educational administrators must assume the lead in clarifying cultural misunderstanding and fostering positive cross-cultural relationships. *Identify, Prepare, and Support Culturally Proficient Educational Leaders.* One way to engage the challenges presented by a history of discrimination, segregation, and oppression in U.S. education is to actively locate, hire, mentor, and promote culturally proficient leaders at every point along the P-20 educational pipeline. Schools should remember that, as organizations, heterogeneity and diverse perspectives often promote the creativity necessary to engaging a higher level of critical analysis and thoughtful solutions to complex problems (Dancy, 2010).

Toward a non-disastrous end: concluding thoughts

We argue here as we have argued elsewhere (Brown et al., 2006; Brown et al., 2007) that the federal government continues to operate in hypocrisy, commanding American children to endure the woes of disparate public education. Unfortunately, the national conglomeration of educational associations and affiliations has by and large conjoined in silence with the amorphous conclave of "privileged" parents whose children attend "good" schools. Education in the United States must be redefined and revamped to accommodate diverse student populations. Radical systemic change is required in order to move from the equality of educational outcomes demanded by the global economy.

We recall our observation (2007) that Hurricane Katrina did not simply tear the roofs from homes but it tore the roof off the American educational system to reveal glaring differences between school types, cultures, successes, failures, and national responses—all before a worldwide audience. The education of all students is more critical than ever. Students of color, like other students, must be sufficiently prepared to meet the challenges of an ever-evolving global society. Acknowledging and embracing the full ambitions of education on a massive and broad scale will enable educators to formulate a systemic remedy to the problems that hinder student success. If all students succeed, the world will prosper and benefit. Should our best efforts to improve the quality of schooling for all students fail, the future of the world in general and our nation in specific is woefully uncertain.

References

Alexander, K. L. (2004). Public schools and the public good. In J. H. Ballantine & J. Z. Spade (Eds.), *Schools and society: A sociological approach to education* (2nd ed., pp. 234–249). Belmont, CA: Thomson Wadsworth.

Anyon, J. (1981). Social class and school knowledge. *Curriculum Inquiry, 11*(1), 3–42.

Anyon, J. (1997), *Ghetto schooling: A political economy of urban educational reform.* New York, NY: Teachers College Press.

Apple, M. (1979/1990). *Ideology and curriculum.* New York, NY: Routledge.

Asher, N. (2007). Made in the (Multicultural) U.S.A.: Unpacking tensions of race, culture, gender, and sexuality in education. *Educational Researcher, 36*(2), 65–3.

Banks, J. A. (1995). The historical reconstruction of knowledge about race: Implications for transformative teaching. *Educational Researcher, 24*(2), 15–25.

Banks, J. A. (2002). Race, knowledge construction, and education in the USA: Lessons and history. *Race, Ethnicity and Education, 5*(1), 7–27.

Bourdieu, P., & Passeron, J. (1977). *Reproduction in education, society, and culture.* Beverly Hills, CA: Sage.

Bowles, S., & Gintis, H. (1976). *Schooling in capitalist America.* New York, NY: Basic Books.

Brown, M. C., & Bartee, R. (2007). *Still not equal: Expanding educational opportunity in society.* New York, NY: Peter Lang.

Brown, M. C., Dancy, T. E., & Davis, J. E. (2007). Drowning beneath the rising tide: Common plight of public schools, disadvantaged students, and African American males. In S. P. Robinson & M. C. Brown (Eds.), *The children Hurricane Katrina left behind: Schooling context, professional preparation, and community politics* (pp. 54–72). New York, NY: Peter Lang.

Brown, M. C., Dancy, T. E., & Norfles, N. (2006). A nation still at risk: No child left behind and the salvation of disadvantaged students. In F. Brown (Ed.), *No child left behind and other special programs and urban districts* (pp. 341–64). Oxford, England: Elsevier.

Brown, M. C., & Land, R. R. (2005). *The politics of curricular change: Race, hegemony and power in education.* New York, NY: Peter Lang.

Brown, M. C., & Lane, J. E. (2003). *Studying diverse institutions: Contexts, challenges and considerations.* San Francisco: Jossey-Bass.

Coleman, J. (1988), Social capital and the creation of human capital. *American Journal of Sociology, 94,* 95–120.

Coleman, J. S., Campbell, E. Q., Hobson, C. J., McPartland, J., Mood, A. M., Winfield, F. C., & York, R. L. (1966). *Equality of educational opportunity.* Washington, DC: Government Printing Office.

Coleman, J. S., & Hoffer, T. (1987). *Public and private high school: The impact of communities.* New York, NY: Basic Books.

Collins, R. (1971). Functional and conflict theories of educational stratification. *American Sociological Review. 36,* 1000–1019.

Dancy, T. E. (2010). When and where interests collide: Policy, research, and the case for managing diversity. In T. E. Dancy (Ed.), *Managing diversity: (Re)visioning equity on college campuses.* (pp. 71–95). New York, NY: Peter Lang.

Dancy, T. E. & Horsford, S. D. (2010). Leadership along the P-20 pipeline: Connecting schooling contexts and campus communities. In S. D. Horsford (Ed.), *New perspectives in educational leadership: Exploring social, political, and community contexts and meaning* (pp. 153–172). New York: Peter Lang.

Darling-Hammond, L. (2007). In S. P. Robinson & M. C. Brown (Eds.), *The children Hurricane Katrina left behind: Schooling context, professional preparation, and community politics* (pp. xi–xix). New York, NY: Peter Lang.

Darling-Hammond, L. (2010). *The flat world of education: How America's commitment to equity will determine our future.* New York, NY: Teachers College Press.

Delgado, R., & Stefancic, J. (1997). Imposition. In R. Delgado & J. Stefanic (Eds.), *Critical white studies: Looking behind the mirror.* Philadelphia, PA: Temple University Press.

Delpit, L. (2006). *Other people's children: Cultural conflict in the classroom.* New York, NY: New Press.

Dewan, S. (2006, June 1). For many, education is another storm victim. New *York Times,* 1–12.

Diamond, B. J., & Moore, M. A. (1995). *Multicultural literacy: Mirroring the reality of the classroom.* New York, NY: Longman.

DiMaggio, P. (1982). Cultural capital and school success: The impact of status culture participation on the grades of United States high school students. *American Sociological Review, 47,* 189–201.

Dimaggio, P., & Mohr, J. (1985). Cultural capital, educational attainment, and marital selection. *American Journal of Sociology, 90,* 1231–1261.

DuBois, W. E. B. (1903/2004). *The souls of black folk.* Boulder, CO: Paradigm

Fanon, F. (1963). *The wretched of the earth.* New York, NY: Grove.

Ferguson, R. F. (1991). Paying for public education: New evidence on how and why money matters. *Harvard Journal on Legislation, 28*(2), 465–498.

Freeman, K. (2007). Crossing the waters: Katrina and the other great migration lessons for African American K-12 students' education. In S. P. Robinson & M. C. Brown (Eds.), *The children Hurricane Katrina left behind: Schooling context, professional preparation, and community politics* (pp. 3–13). New York, NY: Peter Lang.

Freire, P. (1982). *Pedagogy of the oppressed.* New York, NY: Continuum.

Gadsden, V. L., & Fuhrman, S. (2007). Reflections on educational equity in post-Katrina New Orleans. In S. P. Robinson & M. C. Brown II (Eds.), *The children Hurricane Katrina left behind* (pp. 73–85). New York, NY: Peter Lang.

Gandara, P., Larson, K., Rumberger, R., & Mehan, H. (1998, May). *Capturing Latino students in the academic pipeline.* California Policy Seminar Brief Series. Retrieved from http://www.ucop.edu/cprc/pipeline.html

Gans, H. (2010). Race as class. In M. L. Andersen & P. H. Collins (Eds.), *Race, class, and gender: An anthology* (pp. 108–114). Belmont, CA: Wadsworth.

Gay, G. (2000). *Culturally responsive teaching: Theory, research, and practice.* New York, NY: Teachers College Press.

Gay, G. (2007). Teaching children of catastrophe. *Multicultural education, 15*(2), 55–61.

Giroux, H. A. (1998). Critical pedagogy as performative practice: Memories of whiteness. In C. A. Torres & T. R. Mitchell (Eds.), *Sociology of education: Emerging perspectives.* New York, NY: SUNY Press.

Gramsci, A. (1971). *Selections from the prison notebooks* (Q. Hoare & G. Nowell-Smith, Trans.). New York, NY: International Press.

Grant, C. A., & Sleeter, C. E. (2006). *Turning on learning: Five approaches for multicultural teaching plans for race, class, gender, and disability* (4th ed.). Hoboken, NJ: Wiley.

Gratz v. Bollinger, 135 F. Supp. 2d 790 (E. D. Mich, 2001).

Grutter v. Bollinger, 137 F. Supp. 2d 821 (E. D. Mich, 2001), appealed, 247 F.3d 631 (6th Cir. 2001).

Higher Education Act of 1965, Section 401(a)(2) of P.L. 105–244(112 Stat. 1650).

Howard, T. C. (2010). *Why race and culture matter in schools: Closing the achievement gap in America's classrooms.* New York, NY: Teachers College Press.

Johnson, L. B. (1967). To fulfill these rights, Commencement address at Howard University, June 4, 1965. In J. H. Franklin & I. S. Franklin (Eds.), *The Negro in 20th century America.* New York: Vintage Books, 225–231.

Ladson-Billings, G. (2007). Now they are wet: Hurricane Katrina as a metaphor for social and educational neglect. In S. P. Robinson & M. C. Brown (Eds.), *The children Hurricane Katrina left behind: Schooling context, professional preparation, and community politics* (pp. 14–20). New York, NY: Peter Lang.

Ladson-Billings, G. (1994). *The dreamkeepers: Successful teachers of African American children.* San Francisco, CA: Jossey-Bass.

Lareau, A. (2000). *Home advantage* (2nd ed.) Lanham, MD: Rowman & Littlefield.

Legters, N. E., Balfauz, R, Jordan, W. J., and McPart-land, J. M. (2004). Comprehensive reform for urban high schools. In J. H. Ballantine & J. Z. Spade (Eds.), *Schools and society: A sociological approach to education* (2nd ed., pp. 220–227). Belmont, CA: Thomson Wadsworth.

Leonardo, Z. (2004). The unhappy marriage between Marxism and race critique: Political economy and the production of knowledge. *Policy futures in education, 2*(3&4), 483–493.

Leonardo, Z. (2009). *Race, whiteness, and education.* New York, NY: Routledge.

Macleod, J. (2005). *Ain't no makin it: Aspirations and attainment in a low-income neighborhood.* Oxford, England: Westview Press.

Marx, S., & Pennington, J. (2003). Pedagogies of critical race theory: Experimentations with white preservice teachers, *Qualitative Studies in Education, 16*(1), 91–110.

McNeil, M. (2010). Edujobs or race to top: What's worth more to states? Education Week. Retrieved July 21, 2011, from http://blogs.edweek.org/edweek/campaign-k-12/2010/07/edujobs_or_ race_to_top_whats_w.html

McWhorter, J. H. (2000). *Losing the race: Self-sabotage in Black America.* New York, NY: Free Press.

Mills, C. (1997). *The racial contract.* Ithaca, NY: Cornell University Press.

Mitchell, R., & Edwards, K. (2010). Power, privilege, and pedagogy: Collegiate classrooms as sites to learn racial equality. In T. E. Dancy (Ed.), *Managing diversity: (Re) visioning equity on college campuses* (pp. 45–70), New York, NY: Peter Lang.

Morris, J. E. (2008). *Troubling the waters: Fulfilling the promise of quality public schooling for black children.* New York, NY: Teachers College Press.

Moses, M. S. (2002). *Embracing race: Why we need race-conscious policy.* New York, NY: Teachers College Press.

Murillo, E. G., Villenas, S. A., Galvan, R. T., Munoz, J. S., Martinez, C., & Macado-Casas, M. (2010). *The handbook of Latinos and education: Theory, research, and practice.* New York, NY: Routledge.

National Center for Education Statistics (NCES). (2003). *The condition of education 2003.* Washington, DC: U.S. Department of Education.

National Center for Education Statistics (NCES). (2007). *The condition of education 2007.* Washington, DC: U.S. Department of Education.

National Commission on Excellence in Education. (1983). *A Nation at Risk.* Retrieved February 1, 2006, from http://www.ed.gov/pubs/NatAtRisk/index.html

Nieto, S. (2004). *Affirming diversity: The sociopolitical context of multicultural education* (4th ed.). Boston, MA: Pearson Education.

Noguera, P., & Wing, J. Y. (2006). *Unfinished business: Closing the racial achievement gap in our schools.* San Francisco, CA: Jossey-Bass.

Oakes, J. (1982). Classroom social relationships: Exploring the Bowles and Gintis hypothesis. *Sociology of Education, 55*(4), 197–212.

Oliver, M., & Shapiro, T. (1996). *Black wealth/white wealth: A new perspective on racial equality.* New York, NY: Routledge.

Omi, M., & Winant, H. (1989). *Racial formation in the United States: From the 1960s to the 1980s.* New York, NY: Routledge.

Raftery, A. E., & Hout, M. (1993). Maximally maintained inequality: Expansion, reform, and opportunity in irish education, 1921–1975. *Sociology of Education. 66*, 22–39.

Robinson, S. P., & Brown, M. C. (2007). *The children Hurricane Katrina left behind: Schooling context, professional preparation, and community politics.* New York, NY: Peter Lang.

Rolòn-Dow, R. (2005). Critical care: A color(ful) analysis of care narratives in the schooling experiences of Puerto Rican girls. *American Educational Research Journal, 42*(1), 77–111.

Solorzano, D. G., & Villalpando, O. (1998). Critical race theory, marginality, and experience of students of color in higher education. In C. A, Torres & T. R. Mitchell (Eds.), *The sociology of education: Emerging perspectives* (pp. 181–209). Albany, NY: SUNY Press.

Smith, P. K., & Williams-Boyd, P. (2007). For they are us: "Tools" for a post-Katrina curriculum and community. In S. P. Robinson & M. C. Brown (Eds.), *The children Hurricane Katrina left behind: Schooling context, professional preparation, and community politics* (pp. 141–151). New York, NY: Peter Lang.

Solorzano, D. G., & Yosso, T. J. (2000). Critical race theory, LatCrit theory and method: Counterstorytelling Chicana and Chicano graduate school experiences. *International Journal of Qualitative Studies in Education, 14*(4), 471–495.

Steele, S. (1990). *The content of our character: A new vision of race in America.* New York, NY: St. Martin's Press.

Swail, W. S., Cabrera, A. F., & Lee, C. (2004). *Latino youth and the pathway to college.* Washington, DC: Pew Hispanic Center.

Tatum, B. D. (1997). *Why are all the Black kids sitting together in the cafeteria? And other conversations about race.* New York, NY: Basic Books.

Thernstrom, A., & Thernstrom, S. (2003). No excuses: Closing the racial gap in learning. In J. E. Morris (Ed.), *Troubling the waters: Fulfilling the promise of quality public schooling for Black children.* New York, NY: Teachers College Press.

U.S. Census Bureau. (2004, July). *Current population survey 2004 annual social and economic supplement.* Retrieved from http://pubdb3.census.gov/macro/032004/pov/new46_100125_03.htm

U.S. Census Bureau. (2007). American fact finder. Retrieved from http://www.census.gov/

U.S. Census Bureau. (2010). *Current population survey, 2010 annual social and economic supplement. Poverty status by state, 2009.* Retrieved from http://www.census.gov/hhes/www/cpstables/032010/pov/new46_100125_01.htm

U.S. Department of Education. (2004). Executive summary of the No Child Left Behind Act of 2001.

Useem, E. L. (1992). Middle schools and math groups: Parents' involvement in children's placement. *Sociology of Education, 65,* 263–279.

Weis, L., & Fine, M. (2000). *Construction sites: Excavating race, class, and gender among urban youth.* New York, NY: Teachers College Press.

Willie, C., Garibaldi, A., & Reed, W (1991). *The education of African Americans.* Westport, CT: Auburn House.

Wilson, W. J. (2009). *More than just race: Being black and poor in the inner city.* New York, NY: W.W. Norton & Company.

Zamani-Gallaher, E. M., & Polite, V. C. (2007). Still waters run deep: Cracks in the educational pipeline for African American students post-hurricane Katrina. In S. P. Robinson & M. C. Brown (Eds.), *The children Hurricane Katrina left behind: Schooling context, professional preparation, and community politics* (pp. 40–53). New York, NY: Peter Lang.

Part 8

RACE, GENDER AND SEXUALITY

31

SPACES AND PLACES OF BLACK EDUCATIONAL DESIRE

Rethinking black supplementary schools as a new social movement

Heidi Safia Mirza and Diane Reay

Source: *Sociology*, 34, 3, 2000, 521–544.

Abstract

Black supplementary schools, as organic grassroots organisations, are not simply a response to mainstream educational exclusion and poor provision, as they are so often described. They are far more radical and subversive than their quiet conformist exterior, indicating the presence of a covert social movement for educational change. In our small-scale, exploratory study of four black supplementary schools, we attempt to uncover their subjugated knowledges and hidden histories in order to illustrate the ways in which they generate Mueller's 'oppositional meanings'. The narratives of the black women educators consistently decentre assumptions of mainstream schooling, as well as providing evidence of thriving black communities, social capital and complex, contradictory pedagogies within which childcentredness remains an important component. Supplementary schools provide a context in which whiteness is displaced as central and blackness is seen as normative. We conclude by arguing that, through their strategies of reworking notions of both community and blackness, their creation of new 'types' of professional intellectuals and their commitment to social transformation, black supplementary schools represent the genesis of a new gendered social movement.

The 'desire' for education is a consuming passion among the African Caribbean, black British community. Evidence of educational urgency within the black community can be mapped at every stage of the educational process. Many, especially women, migrated from the Caribbean to the United Kingdom to give their children the opportunity to do well at school (Foner 1979; Bryan *et al* 1985; Mirza 1992). Black British pupils, in particular the boys, have some of the highest rates of school attendance (Sewell 1997). Many, especially the girls, achieve relatively well compared to their white working-class peers in the same schools (Mirza 1992; Mirza 1997a). Ultimately, black students are present in greater numbers in proportion to their population than their white peers in post-compulsory schooling, further education and university (Modood 1998).

Excluded from an equal place in the educational system by white fear and racism, the black community is quietly engaged in a range of collective educational strategies which fulfil their desire for educational success. In these hidden spaces of educational desire we can find the black community organising conferences and forums around special educational issues, such as school exclusions and 'underachievement'. We find them engaged in vigorous one-off campaigns around school closure. Self-help organisations such as advice centres and parent-run advice groups spring up in response to black parental concerns and anxieties (Vincent and Warren 1999). We even find groups organising around returning to the Caribbean to seek better education opportunities for their children. But the most sustained of all the strategies is the ever growing area of community based supplementary education.

Set up by and for the black community, black supplementary schools are for the most part self-funding, organic grassroots organisations. These schools, which are mainly run by women, have a history that reaches back into the 1950s, ever since the first wave of post-war black migrants arrived and settled in Britain (Reay and Mirza 1997). They are primarily small concerns run after school, on Saturdays or Sundays. They are mainly, though not exclusively for school pupils aged 5–16 years. Though some schools could have as few as five pupils, the average school catered for thirty to forty pupils. However, popular schools could have as many as ninety pupils. There are no official records or national surveys of such schools. We attempted to build up a local database of black supplementary schools by concentrating on the several London boroughs where 58.7 per cent (300,000) of the African Caribbean population in the United Kingdom are known to live. As little or no 'official' information is available on these schools, personal and social networks, 'word of mouth' and tracing advertisements in the black community press were the source of our information. In our limited short-term research we found sixty black supplementary schools across fifteen boroughs in the Inner London and Greater London area. In Lambeth, one of the London Boroughs where black people make up almost 30 per cent of the population we found twelve such schools. By the end of the study we were hearing of more and more schools through word of mouth and personal and social networks.

However, this small-scale study of African-Caribbean supplementary schooling focused on just four of the schools, three London-based schools, Colibri, Community Connections and Ohemaa and one in a provincial city, Scarlet Ibis.[1] To gather qualitative data we carried out participant observation in two of the schools and conducted in-depth interviews with seven black educators involved

212

in running the schools, six women and one man. A repeat interview has recently been conducted with one of the female black educators. In addition, eight mothers whose children attended two of the supplementary schools were interviewed.

Although all four schools saw their clientele as primarily African-Caribbean this did not mean that the schools were mono-cultural in terms of their ethnic composition. As one of the black educators pointed out, the schools were culturally diverse in their intake. Only one school saw including white pupils as an acceptable part of their remit, but all accepted African and mixed-race students and one had a small number of Asian pupils attending.

Our findings, arising as they do out of a very small-scale investigation based on sixteen qualitative interviews and three days of participant observation, are necessarily exploratory and tentative. However, we hope to indicate through our data that black supplementary schools, despite their quiet conformist exterior, contain elements that are both radical and subversive, providing evidence of a covert social movement for educational change.

A different new social movement?
Black supplementary schooling

In this analysis of black supplementary schools our intention is to develop understandings of new social movements within the context of race and gender. In doing so we argue for a very different vision of new social movements from prevailing orthodoxies which give primacy either to class action or, as in those within the small corpus of work on racialised new social movements, male identity.

With regard to the former orthodoxy, most sociology of new social movements in the United States and Europe has concentrated on their class-based nature (Maheu 1995; Castells 1983). Paul Bagguley argues that there is no British sociology of social movements, either because they are deemed not to exist or because they are so insignificant that they do not warrant serious sociological attention (Bagguley 1997:152). Within the small body of work that does exist, the primary focus has either been on the labour market or else has been preoccupied with the activities of the new middle classes (Parkin 1968; Cotgrove and Duff 1981; Day and Robbins 1987). Similarly, Jennifer Somerville in her analysis of women's movements argues that new social movement theory traditionally privileges socioeconomic location and the concept of interests that underlie them (Sommerville 1997). She suggests an adequate analysis of women's new social movements needs to shift attention away from looking at predisposing factors, such as socio-economic deprivation to looking at the construction of interests within the organisational structure of the movement itself, and within public policy and public culture in general.

Our focus on black female-centred collective action rejects rational choice theory in which understandings of collective action were originally embedded (Olson 1965). Here individuals were seen as atomised, self-maximising agents who will not contribute towards collective efforts to realise social profits if they can achieve such profits without participating. The later development of resource mobilisation theory sees individuals as mobilising for similar reasons, resisting within institutional contexts in order to challenge what they deem to be oppressive policies. Both domination and social movement activity to resist that domination revolve around institutional recognition and ultimately social inclusion (McCarty and Zald 1977).

Traditionally, the sociology of new social movements has been primarily concerned with the potential of groups to initiate social transformation. Stacey Young (1997) uses the term 'new social movements' to denote 'activity aimed at transferring large-scale power imbalances' (p. 226). Within this broad category she includes providing education and services to counteract the effects of oppression and discrimination. However, education as a site for collective lay action is often overlooked in the literature on new social movements (Vincent and Warren 1999). Yet as Signithia Fordham (1996) has eloquently written, the desire for education is a driving force among oppressed groups who, 'avenge the dehumanisation of their black ancestors by appropriating and inverting the myth of (black) intellectual inferiority' (p. 329). For a black person to become educated is, therefore, to become 'human'. Fanon writes that 'nothing is more astonishing than to hear a black (wo)man express (her)him self properly, for then (s)he is putting on the white world'(Fanon 1993:36). Education in this sense is not simply about the process of learning, teaching or schooling, it is about 'refutation' – education is a political act (Casey 1993:124). As black feminists Bryan, Dadzie and Scafe explain 'education is central to our political development' (1985:59).

The more recent new social movement theory opens up positive avenues for rethinking covert educational black female collective action. Here, in the postmodern reworking of new social movements, the construction of identity and subjectivity at both the collective and individual level is a primary focus. In particular, collective identity is seen to be constructed through and by social movements in processes of negotiation and affirmation designed to counter the negative impact of oppression on the basis of those identities. New social movements are seen to be much more interested in the production of symbolic action and cultural conflict than their own material reproduction (Melucci 1988; 1994; 1995). The mere existence of a symbolic challenge is in itself a method of unmasking dominant codes. Thus the concept of new social movements is centrally concerned with the 'generation of oppositional meanings' (Mueller 1992). As Eyerman and Jamieson (1991:161) argue:

> The forms of consciousness that are articulated in social movements provide something crucial in the constitution of modern societies: public spaces for thinking new thoughts, activating new actors, generating new ideas, in short, constructing new intellectual 'projects'.

While 'race' has been invisible in the new social movement theory on class, black female agency has remained largely invisible within the field of 'race'

214

and social movements (cf. Gilroy 1987; Omi and Winant 1994). In the writing on 'race', the assumption has been that the struggle against racist exclusion is contested and fought over in the masculine arena of the streets (Gilroy 1987; Solomos and Back 1995; Keith 1995). Thus, while the literature on 'race' presents us with a gendered picture, it is one wholly preoccupied with the young males. In this masculinised discourse of race and social change, what becomes publicly acknowledged as new social movements are those collectivities in which action and agency are highly visible and always accompanied by overt acts for clamour and recognition. As one of us has argued in an earlier article (Mirza 1997a:272):

> Urban social movements, we are told, mobilise in protest, riots, local politics and community organisations. We are told that it is their action, and not the subversive, covert action of women that gives rise to so-called 'neo-populist, liberatory, authentic politics' (Gilroy 1987:245). This is the masculinist version of radical social change; visible, radical, confrontational, collective action, powerfully expressed in the politics of the inner city, where class consciousness evolves in response to urban struggle.

However, as we illustrate in this paper through the work of women in black supplementary schools, there are ways of attempting to transform structure through agency other than visible clashes in the street. The low-profile industriousness of the women in our study raises questions around visibility: what is noticed and by whom. For the women in this study publicity is a low priority. They are often too busy working at a grassroots level to seek to capture the public eye. Rather, they are part of submerged networks operating beyond public scrutiny to articulate identities and agendas (Melucci 1994; Mueller 1992). In generating oppositional meanings the women produce 'alternative frameworks of sense' (Melucci 1988:248). For example, the discursive constructions of community and blackness within these schools contribute to the formation of collective black identities which work against the hegemony of whiteness and individualism within wider society. Such 'alternative frameworks' create new sites of conflict which symbolically challenge the dominant codes upon which social relationships are 'normatively' founded.

Black female social action occupies a theoretical blind spot. Black supplementary schools which are gendered, raced, classed and located within the terrain of education are thus invisible as sites of racial social change in the literature on new social movements. Similarly black women educators are marginal in research on black supplementary schooling. Yet the black women educators in our study were putting enormous amounts of energy into attempts to create oppositional meaning and facilitate social transformation. In the following three sections of the paper we examine three key discursive arenas of black female collective social action: community building, visions of blackness and radical pedagogic practice.

Reinvoking traditional conceptions of community
in an age of communitarianism

Issues of gender have frequently been overlooked in those few studies which do research black supplementary schooling (cf. Chevannes and Reeves 1987; Dove 1993). In one study that acknowledges the role of women, gender still remains submerged in an analysis that privileges the racial dynamics of black supplementary schools (Mac an Ghaill 1991). However, our finding that running black supplementary schools was primarily women's work is supported by a growing body of research both here and in the United States which asserts that children's education is predominantly the concern and responsibility of mothers (Smith 1988; Griffith and Smith 1990; Lareau 1989; David 1993; Reay 1995; Luttrell 1997). Often, as in this study, collective black agency is generated through the efforts of particular women (Sudbury 1998:87):

> The translation of common experience into collective action requires some additional impetus. That impetus frequently comes from one or more pioneer women. These women have a catalytic impact on the women in a given community or locality and begin the process of awareness raising and mobilisation.

The six black women educators whose in-depth interviews form the main data for this study had been involved in supplementary schooling for periods ranging from four to sixteen years. They had often started out as a member of a small group of black parents, talking in terms of themselves 'and a few other mothers getting together'. As Charity points out:

> It's mainly women who are the ones who are involved in education in this country. Within the Afro-Caribbean community it tends to be mainly women. In my family that was the case and at Colibri it was mainly women who came and that was fine. Obviously, there were a few fathers who were involved and there were a couple of men on the committee, but it was mainly women.

Charity's narrative not only highlights the key contribution of women it also presents a very different version of urban black community to those endemic in popular media and political discourses:

> The school started off in someone's front room on Saturday mornings. The parents were doing all the teaching themselves to start with and it was very much focused on what was their main concern: their children not being able to read and write properly. Then these parents found the group of children grew from ten to fifteen and soon it was twenty and at this point it was unmanageable running a Saturday school in someone's front room, so they petitioned the council for accommodation and finally

got one of the council's derelict properties. They spent their spare time shovelling rubbish out of the room, tramps had been living there, doing building, repair work, getting groups of parents together to decorate. They pulled together and did all this work themselves, used the expertise they had to get the school on its feet and it was mainly the women organising things, making sure it got done.

As Charity's words indicate, these four black supplementary schools generate rich opportunities for contesting prevalent discourses about contemporary urban communities. There is none of the apathy, recalcitrance, fecklessness and aggression which permeate both popular and political discourses. Dominant discourses of the urban working class, both black and white, paint pictures of apathetic masses, inactive and uninformed. Once named 'the underclass' by the socially and politically privileged, and now renamed the 'socially excluded' by the New Labour elite, these urban communities have been ritually pathologised as disengaged, disadvantaged and inherent underachievers (SEU1998). Charity tells a very different story: one of effective agency. The agency she speaks of is not the individualised agency of the white middle classes (Jordan *et al.* 1994; Reay 1998a), but rather a collectivised agency grounded in communal responses to a mainstream educational system which is perceived to be failing black children. In her narrative we hear commitment, reciprocity and continuity.

Verna's text also speaks of community: a community grounded in her own labour:

I really wanted to do Saturday school because so much was given to me when I was a child. I had so much positive input I wanted to give some of it back. I also wanted to challenge this Government's views on community – that community isn't important. Not that I'm interested in politics. I keep my head down. My work is on the ground with children, doing my bit here and it has been rewarding, very rewarding. Children have gone through the school that others have given up on and they are doing very well.

Verna is not 'interested in politics', rather her focus is intensive work 'on the ground with children'. She is engaged in, dare we say, a variant of motherwork (Hill Collins 1994), but one, despite her protestations, that ultimately has a political edge. Community as a concept may be out of favour within academic circles (cf. Young 1990), but all the women used the term extensively in their narratives as something they were not simply a part of but were also actively engaged in constructing through their work as educators. As Rose stated emphatically, 'An important part of Saturday school is about creating community. That's part of what we're here for.'

In order to make sense of the enormous chasm between popular and elite prejudices in relation to urban communities and the actual practices going on within them we need to inject a gendered analysis (see also Burlet and Reid 1998). So many successful communities across all fields of society are founded on women's invisible unpaid labour despite the high profile of *male* leaders. In her exemplary work on 'reading the community' Valerie Hey differentiates between male strategies of commandeering social resources and female strategies of constructing social capital in order to develop effective community links (Hey 1998). The black women educators had minimal possibilities of commandeering social resources. Rather, they all worked incredibly hard to generate a sense of community and develop social capital out of friends and neighbour social relationships. As Hey succinctly puts it 'There are at least two versions of community – his and hers' (Hey 1998:2) and these four Saturday schools were all built on 'her version'.

Similarly Patricia Hill Collins makes a case for appreciating the specific nature of black female 'community connectedness'. She suggests we should rearticulate black women's experiences with Afrocentric feminist thought in order to challenge prevailing definitions of community. She writes (1990:223):

> The definition of community implicit in the market model sees community as arbitrary and fragile, structured fundamentally by competition and domination. In contrast, Afrocentric models stress connections, caring, and personal accountability . . . Denied access to the podium, black women have been unable to spend time theorising about alternative conceptualisations of community. Instead through daily actions African American women have created alternative communities that empower.

Patricia Hill Collins shows that through re-conceptualising the work of mothers, women educators, church and union leaders, community power is not about domination as in the Eurocentric perspective, but about energy which is fostered by creative acts of resistance. Bourdieu has developed the concept of social capital which illuminates this point of gendered community participation. For Bourdieu social capital is the aggregate of all the contacts and group memberships which, through the accumulation of exchanges, obligations and shared identities, provide actual or potential support and access to valued resources (Bourdieu 1986). Social capital is underpinned by practices of sociability which require specific skills and dispositions. However, we suggest that there are gender implications which Bourdieu ignores but which would point to a connection between social capital and Helga Nowotny's concept of emotional capital.

Nowotny develops the concept of emotional capital which she defines as 'knowledge, contacts and relations as well as the emotionally valued skills and assets, which hold within any social network characterised at least partly by affective ties' (Nowotny 1981:148). As Virginia Morrow points out 'this concept should alert us to the invisibility of women's work in creating and sustaining social networks and hence social capital' (Morrow 1999:10). The black women through their involvement in supplementary schooling were producing resources to compensate for perceived deficits in state educational provision and thereby enhancing the black community's stock of both social and cultural capital.

All six women were extensively involved in the wider black community, as well as the community they saw themselves as actively constructing through black supplementary schooling. They were all facilitating black parents' groups and working with local black arts and business collectives. Two of the women were involved in national black women's networks. The social capital generated through such contacts was fed back into the schools benefiting the pupils in a variety of ways – through additional funding, sponsorship and curriculum enhancement. For example in Scarlet Ibis a local black business had paid for computing equipment, while members of the black arts collective had volunteered their services and provided sessions on pottery making, set design and printing.

There are a variety of competing tensions within representations of black supplementary schools as forms of private sector schooling and evidence of black enterprise. They can be depicted as autonomous self-sufficient organisations; part of a vibrant growing largely unacknowledged black enterprise culture which spans commerce, the voluntary sector and the fields of arts and education. Aligned with such understandings of black supplementary schools are views of them as predominantly community self-help projects. Such representations coalesce around new right and, increasingly, New Labour emphases on enterprise and local initiatives. Yet at the same time, there are other images which cut across and powerfully contradict such representations, in particular, black supplementary schooling's association with the political left's project of anti-racism and the rediscovery of marginalised groups' histories.

The desire to maintain a black social reality also meant that the schools were tentative about accepting public funding. As a number of the black women educators pointed out becoming high profile, especially in relation to the local education authority (LEA) was often problematic. It could lead to the locus of control shifting from the school to the LEA. As a consequence two of the schools deliberately avoided LEA funding, opting to finance schools through parental contributions and private fund-raising. They did not want to sacrifice activism for funding (see Sudbury 1998:82–3). But whether they were publicly or privately funded all the women in the study were still engaged in community and political activism. They exemplified a frequently invisible gendered black agency which spoke primarily to a black audience, but also sought at times to engage with mainstream white educational processes (Sudbury 1998).

In addition to extensive links within and beyond the immediate community, the women were firmly rooted in the localities their supplementary schools served. Both Rose and Verna lived on the large sprawling council estate where Scarlet Ibis was situated, while Charity, Nadine and Maxine all lived with walking distance of the schools they helped to run. The women's narratives, with their emphases on material notions of community grounded in a specific geographical locale, render problematic new notions of 'community' in which the developing agenda of communitarianism has detached understandings of community from its grassroots connotations (Reay 1998c). In this new notion of community the association of community with groups of working-class workers has been prised apart and into the gap has been inserted a 1990s view of communities as diasporic collectivities of individuals who share one or maybe two or three characteristics in common (Etzioni 1993). It is important not to overlook the work of regulation and governance such changes achieve. As Hennessy (1993:104) puts it:

> One of the ways the discourse of the new works to maintain the symbolic order is through a strategy of transference. Under pressure from over-determined shifts in the social formation, modes of thinking and desiring which had been thoroughly sanctioned in one ideological formation become inadequate to the reproduction of social subjects in another.

As a result, the circulation of new modes of thinking and desiring in the social imaginary must be publicly inhibited and repressed. Community in the sense of any 'true' sense of collectivity has been discursively reworked to fit the competitive individualism of the 1990s. Through the 'third way' rhetoric of self-help, choice, and individual and family responsibility, community has been remodelled and appropriated by the intellectual elite and white middle classes (cf. Hargreaves and Christie 1998). It is an ironic reversal of 'community' which obscures the unspoken self-interested individualism that has always accompanied middle-class activities (Jordan *et al.* 1994) and renders any understandings of middle-class community paradoxical. The classic ethnography of a working-class English community (Young and Willmott 1957:113) described Bethnal Green in the 1950s as:

> a community which has some sense of being one. There is a sense of community that is a feeling of solidarity between people who occupy the common territory which springs from the fact that people and their families have lived there a long time.

The associations implicit in Young and Willmott's work – of family, kinship, rootedness, localism and collectivity – are no longer apparent in contemporary understandings of community. Community in the Young and Willmott sense is perceived to have disappeared. Yet, paradoxically it is in 1990s Bethnal Green that we actually do have a community in the Young and Willmott mould. The difference is that this community is no longer a white working-class one but a new urban Bengali working-class one.

We argue that similar notions of working-class community are to be found in the discourses of both black women educators and of parents whose children attend supplementary schools. The use of community in the discourses of these black women educators operates as a challenge to the consumerist individualism of the late 1990s communitarianism. Ferree has argued that women, working-class people and black groups in society are especially likely to reject competitive individualism as a feasible value, instead emphasising the construction and maintenance of viable networks of relationships (Ferree 1992:37).

The sense of community engendered through these black women's activities, embracing as it does an interdependency of the individual and the necessity of the communal, is very different to the sterility of academic injunctions of communitarianism. It is also a gendered form of black activism quietly taken up by women that sharply contrasts with the far more high profile agitations valorised by black male activism. However, we would argue black female activism shares neither the inherent ephemerality usually attributed to the former nor the self-defeating qualities often assumed of the latter. Iris Marion Young warns against the tendency to ascribe essentialist male and female ways of working to notions of community and individualism respectively. She argues (1990:306–7) that modern political theory and bourgeois culture identify

> masculinity with values associated with individualism – self-sufficiency, competition, separation and the formal equality of rights. The culture identifies femininity, on the other hand, with the values associated with community – affective relations of care, mutual aid, and cooperation . . . Asserting the value of community over individualism, the feminine over the masculine . . . does have some critical force with respect to dominant ideology and social relations . . . [But] merely revising their valuation does not constitute a genuine alternative to capitalist patriarchal society.

Black supplementary schools paradoxically embody elements of both masculine individualism and feminine co-operation. Within a wider social context in which British consciousness, whether black or white, is currently preoccupied with individualism, black supplementary schools are simultaneously places of collectivity at the same time as they focus on individual achievement. hooks discusses the trend in the United States for black people to buy into liberal individualism and cease to see their fate as in any way linked to a collective fate (hooks 1995). Similar discursive shifts are happening in Britain across racial divisions and within all sectors of society. According to Shotter (1993), processes of postmaterialism are breaking down traditionally homogeneous notions of culture and identity, allowing individuals to free themselves from the constraints of religion, class and traditional community bonds. However, the ability to surrender the familiarity of the (national, ethnic, religious) community in favour of unknown, individualistic autonomy appears to be the preserve of the few. It is these few, for example, web surfers and nomadic academics, who are used to justify postmodern explanations of the obsolescence of traditional means of social organisation. Yet, contrary to the fragmenting forces of postmodernity, in black supplementary schooling a traditional means of organising the community (Johnson 1979) can be seen to be flourishing. It would seem that: 'In spite of postmodernism, little has changed for the majority of black women, globally and nationally. For them power is not diffuse, localised and particular. Power is as centralised and secure as it has always been, excluding, defining and self-legitimating' (Mirza 1997b:20).

At a historical juncture when there is little actual educational collegiality, in spite of its pre-eminence in contemporary managerial rhetoric and the frequent use of the term as window dressing in institutional brochures (Gewirtz *et al.* 1995; Reay 1998b), black supplementary schools offer a very different educational vision. This is not to deny that black supplementary schools are not heavily contested and contradictory spaces. They are, and we discuss some aspects of contestation later. Rather, embedded in the extremely complex and contradictory culture and social positioning of black supplementary schools lies paradoxically one of the few challenges to individualism and free markets within the field of education. Black supplementary schools such as Scarlet Ibis and Community Connections operate as sites for what Mueller (1992) argues is a central component of new social movements 'the generation of oppositional meanings' in relation to a wide range of hegemonic social and educational values.

We have in this section discussed black supplementary schools' reinscription and revitalisation of traditional notions of community. Below we focus on two further challenges; firstly, the black supplementary schools' valorisation of blackness and contestation of whiteness as normative and, secondly, their disruption of prevailing views of correct pedagogy which pathologise child centredness.

Spaces of blackness: contesting whiteness as normative

White bias is everywhere in education, everywhere except in Saturday school, that is.

Brenda

Nancy Fraser writes about 'hidden' public spheres which have always existed, including women's voluntary associations and working-class organisations. In earlier work (Reay and Mirza 1997) we have argued that there are commonalities between black supplementary schools and the socialist Sunday schools at the turn of the century. Both constitute 'counter-publics'. Whereas the socialist Sunday schools struggled to produce working-class discourses to counter hegemonic middle-class views on education, black groups in society have repeatedly found it necessary within a wider social context of white hegemony to form 'subaltern counter-publics': 'in order to signal that they are parallel discursive arenas where members of subordinated social groups invent and circulate counterdiscourses, which in turn permit them to formulate oppositional interpretations of their identities, interests and needs' (Fraser 1994:84).

As Fraser goes on to argue subaltern counter-publics provide spaces of discursive contestation, generating challenges to the discursive status quo. On the surface black supplementary schools appear as sites for conformist reinscriptions of dominant discourses, in particular, those of meritocracy and traditional pedagogy. Yet, there exist parallel spaces of contestation within supplementary schooling. In all four black supplementary schools could be found a reworking of dominant discursive notions of blackness. They demarcate the limits of white hegemony offering a disruptive discursive space:

> I think one of the things we really succeed in is giving the children a positive sense of self. We help them feel comfortable with their blackness when out there they are bound to come up against situations in which they are made to feel uncomfortable about being black.
>
> Verna

As Verna's words exemplify, in black supplementary schools can be found a blackness neither vulnerable nor under threat: rather a blackness comfortable with itself. The sense of community evoked by black supplementary schooling aspires to a positive sense of blackness. Other black women educators also gave a sense of supplementary schools as spaces of blackness that held transformative potential for black children:

> Our children have said that there's something special about being in an all black environment. Its difficult to explain – that they have this sense of being able to unwind, to be themselves, relax, so that's part of what we provide – a safe environment.
>
> Charity

As spaces of blackness these four supplementary schools provided their black pupils with familiarity and a sense of centrality often missing from their experience of mainstream schooling. This feeling of comfortable centrality was one in which materiality (the all black context) and the discursive (the valorisation of blackness) were crucially intertwined:

> The first time I took him to Saturday school it was amazing. We discussed the Saturday school a lot. I saw Saturday school as at times a black home. . . . When I came back with him from Saturday school Akin was jumping all over the place and saying 'Mum, why can't I go to this school five days a week?' He loved it, he was really really excited. He said I know all about so and so and about so and so, all these people from black history. He was fascinated and up to now if he's going to do black history he's really excited.
>
> Cassie

In Cassie's words we find a sense of black supplementary schooling as a space of belonging and collectivity. For Cassie black supplementary school represents another home with all the connotations of familiarity and safety that this encapsulates. But at the same time she stresses the educational gains. It is both home and school, a combination black children rarely find in mainstream schooling. Valerie Hey stresses the crucial importance of discourse in constructing 'permissible' places from which to speak arguing that: 'we urgently need to interrogate which forms of discourse create what sort of places and how these positions encode cultural and social powers for their speakers and forms of powerlessness for those silenced' (Hey 1997:137).

Black supplementary schools provide places and spaces in which counter-hegemonic discourses of blackness can be created; discourses which construct blackness as a positive and powerful identification in contrast to mainstream schooling where, regardless of how many anti-racist policies are written, blackness is still constructed, at best as marginal, at worst as pathological (Gillborn 1995).

As Verna's, Cassie's and Charity's words above illustrate, black supplementary schools provide alternative, autonomous spaces where teachers and pupils can create oppositional and empowering narratives of blackness. Signithia Fordham (1996) has written about the psychological costs incurred when black pupils attempt to achieve academically in mainstream schooling. Because dominant discursive constructions of intellectual ability conflate blackness with being less intelligent she argues that these black pupils are forced into a situation where they must 'act white' if they are to succeed, so as not to run the risk of 'liquidating the self'. In contrast, these black supplementary schools were attempting to provide 'sacred black spaces' where children could achieve educationally and still 'act black'.

In recent work bell hooks expresses regret at the passing of separate black spaces, arguing that it has become fashionable to deny any need for black segregation in a world where black people are surrounded by whiteness (1995:6): 'In the past separate space meant down time, time for recovery and renewal. It was the time to dream resistance, time to theorise, plan, create strategies and go forward. The time to go forward is still upon us and we have long surrendered segregated spaces of radical opposition.' We argue that in black supplementary schooling lies the genesis of hooks' 'segregated spaces of radical opposition'; not in the sense of confrontational male agitation but in a more reflexive, discursive sense. The black women educators were all engaged in various ways in rewriting blackness as a positive social identity in its own right. Such reconstructions while not oppositional in any traditional sense are written against the grain of the dominant discursive constructions of blackness as a negative reflection of whiteness which still prevail across British society.

It could be argued that in a key sense black supplementary schools are a response to black people's continuing exclusion from mainstream public spheres, which in turn is primarily a consequence of endemic social and institutional racism. Indeed, all the black women educators talked about the racism their pupils and their parents encountered outside of the black communities:

> The kids meet so much racism in their everyday lives racism is definitely on the agenda here. We wouldn't be doing our duty by the kids if it wasn't.
>
> Natasha

Black supplementary schools as 'counter institutional buffers' (Hill Collins 1990) are not simply defensive institutions – the product of racial oppression which fosters historically concrete communities among black people and other racial and ethnic groups. The black supplementary school is much more than simply a reaction to racism. Like other black community spaces they do not just provide a respite from oppressive situations or retreat from their effects. Rather, as Patricia Hill Collins (1990:223) suggests 'black female spheres of influence constitute potential sanctuaries where individual black women are nurtured in order to confront oppressive social institutions.' In creating a sanctuary in which the black child is recentred black women decentre the popular pervasive public myth of black underachievement and educational alienation. As radical educators black women challenge the knowledge claims, pedagogy and praxis of mainstream schooling and harness their own radical version of education as a means of transforming their lives.

However, the very thing – spaces of blackness – which makes black supplementary schools so inviting for black pupils and the women who create and nurture them constitutes its threat for the white majority. Unlike 'separatist' private independent white schools which are welcomed as standard bearers and examples of good educational practice, black supplementary schools as sites of black solidarity are often perceived by the white majority as threatening (Tomlinson 1985).

This threat is conceived on a number of different levels, from crude fears of the 'rising up of the oppressed', to slightly more sophisticated critiques which accept the validity of black supplementary schooling yet criticise them as segregationalist and isolationist. At the heart of this white fear is the simple fact that within black supplementary schools lie powerful evocations of difference and 'otherness' that challenge white dominant hegemonic values. The variety of ways in which black supplementary schools are seen by both the educational establishment and the broader British public raises questions around power, normativity and the fear of blackness that lurks deep within the white psyche (Mirza 1999).

Reaffirmation or challenge? Black supplementary schooling's relationship to dominant perspectives on pedagogy

We have examined black supplementary schools as places for the inscription of positive black identities. We now want to explore blackness as it is configured epistemologically within black supplementary schooling. Beyond this we also wish to look at pedagogic approaches within the four schools and how they relate to mainstream approaches. Educational sites are always political and cultural places 'that represent accommodations and contestations over knowledge by differently empowered social constituencies. Thus teachers and students produce, reinforce, recreate, resist and transform ideas about race, gender and difference in the classroom' (Mohanty 1994:147). Mohanty reiterates Paulo Freire's argument that education represents both a struggle for meaning as well as a struggle over power relations 'thus education becomes a central terrain where power and politics operate out of the lived culture of individuals and groups situated in asymmetrical social and political positions' (Mohanty 1994:147).

However, any power differentials between teachers and pupils in black supplementary schools are overshadowed by the far greater power differentials between mainstream and supplementary schooling within the field of education. Although Mohanty's area of research is Women's Studies within the academy, black supplementary schools are similarly grounded in definitions of difference that attempt to resist incorporation and appropriation by providing a space for historically racialised silenced peoples to construct knowledge.

The four schools all emphasized black history and black studies as part of their curriculum offer:

> We focus on English and Maths but integrate Black studies into our curriculum offer. For example we'll do a project on black women writers and that will be part of our English curriculum.
>
> Maxine

But more than that they offered a space for what Rose called 'thinking black':

> You know you've got a maths problem about money and you don't even think about it – it's how much do three yams cost, not three pounds of carrots. It's as natural as that – just thinking black.
>
> Rose

While we expected black supplementary schools to generate oppositional discourses on blackness to those prevalent in wider white society, we did not expect our black women educators to espouse child-centred philosophies which ran counter to dominant views on pedagogy within the educational field, however they did:

> Well, we have to be versatile. For example, with Shona who teaches here she uses different types of groupwork. She has this group who are very bright and sometimes they'll work together, then sometimes she'll put them with the slower children so they can learn from them. We try different ways. And really it is about helping these children realise their learning potential, because – no matter what the experts say – different children have different learning styles, so you can't just use one. You have to keep trying until you find one to suit the child. We are very conscious of that here. We think it's very important to match teaching styles to the child's learning needs.
>
> Maxine

> I have a very strong philosophy of child centredness. I have always been very committed to supporting the child. In our society children often don't have a voice. I suppose parents might have expected Saturday school to be more formal. I mean we work in groups – there is no sitting

226

in rows. But I believe in working in ways that are best for the child, so there is a strong focus on three Rs but also on making the work really interesting for the child, starting from where the child is and integrating things around culture and history.

Verna

We are not simply arguing that black supplementary schools are 'havens' of progressive educational practice and we recognise the troubled history of child-centredness within the mainstream British educational system. Childcentredness has increasingly become pathologised within dominant educational discourses (Gipps and MacGilchrist 1999) and has always been problematic because of the ways in which it can be used to decontextualise the child and pedagogic practice from wider social structures. However, within the situated context of black sup-plementary schooling, as Verna argues, 'starting from where the child is' requires an explicit recognition of racialised commonality. We suggest that all four sup-plementary schools draw on complex, contradictory pedagogical strands within which childcentredness remains an important component. This is particularly sur-prising during a historical period in which progressivism has been discredited and superseded within mainstream schooling by more teacher-directed approaches which are increasingly reliant on textbooks and whole class teaching.

There is research which indicates that mainstream schooling practice, even during the supposed heyday of progressivism in the 1960s and 1970s, was rarely childcentred (Galton et al. 1980; Galton 1989). Such evidence makes the responses of the black women educators even more unanticipated. The only one of our seven respondents to prioritise formal ways of teaching over child-centred approaches was the one male in the sample but he too recognised the contradictions. He talked at length about the importance of differentiation but saw child-centred approaches as too idealistic and time consuming. While the women's solution was a focus on meeting the needs of the individual child, Michael felt the only practical response was ability grouping.

However, the women's words need to be contextualised within a very real ten-sion between the reinscription of traditional curricula through the strong focus on basic skills and the '3 Rs' in all four schools, and competing progressive ten-dencies which prioritised children's initiative and creativity, and their autonomy as learners. All seven black educators were juggling difficult tensions between fitting in with the mainstream and a clear conviction that they could meet the children's needs more effectively. For the black women educators there were additional tensions between parental demands and their own educational phi-losophies and between their often explicit focus on empowerment and the need to raise educational standards.

Our focus is on four schools and we cannot argue that they are typical of black supplementary schooling as a whole. As Sewell's research would seem to indicate the field of supplementary schooling is characterised by heterogeneity and difference (Sewell 1996). However, we do argue that our data reveals strands of progressivism and child centredness in all four schools. For example, all the schools had a regular circle time and a focus on black studies, while two of the schools had a strong commitment to child centredness that infused all of the curriculum offer. Thus we suggest, in contrast to mainstream schooling, these four black supplementary schools demonstrate in their praxis that high standards, a child-centred approach and a relevant curriculum, for black as well as white pupils, are all possible to achieve.

Conclusion: from black educational desire to a new social movement

Eyerman and Jamieson (1991:166) define a social movement as follows:

> All social movements, by definition, bring about some kind of identity transformation. On one level, they do this by setting new kinds of problems for societies to solve, by putting new issues on the historical agenda. On another level, they do this by proposing new 'cosmologies' or Values' which enter into the ethical identities of individuals. And on a more institutional level, they do this by creating new 'types' of professional intellectuals, who, as it were carry the cognitive praxis of the movement on into the larger society.

Our findings of the radical and transformative work of black women in supplementary schools appear to fulfil Eyerman and Jamieson's criteria of what constitutes a new social movement.

Firstly, the four black supplementary schools are struggling to bring about identity transformation. The black women educators work ceaselessly to create 'oppositional meaning' and facilitate social transformation through their sustained efforts in the three areas of community building, visions of blackness and radical pedagogic practice. These black supplementary schools, as sites of female collective action, engage in covert yet radical acts of social transformation which challenge the dominant codes and expectations that hegemonic white-dominated societies have of black people. Thus it can be argued, in opposition to those who suggest black struggles for educational opportunities are too fragile, defensive, and powerless to constitute stable forms of political action (Gilroy 1987:230), that black supplementary schools as political, social and symbolic sites of refusal and transformation of meaning form the genesis of a new social movement.

Secondly, in their implicit critique of the pervasive unspoken whiteness of mainstream schooling black supplementary schools put on the historical agenda new problems for society to solve. Black supplementary schools provide a 'sacred space of blackness' (Foley 1998) that enables the affirming of selfhood that the white majority take for granted in their privileged spaces of whiteness in mainstream schools. The black women educators were all engaged in various ways in rewriting blackness as a positive 'normative' social identity in its own right. Such reconstructions, while not oppositional in any traditional confrontational (masculine) sense, are written in opposition to the dominant discursive constructions of blackness as a negative reflection of whiteness which still prevail across British society.

Thirdly, black supplementary schools propose new 'cosmologies' or 'values' which enter into the ethical identities of others through the women's reworking of the notion of community. The sense of community engendered through these black women's activities, embracing as it does an interdependency of the individual and the necessity of the communal, is very different from the traditional notion of community as defined through market forces. The mission of the four supplementary schools in our study is to integrate educational success with a commitment to remaining true to one's origins. On the surface, black supplementary schools appear as sites for conformist reinscriptions of dominant discourses, in particular, those of meritocracy and traditional pedagogy. Yet, there exist parallel spaces of contestation within supplementary schooling. They combine goals of enabling young black people to achieve academically with a simultaneous opposition to the system, an opposition which is encoded discursively rather than enacted antagonistically. Embedded in the extremely complex and contradictory culture and social positioning of black supplementary schools lies paradoxically one of the few challenges to individualism and free markets within the field of education.

Fourthly, on a more institutional level, black supplementary schools create new 'types' of professional intellectuals, who carry the 'cognitive praxis' of the movement on into the larger society. In their quiet female ways of working, black women in our study of supplementary schools have successfully tapped the spontaneous black desire for education and learning that has been contained and restricted by white fear, hostility and ignorance for the 'other' that lies at the heart of racism and its exclusionary practices both in the classroom and in the wider educational institutions in Britain.

It would appear, therefore, in the formal sense of measured tangible outcome, the black supplementary schools in our study fulfil the criteria expected of a new social movement. However, as we have argued black supplementary schools, as gendered spaces of collective action have been overlooked in the literature on new social movements. Hidden from view, in covert quiet ways, black women work to keep alive the black communities' collective desire for self-knowledge and 'belief in the power of schooling to mitigate racial barriers . . . and make dreams come true' (Fordham 1996:63).

However, in re-envisioning black female collective community action as transformative and radical we must acknowledge that there are theoretical and practical problems with the traditional (masculinised) notion of community in general, and 'black' community in particular that need to be resolved. Floya Anthias and Nira Yuval-Davis (1993:165–7) in their work on 'black' communities in Britain, point to the ambivalence of the concept of community as having both strength and weakness. On the one hand 'black community' can be used as part of an oppositional statement of solidarity – organic and naturalised. On the other it can be equated with the negative image of what that 'community' has come to represent – a pathologised, stigmatised repository of cultural disadvantage from which many wish to disassociate themselves if they are to achieve any social mobility.

Nevertheless the idea of the 'black community' still remains a potent force. Claire Alexander argues that both black people and the wider society perceive it as a unified and largely separate entity, projecting onto it illusions of fixity and absolute identification premised on the correlation of 'community' with 'race'. She writes: 'Community becomes a symbol for the presence of black people in Britain, at once both reducing and objectifying the group as a social category, and consolidated through the use of "markers" or symbolic border guards' (Alexander 1996:33). However, we found that the idea of 'community', as practised among the women, was less about creating symbolic markers and more about the conscious, pragmatic construction of a 'black home'. While the schools themselves were set up as physically bounded 'spaces of safety', these 'sacred spaces of blackness' were not just symbolic – they were a lived reality in which the women's energy and creativity generated 'social capital' in relation to education (Bourdieu 1993). Notions of community were thus grounded in the women's own labour. They were not simply a part of the community, they were also actively engaged in constructing it through their work as radical black educators.

Ironically, the concept of 'community', while central to political strategy is marginal in contemporary academic debate. Collective action appears to undermine the theoretical purity of de-essentialised notions of postmodern identity and subjectivity (Fuss 1989). Indeed, community and collective action implies the social construction of a unified consciousness and identity. Iris Marion Young argues the desire for mutual identification which the 'ideal of community' must require generates social exclusions in itself. The urge to unity fostered by the ideal of community and the homogeneity deliberately engendered by 'movement' denies 'difference' and diversity by positing itself as a solid self-sufficient unity and an excluding totality. She argues that a radical politics cannot be achieved within the 'ideal of community' as currently posited. Young (1990:320) writes: 'Radical politics must develop discourse and institutions which bring differently identified groups together without suppressing or subsuming the "differences"'. Young suggests we move from the 'face-to-face' ideal of community to a 'politics of difference' built around the positive experience of city life and vision of the 'good society', which comes about through a process of people relating to each other and an 'openness to unassimilated otherness' (p. 320).

However, our study, though small-scale, indicates that 'community' as practised by the black women did at once both embrace unity and difference. While the schools had a distinct identity forged by the need to escape and transform the confines of subordination which has been externally ascribed to them as racialised 'others', the schools were not exclusive to the black community and their children. As a space of radical blackness the schools' decentring of whiteness did not exclude an understanding of 'whiteness'. Moreover, the schools' emphasis on 'fitting in with the mainstream' and the holistic and progressive childcentred vision of education was based on openness, mutuality, co-operation and symbiosis with the mainstream schools. The 'radical' pedagogy and practice that we found in our small-scale study suggests that female-centred black supplementary schools can be a 'blue print' of 'real' community action and ultimately have the potential to form the basis of a transformative social movement.

Note

1 This research was made possible only by the kind and open participation of all the black women and the one black man who were interviewed. Their names, and the names of the schools, have been changed.

References

Alexander, C. 1996. *The Art of Being Black.* Oxford: Clarendon Press.

Anthias, F. and Yuval-Davis, N. 1993. *Racialised Boundaries: Race, Nation, Gender, Colour and Class and the Anti-Racist Struggle.* London: Routledge.

Bagguley, P. 1997. 'Beyond Political Sociology: Developments in the Sociology of Social Movements'. *Sociological Review* 45:147–61.

Bourdieu, P. 1986. 'The Forms of Capital', pp. 241–58 in J. G. Richardson (ed.), *Handbook of Theory for the Sociology of Education.* New York: Greenwood Press.

Bourdieu, P. 1993. *Sociology in Question.* London: Sage.

Bryan, B., Dadzie, S. and Scafe, S. 1985. *The Heart of the Race: Black Women's Lives in Britain.* London: Virago.

Burlet, S. and Reid, H. 1998. 'A Gendered Uprising: Political Representation and Minority Ethnic Communities'. *Ethnic and Racial Studies* 21:270–87.

Casey, K. 1993. *I Answer with my Life: Life Histories of Women Teachers Working for Social Change.* London: Routledge.

Castells, M. 1983. *The City and the Grassroots.* London: Edward Arnold.

Chevannes, M. and Reeves, F. 1987. 'The Black Voluntary School Movement: Definition, Context and Prospects', in B. Troyna (ed.), *Racial Inequality in Education.* London: Tavistock.

Cotgrove, S. and Duff, A. 1981. 'Environmentalism, Values and Social Change'. *British Journal of Sociology* 1:91–110.

David, M. E. 1993. *Parents, Gender and Education Reform.* Cambridge: Polity Press.

Day, G. and Robbins, D. 1987. 'Activists for Peace: The Social Basis of a Local Peace Movement', in C. Creighton and M. Shaw (eds.), *The Sociology of War and Peace.* London: Macmillan.

Dove, N. 1993. 'The Emergence of Black Supplementary Schools: Resistance to Racism in the United Kingdom'. *Urban Education* 27:430–47.

Etzioni, A. 1993. *The Spirit of Community.* New York: Crown.

Eyerman, R. and Jamieson, A. 1991. *Social Movements: A Cognitive Approach.* University Park: The Pennsylvania State University Press.

Fanon, F. 1993 [1st edn 1952]. *Black Skin, White Masks.* London: Pluto.

Ferree, M. M. 1992. 'The Political Context of Rationality: Rational Choice Theory and Resource Mobilisation', pp. 29–52 in A. D. Morris and C. McClurg Mueller (eds.), *Frontiers in Social Movement Theory.* New Haven: Yale University Press.

Foley, D. 1998. 'Review Symposium; Blacked Out: Dilemmas of Race, Identity and Success at Capital High'. *Race, Ethnicity and Education* 11:131–5.

Foner, N. 1979. *Jamaica Farewell: Jamaican Migrants in London.* London: Routledge and Kegan Paul.

Fordham, S. 1996. *Blacked-Out: Dilemmas of Race, Identity and Success at Capital High.* Chicago: University of Chicago Press.

Fraser, N. 1994. 'Rethinking the Public Sphere: A Contribution to the Critique of Actually Existing Democracy', pp. 74–98 in H. A. Giroux and P. McLaren (eds.), *Between Borders: Pedagogy and the Politics of Cultural Studies.* New York: Routledge.

Fuss, D. 1989. *Essentially Speaking.* New York: Routledge.

Galton, M. 1989. *Teaching in the Primary School.* London: David Fulton Publishers.

Galton, M., Simon, B. and Croll, P. 1980. *Inside the Primary Classroom.* London: Routledge and Kegan Paul.

Gewirtz, S., Ball, S. J. and Bowe, R. 1995. *Markets, Choice and Equity in Education.* Buckingham: Open University Press.

Gillborn, D. 1995. *Racism and Anti-racism in Real Schools.* Buckingham: Open University Press.

Gilroy, P. 1987. *There Ain't No Black in the Union Jack.* London: Hutchinson.

Gipps, C. and MacGilchrist, B. 1999. 'Primary School Learners', in P. Mortimore (ed.), *Understanding Pedagogy and Its Impact on Learning.* London: Paul Chapman.

Griffith, A. and Smith, D. E. 1990. 'What Did You Do in School Today?' *Mothering, Schooling and Social Class Perspectives on Social Problems* 2:3–24.

Hargreaves, I. and Christie, I. (eds.) 1998. *The Third Way and Beyond.* London: Demos.

Hennessy, R. 1993. *Materialist Feminism and the Politics of Discourse.* London: Routledge.

Hey, V. 1996. 'A Game of Two Halves – A Critique of Some Complicities: Between Hegemonic and Counter-hegemonic Discourses Concerning Marketisation and Education'. *Discourse: Studies in the Cultural Politics of Education* 17:351–62.

Hey, V. 1997. *The Company She Keeps: An Ethnography of Girls' Friendship.* Buckingham: Open University Press.

Hey, V. 1998. 'Reading the Community: A Critique of Some Post/modern Narratives about Citizenship and Civil Society', in P. Bagguley and G. Hearn (eds.), *Transforming the Political.* London: Macmillan.

Hill Collins, P. 1990. *Black Feminist Thought: Knowledge, Conciousness and the Politics of Empowerment.* London: Routledge.

Hill Collins, P, 1994. 'Shifting the Center: Race, Class, and Feminist Theorising about Motherhood', in D. Bassin, M. Honey and M. Mahrer Kaplin (eds.), *Representations of Motherhood.* New Haven: Yale University Press.

hooks, bell. 1995. *Killing Rage: Ending Racism.* London: Penguin Books.

Johnson, R. 1979. 'Really Useful Knowledge: Radical Education and Working-class Culture 1790–1848', in J. Clarke, C. Critcher and R. Johnson (eds.), *Working Class Culture: Studies in History and Theory.* New York: St Martin's Press.

Jordan, B., Redley, M. and James, S. 1994. *Putting the Family First: Identities, Decisions, Citizenship.* London: UCL Press.

Keith, M. 1995. 'Shouts of the Street: Identity and Spaces of Authenticity'. *Social Identities* 1:297–315.

Lareau, A. 1989. *Home Advantage.* London: Falmer Press.

Luttrell, W. 1997. *School-smart and Mother-wise: Working-class Women's Identity and Schooling.* London: Routledge.

Mac an Ghaill, M. 1991. 'Black Voluntary Schools: The "Invisible" Private Sector', in G. Walford (ed.), *Private Schooling: Tradition, Change and Diversity*. London: Paul Chapman.

McCarty, J. and Zald, M. 1977. 'Resource Mobilisation and Social Movements'. *American Journal of Sociology* 82:1212–41.

Maheu, L. (ed.) 1995. *Social Movements and Social Classes: The Future of Collective Action*. London: International Sociological Association/Sage.

Melucci, A. 1988. 'Social Movements and the Democratisation of Everyday Life', in J. Kean (ed.), *Civil Society and the State*. London: Verso.

Melucci, A. 1994. 'A Strange Kind of Newness: What's "New" in New Social Movements', in E. Larana *et al.* (eds.), *New Social Movements: From Ideology to Identity*. Philadelphia: Temple University Press.

Melucci, A. 1995. 'The New Social Movements Revisited: Reflections on a Sociological Misunderstanding', in L. Maheu (ed.), *Social Movements and Social Classes: the Future of Collective Action*. London: International Sociological Association/Sage.

Mirza, H. S. 1992. *Young, Female and Black*. London: Routledge.

Mirza, H. S. 1997a. 'Black Women in Education: A Collective Movement for Social Change', in H. S. Mirza (ed.), *Black British Feminism*. London: Routledge.

Mirza, H. S. 1997b. 'Mapping a Genealogy of Black British Feminism', in H. S. Mirza, *Black British Feminism*. London: Routledge.

Mirza, H. S. 1999. 'Black Masculinity and Schooling: A Black Feminist Response'. *British Journal of Sociology of Education* 20:137–47.

Modood, T. 1998. 'Ethnic Minorities' Drive for Qualifications', in T. Modood and T. Acland (eds.), *Race and Higher Education*. London, PSI.

Mohanty, C. T. 1994. 'On Race and Voice: Challenges for Liberal Education in the 1990s', pp. 145–66 in H. A. Giroux and P. McLaren (eds.), *Between Borders: Pedagogy and the Politics of Cultural Studies*. New York: Routledge.

Morrow, V. 1999. 'Conceptualising Social Capital in Relation to Health and Well-being for Children and Young People: A Critical Review'. *Sociological Review* 47:744–65.

Mueller, C. M. 1992. 'Building Social Movement Theory', in A. D. Morris and C. M. Mueller (eds.), *Frontiers in Social Movement Theory*. New Haven: Yale University Press.

Nowotny, H. 1981. 'Women in Public Life in Austria', in C. F. Epstein and R. L. Coser (eds.), *Access to Power: Cross-National Studies of Women and Elites*. London: George Allen & Unwin.

Olson, M. 1965. *The Logic of Collective Action: Public Goods and the Theory of Groups*. Cambridge, Mass.: Harvard University Press.

Omi, M. and Winant, H. 1994. *Racial Formation in the United States: From 1960s to 1990s*. New York: Routledge.

Parkin, F. 1968. *Middle Class Radicalism*. Manchester: Manchester University Press.

Reay, D. 1995. 'A Silent Majority: Mothers in Parental Involvement', in R. Edwards and J. Ribbens (eds.), *Women in Families and Households: Qualitative Research. Women's Studies International Forum Special Issue* 18:337–48.

Reay, D. 1998a. *Class Work: Mothers' Involvement in Their Children's Primary Schooling*. London: University College Press.

Reay, D. 1998b. 'Setting the Agenda: The Growing Impact of Market Forces on Pupil Grouping in British Secondary Schooling'. *Journal of Curriculum Studies* 30:545–58.

Reay, D. 1998c. 'Rethinking Social Class: Qualitative Perspectives on Class and Gender'. *Sociology* 32: 259–76.

Reay, D. and Mirza, H. S. 1997. 'Uncovering Genealogies of the Margins: Black Supplementary Schooling'. *British Journal of Sociology of Education* 18:477–99.

SEU. 1998. *Bringing Britian Together: A National Strategy for Neighbourhood Renewal.* Report by the Social Exclusion Unit, Cmd 4045. London: HMSO.

Sewell, T. 1996. 'South London Supplementary/Heritage Schools: Shifting out of Dominance'. Paper presented at British Educational Research Association Conference.

Sewell, T. 1997. *Black Masculinities and Schooling: How Black Boys Survive Modern Schooling.* Staffordshire: Trentham.

Shotter, J. 1993. *The Cultural Politics of Everyday Life.* Buckingham: Open University Press.

Smith, D. E. 1988. *The Everyday World as Problematic: A Feminist Sociology.* Milton Keynes: Open University Press.

Solomos, J. and Back, L. 1995. *Race Politics and Social Change.* London: Routledge.

Sommerville, J. 1997. 'Social Movement Theory, Women and the Question of Interests' *Sociology* 31: 673–95.

Sudbury, J. 1998. *'Other Kinds of Dreams': Black Women's Organisations and the Politics of Transformation.* London: Routledge.

Tomlinson, S. 1985. 'The Black Education Movement', in M. Arnot (ed.), *Race and Gender.* Oxford: Pergamon Press.

Vincent, C. and Warren, S. 1999. 'Class, Race and Collective Action', in S. Riddell and J. Salisbury (eds.), *Gender Equality Policies and Educational Reforms in the United Kingdom.* London: Routledge.

Young, I. M. 1990. 'The Ideal of Community and the Politics of Difference', in L. Nicolson (ed.), *Feminism/Postmodernism.* London: Routledge.

Young, S. 1997. *Changing the Wor(l)d: Discourse, Politics and the Feminist Movement.* London: Routledge.

Young, M. and Willmott, D. 1957. *Family and Kinship in East London.* Harmondsworth: Penguin.

32

AIN'T I A WOMAN?

Revisiting intersectionality

Avtar Brah and Ann Phoenix

Source: *Journal of International Women's Studies*, 5, 3, 2004, 75–86.

In the context of the second Gulf war and US and the British occu-
pation of Iraq, many 'old' debates about the category 'woman'
have assumed a new critical urgency. This paper revisits debates
on intersectionality in order to show that they can shed new light
on how we might approach some current issues. It first discusses
the 19th century contestations among feminists involved in anti-
slavery struggles and campaigns for women's suffrage. The second part of the paper uses autobiography and empirical studies
to demonstrate that social class (and its intersections with gender
and 'race' or sexuality) are simultaneously subjective, structural
and about social positioning and everyday practices. It argues that
studying these intersections allows a more complex and dynamic
understanding than a focus on social class alone. The conclusion
to the paper considers the potential contributions to intersectional
analysis of theoretical and political approaches such as those associated with post structuralism, postcolonial feminist analysis, and
diaspora studies.

Introduction

At the time of the 1991 war against Iraq, feminist critiques of the then familiar
discourse of 'global sisterhood' were a commonplace. As American and British
bombs fell over Iraq once again in March 2003, many of the 'old' questions that
we have debated about the category 'woman' assume critical urgency once again,
albeit they now bear the weight of global circumstances of the early twenty first
century.

This paper aims briefly to discuss some 'old' issues that continue to be central
to making feminist agenda currently relevant. In order to do so, it revisits debates
on 'intersectionality' that helped to take forward feminisms in previous decades.
The first part of the paper discusses some long-standing internal conversations

among different strands of feminisms which have already furnished important insights into contemporary problems. By revisiting these historical developments, we do not wish to suggest that the past unproblematically provides an answer to the present. On the contrary, we would wish to learn from and build upon these insights through critique so that they can shed new light on current predicaments. Hence, when we start with the 19th century debates, it is not because there is a direct correspondence between slavery and 21st century forms of governmentality, but rather to indicate that some issues that emerged then can help illuminate and elucidate our current entanglements with similar problematics.

The second part of the paper comments on intersections as they have been analysed in some autobiographical and empirical research based texts. We argue that the need for understanding complexities posed by intersections of different axis of differentiation is as pressing today as it has always been. In the final section we briefly examine the contribution of recent theoretical developments to the analysis of 'intersectionality' which could potentially nurture fruitful new feminist agendas.

Ain't I a woman? Sojourner's 'Truth'

One critical thematic of feminism that is perennially relevant is the important question of what it means to be a woman under different historical circumstances. Throughout the 1970s and the 1980s, this concern was the subject of major debate as the concept of 'global sisterhood' was critiqued for its failure to fully take on board the power relations that divided us (Haraway, 1991, Davis 1981, Feminist Review, 1984, Talpade-Mohanty 1988). A century earlier, contestations among feminists involved in anti-slavery struggles and campaigns for women's suffrage also foregrounded similar conflicts. Their memory still resonates with us because the interrelationships between racism, gender, sexuality, and social class were at the heart of these contestations. Indeed, we begin this paper with the 19th century political locution '*Ain't I a Woman?*' precisely because – by fundamentally challenging all ahistoric or essentialist notions of 'woman' – it neatly captures all the main elements of the debate on 'intersectionality'. We regard the concept of 'intersectionality' as signifying the complex, irreducible, varied, and variable effects which ensue when multiple axis of differentiation – economic, political, cultural, psychic, subjective and experiential – intersect in historically specific contexts. The concept emphasizes that different dimensions of social life cannot be separated out into discrete and pure strands.

It is worth bearing in mind that the phrase, 'Ain't I a Woman?' was first introduced into North American and British feminist lexicon by an enslaved woman Sojourner Truth (the name she took, instead of her original name Isabella, when she became a travelling preacher). It predates by a century some of our more recent feminist texts on the subject such as Denise Riley's (2003/1988) 'Am I that name?' or Judith Butler's 'Gender Trouble' (Butler, 1990). It is as well to remember in this regard, that the first women's antislavery society was formed in 1832 by black women in Salem, Massachusetts in the USA. Yet, black women were conspicuous by their absence at the Seneca Falls Anti-Slavery Convention of 1848 where the mainly middle class white delegates debated the motion for women's suffrage. Several questions arise when we reflect on black women's absence at the Convention. What, for instance, are the implications of an event which occludes the black female subject from the political imaginary of a feminism designed to campaign for the abolition of slavery? What consequences did such disavowals have for the constitution of gendered forms of 'whiteness' as the normative subject of western imagination? How did events like these mark black and white women's relational sense of themselves? Importantly, what happens when the subaltern subject – black woman in this case – repudiate such silencing gestures?

We know from the biographies of black women such as Sojourner Truth that many of them spoke loud and clear. They would not be caged by the violence of slavery even as they were violently marked by it. Sojourner Truth's 1851 speech at the Women's Rights Convention in Akron, Ohio, very well demonstrates the historical power of a political subject who challenges imperatives of subordination and thereby creates new visions. This power (which, according to Foucault, simultaneously disciplines and creates new subjects) and its consequences are much bigger than the gains or losses of an individual life who articulates a particular political subject position. Sojourner Truth was born into enslavement (to a wealthy Dutch slave-owner living in New York). She campaigned for both the abolition of slavery and for equal rights for women. Since she was illiterate throughout her life, no formal record of the speech exists and, indeed, two different versions of it are in existence (Gates and McKay, 1997). The first was published in The Anti-Slavery Bugle, Salem, Ohio, in June 21, 1851. However, it is the more dramatic account, recounted in 1863 by the abolitionist and president of the Convention, Frances Gage, which is in common circulation. What is clear is that the words of Sojourner Truth had an enormous impact at the Convention and that the challenge they express foreshadowed campaigns by black feminists more than a century later:

"Well, children, where there is so much racket, there must be something out of kilter, I think between the Negroes of the South and the women of the North – all talking about rights – the white men will be in a fix pretty soon. But what's all this talking about? That man over there says that women need to be helped into carriages, and lifted over ditches, and to have the best place everywhere. Nobody helps me any best place. And ain't I a woman? Look at me! Look at my arm. I have plowed (sic), I have planted and I have gathered into barns. And no man could head me. And ain't I a woman? I could work as much, and eat as much as any man – when I could get it – and bear the lash as well! And ain't I a woman? I have borne children and seen most of them sold into slavery, and when I cried out with a mother's grief, none but Jesus heard me. And ain't I a woman? . . ."

This cutting edge speech (in all senses of the term) deconstructs every single major truth-claim about gender in a patriarchal slave social formation. More generally, the discourse offers a devastating critique of socio-political, economic and cultural processes of 'othering' whilst drawing attention to the simultaneous importance of subjectivity – of subjective pain and violence that the inflictors do not often wish to hear about or acknowledge. Simultaneously, the discourse foregrounds the importance of spirituality to this form of political activism when existential grief touches ground with its unconscious and finds affirmation through a belief in the figure of a Jesus who listens. Political identity here is never taken as a given but is performed through rhetoric and narration. Sojourner Truth's identity claims are thus relational, constructed in relation to white women and all men and clearly demonstrate that what we call 'identities' are not objects but processes constituted in and through power relations.

It is in this sense of critique, practice and inspiration that this discourse holds crucial lessons for us today. Part lament, but defiant, articulating razor sharp politics but with the sensibility of a poet, the discourse performs the analytic moves of a 'decolonised mind', to use Wa Thiongo's (1986) critical insight. It refuses all final closures. We are all in dire need of decolonised open minds today. Furthermore, Sojourner Truth powerfully challenges essentialist thinking that a particular category of woman is essentially this or essentially that (e.g. that women are necessarily weaker than men or that enslaved black women were not real women). This point holds critical importance today when the allure of new Orientalisms and their concomitant desire to 'unveil' Muslim women has proved to be attractive even to some feminists in a 'post September 11' world.

There are millions of women today who remain marginalized, treated as a 'problem', or construed as the focal point of a moral panic – women suffering poverty, disease, lack of water, proper sanitation; women who themselves or their households are scattered across the globe as economic migrants, undocumented workers, as refugees and asylum seekers; women whose bodies and sexualities are commodified, fetishised, criminalized, racialised, disciplined and regulated through a myriad of representational regimes and social practices. So many of us, indeed, perhaps, all of us one way or another, continue to be 'hailed' as subjects within Sojourner Truth's diasporic imagination with its massive potential for undoing the hegemonic moves of social orders confronting us today. She enacts dispersal and dissemination both in terms of being members of a historical diaspora but equally, in the sense of disarticulating, rupturing and de-centring the precariously sutured complacency and self-importance of certain feminisms.

Late modern decentrings

Since Sojourner Truth many feminists have consistently argued for the importance of examining 'intersectionality'. A key feature of feminist analysis of 'intersectionality' is that they are concerned with 'decentring' of the 'normative subject' of feminism. Such decentring activities scaled new heights when fuelled by political energies generated by the social movements of the second half of the last century – anti-colonial movements for independence, Civil Rights and the Black Power movements, the Peace movement, student protests and the Workers' movements, the Women's Movement or the Gay and Lesbian Movement. Whichever set of hegemonic moves became the focus of contestation in a specific debate – whether it was the plight of subordinated sexualities, class injustices, or other subaltern realities – the concept of a self-referencing, unified subject of modernity now became the subject of overt and explicit political critique. Political projects such as that of the Combahee River Collective, the black lesbian feminist organisation from Boston, pointed, as early as 1977, to the futility of privileging a single dimension of experience as if it constituted the whole of life. Instead, they spoke of being "actively committed to struggling against racial, sexual, heterosexual and class oppression" and advocated "the development of integrated analysis and practice based upon the fact that the major systems of oppression are interlocking (ibid: 272).

The concept of 'simultaneously interlocking oppressions' that were local at the same time as they were global was one of the earliest and most productive formulations of the subsequent theorisation of a "decentred subject" (see, e.g. hooks, 1981). As Norma Alacorn, in her analysis of the book 'The Bridge Called My Back' – a North American collection of political writings by women of colour – later suggested, the theoretical subject of 'Bridge' is a figure of multiplicity, representing consciousness as a "site of multiple voicings" seen "not as necessarily originating with the subject but as discourses that traverse consciousness and which the subject must struggle with constantly". This figure is the bearer of modes of subjectivity that are deeply marked by "psychic and material violence" and it demands a thorough "reconfiguration of feminist theory" (Alacorn in Anzaldua 1990: 359–365).

In Britain, we were making similar claims when women of African, Caribbean, and South Asian background came to be figured as 'black' through political coalitions, challenging the essentialist connotations of racism (Grewal et al., 1988, Brah 1996, Mirza 1997). This particular project of Black British feminism was forged through the work of local women's organisations around issues such as wages and conditions of work, immigration law, fascist violence, reproductive rights, and domestic violence. By 1978, local groups had combined to form a national body called the Organisation of Women of Asian and African Descent (OWAAD). This network held annual conferences, published a newsletter, and served as an active conduit for information, intellectual conversations and political mobilisation. The ensuing dialogue entailed sustained analysis of racism, class, and gender with much debate as to the best means of confronting their outcomes whilst remaining alive to cultural specificities:

> Our group organises on the basis of Afro-Asian unity, and although that principle is maintained, we don't deal with it by avoiding the problems this might present, but by having on-going discussions..........Obviously,

we have to take into account our cultural differences, and that has affected the way we are able to organise.

(OWAAD cited in Mirza 1997:43)

This careful attention to working within, through and across cultural differences is a highly significant heritage of this feminism and it is one that can be used as a resource for working with the question of cultural difference in the present moment when, for example, differences between Muslim and non-Muslim women are constructed as posing insurmountable cultural differences. Internal conflicts within OWAAD, as amongst white women's groups, especially around homophobia, proved salutary so that, even as British 'black feminism' assumed a distinctive political identity separate from 'white feminism', engaging the latter in critical theoretical and political debate, it was not immune to the contradictions of its own internal heterogeneity. These internal conflicts within and between different feminisms prefigured later theories of 'difference'.

Gender, race, class and sexuality

During the 1980s, there was much controversy about the best way to theorise the relationship between the above dimensions. The main differences in feminist approaches tended to be understood broadly in terms of socialist, liberal and radical feminisms, with the question of racism forming a point of conflict across all three. We do not wish to rehearse that debate here. Instead, this section discusses the importance of an intersectional approach by first addressing the contributions made by feminist work on gender and class, followed by an exploration of the gains made when the focus shifted to encompass other dimensions. We are aware that social class remains a contested category with its meaning varying with different theoretical and political perspectives. Our focus is somewhat different. We are primarily concerned with the ways in which class and its intersections are narrated in some autobiographical and empirical studies.

In the introduction to a now classic book *Truth, Dare or Promise: Girls Growing-Up in the Fifties*, Liz Heron (1985) discusses how the provision of free orange juice gave working class children the sense that they had a right to exist. The implication of this – that social class produces entitlement/lack of entitlement to exist and that social policy decisions affect this – is vividly demonstrated in this example. In the same book, Valerie Walkerdine (who has consistently discussed social class over the last 20 years), describes walking with a middle class friend on a seaside pier and seeing a working class family adding brown sauce to their chips. When her friend asks, 'how could they do that?' Walkerdine is immediately interpellated as working class, drawn into recognising the 'othering' of her working class background in this class inflected discourse on culinary habits. In later work Walkerdine also discusses middle class tendencies to view working classes as 'animals in a zoo' (with Helen Lucey,

1989) and with Helen Lucey and June Melody (2002) she considers the ways in which social class is lived in everyday practices and the emotional investments and issues it produces. Some of the middle class young women, for example, were subjected to expectations that meant that they could never perform sufficiently well to please their parents.

While the intersection of 'race' with social class is not analysed in Walkerdine's example, it is a silent presence in that it is white, working class practices that are subject, in the 1985 example, to the fascinated scopophilic gaze. In a similar way, Beverley Skeggs' (1997) work on young, white, working class women in North-West England showed their struggle for respectability and their often painful awareness of being judged more severely than middle class women. In these examples, social class (and its intersections with gender) are simultaneously subjective, structural, about social positioning and everyday practices. If we consider the intersections of 'race' and gender with social class, however, the picture becomes even more complex and dynamic.

> '"Race matters" writes the African American philosopher Cornel West (1993). Actually, class, gender and race matter, and they matter because they structure interactions, opportunities, consciousness, ideology and the forms of resistance that characterize American life. . . They matter in shaping the social location of different groups in contemporary society.' (Andersen, 1996: ix)

Anne McClintock (1995) uses an intersectional analysis to argue that to understand colonialism and postcolonialism, one must first recognize that 'race', gender and class are not distinct and isolated realms of experience. Instead, they come into existence in and through contradictory and conflictual relations to each other. In keeping with Catherine Hall's (1992, 2002) argument, McClintock shows that the Victorians connected 'race', class, and gender in ways that promoted imperialism abroad and class distinction in Britain.

> 'Imperialism. . . is not something that happened elsewhere – a disagreeable fact of history external to Western identity. Rather, imperialism and the invention of race were fundamental aspects of Western, industrial modernity. The invention of race in the urban metropoles . . . became central not only to the self-definition of the middle class but also to the policing of the "dangerous classes": the working class, the Irish, Jews, prostitutes, feminists, gays and lesbians, criminals, the militant crowd and so on. At the same time, the cult of domesticity was not simply a trivial and fleeting irrelevance, belonging properly in the private, "natural" realm of the family. Rather, I argue that the cult of domesticity was a crucial, if concealed, dimension of male as well as female identities – shifting and unstable as these were.'
>
> (Mclintock, 1995: 5)

At the level of everyday practices and subjectivity, Gail Lewis (1985) demonstrates how 'race' and gender intersected with the working class positioning of her parents so that their shifting power relations were only understandable as locally situated, albeit with global underpinnings. Her mother (a white woman) was responsible for dealing with public officials because of her parents' experiences of racism in relation to her father (a black man). In these instances, mother's 'whiteness' (Frankenberg, 1993), becomes a signifier of superiority over her black husband. On the other hand, since both parents – marked by patriarchal conventions of the time surrounding heteronormativity – believed that men ought to deal with the outside world, this had implications for their relationship at home, where her father prevailed. Lewis (2000) develops her analysis of the intersections of 'race', gender and class in studying the diverse everyday practices of black women social workers in relation to black and white clients and colleagues and white line managers. She demonstrates that the intersection of 'race', gender and class is subjectively lived, that it is part of social structure and involves differential (and sometimes discriminatory) treatment (see also Dill, 1993).

Other autobiographical pieces of work also demonstrate these intersections. For example, bell hooks (1994) writes of how she quickly learned that working class black people around Yale University greeted her on the street, while middle class ones ignored her. Using her own experience as a white, Jewish, middle class woman, Paula Rothenberg (2000) examines the intersections of 'race', gender and social class. She argues that people generally do not see the ways in which they are privileged, and so well-intentioned, middle class, white liberals often strive to maintain privilege for their children, while denying that they are doing so. Yet, the dynamics of power and privilege shape the key experiences of their lives. From a different class position, Nancie Caraway (1991) argues that a simplistically racialised notion of privilege is highly unsatisfactory for analysing the experiences of working class white women living in poverty.

Over the last twenty years, the manner in which class is discussed in political, popular and academic discourse has radically changed to the point that, as Sayer (2002) notes, some sociologists have found it embarrassing to talk to research participants about class. This tendency is also evident in government circles as when the discourse on child poverty comes to substitute analysis of wider inequalities of class. While the current government does not wish to use the language of class inequality, it has pledged itself to eradicate child poverty within twenty years. However, it is important to ask whether a commitment to eradicating poverty in children can ever be fully achieved without the eradication of poverty among their parents. For example, a study by Middleton et al. (1997) found that one per cent of children do not have a bed and mattress to themselves, five per cent live in damp housing and do not have access to fresh fruit each day or new shoes that fit. More than ten per cent of children over the age of 10 share a bedroom with a sibling of the opposite sex. Yet, counter-intuitively, over half the children who were defined as 'not poor' had parents who were defined as 'poor'. Their parents reported that they sometimes went without clothes, shoes and entertainment in order to make sure that their children are provided for. One in twenty mothers reported that they sometimes go without food in order to provide for their children. Lone mothers were particularly likely to report this. In Britain and the USA, recent studies by Ehrenreich (2002) and Toynbee (2003) provide another timely reminder of how grinding, poorly-paid, working class jobs continue to differentiate women's experiences.

From their analyses of data from 118 British Local Education Authorities, Gillborn and Mirza (2000) found that social class makes the biggest difference to educational attainment, followed by 'race' and then by gender – although they recognised that class outcomes are always intertwined with gender and 'race'. The processes by which social class continues to operate (for the middle as well as the working classes) require more attention if processes of social inclusion and exclusion are to be taken seriously. As Diane Reay (1998) points out in relation to education, this is not because different social classes view the importance of education differently – middle class position is commonly seen by both sections as central to social mobility and success. However, middle class mothers can draw upon more success-related cultural capital than their working class peers – e.g. they are better positioned to provide their children with 'compensatory education' (help with school work, for example) and having the status (and confidence) to confront teachers when they feel their children are not being pushed hard enough or taught well enough.

Similarly, The Social Class and Widening Participation in HE Project, based at the then University of North London (Archer and Hutchings, 2000; Archer et al., 2001), found that class has an enormous impact on participation in higher education. However, 'working class' people do not constitute a unitary, homogeneous category, and participation in higher education varies between different working class groups. Participation is lowest amongst those from unskilled occupational backgrounds and for inner-city working class groups. These class factors articulate with 'race' and ethnicity to produce complex patterns of participation in higher education (CVCP, 1998; Modood, 1993).

Recognition of the importance of intersectionality has impelled new ways of thinking about complexity and multiplicity in power relations as well as emotional investments (e.g. Arrighi, 2001; Kenny, 2000; Pattillo-McCoy, 1999). In particular, recognition that 'race', social class and sexuality differentiated women's experiences has disrupted notions of a homogeneous category 'woman' with its attendant assumptions of universality that served to maintain the status quo in relation to 'race', social class and sexuality, while challenging gendered assumptions. As such, intersectionality fits with the disruption of modernist thinking produced by postcolonial and poststructuralist theoretical ideas.

Postcoloniality, poststructuralism, diaspora and difference

Feminist theories of the 1970s and 1980 were informed by conceptual repertoires drawn largely from 'modernist' theoretical and philosophical traditions of European Enlightenment such as liberalism and Marxism. The 'postmodernist' critique of these perspectives, including their claims to universal applicability, had precursors, within anticolonial, antiracist, and feminist critical practice. Postmodern theoretical approaches found sporadic expression in Anglophone feminist works from the late 1970s. But, during the 1990s they became a significant influence, in particular their poststructuralist variant. The work of scholars who found poststructuralist insights productive traversed theoretical ground that ranged from discourse theory, deconstruction, psychoanalysis, queer theory, and postcolonial criticism. Contrary to analysis where process may be reified and understood as personified in some essential way in the bodies of individuals, different feminisms could now be viewed as representing historically contingent relationships, contesting fields of discourses, and sites of multiple subject positions. The concept of 'agency' was substantially reconfigured, especially through poststructuralist appropriations of psychoanalysis. New theories of subjectivity attempted to take account of psychic and emotional life without recourse to the idea of an inner/outer divide. Whilst all this intellectual flux led to a reassessment of the notion of experiential 'authenticity', highlighting the limitations of 'identity politics', the debate also demonstrated that experience itself could not become a redundant category. Indeed, it remains crucial in analysis as a 'signifying practice' at the heart of the way we make sense of the world symbolically and narratively.

Overall, critical but productive conversations with poststructuralism have resulted in new theories for refashioning the analysis of 'difference' (Butler, 1990; Grewal and Kaplan 1994; Weedon 1996; Spivak, 1999). One distinctive strand of this work is concerned with the potential of combining strengths of modern theory with postmodern insights. This approach has taken several forms. Some developments, especially in the field of literary criticism have led to 'postcolonial' studies with their particular emphasis upon the insight that both the 'metropolis' and the 'colony' were deeply altered by the colonial process and that these articulating histories have a mutually constitutive role in the present. Postcolonial feminist studies foreground processes underlying colonial and postcolonial discourses of gender. Frequently, such work uses poststructuralist frameworks, especially Foucauldian discourse analysis or Derridean deconstruction. Some scholars have attempted to combine poststructualist approaches with neo-Marxist or psychoanalytic theories. Others have transformed 'border theory' (Anzaldua 1987; Young, 1994, Lewis 1996; Alexander and Mohanty-Talpade 1997; Gedalof, 1999; Mani, 1999; Lewis, 2000). A related development is associated with valorisation of the term diaspora. The concept of diaspora is increasingly used in analysing the mobility of peoples, commodities, capital and cultures in the context of globalisaton and transnationalism. The concept is designed to analyse configurations of power – both productive and coercive – in 'local' and 'global' encounters in specific spaces and historical moments. In her work (Brah 1996, 2002) addresses the concept of 'diaspora' alongside that of Gloria Anzaldua's theorisation of 'border' and the widely debated feminist concept of 'politics of home'. The intersection of these three terms is understood through the concept of 'diaspora space' which covers the entanglements of gene-alogies of dispersal with those of 'staying put'. The term 'homing desire' is used to think through the question of home and belonging; and, both power and time are viewed as multidimensional processes. Importantly, the concept of 'diaspora space' embraces the intersection of 'difference' in its variable forms, placing emphasis upon emotional and psychic dynamics as much as socio-economic, political and cultural differences. Difference is thus conceptualised as social rela-tion; experience; subjectivity; and, identity. Home and belonging is also a theme of emerging literature on 'mixed-race' identities which interrogates the concept of 'race' as an essentialist discourse with racist effects (Tizard and Phoenix 2002/1993, Zack 1993; Ifekwunige 1999; Dalmage, 2000). Accordingly, the idea that you are mixed-race if you have black and white parents is problematised. Instead the analytical focus is upon varying and variable subjectivities, identities, and the specific meanings attached to 'differences'.

Raising new and pressing questions

In 2003, the second war against Iraq has brought into relief many continuing femi-nist concerns such as the growing militarization of the world, the critical role of the military industrial complex as a technology of imperial governance, the feminisa-tion of global labour markets and migration flows, the reconstitution of differen-tially racialised forms of sexuality as a constitutive part of developing regimes of 'globalisation', and the deepening inequalities of power and wealth across different regions of the world. A historically-rooted and forward looking consideration of intersectionality raises many pressing questions. For example: What are the impli-cations for feminisms of the latest forms of postmodern imperialisms that stalk the globe? What kinds of subjects, subjectivities, and political identities are produced by this juncture when the fantasy of the veiled Muslim woman "in need of rescue", the rhetoric of the 'terrorist', and the ubiquitous discourse of democracy becomes an alibi for constructing new global hegemonies? How do we challenge simplistic binaries which posit secularism and fundamentalism as mutually exclusive polar opposites? What is the impact of these new modes of governmentality on the lives of differentially exploited, racialised, ethnicised, sexualised, and religionised humans living in different parts of the world? What do these lived experiences say to us – living as we do in this space called the west – about our own positionalities, responsibilities, politics, and ethics? We have tried to indicate that feminist dia-logues and dialogic imaginations provide powerful tools for challenging the power games currently played out on the world stage.

References

Alexander Jacqi & Mohanty, Chandra Talpade (1997) *Feminist Genealogies, Colonial legacies, Democratic Futures*, London & New York: Routledge

Anzaldua Gloria (1990) *Making Face, Making Soul*, San Francisco: Aunt Lute Foundation Books

Archer, Louise and Hutchings, Merryn (2000) '"Bettering Yourself"? Discourses of Risk, Cost and Benefit in Ethnically Diverse, Young Working Class Non-Participants' Constructions of HE' *British Journal of Sociology of Education, 21*(4), 553–572

Archer, Louise; Pratt, Simon and Phillips, Dave (2001) 'Working class men's constructions of masculinity and negotiations of (non)participation in higher education' in *Gender and Education, 13*, (4), pp. 431–449

Andersen, Margaret (1996) 'Introduction', in Esther Ngan-Ling Chow, Doris Wilkinson and Maxine Baca Zinn (eds) *Race, Class & Gender: Common Bonds, Different Voices*, Thousand Oaks, CA: Sage

Arrighi, Barbara (2001) *Understanding Inequality: the intersection of race/ethnicity, class, and gender*, New York: Rowman and Littlefield

Brah Avtar (1996) *Cartographies of Diaspora, Contesting Identities*, London & New York: Routledge

Brah, Avtar (2002) Global mobilities, local predicaments: globalization and the critical imagination, *Feminist Review, 70*, pp. 30–45

Butler, Judith (1990) *Gender Trouble*, New York: Routledge

Caraway, Nancie (1991) *Segregated Sisterhood*, Knoxville, TN: The University of Tennessee Press

Collins-Hill Patricia (1990) *Black Feminist Thought*, Boston: Unwin Hyam

Combahee River Collective (1977) 'A black feminist statement' Reprinted in Linda Nicolson (ed.) (1997) *The Second Wave: A Reader in Feminist Theory*, New York: Routledge

Committee of Vice Chancellors and Principals (1998) *From Elitism to Inclusion: good practice in widening access to higher education Main Report*, London, CVCP

Dalmage, Heather (2000), *Tripping on the Color Line: Black-White Multiracial Families in a Racially Divided World*, New Brunswick, NJ: Rutgers University Press

Davis Angela (1981) *Women, Race and Class*, London: Women's Press

Dill, Barbara Thornton (1993) *Across the Boundaries of Race and Class: An Exploration of Work and Family among Black Female Domestic Servants*, USA: Garland

Ehrenreich, Barbara (2002), *Nickel and Dimed: On (Not) Getting by in America*, USA: Granta

Frankenberg, Ruth (1993) *White Women Race Matters: The construction of whiteness*, London: Routledge

Feminist Review (1984) 'Many Voices, One Chant: Black feminist perspectives', *Feminist Review, 17*

Gates, Henry Louis and Mckay, Nelly (1997) *The Norton Anthology of African American Literature*, New York: Norton

Gedalof, Irene (1999) *Against Purity*, London: Routledge

Gillborn, David & Mirza, Heidi Safia (2000) *Educational Inequality: mapping race, class and gender. A synthesis of evidence*, London: Ofsted

Grewal, Inderpal and Kaplan, Caren (ed) (1994) *Scattered Hegemonies*, Minnesota: University of Minnesota Press

Grewal Shabnam, Kay, Jackie, Landor, Lilianne, Lewis, Gail and Parmar, Pratibha (eds) (1988) *Charting the Journey*, London: Sheba

Hall, Catherine (1992) *White, Male and Middle-Class: Explorations in Feminism and History*, London: Routledge

Hall, Catherine (2002) *Civilising Subjects: Colony and Metropole in the English Imagination, 1830–1867*, Chicago: University of Chicago Press

Haraway, Donna (1991) *Simians, Cyborgs and Women: the reinvention of nature*, London Free Association Books

Heron, Liz (1985) 'Introduction' in Liz Heron (ed.) *Truth, Dare or Promise: Girls Growing-Up in the Fifties*, London: Virago

hooks, bell (1981) *Ain't I a Woman: Black Women and Feminism*, Boston: South End Press

hooks, bell (1994) *Teaching to Transgress: Education as the Practice of Freedom*, New York: Routledge

Ifekwunige Jayne (1999) *Scattered Belongings*, London & New York: Routledge

Kenny, Lorraine, Delia (2000) *Daughters of Suburbia: Growing Up White, Middle Class, and Female*, New Brunswick, New Jersey: Rutgers University Press

Lewis, Gail (1985) 'From deepest Kilburn' in L. Heron (ed.) *Truth, Dare or Promise: Girls Growing-Up in the Fifties*, London: Virago

Lewis, Gail (2000) *Race, Gender, Social Welfare*, Cambridge: Polity

Lewis, Reina (1996) *Gendering Orientalism*, London: Routledge

Mani Lata (1999) *Contentious Traditions*, Indiana: Indiana University Press

Mclintock, Ann (1995) *Imperial Leather: Race, Gender, and Sexuality in the Colonial Contex*, New York: Routledge

Middleton, S., Ashworth, Karl and Braithwaite, Ian (1997) *Small Fortunes: spending on children, childhood poverty and parental sacrifice*, York: Joseph Rowntree Foundation

Mirza Heidi Safia (ed.) (1991) *Black British Feminism*, London & New York: Routledge

Modood, Tariq (1993) 'The number of ethnic minority students in British Higher Education: some grounds for optimism,' *Oxford Review of Education, 19*, 2, pp 167–182

Mohanty, Chandra Talpade (1988) 'Under Western Eyes: feminist scholarships and colonial discourses', Feminist Review *30*, pp 61–88

Pattillo-McCoy, Mary (1999) *Black Picket Fences: privilege and peril among the Black middle class*, Chicago, University of Chicago Press

Reay, Diane (1998) "'Always knowing' and 'never being sure': Familial and institutional habituses and higher education choice", *Journal of Education Policy, 13*, 4, 519–529

Riley Denise (2003/1988) *"'Am I That Name?' Feminism and the Category of Women" in History.* 2nd edition, Minnesota: University of Minnesota Press

Rothenberg, Paula (2000) *Invisible Privilege,* Lawrence KS: University of Kansas Press

Sayer, Andrew (2002) 'What Are You Worth?: Why Class is an Embarrassing Subject'. *Sociological Research Online, vol. 7, no. 3*, http://www.socresonline.org.Uk/7/3/sayer.html

Skeggs, Beverly (1997) *Formations of Class and Gender*, London, Sage

Spivak, Gayatri Chakravorty (1999) *A Critique of Postcolonial Reason*, Harvard University Press

Sudbury Julia (1998) *Other Kinds of Dreams*, New York & London: Routledge Tizard, Barbara and Phoenix Ann (1993/2002) *Black, White or Mixed Race?* 2nd edition London: Routledge

Toynbee, Polly (2003) *Hard Work: Life in Low-pay Britain*, London: Bloomsbury

Wa Thiongo, Ngugi (1986) *Decolonizing the Mind: The Politics of Language in African Literature*, London: Currey

Walkerdine, Valerie (1985) 'Dreams from an ordinary childhood' in Heron L (ed.) *Truth, Dare or Promise: Girls Growing-Up in the Fifties*, London: Virago

Walkerdine, Valerie and Lucey, Helen (1989) *Democracy in the Kitchen*, London Virago

Walkerdine, Valerie, Lucey, Helen and Melody, June (2002) *Growing Up Girl*, London: Palgrave

Weedon, Chris (1996) *Feminist Practice and Poststructuralist Theory. 2nd edition,* Oxford: Blackwell

Young, Iris Marion (1990) *Justice and the Politics of Difference*, Princeton: Princeton University Press

Young, Lola (1994) *Fear of the Dark*, London: Routledge

Zack, Naomi (1993) *Race and Mixed Race*, USA: Temple University Press

33

THE TROUBLE WITH
BLACK BOYS

The role and influence of environmental and cultural factors on the academic performance of African American males

Pedro A. Noguera

Source: *Urban Education*, 38, 4, 2003, 431–459.

There is considerable confusion regarding why Black males are overrepresented in categories typically associated with negative behavioral outcomes. Drawing on research from a variety of disciplines, this article explores the influence of environmental and cultural factors on the academic performance of Black males. The article also examines the ways in which environmental and cultural forces shape the relationship between identity, particularly related to race and gender, and school performance. Finally, strategies for countering harmful environmental and cultural influences, both the diffuse and the direct, are explored with particular attention paid to recommendations for educators, parents, and youth service providers who seek to support young African American males.

All of the most important quality-of-life indicators suggest that African American males are in deep trouble. They lead the nation in homicides, both as victims and perpetrators (Skolnick & Currie, 1994), and in what observers regard as an alarming trend, they now have the fastest growing rate for suicide (National Research Council, 1989; Poussaint & Alexander, 2000). For the past several years, Black males have been contracting HIV and AIDS at a faster rate than any other segment of the population (Auerbach, Krimgold, & Lefkowitz, 2000; Centers for Disease Control, 1988; Kaplan, Johnson, Bailey, & Simon, 1987), and their incarceration, conviction, and arrest rates have been at the top of the charts in most states for some time (Roper, 1991; Skolnick & Currie, 1994). Even as babies, Black males have the highest probability of dying in the 1st year of life (Auerbach et al., 2000;

249

National Research Council, 1989), and as they grow older they face the unfortunate reality of being the only group in the United States experiencing a decline in life expectancy (Spivak, Prothrow-Stith, & Hausman, 1988). In the labor market, they are the least likely to be hired and in many cities, the most likely to be unemployed (Feagin & Sikes, 1994; Hacker, 1992; Massey & Denton, 1993; Moss & Tilly, 1995; Wilson, 1987).

Beset with such an ominous array of social and economic hardships, it is hardly surprising that the experience of Black males in education, with respect to attainment and most indicators of academic performance, also shows signs of trouble and distress. In many school districts throughout the United States, Black males are more likely than any other group to be suspended and expelled from school (Meier, Stewart, & England, 1989). From 1973 to 1977 there was a steady increase in African American enrollment in college. However, since 1977 there has been a sharp and continuous decline, especially among males (Carnoy, 1994; National Research Council, 1989). Black males are more likely to be classified as mentally retarded or suffering from a learning disability, more likely to be placed in special education (Milofsky, 1974), and more likely to be absent from advanced-placement and honors courses (Oakes, 1985; Pollard, 1993). In contrast to most other groups where males commonly perform at higher levels, such as in math- and science-related courses, the reverse is true for Black males (Pollard, 1993). Even class privilege and the material benefits that accompany it fail to inoculate Black males from low academic performance. When compared with their White peers, middle-class African American males lag significantly behind in both grade point average and on standardized tests (Jencks & Phillips, 1998).

It is not surprising that there is a connection between the educational performance of African American males and the hardships they endure within the larger society (Coleman et al., 1966). In fact, it would be more surprising if Black males were doing well academically in spite of the broad array of difficulties that confront them. Scholars and researchers commonly understand that environmental and cultural factors have a profound influence on human behaviors, including academic performance (Brookover & Erickson, 1969; Morrow & Torres, 1995). What is less understood is how environmental and cultural forces influence the way in which Black males come to perceive schooling and how those perceptions influence their behavior and performance in school. There is considerable evidence that the ethnic and socioeconomic backgrounds of students have bearing on how students are perceived and treated by the adults who work with them within schools (Brookover & Erickson, 1969; Morrow & Torres, 1995). However, we know less about the specific nature of the perceptions and expectations that are held toward Black males and how these may in turn affect their performance within schools. More to the point, there is considerable confusion regarding why being Black and male causes this segment of the population to stand out in the most negative and alarming ways, both in school and in the larger society.

This article is rooted in the notion that it is possible to educate all children, including Black males, at high levels. This idea is not an articulation of faith but rather a conclusion drawn from a vast body of research on human development and from research on the learning styles of Black children (Lee, 2000). Therefore, it is possible for schools to take actions that can reverse the patterns of low achievement among African American males. The fact that some schools and programs manage to do so already is further evidence that there exists a possibility of altering these trends (Edmonds, 1979). To the degree that we accept the idea that human beings have the capacity to resist submission to cultural patterns, demographic trends, environmental pressures and constraints, bringing greater clarity to the actions that can be taken by schools and community organizations to support the academic achievement of African American males could be the key to changing academic outcomes and altering the direction of negative trends for this segment of the population (Freire, 1972).

This article explores the possibility that the academic performance of African American males can be improved by devising strategies that counter the effects of harmful environmental and cultural forces. Drawing on research from a variety of disciplines, the article begins with an analysis of the factors that place certain individuals (i.e., African American males) at greater risk than others. This is followed by an analysis of the ways in which environmental and cultural forces interact and influence academic outcomes and how these factors shape the relationship between identity, particularly related to race and gender, and school performance. Finally, strategies for countering harmful environmental and cultural influences, both the diffuse and the direct, are explored with particular attention paid to recommendations for educators, parents, and youth service providers who seek to support young African American males.

The nature of the "risk"

The good news is that not all Black males are at risk. I was reminded of this fact on my way to work one morning. Before driving to San Francisco with a colleague, another Black male academic, we stopped to pick up a commuter so that we could make the trip across the Bay Bridge in the faster carpool lane during the middle of the rush hour. As it turned out, the first carpooler to approach our car was another Black male. As we drove across the bridge, we made small talk, going from basketball to the merits of living in the Bay Area, until finally we approached the subject of our careers. The rider informed us that he managed a highly profitable telecommunications firm, and if his plans progressed as he hoped, he would be retiring on a very lucrative pension in Hawaii before the age of 50. Contemplating his financial good fortune and that of my colleague and myself (although the two of us had no plans for early retirement), I posed the question, "What explains why we are doing so well and so many brothers like us are not?"

The answer was not obvious. All three of us were raised in working-class families, had grown up in tough neighborhoods, had close friends and family members who had been killed while they were young, and knew others who were serving time in prison. What made our lives, with our promising careers and growing families, so fortunate and so different? All three of us were raised by both of our parents, but further exploration revealed that none of us had regular contact with our fathers. We all attended public schools, but each of us felt that we had succeeded in spite of, and not because of, the schools we attended. With time running out as we approached our rider's stop, we threw out the possibility that the only thing that spared us the fate of so many of our brethren was luck, not getting caught for past indiscretions and not being in the wrong place at the wrong time.

Viewed in the context of the negative social patterns cited previously, the explanation for our apparent good luck does not seem mysterious. Although it is true that many Black males are confronted with a vast array of risks, obstacles, and social pressures, the majority manages to navigate these with some degree of success. The good news is that most Black males are not in prison, do not commit suicide, and have not contracted HIV/AIDS. These facts do not negate the significance of the problems that confront Black males, but they do help to keep the problems in perspective. Understanding how and why many Black males avoid the pitfalls and hardships that beset others may help us to devise ways to protect and provide support for more of them.

The effects of growing up in poverty, particularly for children raised in socially isolated, economically depressed urban areas, warrants greater concern, especially given that 1 out of every 3 Black children is raised in a poor household (Carnoy, 1994). Here the evidence is clear that the risks faced by children, particularly African American males, in terms of health, welfare, and education are substantially greater (Gibbs, 1988). A recent longitudinal study on the development of children whose mothers used drugs (particularly crack cocaine) during pregnancy found that when compared to children residing in similar neighborhoods from similar socioeconomic backgrounds, the children in the sample showed no greater evidence of long-term negative effects. This is not because the incidence of physical and cognitive problems among the sample was not high, but because it was equally high for the control group. The stunned researchers, who fully expected to observe noticeable differences between the two groups, were compelled to conclude that the harmful effects of living within an impoverished inner-city environment outweighed the damage inflicted by early exposure to drugs (Jackson, 1998).

A vast body of research on children in poverty shows that impoverished conditions greatly increase the multiplier effect on risk variables (i.e., single-parent household, low birth weight, low educational attainment of parents, etc.) (Gabarino, 1999). Poor children generally receive inferior services from schools and agencies that are located in the inner city, and poor children often have many unmet basic needs. This combination of risk factors means it is nearly impossible to establish cause and effect relationships among them. For example, research has shown that a disproportionate number of poor children suffer from a variety of sight disorders (Harry, Klingner, & Moore, 2000). However, the disabilities experienced by children are often related to poverty rather than a biological disorder. For example, because poor children often lack access to preventive health care, their untreated vision problems are inaccurately diagnosed as reading problems, and as a consequence, large numbers are placed in remedial and special education programs (Harry et al., 2000). Throughout the country, Black children are over-represented in special education programs. Those most likely to be placed in such programs are overwhelmingly Black, male, and poor (Harry et al., 2000).

The situation in special education mirrors a larger trend in education for African Americans generally and males in particular. Rather than serving as a source of hope and opportunity, some schools are sites where Black males are marginalized and stigmatized (Meier et al., 1989). In school, Black males are more likely to be labeled with behavior problems and as less intelligent even while they are still very young (Hilliard, 1991). Black males are also more likely to be punished with severity, even for minor offenses, for violating school rules (Sandler, Wilcox, & Everson, 1985, p. 16) and often without regard for their welfare. They are more likely to be excluded from rigorous classes and prevented from accessing educational opportunities that might otherwise support and encourage them (Oakes, 1985, p. 53). Consistently, schools that serve Black males fail to nurture, support, or protect them.

However, changing academic outcomes and countering the risks experienced by Black males is not simply a matter of developing programs to provide support or bringing an end to unfair educational policies and practices. Black males often adopt behaviors that make them complicit in their own failure. It is not just that they are more likely to be punished or placed in remedial classes, it is also that they are more likely to act out in the classroom and to avoid challenging themselves academically. Recognizing that Black males are not merely passive victims but may also be active agents in their own failure, means that interventions designed to help them must take this into account. Changing policies, creating new programs, and opening new opportunities will accomplish little if such efforts are not accompanied by strategies to actively engage Black males and their families in taking responsibility to improve their circumstances. Institutionally, this may require programmatic interventions aimed at buffering and offsetting the various risks to which Black males are particularly vulnerable. However, to be effective such initiatives must also involve efforts to counter and transform cultural patterns and what Ogbu (1987) has called the "oppositional identities" adopted by Black males that undermine the importance they attach to education.

As I will illustrate, one of the best ways to learn how this can be done is to study those schools and programs that have proven successful in accomplishing this goal. Additionally, it is important for such work to be anchored in a theoretical understanding of how the pressures exerted on Black males in American society can be contested. Without such an intellectual underpinning, it is unlikely that new interventions and initiatives will succeed at countering the hazardous direction of trends for African American males.

Structural versus cultural explanations

Epidemiologists and psychologists have identified a number of risk factors within the social environment that when combined, are thought to have a multiplier effect on risk behavior. Lack of access to health care, adequate nutrition, and decent housing, growing up poor and in a single-parent household, being exposed to substance abuse at a young age, and living in a crime-ridden neighborhood are some of the variables most commonly cited (Earls, 1991, p. 14). Similarly, anthropologists and sociologists have documented ways in which certain cultural influences can lower the aspirations of Black males and contribute to the adoption of self-destructive behavior. Ogbu (1987) argued that community-based "folk theories" that suggest that because of the history of discrimination against Black people, even those who work hard will never reap rewards equivalent to Whites, could contribute to self-defeating behaviors (p. 23). There is also evidence that many Black males view sports or music as more promising routes to upward mobility than academic pursuits (Hoberman, 1997, pp. 48–49). Finally, some researchers have found that for some African American students, doing well in school is perceived as a sign that one has "sold out" or opted to "act White" for the sake of individual gain (Fordham, 1996, p. 12; Ogbu, 1990, p. 29).

Despite their importance and relevance to academic performance, risk variables and cultural pressures cannot explain individual behavior. Confronted with a variety of obstacles and challenges, some Black males still find ways to survive and in some cases, to excel. Interestingly, we know much less about resilience, perseverance, and the coping strategies employed by individuals whose lives are surrounded by hardships than we know about those who succumb and become victims of their environment. Deepening our understanding of how individuals cope with, and respond to, their social and cultural environments is an important part of finding ways to assist Black males with living healthy and productive lives.

In the social sciences, explanations of human behavior, especially that of the poor, have been the subject of considerable debate. Most often, the debate centers on those who favor structural explanations of behavior and those who prefer cultural explanations of behavior. Structuralists generally focus on political economy, the availability of jobs and economic opportunities, class structure, and social geography (Massey & Denton, 1993, pp. 7–24; Tabb, 1970, pp. 11–36; Wilson, 1978, pp. 22–46; Wilson, 1987, pp. 12–35). From this perspective, individuals are viewed as products of their environment, and changes in individual behavior are made possible by changes in the structure of opportunity. From this theoretical perspective, holding an individual responsible for their behavior makes little sense because behavior is shaped by forces beyond the control of any particular individual. Drug abuse, crime, and dropping out of school are largely seen as social consequences of inequality. According to this view, the most effective way to reduce objectionable behavior is to reduce the degree and extent of inequality in society.

In contrast, culturalists downplay the significance of environmental factors and treat human behavior as a product of beliefs, values, norms, and socialization. Cultural explanations of behavior focus on the moral codes that operate within particular families, communities, or groups (Anderson, 1990, p. 34). For example, the idea that poor people are trapped within a "culture of poverty," which has the effect of legitimizing criminal and immoral behavior, has dominated the culturalists' perspective of poverty (Glazer & Moynihan, 1963, pp. 221–267; Lewis, 1966, pp. 74–88). For the culturalists, change in behavior can only be brought about through cultural change. Hence, providing more money to inner-city schools or busing inner-city children to affluent suburban schools will do little to improve their academic performance because their attitudes toward school are shaped by the culture they brought from home and the neighborhood in which they live (Murray, 1984, pp. 147–254). According to this view, culture provides the rationale and motivation for behavior, and cultural change cannot be brought about through changes in governmental policy or by expanding opportunities.

A growing number of researchers are trying to find ways to work between the two sides of the debate. Dissatisfied with the determinism of the structuralists, which renders individuals as passive objects of larger forces, and with the "blame the victim" perspective of the culturalists, which views individuals as hopelessly trapped within a particular social/cultural milieu (Ryan, 1976, pp. 32–46), some researchers have sought to synthesize important elements from both perspectives while simultaneously paying greater attention to the importance of individual choice and agency (McLeod, 1987). From this perspective, the importance of both structure and culture is acknowledged, but so too is the understanding that individuals have the capacity to act and make choices that cannot be explained through the reductionism inherent in either framework (Morrow & Torres, 1995, pp. 112–134). The choices made by an individual may be shaped by both the available opportunities and the norms present within the cultural milieu in which they are situated. However, culture is not static and individual responses to their environment cannot be easily predicted. Both structural and cultural forces influence choices and actions, but neither has the power to act as the sole determinant of behavior because human beings also have the ability to produce cultural forms that can counter these pressures (Levinson, Foley, & Holland, 1996, pp. 21–26; Willis, 1977, pp. 62–81).

This is not to suggest that because individuals have the capacity to counter these forces, many will choose or be able to do so. The effects of poverty can be so debilitating that a child's life chances can literally be determined by a number of environmental and cultural factors such as the quality of prenatal care, housing, and food available to their mothers that are simply beyond the control of an individual or even of concerted community action. It would be naive and erroneous to conclude that strength of character and the possibility of individual agency can enable one to avoid the perils present within the environment or that it is easy for individuals to choose to act outside the cultural milieu in which they were raised. Even as we recognize that individuals make choices that influence the character of their lives, we must also recognize that the range of choices available are profoundly constrained and shaped by external forces. For this reason, efforts to counter behaviors that are viewed as injurious—whether dropping out of school, selling drugs, or engaging in violent behavior—must include efforts to comprehend the logic and motivations behind the behavior. Given the importance of agency and choice, the only way to change behavioral outcomes is to understand the cognitive processes that influence how individuals adapt, cope, and respond.

In a comprehensive study of teen pregnancy, Kristen Luker (1996) demonstrated the possibility for synthesizing the two perspectives—structural and cultural explanations of human behaviors that traditionally have been seen as irreconcilable. Teen pregnancy, which for years has been much more prevalent among low-income females than middle-class White females, has traditionally been explained as either the product of welfare dependency and permissive sexual mores (the culturalists) or the unfortunate result of inadequate access to birth control and economic opportunities (the structuralists). Through detailed interviews with a diverse sample of teen mothers, Luker put forward a different explanation that draws from both the cultural and the structural perspectives and acknowledges the role and importance of individual choice. She pointed out that although both middle-class and lower-class girls engage in premarital sex and sometimes become pregnant, middle-class girls are less likely to have babies during adolescence because they have a clear sense that it will harm their chance for future success. In contrast, when confronted with an unexpected pregnancy, poor girls are more likely to have babies; they do not perceive it as negatively affecting their future because college and a good job are already perceived as being out of reach. In fact, many girls in this situation actually believe that having a baby during adolescence will help them to settle down because they will now be responsible for another life (Luker, 1996, pp. 223–236).

Given the importance of individual "choice" to this particular behavior, any effort to reduce teen pregnancy that does not take into account the reasoning that guides decision making is unlikely to succeed. Similarly, efforts to improve the academic performance of African American males must begin by understanding the attitudes that influence how they perceive schooling and academic pursuits. To the extent that this does not happen, attempts to help Black males based primarily on the sensibilities of those who initiate them are unlikely to be effective and may be no more successful than campaigns that attempt to reduce drug use or violence by urging kids to "just say no" (Skolnick & Currie, 1994, p. 429).

Investigations into the academic orientation of Black male students must focus on the ways in which the subjective and objective dimensions of identity related to race and gender are constructed within schools and how these influence academic performance. Although psychologists have generally conceived of identity construction as a natural feature of human development (Cross, Parnham, & Helms, 1991, pp. 13–19; Erickson, 1968, p. 32), sociologists have long recognized that identities, like social roles, are imposed on individuals through various socialization processes (Goffman, 1959, pp. 23–34). The processes and influences involved in the construction of Black male identity should be at the center of analyses of school performance because it is on the basis of their identities that Black males are presumed to be at risk, marginal, and endangered in school and throughout American society (Anderson, 1990, pp. 23–36; Gibbs, 1988, pp. 113–124; Kunjufu, 1985, p. 23).

Structural and cultural forces combine in complex ways to influence the formation of individual and collective identities, even as individuals may resist, actively
or passively, the various processes involved in the molding of the "self." The
fact that individuals can resist, subvert, and react against the cultural and structural forces which shape social identities compels us to recognize that individual
choice, or what many scholars refer to as agency, also plays a major role in the
way identities are constructed and formed (Giroux, 1983, pp. 23–36). For this
reason, research on identity must pay careful attention to the attitudes and styles
of behavior that African American males adopt and produce in reaction to the
social environment and how these influence how they are seen and how they see
themselves within the context of school. Writing on the general importance of
identity to studies of schooling, Levinson et al. (1996) argued that "student identity formation within school is a kind of social practice and cultural production
which both responds to, and simultaneously constitutes, movements, structures,
and discourses beyond school" (p. 12).

Students can be unfairly victimized by the labeling and sorting processes that
occur within school in addition to being harmed by the attitudes and behavior they
adopt in reaction to these processes. For this reason, it is important to understand
the factors that may enable them to resist these pressures and respond positively to
various forms of assistance that may be provided within school or in the communities where they reside. By linking a focus on identity construction to an analysis
of cultural production, it is the goal of this article to gain greater insight into how
schools can be changed and how support programs can be designed to positively
alter academic outcomes for African American males.

Identity and academic performance

It has long been recognized that schools are important sites of socialization.
Schools are places where children learn how to follow instructions and obey
rules, how to interact with others, and how to deal with authority (Apple, 1982, p.
47; Spring, 1994, p. 34). Schools are important sites for gender role socialization
(Thorne, 1993, p. 22), and in most societies, they are primary sites for instruction
about the values and norms associated with citizenship (Loewen, 1995, pp. 43–51;
Spring, 1994, p. 16).

For many children, schools are also places where they learn about the meaning of race. Although this may occur through lesson plans adopted by teachers,
it is even more likely that children learn about race through the hidden or informal curriculum (Apple, 1982, p. 64) and through nonstructured school activities
such as recess (Dyson, 1994, p. 21). Even when teachers do not speak explicitly
about race and racial issues with children, children become aware of physical differences related to race quite early (Tronyna & Carington, 1990, p. 18).
However, children do not become aware of the significance attached to these
physical differences until they start to understand the ideological dimensions of
race and become cognizant of differential treatment that appears to be based on

race (Miles, 1989, pp. 32–47). Name-calling, including the use of racial epithets, serves as one way of establishing racial boundaries even when children do not fully understand the meaning of the words that are used (Tronyna & Carington, 1990, p. 73). Similarly, school practices that isolate and separate children on the basis of race and gender also send children important messages about the significance of race and racial differences (Dyson, 1994, p. 34; Thome, 1993, p. 45). Schools certainly are not the only places where children formulate views about race, but because schools are often sites where children are more likely to encounter persons of another race or ethnic group, they play a central role in influencing the character of race relations in communities and the larger society (Peshkin, 1991, p. 65).

As young people enter into adolescence and develop a stronger sense of their individual identities (Erickson, 1968, p. 18), the meaning and significance of race also change. Where it was once an ambiguous concept based largely on differences in physical appearance, language, and styles of behavior, race becomes a more rigid identity construct as children learn the historical, ideological, and cultural dimensions associated with racial group membership (Cross et al., 1991, pp. 34–49; Tatum, 1992, p. 39). Even children who once played and interacted freely across racial lines when they were younger often experience a tightening of racial boundaries and racial identities as they get older and begin following patterns of interaction modeled by adults (Metz, 1978, p. 221; Peshkin, 1991, p. 46). Peer groups play a powerful role in shaping identity because the desire to be accepted by one's peers and "fit in" with one's peers often becomes a paramount concern for most adolescents. Research has shown that in secondary school, peer groups assume a great influence over the orientation young people adopt toward achievement (Phelan, Davidson, & Ya, 1998, pp. 10–18), and they profoundly shape the way identities are constituted in school settings (Steinberg, 1996). As adolescents become clearer about the nature of their racial and gender identities, they begin to play a more active role in maintaining and policing these identities. Peer groups are also likely to impose negative sanctions on those who violate what are perceived as established norms of behavior and who attempt to construct identities that deviate significantly from prevailing conceptions of racial and gender identity (Peshkin, 1991).

Despite the importance that several researchers have placed on the role of peer groups in the socialization process, peer groups are by no means the only forces that shape the social construction of identity within schools (Fordham, 1996, p. 47; Ogbu, 1987, p. 87; Solomon, 1992, p. 22; Steinberg, 1996, p. 185). The structure and culture of school plays a major role in reinforcing and maintaining racial categories and the stereotypes associated with them. As schools sort children by perceived measures of their ability and as they single out certain children for discipline, implicit and explicit messages about racial and gender identities are conveyed. To the degree that White or Asian children are disproportionately placed in gifted and honors classes, the idea that such children are inherently smarter may be inadvertently reinforced. Similarly, when African American and Latino children are overrepresented in remedial classes, special education programs, or on the lists for suspension or expulsion, the idea that these children are not as smart or as well behaved is also reinforced (Ferguson, 2000, p. 134). Such messages are conveyed even when responsible adults attempt to be as fair as possible in their handling of sorting and disciplinary activities. Because the outcomes of such practices often closely resemble larger patterns of success and failure that correspond with racial differences in American society, they invariably have the effect of reinforcing existing attitudes and beliefs about the nature and significance of race.

For African American males, who are more likely than any other group to be subjected to negative forms of treatment in school, the message is clear: Individuals of their race and gender may excel in sports, but not in math or history. The location of Black males within school, in remedial classes or waiting for punishment outside the principal's office, and the roles they perform within school suggest that they are good at playing basketball or rapping, but debating, writing for the school newspaper, or participating in the science club are strictly out of bounds. Such activities are out of bounds not just because Black males may perceive them as being inconsistent with who they think they are but also because there simply are not enough examples of individuals who manage to participate in such activities without compromising their sense of self. Even when there are small numbers of Black males who do engage in activities that violate established norms, their deviation from established patterns often places them under considerable scrutiny from their peers who are likely to regard their transgression of group norms as a sign of "selling out."

Researchers such as Ogbu and Fordham have attributed the marginality of Black students to oppositional behavior (Fordham, 1996, p. 46; Ogbu, 1987, p. 34). They argue that Black students hold themselves back out of fear that they will be ostracized by their peers. Yet, what these researchers do not acknowledge is the dynamic that occurs between Black students, males in particular, and the culture that is operative within schools. Black males may engage in behaviors that contribute to their underachievement and marginality, but they are also more likely to be channeled into marginal roles and to be discouraged from challenging themselves by adults who are supposed to help them. Finally, and most important, Ogbu and Fordham fail to take into account the fact that some Black students, including males, find ways to overcome the pressures exerted on them and manage to avoid choosing between their racial and gender identity and academic success. Even if few in number, there are students who manage to maintain their identities and achieve academically without being ostracized by their peers. Understanding how such students navigate this difficult terrain may be the key to figuring out how to support the achievement of larger numbers of Black students.

A recent experience at a high school in the Bay Area illustrates how the interplay of these two socializing forces, peer groups and school sorting practices, can play out for individual students. I was approached by a Black male student who needed assistance with a paper on *Huckleberry Finn* that he was writing for his 11th-grade English class. After reading what he had written, I asked why he had not discussed the plight of Jim, the runaway slave who is one of the central characters of the novel. The student informed me that his teacher had instructed the class to focus on the plot and not to get into issues about race because according to the teacher, that was not the main point of the story. He explained that two students in the class, both Black males, had objected to the use of the word "nigger" throughout the novel and had been told by the teacher that if they insisted on making it an issue they would have to leave the course. Both of these students opted to leave the course even though it meant that they would have to take another course that did not meet the college preparatory requirements. The student I was helping explained that because he needed the class he would just "tell the teacher what she wanted to hear." After our meeting, I looked into the issue further and discovered that one student, a Black female, had chosen a third option: she stayed in the class but wrote a paper focused on race and racial injustice, even though she knew it might result in her being penalized by the teacher.

This example reveals a number of important lessons about the intersection of identity, school practices, and academic performance. Confronted by organizational practices, which disproportionately place Black students in marginal roles and groupings, and pressure from peers, which may undermine the importance attached to academic achievement, it will take considerable confidence and courage for Black students to succeed. The four Black students in this English class were already removed from their Black peers by their placement in this honors course. In such a context, one seemed to adopt what Fordham (1996) described as a "raceless" persona (the student I was assisting) to satisfy the demands of the teacher, but this is only one of many available options. Two others responded by choosing to leave for a lower level class where they would be reunited with their peers with their identities intact but with diminished academic prospects. The option exercised by the female student in the class is perhaps the most enlightening yet difficult to enact. She challenged her teacher's instructions, choosing to write about race and racism, even though she knew she would be penalized for doing so. Yet she also had no intention of leaving the class, despite the isolation she experienced, to seek out the support of her peers.

This case reveals just some of the ways Black students may respond to the social pressures that are inherent in school experiences. Some actively resist succumbing to stereotypes or the pressure of peers, whereas others give in to these pressures in search of affirmation of their social identity. For those who seek to help Black students and males in particular, the challenge is to find ways to support their resistance to negative stereotypes and school sorting practices and to make choosing failure a less likely option for them. The teacher mentioned in the case just described may or may not have even realized how her actions in relation to the curriculum led her Black students to make choices that would profoundly influence their education. As the following section will illustrate, when educators are aware of the social and cultural pressures exerted on students, the need to choose between one's identity and academic success can be eliminated.

Learning from students and the schools that serve them well

Fortunately, there is considerable evidence that the vast majority of Black students, including males, would like to do well in school (Anderson, 1990, p. 249; Kao & Tienda, 1998, p. 36). Additionally, there are schools where academic success for Black students is the norm and not the exception (Edmonds, 1979, p. 11; Sizemore, 1988, p. 45). Both of these facts provide a basis for hope that achievement patterns can be reversed if there is a willingness to provide the resources and support to create the conditions that nurture academic success.

In my own research at high schools in northern California, I have obtained consistent evidence that most Black students value education and would like to succeed in school. In response to a survey about their experiences in school, nearly 90% of the Black male respondents ($N = 147$) responded "agree" or "strongly agree" to the questions "I think education is important" and "I want to go to college." However, in response to the questions "I work hard to achieve good grades" and "My teachers treat me fairly," less than a quarter of the respondents, 22% and 18% respectively, responded affirmatively. An analysis of just these responses to the survey suggests a disturbing discrepancy between what students claim they feel about the importance of education, the effort they expend, and the support they receive from teachers (Noguera, 2001). Similar results were obtained from a survey of 537 seniors at an academic magnet high school. African American males were least likely to indicate that they agreed or strongly agreed with the statement "My teachers support me and care about my success in their class" (see Table 1).

Rosalind Mickelson (1990) found similar discrepancies between expressed support for education and a commitment to hard work. Her research findings led her to conclude that some Black students experience what she referred to as an "attitude-achievement paradox." For Mickelson, the reason for the discrepancy is that although many Black students say they value education, such an expression is little more than an "abstract" articulation of belief. However, when pressed to state whether they believe that education will actually lead to a better life for them, the Black students in Mickelson's study expressed the "concrete" belief that it would not. Mickelson concluded that the contradiction between abstract and concrete beliefs toward education explains why there is a discrepancy between the attitudes expressed by Black students and their academic outcomes (pp. 42–49).

Table 1 "My teachers support me and care about my success in their class" (in percentages) ($N = 537$)

	Black Male	Black Female	Asian Male	Asian Female	White Male	White Female
Strongly agree	8	12	24	36	33	44
Agree	12	16	42	33	21	27
Disagree	38	45	16	15	18	11
Strongly disagree	42	27	18	16	28	18

Although Mickelson's (1990) findings seem plausible, I think it is also important to consider how the experiences of Black students in schools, especially males, may result in a leveling of aspirations. If students do not believe that their teachers care about them and are actively concerned about their academic performance, the likelihood that they will succeed is greatly reduced. In MetLife's annual survey on teaching, 39% of students surveyed ($N = 3,961$) indicated that they trust their teachers "only a little or not at all"; when the data from the survey were disaggregated by race and class, minority and poor students indicated significantly higher levels of distrust (47% of minorities and 53% of poor students stated that they trusted their teachers only a little or not at all) (MetLife, 2000, p. 184). Though it is still possible that some students will succeed even if they do not trust or feel supported by their teachers, research on teacher expectations suggests that these feelings have a powerful effect on student performance (Weinstein, Madison, & Kuklinski, 1995, pp. 124–125). Moreover, there is research that suggests that the performance of African Americans, more so than other students, is influenced to a large degree by the social support and encouragement that they receive from teachers (Foster, 1997, p. 122; Ladson-Billings, 1994, p. 36; Lee, 2000, p. 57). To the extent that this is true, and if the nature of interactions between many Black male students and their teachers tends to be negative, it is unlikely that it will be possible to elevate their achievement without changing the ways in which they are treated by teachers and the ways in which they respond to those who try to help them.

However, there are schools where African American male students do well and where high levels of achievement are common. For example, a recent analysis of the academic performance indicators of public schools in California revealed that there are 22 schools in the state where Black students compose 50% or more of the student population and have aggregate test scores of 750 or greater (1,000 is the highest possible score) (Foster, 2001). Most significantly, when the test-score data for these schools were disaggregated on the basis of race and gender, there was no evidence of an achievement gap. Though schools such as these are few in number, given the fact that there are more than 2,000 public schools in California, the fact that they exist suggests that similar results should be possible elsewhere.

Researchers who have studied effective schools have found that such schools possess the following characteristics: (a) a clear sense of purpose, (b) core standards within a rigorous curriculum, (c) high expectations, (d) a commitment to educate all students, (e) a safe and orderly learning environment, (f) strong partnerships with parents, and (g) a problem-solving attitude (Murphy & Hallinger, 1985; Sizemore, 1988). Though the criteria used to determine effectiveness rely almost exclusively on data from standardized tests and ignore other criteria, there is no disagreement that such schools consistently produce high levels of academic achievement among minority students. Researchers on effective schools for low-income African American students also cite the supportive relations that exist between teachers and students and the ethos of caring and accountability that pervade such schools as other essential ingredients of their success (Sizemore, 1988). Educational reformers and researchers must do more to investigate ways to adopt strategies that have proven successful at schools where achievement is less likely. As Ron Edmonds (1979), formerly one of the leading researchers on effective schools, stated, "We already know more than enough to successfully educate all students" (p. 26). The challenge before educators and policy makers is to find ways to build on existing models of success.

Unfortunately, most African American children are not enrolled in effective schools that nurture and support them while simultaneously providing high quality instruction. Even as pressure is exerted to improve the quality of public education so that the supply of good schools is increased, other strategies must be devised at the community level to provide Black children with support. For example, there are long-standing traditions within Jewish and many Asian communities to provide children with religious and cultural instruction outside of school. In several communities throughout the United States, Black parents are turning to churches and community organizations as one possible source of such support (McPartland & Nettles, 1991). In northern California, organizations such as Simba and the Omega Boys Club (both community-based mentoring programs) provide African American males with academic support and adult mentors outside of school (Watson & Smitherman, 1996). Organizations such as these affirm the identities of Black males by providing them with knowledge and information about African and African American history and culture and by instilling a sense of social responsibility toward their families and communities (Ampim, 1993; Myers, 1988). Unfortunately, these organizations are small and are largely unable to serve the vast numbers of young people in need. Moreover, it is unlikely that such organizations can completely counter the harmful effects of attendance in unsupportive and even hostile schools because they are designed to complement learning that is supposed to take place in school. Still, the model they provide demonstrates that it is possible to work outside of schools to have a positive influence on the academic performance of African American youth. Given their relative success but small size, it would be advisable to find ways to replicate them elsewhere.

Drawing from the research on mentoring and student resilience that has identified strategies that are effective in supporting the academic achievement of African American students, community organizations and churches can attempt to compensate for the failings of schools. Through after-school and summer school programs, these groups can provide young people with access to positive role models and social support that can help buffer young people from the pressures within their schools and communities (Boykin, 1983). Although such activities should not be seen as a substitute for making public schools more responsive to the communities that they serve, they do represent a tangible action that can be taken immediately to respond to the needs of Black youth, particularly males who often face the greatest perils.

Conclusion: the need for further research

Although this article made reference to the cultural norms, attitudes, and styles of behavior African American males may adopt and produce that can diminish the importance they attach to academic achievement, the emphasis of this paper has been on the ways in which schools disserve and underserve this population of students. Such an emphasis is necessary because research on effective schools has shown that when optimal conditions for teaching and learning are provided, high levels of academic success for students, including African American males, can be achieved. Put differently, if we can find ways to increase the supply of effective schools, it may be possible to mitigate against some of the risks confronting Black males. This does not mean the question of how to influence the attitudes, behaviors, and stances of Black males toward school and education generally does not need to be addressed or that it does not require further investigation. To the extent that we recognize that all students are active participants in their own education and not passive objects whose behavior can be manipulated by adults and reform measures, then the importance of understanding how to influence behavior cannot be understated. Learning how to influence the attitudes and behaviors of African American males must begin with an understanding of the ways in which structural and cultural forces shape their experiences in school and influence the construction of their identities. In this regard, it is especially important that future research be directed toward a greater understanding of youth culture and the processes related to cultural production.

Like popular culture, youth culture—and all of the styles and symbols associated with it—is dynamic and constantly changing. This is particularly true for inner-city African American youth whose speech, dress, music, and tastes often establish trends for young people across America. For many adults, this culture is also impenetrable and often incomprehensible. Yet, despite the difficulty of understanding and interpreting youth culture, it is imperative that efforts to help Black youth be guided by ongoing attempts at understanding the cultural forms they produce and the ways in which they respond and adapt to their social and cultural environment. Without such an understanding, efforts to influence the attitudes and behaviors of African American males will most likely fail to capture their imaginations and be ignored.

The importance of understanding youth culture became clear when embarking on research on how the popular media influences the attitudes of young people toward violence. Part of this research attempted to study how young people react to violent imagery in films by watching segments of popular movies with groups of middle school students and discussing their interpretations and responses to the ways violence was depicted. Following a series of discussions of their moral and ethical judgments of the violence conveyed in the films, the students asked to watch the film *Menace to Society* as part of the research exercise. Surprisingly, several of the students owned copies of the film and many had seen the film so many times that they had memorized parts of the dialogue. The film, which tells the story of a young man growing up in south central Los Angeles, is filled with graphic images of violence. After viewing, it became apparent that there might be some truth to the idea that violent films do condition young people to rationalize violent behavior as a legitimate and appropriate way for resolving conflicts and getting what they want. However, when discussing the film, it became clear that most were repulsed by the violence even though they were entertained by it, and rather than identifying with perpetrators of violence in the film, they identified most strongly with those characters who sought to avoid it (Noguera, 1995).

This experience and others like it made me realize how easy it is for adults to misinterpret and misunderstand the attitudes and behavior of young people. Generational differences, especially when compounded by differences in race and class, often make it difficult for adults to communicate effectively with youth. Many adults are aware of the chasm that separates them from young people, yet adults typically take actions intended to benefit young people without ever investigating whether the interventions meet the needs or concerns of youth. There is a need to consult with young people on how the structure and culture of schools contribute to low academic achievement and to enlist their input when interventions to improve student performance are being designed and implemented.

In addition to research on youth culture, there is a pressing need for further research on how identities—especially related to the intersection of race, class, and gender—are constructed within schools and how these identities affect students' attitudes and dispositions toward school, learning, and life in general. Presently such an analysis is largely absent from the policies and measures that are pursued to reform schools and improve classroom practice. Consistently, the focus of reform is on what adults and schools should do to improve student achievement, with students treated as passive subjects who can easily be molded to conform to our expectations. To devise a policy that will enable successes achieved in a particular program, classroom, or school to be replicated elsewhere, we must be equipped with an understanding of the process through which identities are shaped and formed within schools. There is also a need for further research on peer groups and their role in influencing the academic orientation of students.

Much of what I know about the plight of African American males comes from my personal experience growing up as a Black male and raising two sons. I have an intuitive sense that the way we are socialized to enact our masculinity, especially during adolescence, is a major piece of the problem. Researchers such as Geneva Smitherman (1977) and others have argued that Black children, and males in particular, often behave in ways that are perceived as hostile and insubordinate by adults (p. 234). Others suggest that males generally, and Black males especially, have particularly fragile egos and are susceptible to treating even minor slights and transgressions as an affront to their dignity and sense of self-respect (Kunjufu, 1985, p. 16; Madhubuti, 1990, p. 88; Majors & Billson, 1992, p. 92; West, 1993, p. 47). Such interpretations resonate with my own experience, but it is still not clear how such knowledge can be used to intervene effectively on behalf of African American males.

I recall that as a young man, I often felt a form of anger and hostility that I could not attribute to a particular incident or cause. As a teacher, I have observed similar forms of hostility among Black male students, and for the past 3 years, I have witnessed my eldest son exhibit the same kinds of attitudes and behavior. Undoubtedly, some of this can be explained as a coping strategy: Black males learn at an early age that by presenting a tough exterior it is easier to avoid threats or attacks (Anderson, 1990, p. 38). It may also be true, and this is clearly speculation, that the various ways in which Black males are targeted and singled out for harsh treatment (at school or on the streets by hostile peers or by the police) elicit postures of aggression and ferocity toward the world.

Given the range and extent of the hardships that beset this segment of the population, there is no doubt that there are some legitimate reasons for young Black males to be angry. Yet, it is also clear that this thinly veiled rage and readiness for conflict can be self-defeating and harmful to their well-being. One of the consequences of this hostility and anger may be that such attitudes and behaviors have a negative effect on their academic performance. Adults, especially women, may be less willing to assist a young male who appears angry or aggressive. A colleague of mine has argued that what some refer to as the "fourth grade syndrome," the tendency for the academic performance of Black males to take a decisive downward turn at the age of 9 or 10, may be explained by the fact that this is the age when Black boys start to look like young men (Hilliard, 1991, p. 113; Kunjufu, 1985, p. 18). Ferguson (2000) found in his research in Shaker Heights, Ohio, that Black students were more likely than White students to cite "toughness" as a trait they admired in others (p. 23). If these researchers are correct, and if the toughness admired by Black males evokes feelings of fear among some of their teachers, it is not surprising that trouble in school would be common. Gaining a clearer understanding of this phenomenon may be one important part of the process needed for altering academic trends among Black males.

Still, it would be a mistake to conclude that until we find ways to change the attitudes and behaviors of Black males, nothing can be done to improve their academic performance. There is no doubt that if schools were to become more nurturing and supportive, students would be more likely to perceive schools as a source of help and opportunity rather than an inhospitable place that one should seek to escape and actively avoid. Changing the culture and structure of schools such that African American male students come to regard them as sources of support for their aspirations and identities will undoubtedly be the most important step that can be taken to make high levels of academic achievement the norm rather than the exception.

References

Ampim, M. (1993). *Towards an understanding of Black community development.* Oakland, CA: Advancing the Research.

Anderson, E. (1990). *Streetwise: Race, class, and change in an urban community.* Chicago: University of Chicago Press.

Apple, M. (1982). *Education and power.* Boston: ARK.

Auerbach, J. A., Krimgold, B. K., & Lefkowitz, B. (2000). *Improving health: It doesn't take a revolution. Health and social inequality.* Washington, DC: Kellogg Foundation.

Boykin, W. (1983). On the academic task performance and African American children. In J. Spencer (Ed.), *Achievement and achievement motives* (pp. 16–36). Boston: Freeman.

Brookover, W. B., & Erickson, E. L. (1969). *Society, schools, and learning.* Boston: Allyn and Bacon.

Carnoy, M. (1994). *Faded dreams: The politics and economics of race in America.* New York: Cambridge University Press.

Centers for Disease Control. (1988). Distribution of AIDS cases by racial/ethnic group and exposure category: United States (June 1, 1981 to July 4, 1988). *Morbidity and Mortality Weekly Report, 55,* 1–10.

Coleman, J., Campbell, E., Hobson, C., McPartland, J., Mood, A., Weinfeld, F., et al. (1966). *Equality of educational opportunity.* Washington, DC: Government Printing Office.

Cross, W., Parnham, T., & Helms, J. (1991). *Shades of Black: Diversity in African American identity.* Philadelphia: Temple University Press.

Dyson, A. H. (1994). The Ninjas, the X-Men, and the Ladies: Playing with power and identity in an urban primary school. *Teachers College Record, 96*(2), 219–239.

Earls, F. (1991). Not fear, nor quarantine, but science: Preparation for a decade of research to advance knowledge about causes and control of violence in youths. *Journal of Adolescent Health, 12,* 619–629.

Edmonds, R. (1979). Effective schools for the urban poor. *Educational Leadership, 37*(1), 15–27.

Erickson, E. (1968). *Identity: Youth and crisis.* New York: Norton.

Feagin, J. R., & Sikes, M. P. (1994). *Living with racism: The Black middle class experience.* Boston: Beacon.

Ferguson, R. (2000). *A diagnostic analysis of Black-White GPA disparities in Shaker Heights, Ohio.* Washington, DC: Brookings Institution.

Fordham, S. (1996). *Blacked out: Dilemmas of race, identity, and success at Capital High.* Chicago: University of Chicago Press.

Foster, M. (1997). *Black teachers on teaching.* New York: New Press.

Foster, M. (2001). *University of California report of Black student achievement.* Unpublished manuscript, University of California, Santa Barbara.

Freire, P. (1972). *Pedagogy of the oppressed.* New York: Continuum Publishing.

Gabarino, J. (1999). *Lost boys: Why our sons turn to violence and how to save them.* New York: Free Press.

Gibbs, J. T. (1988). *Young, Black, and male in America: An endangered species.* New York: Auburn House.

Giroux, H. (1983). *Theory and resistance in education.* New York: Bergin and Harvey.

Glazer, N., & Moynihan, D. (1963). *Beyond the melting pot.* Cambridge, MA: MIT Press.

Goffman, E. (1959). *The presentation of self in everyday life.* Garden City, NY: Doubleday.

Hacker, A. (1992). *Two nations: Black, White, separate, hostile, unequal.* New York: Scribner.

Harry, B., Klingner, J., & Moore, R. (2000, November). *Of rocks and soft places: Using qualitative methods to investigate the processes that result in disproportionality.* Paper presented at the Minority Issues in Special Education Symposium, Harvard University, Cambridge, MA.

Hilliard, A. (1991). Do we have the will to educate all children? *Educational Leadership, 49*(1), 31–36.

Hoberman, J. (1997). *Darwin's athletes.* New York: Houghton Mifflin.

Jackson, J. (1998). The myth of the crack baby. *Family Watch Library, September/October,* 4–12.

Jencks, C., & Phillips, M. (Eds.). (1998). *The Black-White test score gap.* Washington, DC: Brookings Institution.

Kao, G., & Tienda, M. (1998). Educational aspirations among minority youth. *American Journal of Education, 106,* 349–384.

Kaplan, H., Johnson, R., Bailey, C., & Simon, W. (1987). The sociological study of AIDS: A critical review of the literature and suggested research agenda. *Journal of Health and Social Science Behavior, 28,* 140–157.

Kunjufu, J. (1985). *Countering the conspiracy to destroy Black boys.* Chicago: African American Images.

Ladson-Billings, G. (1994). *The dreamkeepers: Successful teachers of African American children.* San Francisco: Jossey-Bass.

Lee, C. (2000). *The state of knowledge about the education of African Americans.* Washington, DC: American Educational Research Association, Commission on Black Education.

Levinson, B., Foley, D., & Holland, D. (1996). *The cultural production of the educated person.* Albany: SUNY Press.

Lewis, O. (1966). *La vida: A Puerto Rican family in the culture of poverty—San Juan and New York.* New York: Random House.

Loewen, J. (1995). *Lies my teacher told me.* New York: New Press.

Luker, K. (1996). *Dubious conceptions: The politics of teenage pregnancy.* Cambridge, MA: Harvard University Press.

Madhubuti, H. R. (1990). *Black men, obsolete, single, dangerous? The Afrikan American family in transition: Essays in discovery, solution, and hope.* Chicago: Third World Press.

Majors, R., & Billson, M. (1992). *Cool pose: Dilemmas of Black manhood in America.* New York: Simon & Schuster.

Massey, D., & Denton, N. (1993). *American apartheid.* Cambridge, MA: Harvard University Press.

McLeod, J. (1987). *Ain't no makin' it.* Boulder, CO: Westview.

McPartland, J., & Nettles, S. (1991). Using community adults as advocates or mentors for at-risk middle school students: A two-year evaluation of Project RAISE. *American Journal of Education, August,* 28–47.

Meier, K., Stewart, J., & England, R. (1989). *Race, class and education: The politics of second generation discrimination.* Madison: University of Wisconsin Press.

Metz, M. (1978). *Classrooms and corridors.* Berkeley: University of California Press.

MetLife. (2000). *The MetLife survey of the American teacher, 2000: Are we preparing students for the 21st century?* New York: Author.

Mickelson, R. (1990). The attitude achievement paradox among Black adolescents. *Sociology of Education, 63*(1), 37–62.

Miles, R. (1989). *Racism.* London: Routledge Kegan Paul.

Milofsky, C. (1974). Why special education isn't special. *Harvard Educational Review, 44*(4), 437–458.

Morrow, R. A., & Torres, C. A. (1995). *Social theory and education: A critique of theories of social and cultural reproduction.* Albany: SUNY Press.

268

Moss, P., & Tilly, C. (1995). *Raised hurdles for Black men: Evidence from interviews with employers* (Working Paper). New York: Russell Sage.

Murphy, J., & Hallinger, P. (1985). Effective high schools: What are the common characteristics? *NASSP Bulletin, 69*(477), 18–22.

Murray, C. A. (1984). *Losing ground: American social policy, 1950–1980.* New York: Basic Books,

Myers, L. J. (1988). *Understanding an Afrocentric worldview: Introduction to an optimal psychology.* Dubuque, IA: Kendall/Hunt.

National Research Council. (1989). *A common destiny: Blacks and American society.* Washington, DC: National Academy Press.

Noguera, P. (1995). Reducing and preventing youth violence: An analysis of causes and an assessment of successful programs. In California Wellness Foundation (Ed.), *1995 Wellness Lectures* (pp. 25–43). Oakland: California Wellness Foundation and the University of California, Berkeley.

Noguera, P. (2001). Racial politics and the elusive quest for equity and excellence in education. *Education and Urban Society, 34*(1), 27–42.

Oakes, J. (1985). *Keeping track: How schools structure inequality.* New Haven, CT: Yale University Press.

Ogbu, J. (1987). Opportunity structure, cultural boundaries, and literacy. In J. Langer (Ed.), *In language, literacy and culture: Issues of society and schooling* (pp. 42–57). Norwood, NJ: Ablex.

Ogbu, J. (1990). Literacy and schooling in subordinate cultures: The case of Black Americans. In K. Lomotey (Ed.), *Going to school* (pp. 3–21). Albany: SUNY Press.

Peshkin, A. (1991). *The color of strangers, the color of friends.* Chicago: University of Chicago Press.

Phelan, P. A., Davidson, H., & Ya, C. (1998). *Adolescent worlds.* Albany: SUNY Press.

Pollard, D. S. (1993). Gender, achievement and African American students' perceptions of their school experience. *Educational Psychologist, 28*(4), 294–303.

Poussaint, A., & Alexander, A. (2000). *Lay my burden down: Unraveling suicide and the mental health crisis among African Americans.* Boston: Beacon.

Roper, W. L. (1991). The prevention of minority youth violence must begin despite risks and imperfect understanding. *Public Health Reports, 106*(3), 229–231.

Ryan, W. (1976). *Blaming the victim.* New York: Vintage.

Sandler, D. P., Wilcox, A. J., & Everson, R. B. (1985). Cumulative effects of lifetime passive smoking on cancer risks. *Lancet, 1*(24), 312–315.

Sizemore, B. (1988). The Madison School: A turnaround case. *Journal of Negro Education, 57*(3), 243–266.

Skolnick, J. H., & Currie, E. (Eds.). (1994). *Crisis in American institutions* (9th ed.). New York: HarperCollins.

Smitherman, G. (1977). *Talkin' and testifyin': The language of Black America.* Boston: Houghton Mifflin.

Solomon, P. (1992). *Black resistance in high school.* Albany: SUNY press.

Spivak, H., Prothrow-Stith, D., & Hausman, A. (1988). Dying is no accident: Adolescents, violence, and intentional injury. *Pediatric Clinics of North America, 35*(6), 1339–1347.

Spring, J. (1994). *American Education.* New York: McGraw-Hill.

Steinberg, L. (1996). *Beyond the classroom.* New York: Simon & Schuster.

Tabb, W. (1970). *The political economy of the Black ghetto.* New York: Norton.

Tatum, B. D. (1992). Talking about race, learning about racism: The application of racial identity development theory in the classroom. *Harvard Educational Review, 62*(1), 1–24.

Thorne, B. (1993). *Gender play.* New Brunswick, NJ: Rutgers University Press.

Tronyna, B., & Carington, B. (1990). *Education, racism and reform.* London: Routledge Kegan Paul.

Watson, C., & Smitherman, G. (1996). *Educating African American males: Detroit's Malcom X Academy.* Chicago: Third World Press.

Weinstein, R. S., Madison, S., & Kuklinski, M. (1995). Raising expectations in schooling: Obstacles and opportunities for change. *American Educational Research Journal, 32*(1), 121–159.

West, C. (1993). *Race matters.* Boston: Beacon.

Willis, P. (1977). *Learning to labor.* New York: Columbia University Press.

Wilson, W. (1978). *The declining significance of race.* Chicago: University of Chicago Press.

Wilson, W. (1987). *The truly disadvantaged.* Chicago: University of Chicago Press.

34

SOME CHALLENGES FACING QUEER YOUTH PROGRAMS IN URBAN HIGH SCHOOLS

Racial segregation and de-normalizing Whiteness

Lance Trevor McCready

Source: *Journal of Gay & Lesbian Issues in Education*, 1, 3, 2003, 37–51.

Abstract

Relatively little is known about the unique challenges facing queer youth programs such as Project 10 and Gay-Straight Alliances, housed in urban high schools where the majority of students are poor, non-White, and/or non-native English speakers. This article begins a conversation about two important issues that the author believes have an impact on queer youth programs in urban schools: racial segregation and the normalization of Whiteness. Data for the article are based on the author's participation in a school-university collaborative action research project at California High School (CHS) between 1996 and 2000. The project's research on participation in extracurricular activities led to the author's independent participant-observation in Project 10, the school's social/support group for lesbian, gay, bisexual, transgender, and questioning students. The results of these investigations suggest that the racially segregated social environment of CHS greatly affects the participation of queer students of color in Project 10. Additionally, faculty advisors for this program seemed less aware of the social/support needs of queer youth of color. In conclusion, the author suggests that through collaborative inquiry, students, teachers, and queer youth advocates develop awareness of the relationship between the social context of urban schools and participation in extracurricular activities. He also suggests that faculty advisors and queer youth advocates become more aware of the identities of queer youth of color by diversifying the curriculum and building coalitions with students and teachers who are broadly concerned with the ways multiple forms of oppression make urban schools ineffective and unsafe.

Relatively little is known about queer youth programs in urban schools and the unique challenges they face as a result of being housed in inner-city schools where the majority of students are poor, non-White and/or non-native English speakers. Here, I discuss my experiences working on a school-university collaborative action research project (CARP) at a California High School (CHS) located in a small urban community in the Bay Area of California.[1] My work on CARP led to independent participant-observation of Project 10. This social/support group for lesbian, gay, bisexual, transgender, and questioning students developed, by Dr. Virginia Uribe in 1984, as a school-based dropout prevention program and later evolved into the school's GSA.[2] During the four years I worked on CARP, between 1996 and 2000, I became intrigued with the way the school's racially segregated academic and social environment(s) affected student participation in extracurricular activities. As an out Black, gay, male educator, I was drawn to the question of why, in a school where over 60 percent of the students were non-White, Project 10 participants tended to be White female students. I conducted in-depth interviews with four openly gay, Black male students, two of which are excerpted in this article. These interviews, coupled with my own participant-observation in Project 10, lead me to conclude that two important challenges face queer youth programs in urban schools: racial segregation and de-normalizing Whiteness.

Racial segregation

Like many Bay Area educators, I was initially attracted to CHS because of its racially diverse student body and extensive curriculum. Soon after I began working there, meeting and spending time with various faculty members and students, I learned that this famed diversity had a down side. Jerome Pettigew,[3] a Black gay male English teacher, described CHS as "two schools under one roof." One school, he claimed, serves the needs of academically elite students who are predominantly White and Asian American (Chinese American and Japanese American) through extensive AP programs, extracurricular clubs and activities, and college preparatory classes. The other school serves lower achieving students, who are predominantly Black and Latino, with fewer programs to meet their academic and social needs. In short, persistent racial segregation in core and extracurricular programs continues to tarnish the otherwise hopeful integrated atmosphere of CHS.

While it was common knowledge that the football and basketball teams at CHS were predominantly Black, I was less attentive to the student demographics of non-athletic extracurricular activities until Fran Thompson, the faculty adviser for Project 10, invited me to speak at a Project 10 meeting during the 1996–97 academic year. On the day of the meeting, I walked into Fran's classroom expecting to see a collage of race and ethnicity. Instead of diversity, I found homogeneity: twelve White, female, lesbian and bisexual-identified students. So why didn't queer students of color attend Project 10 meetings at CHS?[4]

During the summer of 1996, CARP established the Taking Stock Committee (TSC) to investigate how CHS's racially segregated environment affects the academic performance of students, particularly low-achieving Black and Latino students. Several participants in CARP suspected that segregated patterns of participation in academic and extracurricular programs created the impression that students' racial identities determined their level of academic success. Understanding how this link was created, we felt, was a first step toward undoing it.

Because data on racial segregation in extracurricular activities had not yet been formally documented, the TSC decided to survey faculty on the extracurricular activities for which they served as advisors. Questions included the racial and gender breakdown of students participating, target populations, recruitment strategies, and purposes of the activities. These data could not be obtained through traditional school records of attendance, discipline, or standardized tests. TSC also administered the survey through face-to-face interviews to increase the faculty advisor response rate.

Table 1, organized by type of club and racial composition, summarizes data on the extracurricular activities. Figure 1 represents racial demographic data by

Table 1 Extracurricular Activities Organized by Type and Racial Composition

Academic/Career Clubs

Name of Club	*Racial Composition*
9th Grade Orientation	Not available
B.E.S.T.	Predominantly White
Close Up	Predominantly White
Community Service Resource Center	Predominantly students of color
CSF	Not available
ESL Yearbook	Predominantly students of color
Field Studies	Predominantly White
Homework Center	Predominantly students of color
Jacket (student newspaper)	Predominantly White
Junior Classical League	Predominantly White
Junior Statesman	Predominantly White
Key Club	Mixed
Literary Magazine	Predominantly White
Mock Trial	Predominantly White
Student Leadership	Predominantly White
UCO/MESA	Predominantly students of color
Uiamaa (Black student newpaper)	Predominantly students of color
Work Experience	Predominantly students of color
Yearbook	Predominantly White

Athletic

Badminton	Predominantly students of color
Baseball (JV & VAR)–boys	Mixed
Basketball (VAR)–boys	Predominantly students of color
Basketball (Frosh, JV & VAR)–girls	Predominantly students of color
Crew–boys	Predominantly White
Crew–girls	Predominantly White
Cross-Country–boys	Not available
Cross-Country–girls	Predominantly White
Diving–coed	Not available

(Continued)

273

Table 1 (Continued)

Name of Club	Racial Composition
Field Hockey–girls	Not available
Football (Frosh, JV & VAR)	Predominantly students of color
Golf–boys	Not available
Golf–girls	Not available
Lacrosse–boys	Not available
Lacrosse–girls	Not available
Soccer (JV & VAR)–boys	Not available
Soccer (JV & VAR)–girls	Predominantly White
Softball (JV & VAR)–girls	Predominantly White
Swim Team–boys	Not available
Swim Team–girls	Not available
Tennis–boys	Not available
Tennis–girls	Predominantly White
Track & Field–boys	Predominantly students of color
Track & Field–girls	Not available
Volleyball–boys	Predominantly White
Volleyball–girls	Not available
Wrestling–coed	Not available
Waterpolo–boys	Not available
Waterpolo–girls	Not available

Cultural

African Students Association	Predominantly students of color
Chicano-Latino Graduation	Predominantly students of color
German Exchange	Not available
International Ambassadors Club	Predominantly students of color
Islamic Student Union	Not available
Jewish Student Union	Predominantly White
Kiswahili	Predominantly students of color
Mexico Exchange	Predominantly White
Project 10	Predominantly White
Vietnamese Students Association	Predominantly students of color

Performing and Visual Arts

Acting Workshop	Predominantly White
Baile Folklorico	Predominantly students of color
CHS Voices of Joy	Predominantly students of color
Cheerleaders	Predominantly students of color
Choreography	Predominantly White
Concert Chorale	Predominantly White
Dance Projects	Predominantly White
Dramatic Art	Predominantly White
Jazz Band	Predominantly White
Magic Club	Predominantly White
Afro-Haitian Dance	Predominantly students of color
Production Acting	Predominantly White
Students Artists League	Predominantly White

Social Clubs

Bubbles Club	Predominantly White
Star Trek Club	Predominantly White

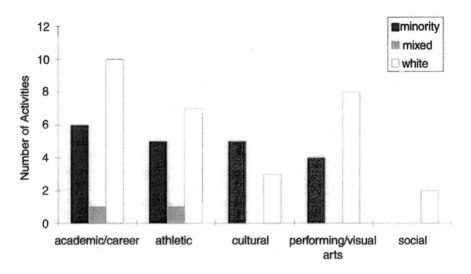

Figure 1 Taking Stock Clubs and Activities, by Race

the number of activities that are racially mixed, predominantly students of color, or predominantly White. Immediately noticeable is the small number of activities that are "mixed" in terms of race. Of the 73 activities surveyed, only two (three percent)–the Key Club, an activity that focuses on community service projects, and the boy's baseball team–were racially mixed.

Overall, extracurricular activities at CHS were racially segregated. Only 22 (the number of activities that are racially mixed + the number of activities that are predominantly students of color), or 30 percent, were activities where Black students might see themselves represented in any significant numbers. Moreover, excluding those activities geared towards students from other non-Black racial/ethnic backgrounds such as ESL Yearbook, Chicano-Latino Graduation, and Vietnamese Students Association, only eight or 11 percent of the activities were ones where Black students might interact with one another in any significant numbers.

Project 10 was one of the predominantly White extracurricular activities. Seeking an explanation, I interviewed two Black gay male students, Jamal and David, who attended CHS between the years 1992 and 2000. Their narratives revealed how they felt themselves under surveillance by their heterosexual Black peers who monitored the sexual "boundaries of blackness" (Cohen, 2001). For example, Jamal, who graduated from CHS in 1994, claimed that particularly among Black students, to align oneself with Project 10 meant to invite unnecessary scrutiny. Jamal believed these dynamics were particularly evident when students read the daily Bulletin announcing school-wide events, including Project 10:

[T]hey used to have announcements in the Bulletin, "Are you gay, bisexual, queer, questioning?" And then like I guess there would always be a designated reader for the class Bulletin everyday. . . . [I]t was interesting because when I would have a predominantly White class in morning second period when the Bulletin was read, like they would read it, they would read it. And people were just kinda like, just listen to it. There might be little side comments here and there, but they would listen and like, "That's a club in the school." But in the Black classes that I had, that same period? Ohhh my god, they would skip over it like the club did not exist. They would either speak through it [the announcement], or it was just treated differently than the other club announcements . . . [T]here was a running joke at school like people wanted to go and actually see who actually went to the club. . . . [I]t probably stopped a lot of people from going, the thought of someone seeing them go. Like you don't want to be seen walking up to the third floor on the day that Project 10 is meeting. Although Project 10 existed, as Jamal's memories suggest, it was not particularly safe or confidential.

Jamal's desire to display an appropriate Black identity that maintained social ties with his Black peers reflects what Signithia Fordham describes as the power of "fictive kinship" (Fordham, 1996). In studying the social identities and cultural frames of reference among Black students at Capital High School in Washington, D.C., Fordham observed that Black students may or may not have been related by blood, but they maintained essential social relationships that served a political function as well. When Black students used kinship terms such as "brother" or "sister" to refer to one another, it conveyed a sense of peoplehood or collective social identity. The fictive kinship systems of Black students at Capital High School included strategies for protecting their identity and maintaining boundaries between themselves and White students. Black students perceived certain behaviors and certain activities or events as inappropriate because Whites had established the performance criteria in those areas. Academic tasks and school-related activities represented one such area.

According to Fordham, since Black students at Capital High were involved in the evaluation of group members' eligibility for membership in the fictive kinship system, they controlled the criteria used to judge one's worthiness for membership. The determination and control of the criteria for membership in the fictive kinship system are in contrast to those for earning grades in school. From Fordham's point of view, fictive kinship means a lot to Black students because they regard it as the ideal by which members of the group are judged.

"Fictive kinship" may partially explain why Jamal stayed away from Project 10. Based on more than five years of participant-observation at CHS, I conclude that most peer groups, including those of Black students, viewed heterosexuality as the ideal. Any Black student daring to participate openly in Project 10 challenged this

276

ideal. At CHS, identifying as Black meant participating in extracurricular activities that were predominantly Black and heterosexual.[5]

Heterosexist fictive kinship networks, however, were not the only reason why Jamal and other Black gay male students avoided Project 10. Another invisible dynamic was the normalization of Whiteness.

Normalization of Whiteness

David, an openly gay, Black, biracial male student stayed away from Project 10 because the group's predominantly White, female composition alienated him:

D: [Project 10] is pretty much a select group of White girls. I've only been a few times. It's about four or five girls who all know each other. They're all out, you know, within that group. And they go there I guess for social support. That pretty much seems to be Project 10 at this point at CHS.

L: Has it always been that way?

D: Well for one thing I think it's important to say that the people who are in Project 10 are all pretty close. I don't know if whether or not that's because Project 10 creates relationships or because they all knew each other before Project 10. . . . And friends of theirs who may or may not be straight-identified may drop in and just hang out with them. But usually it's not related to queer support. It's usually just a social place where I guess they can talk about their girlfriends or whatever. But, even then, the few times that I went they were talking about upcoming events as far as queer activism or a ski trip. . . . I went two consecutive weeks and then I stopped going because it wasn't doing anything for me. There's nothing there for me; right now it's just teatime for a few lesbians and their friends.

David's statement reflects the tendency of White female students, like their black peers, to socialize with one another around a distinct set of racially-defined concerns, rather than build coalitions with students from different racial backgrounds, who may have an entirely different set of interests. In the racially segregated environment of CHS, the lack of a social/support agenda regarding race seemed inadvertently to privilege those students who de-emphasized their racial identity. In fact, both the original Project 10 at Fairfax High School in Los Angeles and CHS Project 10 lack a clear purpose regarding issues of racial equity.

Virginia Uribe, a White female counsellor at Fairfax High School, always recognized that queer youth were a diverse group. She wrote:

Crossing every boundary of race, religion and class, they have sat through years of public school education in which their identities have been overlooked, denied, or abused. They have been quiet due to their own fear and sense of isolation, as well as the failure of their parents and adult gay

277

men and women to be their advocates. The result has been a creation of a group of youngsters within our schools who are at significantly high risk of dropping out of school. (Uribe, 1995, p. 203)

However, she seemed less clear about how to address the needs of queer youth of color within the space of Project 10. Uribe implies that queer students of color should get their needs met by familiarizing themselves with resources in the community beyond the walls of school:

> The various cultures and races reflected in the United States are also reflected in the lesbian and gay population. Such adolescents face the prospect of living their lives within three rigidly defined and strongly independent communities: the lesbian and gay community, their ethnic or racial community, and the society at large. Each community fulfills basic needs which often would be imperiled if such communities would be visibly integrated. A common result is the constant effort to maintain a manner of living that keeps the three communities separate. This is a process that leads to increased isolation, depression, and anger, centered around the fear of being separated from all support systems, including the family. . . . As with parent issues, school personnel need to recognize the special issues that exist among minority lesbian and gays, and they should familiarize themselves with any community resources that may exist. (Uribe, 1995, p. 207)

By defining the complexities of identifying in society as queer and of color as a "special issue," Uribe, perhaps unconsciously, designated Project 10 at Fairfax High School as a space where Whiteness was normalized. One could interpret her suggestion that school personnel familiarize themselves with community resources outside the school as an acknowledgement of the limitations of Project 10 to provide support for students with complex social/support needs. On the other hand, given that Fairfax High School is predominantly students of color, to suggest that school personnel seek "community resources" for queer students suggests that Project 10's goals are politically narrow and deficient with regard to race.

Fran Thompson, faculty advisor for CHS Project 10, faced similar dilemmas trying to create and sustain a social/support group for queer youth that affirmed the identities of queer youth of color. Thompson suggested that the strong participation of White female students was related to the fact that they were the most concerned about encountering discrimination for being openly queer. In contrast, queer students of color seemed to relate more to groups outside of CHS such as Lavender, a support group run by the lesbian and gay community center. Admitting that "Diversifying the ethnic composition of the group is very complicated," Fran questioned her own ability to comprehend fully the multitude of pressures that queer students of color face.

Like Uribe, Thompson's limited understanding of the social/support needs of queer youth of color may have unintentionally alienated these youth, encouraging them to seek resources outside the school. In this way, Project 10 and other queer youth programs privilege White students whose identities are viewed as normal and more understandable compared to queer youth of color.

Developing an awareness of the relationship between contexts and participation

American public schools are now twelve years into the process of continuous resegregation. The desegregation of Black students, which increased continuously from the 1950s to the late 1980s, has now receded to levels not seen in three decades (Orfield, Eaton & Harvard Project on School Desegregation, 1996).

The social context of urban schools has an impact on participation in queer youth programs. Yet, too often the classroom or the club is viewed as island unto itself, independent of the social and cultural context of the school. Students and teachers who endeavor to establish and/or maintain urban queer youth programs that reflect the school's race and class diversity need to become aware of the social and cultural contexts of inner cities and the way these contexts affect participation in extracurricular activities.

CHS, like many high schools, is characterized by persistent racial segregation in academic and extracurricular programs. One of the most valuable outcomes of CARP was the positive awareness it brought to CHS faculty and staff regarding both formal and more casual belief systems and social practices that reproduce racial segregation in academic classes and extracurricular activities. When faculty, staff, students, parents, and administrators on TSC were given the opportunity to research the origins of racial segregation, they witnessed some of the social dynamics such as "fictive kinship" that produces racial segregation. They, too, had an all-too-rare opportunity to reflect on how their practices (teaching, advising, counseling, etc.) might reinforce or could interrupt social boundaries defined by race, gender, class, and sexual identity.

Collaborative action research that is respectful of the knowledge that faculty, staff, and students bring to the table can open the door for more effective school reforms. Before starting a social/support program for queer youth in an urban school or when seeking to strengthen these programs, students and educators should consider investigating the social and cultural context of the school and surrounding community, and exploring how these contexts are having an impact on participation in school programs and activities.

De-normalizing Whiteness

When Fran Thompson admitted that "Diversifying the ethnic composition of the group is very complicated," she questioned her ability to understand the multitude of pressures facing queer students of color. In doing so, she inadvertently normalized the lives of White queer students and relegated queer students of color to the margins of Project 10. Her narrative points to the need to de-normalize the perceived Whiteness of queer youth identity.

When Whiteness continues to be viewed as the norm, even in institutions and communities like CHS that are predominantly non-White, students of color are regarded as second-class citizens. When non-White racial identity is considered equally normal, queer youth programs are more likely to attract the participation of students from diverse backgrounds because the social, political, and support activities of the group are grounded in the concerns of multiple racial and ethnic communities.

More specifically, de-normalizing Whiteness creates opportunities for faculty advisors and queer youth advocates to diversify the curriculum of queer youth programs. Lipkin (1995, p. 35) notes that "if gay youth are exposed to the diversity of gay identities, to the richness of the culture, and to the long history of same-gender attraction, their development will be enhanced." Those who organize and/or facilitate queer youth programs can challenge the normalization of Whiteness by making a conscious effort to use speakers bureaus and workshop facilitators that are racially diverse, decorating the meeting room with queer historical figures from multiple racial and ethnic backgrounds, and having books, magazines, and other reading materials on hand that reflect a range of racial and ethnic experiences about queer identity.

In addition, de-normalizing Whiteness creates opportunities for students, faculty advisors, and queer youth advocates in urban schools to build coalitions. Allying with other students and teachers who are broadly concerned with the ways multiple forms of oppression such as institutional racism, poverty, and heterosexism can make urban schools more effective and safe for all students.

For example, during the 1997–98 academic year, David's frustration with the predominantly White female composition of Project 10 led him to organize a more diverse "political" group of students to fight not only homophobia and heterosexism, but also racism, violence, and other forms of social oppression that typically intersect the lives of queer students of color. This new group successfully organized several forums on homophobia and heterosexism, including one aimed at students of color and another directed at teachers that made connections between the marginalization of students of color and the harassment of queer students.

After David graduated from CHS he became peer leader of a queer youth group housed in the city's Lesbian, Gay, Bisexual, Transgendered Community Services Center (LGBTCSC). During his tenure as peer leader, David succeeded in increasing the involvement of queer youth of color. To make the group more inviting to youth of color he organized dances and other social events that had a "mixed cultural flavor." For example, he made sure that dance parties had two dance floors that played different kinds of music such as hip hop and salsa.

In addition to his work at the LGBTCSC, David began working with the newly formed GSA (that evolved from Project 10) at CHS. He coached the new faculty advisors (Fran "passed the torch" to two new faculty members in 1999) on how create to an environment that felt welcoming to students of color. He taught GSA peer leaders how to plan events that would appeal to racially diverse groups of students. Additionally, David encouraged CHS students of color who were involved with the queer youth group at CSC to become more active at CHS. David's efforts with respect to anti-racism work and diversity is a large reason why, when I attended a GSA meeting in 2001, the room was filled with a diverse group of CHS students that included African American, White, Latino, and multiracial students.

David's work, which emphasized coalition building, anti-racism, and a broad social justice agenda, is a strong indication that de-normalizing Whiteness can lead to stronger, more diverse social/support programs for queer youth that engage the entire school community in a war against the debilitating conditions of inner city schools. In David's words:

> I think we're just fighting against something much larger. You know when you're dealing with issues of homophobia or you know racism or whatever, all the issues that people at this school have to go through day to day, I think its everyone's job to try and remedy these problems.

Notes

1 CARP was a six-year project comprised of collaborative inquiry teams of teachers, students, administrators, parents, professors, and graduate students who investigated the reasons behind two problems CHS has faced since it voluntarily desegregated over 50 years ago: the race-class academic achievement gap and racial segregation in academic and extracurricular programs.

2 During the 1997–1998 school year, Fran Thompson, faculty advisor for CHS Project 10, persuaded the group to change its name to the Gay-Straight Alliance as a way of connecting the group's civic engagement goals to a national network of GSAs working to make schools safe for queer students (Bass & Kaufman, 1996). In addition, Fran felt the name change would improve the group's demographics by increasing the number of heterosexual-identified students present at weekly meetings, which in turn would enable queer students to feel more comfortable being active in the group without "outing" themselves. From Fran's perspective, increased comfort with being openly queer could lead to a broader political agenda that included spreading awareness of homophobia and heterosexism.

3 The names of students and school personnel have been changed to protect their identities.

4 I use the term queer as an umbrella term for lesbian, gay, bisexual, transgendered, and anyone else who claims a non-normative, nonheterosexual identity. I acknowledge that the term "queer" as an identity or statement of social location, does not resonate with everyone. Besides the fact that the term "queer" erases certain sociocultural differences among lesbians, gay men, bisexuals, etc., some also consider the term derogatory. I currently use it, however, to acknowledge the limitless possibilities of one's sexual identity, rather than the misleading stability of sexual orientation terms such as "gay" and "lesbian" seem to imply. Additionally, although most of the examples of queer people of color in this article used are Black, I do not interpret "of color" as a code for Black people.

5 The heterosexism of Black peer groups and the resultant surveillance of nonheterosexual identities by "fictive kin" are often interpreted as meaning the culture of Black people is more homophobic than that of whites. A full discussion of this issue is beyond the scope of this article. My sense, however, is that the idea of Black hyper-homophobia ignores the question of how historical circumstances have led to varied expressions of homophobia in different racial, ethnic, and/or cultural communities. For example, Constantine-Simms (2001) notes that African Americans' expression of homophobia in the Black church is related to the ways 19th century missionaries in Africa pathologized the sexual expression of indigenous Africans. The present article implies that, in urban schools, it is worth exploring the relationship between Black students' experience of racial segregation and other forms of marginalization, and the ways they express homophobia and heterosexism.

References

Bass, E., & Kaufman, K. (1996). *Free your mind: The book for gay, lesbian, and bisexual youth–and their allies.* New York: HarperPerennial.

Constantine-Simms, D. (2001). *The greatest taboo: Homosexuality in Black communities.* Los Angeles, CA: Alyson Books.

Fordham, S. (1996). *Blacked out: Dilemmas of race, identity, and success at Capital High.* Chicago, IL: University of Chicago Press.

Lipkin, A. (1993). The case for a gay and lesbian curriculum. *The High School Journal,* 77(1/2), 95–107.

Orfield, G., Eaton, S., & Harvard Project on School Desegregation. (1996). *Dismantling desegregation: The quiet reversal of Brown v. Board of Education.* New York: New Press.

Uribe, V. (1995). Project 10: A school-based outreach to gay and lesbian youth. In G. Unks (Ed.), *The gay teen* (pp. 203–210). New York: Routledge.

Part 9

RACE AND DIS/ABILITY

35

TOWARD AN INTERDISCIPLINARY UNDERSTANDING OF EDUCATIONAL EQUITY AND DIFFERENCE

The case of the racialization of ability

Alfredo J. Artiles

Source: *Educational Researcher*, 40, 9, 2011, 431–445.

The author argues for an interdisciplinary perspective to study the complexities of educational equity and transcend the limits of previous research. He focuses on the racialization of disability as a case in point; specifically, he reviews the visions of justice that inform the scholarship on racial and ability differences and situates their interlocking in a historical perspective to illustrate how race and ability differences have elicited paradoxical educational responses. The author also examines how the convergence of contemporary reforms is creating fluid markers of difference that change meanings across contexts, thus having distinct consequences for students' identities and schools' responses. He concludes with an outline of guiding ideas for interdisciplinary research on inequities that emerge at the intersections of race and ability differences.

Education researchers, policy makers, and practitioners have worked for generations to understand and change educational inequities. Unfortunately, this project has proved elusive at best, as reflected in various indicators of educational access and outcomes. The purpose of this article is to make the case for the use of interdisciplinary theoretical and methodological perspectives in the study of educational inequity. An interdisciplinary lens will enable us to do justice to the complexity of the equity challenges we face in the United States and transcend the limits of traditional research on educational equity. This is a timely project, for the shifting contemporary landscapes of educational policy and practice offer rich opportunities to study educational inequities from an interdisciplinary perspective. To illustrate, recent educational policy responses to struggling learners are increasing accountability pressures and blurring the boundaries between general and special education through initiatives such as Response to Intervention and through the monitoring of racial disparities in special education. These efforts create conditions for the construction of multiple views of *difference* in which disparate markers change their meanings and gain (or lose) currency across contexts, thus having distinct consequences for students' identities and schools' responses to them.

I focus this analysis of educational inequities on the historical interlocking of race and ability differences, specifically in connection with the so-called high-incidence or subjective disabilities—that is, intellectual disabilities, learning disabilities, speech/language impairments, and emotional/behavioral disorders—as a case in point because of the rich affordances of this topic for an analysis of equity and difference in education. In 2009–2010, these students comprised the majority of the population with disabilities in the nation and represented about 4 million children and youth in U.S. schools, about 69% of the entire special education population (U.S. Department of Education, 2009).

Although some commentators would argue that race and disability have maintained parallel histories in their respective struggles for educational equity, I argue that these notions of difference have been interlaced in complicated ways throughout the history of American education. In fact, the historical intertwining of race and disability has created tensions and paradoxes in educational responses to these differences. For instance, people with disabilities benefited from the momentum built by the civil rights victories of racial minority communities as they mobilized to attain rights and entitlements that culminated in the passage of the Individuals with Disabilities Education Act (IDEA). At the same time, concerns have been raised for more than 40 years about the disproportionate identification of disabilities among some racial groups. Table 1 summarizes key findings of this research that attest to the magnitude of the problem.

An interesting paradox in the racialization of disabilities is that the civil rights response for one group of individuals (i.e., learners with disabilities) has become a potential source of inequities for another group (i.e., racial minority students) despite their shared histories of struggle for equity. Are there productive ways to bridge the growing distance between the civil rights movements for people with disabilities and for racial minorities? Moreover, the inclusive education movement for students with disabilities has not addressed systematically the disproportionate presence of racial minority students in its agenda. How do we reconcile these contradictions? What are potentially useful interdisciplinary resources for the systematic examination and elimination of inequities for these groups across contexts and times? How do we interpret the silence about the layering of student identities and the power of cultural practices in the production of these inequities? In short, an interdisciplinary analysis of the racialization of disabilities opens unique opportunities to grapple with key aspects of the next generation of educational equity research.

Table 1 Highlights from racial disproportionality research

Donovan and Cross reported in 2002 that, at the national level, African Americans were 2.35 times more likely than White peers to receive an ID diagnosis. Native Americans were 24% more likely than their peers to receive an LD label. African Americans were 59% more likely than their counterparts to be identified as E/BD.

The ID category increased by 400% between 1948 and 1966; it was the largest disability group in 1975.

LD prevalence has grown by over 200% since 1975.

Boys represent about 80% of the E/BD population, 70% of LD students, and 60% of students with ID. Poor students are disproportionately represented in these categories.

After students are placed in special education, academic performance remains low, the risk for dropout and juvenile justice placement increases, and access to college is limited compared with that of their nondisabled peers; in adulthood this population tends to stay in low-paying jobs. White students with disabilities tend to do better than their racial minority peers.

Racial minority students have more limited access to related services and are placed in more segregated programs than their White peers with the same disability diagnosis.

Poverty is associated with disability status; however, race is a significant predictor of disability diagnosis after controlling for poverty. Poverty moderates the risk for disability diagnosis in complex ways, depending on school or community poverty levels, student race and gender, disability category, and school location.

Note. ID = intellectual disabilities; LD = learning disabilities; E/BD = emotional/behavioral disorders. From Artiles, Kozleski, et al., 2010; Donovan and Cross, 2002; Skiba et al., 2008.

I organize this article into three sections. First, I delve into the complexities of justice in the context of racial and ability differences, with a critical eye on the visions of justice that inform this scholarship. Second, I situate the interlocking of race and ability differences in a historical perspective as a means to highlight (dis)continuities in the ways that race and ability have elicited paradoxical, and at times problematic, responses from social institutions. I conclude with an outline of guiding ideas for interdisciplinary research on inequities at the intersections of race and ability differences.

Probing the complexities of justice: the case of race and ability differences

I present in this section a critical outline of justice views that have been used in the literature on race and ability differences as a means to identify areas in need of attention in future educational equity scholarship for racial minority learners.

Critiques of justice related to racial differences

Some of the most compelling critiques of justice views are found in scholarship related to racial differences. Charles Mills (1997) explained, for instance, that political philosophy historically has addressed questions about justice in abstract terms, whereas the justice concerns of oppressed and marginalized groups have stressed the material and historical conditions of their oppression. The classic distributive model of justice used in education has been critiqued on comparable terms. This model refers to the "morally proper distribution of social benefits and burdens among society's members" (Young, 1990, p. 16). The model contrasts alternative distribution patterns and decides which one is more just. This perspective has been criticized for focusing solely on end-state patterns (e.g., academic outcomes) at the expense of the social structures, institutional contexts, and decision-making processes that shape distributive practices (Young, 1990). The processes that lead to the end-state patterns are erased. An example is the work on school racial desegregation that is solely concerned with shifting enrollment demographics, because it leaves "intact the meritocratic nature of schools" that created the inequities in the first place (Christensen & Dorn, 1997, p. 187).

Another racial justice approach is concerned with representation and participation. In this view, the goal is *equal participation* (Fraser, 2007); injustices are created by *maldistribution*, that is, unequal access to resources, and *misrecognition*, that is, devalued standings mediated by institutional hierarchies that prevent individuals or groups from full participation (Fraser, 2007). A traditional example is curriculum reforms to improve the representation of racialized groups. A risk is that representation could lead to essentializing groups since the struggle for representation is centered on a particular vision of the group's identity. Epstein's (2007) analysis of the politics of inclusion in medical research illustrates how equity work driven by representation agendas advanced recognition of longstanding invisible differences but also reinscribed essentializing assumptions about the group engaged in the representation struggles.

Participation in justice work can also take on ambiguous shades. Questions arise, for example, related to the telos of participation in a given society (e.g., Is the goal to assimilate racial minorities?). What about the existing structures of oppression in the contexts in which participation will take place? Should participation have a transformative bent? What counts as participation, and who defines it? (See Artiles, Kozleski, Dorn, & Christensen, 2006.)

Critiques about racial justice have been advanced in other disciplines, such as law. Scholars have used the notion of *White innocence* in law as an analytic framework to critique legal texts, decisions, and theories. Gotanda (2004) offered a critique of constitutional law theories building on Laurence Tribe's work. He explained that the justice theorist who tended to "look away from the substantive claims of a subordinated group and to focus upon abstract notions of democracy strips away any of the societal linkages that create real, social, human beings" (p. 668). He argued that the notion of White innocence demands attention to the ideological underpinnings of legal decisions and texts and of legal scholars' work. Gotanda applied the White innocence framework to *Brown v. Board of Education* and concluded that this landmark decision was "an exercise in white innocence" (p. 672). He traced the ambiguous nature of the legal precedents that allowed the court to affirm that a new set of conditions were at play in 1954, thus letting the court off the hook from responsibility for the historical racial segregation that pervaded the country. Gotanda argued that Chief Justice Warren's decision, based largely on *new* psychological evidence, represented a sort of "Aha! Moment" that enabled the court to focus on the present, thus erasing a multigenerational history of racial segregation. "The Aha! Moment has, through the use of a 'new' beginning, cut off the moral, social, economic, and political ties to the past. . . . [It's] the innocence of a new beginning" (Gotanda, 2004, p. 673). The analysis of ideological assumptions in legal decisions along with attention to the benefits accrued from the innocence claimed in the "Aha! Moment" enabled Gotanda to document how this significant legal decision in the history of the United States constituted an exercise in White innocence.

Ross (1990) relied on a rhetorical analysis to examine how race has been treated in the history of law. Ross explained that the field of law, like other disciplines, over time has developed discursive strategies and has crafted theories, artifacts, and practices to define and study its object. Legal rhetoric is a prime example of such a professional vision, and Ross argued that there has been a legal rhetoric of race throughout the history of the United States that strives to "make smooth the cracked surface of the law's response to race . . . obscuring the conflicts and paradoxes, smoothing over choices for which we would later feel nothing but shame" (p. 3). Ross's analysis centers on the work of two rhetorical themes, namely, *White innocence*, that is, "the insistence on the innocence of contemporary whites," and *Black abstraction*, that is, "the refusal to depict blacks in any real and vividly drawn social context" (p. 2). It should be noted that the power of Black abstraction resides largely in the fact that it erases the humanness of African Americans—a recurrent theme in scientific and public discourses in American history (Hammonds & Herzig, 2008)—which in turn erodes empathetic responses from Whites to the suffering of African Americans. Similarly, White innocence's power stems from its intricate connection to cultural archetypes about the nature and positions of the White and Black races across various realms (e.g., religious, sexual, cultural; Ross, 1990).

In his analysis of *Plessy*, Ross quoted Justice Brown's decision to illustrate the work of these rhetorical themes:

> We consider the underlying fallacy of plaintiff's argument to consist in the assumption that the enforced separation of the two races stamps the colored race with a badge of inferiority. If this be so, it is not by reason of anything found in the act, but solely because the colored race chooses to put that construction upon it. (As quoted in Ross, 1990, p. 31)

Through absolution of the act of sanctioning separation and blaming Black folks for supposedly self-imposed inferiority, the legal decision granted innocence to White society and naturalized the segregation of the races (Ross, 1990). Moreover, addressing racial segregation in abstract terms, devoid of any consideration of the socioeconomic, historical, and political situations of Black communities, enabled the court to use effectively the rhetorical theme of Black abstraction. In contrast, Ross (1990) concluded that *Brown v. Board of Education* represented "both a moment of transition and a moment of continuity" (p. 38) in the legal rhetoric of race. "Abstraction from social context was rejected [through the acknowledgment of the social-psychological impact of racial segregation on African American children]; 'white innocence' was left intact" (given the Court's silence about the racist intentions of racial segregation; p. 38).

To conclude, the scholarship on racial differences offers a powerful critique of justice theories and remedies through an engagement with the material conditions of inequity. It dissects the ideological underpinnings of legal decisions and practices and offers analytical tools to confront the role of power in justice questions and dilemmas. This work also raises questions about the role of academic disciplines in generating knowledge that objectifies people into subjects through "dividing practices," in this case those germane to racial differences (Foucault, 1982); this is a recurrent theme in my analysis.

Parallel narratives of justice related to ability differences

The history of ability differences and the role that justice has played in it is not based on a monolithic narrative. The dominant ability difference model (which I describe as canonical) has informed many policies, personnel preparation programs, funding priorities, and research programs and is framed from a medical perspective in which the condition of disability is traceable to individuals' characteristics. Justice in this vision of ability differences historically has been grounded in a distributive paradigm that stresses individual rights. The underlying logic is that people with disabilities are oppressed by virtue of exclusion from access to and use of resources, for example, specialized educational services and access to general education.

The canonical model's reliance on an individual rights discourse has had several key consequences for policy and practice. For instance, the educational outcomes of students with disabilities ultimately depend on their own individual worth and effort (Varenne & McDermott, 1999). Second, the vision of justice embodied in policies and practices erases the histories of marginalization and underservice that many student subgroups (e.g., racial minority) placed in this system experienced across generations (Rizvi & Lingard, 1996). Third, most legal and policy principles of special education do not alter the hierarchical nature of schools (Christensen & Dorn, 1997), thus making special education complicit in the perpetuation of educational inequities for certain subgroups of students, most notably poor students and racial minority learners. Note that the canonical narrative does not weave race systematically and explicitly in its trope, even though the struggles that led to P.L. 94–142 built on the momentum created by the civil rights movement for African Americans (Artiles et al., 2006).

A parallel justice narrative explicitly links disability with race and critiques the justice views embedded in the discourses of special and inclusive education (Artiles et al., 2006). The bulk of that narrative focuses on the racialization of disability and the overidentification of African Americans, Native Americans, and Latinos in special education throughout history (Harry & Klingner, 2006). Although disability and race are framed as social constructions, the narrative places a greater emphasis on cultural historical issues germane to racial differences at the expense of a critique of the social construction of disability, akin to what the disability studies field has produced. In turn, with a few exceptions (e.g., Erevelles & Minear, 2010; Ferri & Connor, 2005), the disability studies community has not systematically woven the role of race into its understanding of disability identity constructions. Tremain (2005) pointed out that the disability studies community has largely theorized power from (borrowing from Foucault) a "juridico-discursive" perspective; in this view, "power is construed as a fundamentally repressive thing, which is possessed by centralized externalized authority such as a particular social group, a class, an institution, or the state, and which reigns over, and down upon, others" (p. 9).

The work on the racialization of disabilities and that on disability studies have critiqued the underlying notions of justice that permeate current policies and the dominant medical paradigm. Both advance a critique based on the limits of a liberal vision of justice because of its reliance on individual rights and its historical amnesia (Artiles, 2003; Ferri & Connor, 2005). The work on the inclusion of students with disabilities framed from a communitarian justice discourse also has been critiqued for its limited engagement with historical legacies of oppression and lack of specificity, among other reasons (Artiles et al., 2006).

In summary, analyses and critiques of justice related to race and ability differences address several of the limits of classic justice theories that are used in the educational equity scholarship. Nevertheless, largely missing in this work is explicit attention to the intersection of markers of difference and a cultural analysis of the conditions that surround the production of inequities. What is needed is an examination of "power relations through the antagonism of strategies," particularly a dissection of various types of struggles (Foucault, 1982, p. 780). In the next section, I present an analytic summary of scholarship on the interlocking of race and ability differences over time as a means to enrich the preceding critique of justice.

Tracing the interlocking of race and ability differences: then and now

Legal and policy issues are discussed in this section from a historical perspective as they affect the racialization of disabilities.

Race, disability, disease, poverty, and the body in historical perspective

Notwithstanding the blind spots and limits of the educational discourses on race and ability differences and justice, insights on their intersectionality have been produced in other disciplines. This work deepens our understanding of the cultural historical and ideological sedimentation of the intersections of race and

291

disability that challenges the medical model and transcends the limits of the social model of disability.

Schweik's (2009) analysis focuses on the so-called ugly law that became increasingly visible at the end of the 19th century (also known as the *unsightly beggar ordinances*), that is,

> a certain strong and unified project shared by and across various city cultures, involving both a judgment about bodily aesthetics and the use of law to repress the visibility of human diversity in social contexts associated with disability and poverty—what we might call the sighting/citing of the ugly. (p. 3)

There was considerable variability in the framing of these ordinances, for neither the beggar nor "the crime of 'unsightliness' appears in all places" (p. 4). Columbus (Ohio), for instance, used the heading (as late as 1972) "exposing self when unsightly." Denver categorized the law in 1886 under the section title "Deformed, Diseased or Maimed Persons" (Section 1009), which stated that a "deformed" person "shall not expose himself to public view." In turn, Chicago's municipal code of 1911 used the heading "Exposing diseased or mutilated limbs" for a law that stated, "Exposure of diseased, mutilated, or deformed portions of the body prohibited" (as quoted in Schweik, 2009, p. 9).

The legal discourses about the ugly, the begging, and the disabled are embroidered in the tapestry of a project to regulate deviant bodies, for they constitute virtually synonymous histories (Schweik, 2009). Layered on this composite of deviance comes race, as part of larger American historical and legal narratives about what Farley (2002) called "nobodyness," which includes other outlaw ontologies (e.g., those of prostitutes and immigrants). Indeed, ugly laws regulated "who could be where, who would be isolated and excluded, who had to be watched, whose comfort mattered" (Schweik, 2009, p. 184). Note that the regulation of disabled and racialized people was intricately entwined in this legal discourse. "It is not accidental," Schweik argues, "that enactment of ugly laws, which peaked in the mid 1890s, emerged with intensity at the moment of statutory Jim Crow" (p. 189). Like ugly laws germane to disabled individuals, the history of racial segregation is full of codes, regulations, and laws about the surveillance of Black bodies on sidewalks and in stores, businesses, trains, and other public spaces.

Health and disease also were enmeshed in the surveillance of deviance as a means to prevent public health threats. Krieger (2011) explained how

> by the early nineteenth century the scientific discourse of human "variety" had morphed into discussion of human "races," ordered by superiority. . . . In this schema, "race" simultaneously and tautologically became a category defined by—and used to explain—racial differentials in morbidity and mortality. . . . "Racial" categories become so entrenched and "naturalized" in scientific thought that, by the early-to-mid

nineteenth century, medical discussion about populations—and research on their health status—without "racial" categories became virtually unimaginable. (pp. 89, 91)

Consequently, scientific outlets and popular media were regularly populated by papers and reports that described biological differences, mental abilities, illness predispositions, and prevalence of diseases (e.g., mental illnesses) among African Americans, as part of their overall portrayal as inferior to White subjects (Krieger, 2011). Debates ensued about the nature of the data and methodological techniques used in these studies. An important consequence was that "debates about Black/White health status were central, not ancillary, to the content, conduct, and validity of the U.S. Census, U.S. health data, and U.S. health research" (Krieger, 2011, p. 92). The fact is that the sociohistorical conditions of African Americans at the end of the 19th century contributed to this "symbolic economy of disease" (Schweik, 2009, p. 193) that led to the interlocking of race, disease, disability, and poverty. Indeed, the health status of African Americans deteriorated markedly after generations under a substandard health care system maintained by the institution of slavery, the effects of the Civil War, and discriminatory policies and treatment.

Eugenic discourses also contributed during this era to the cultural work of deviance regulation and the ranking of bodies that targeted the usual suspect ontologies, namely, disability and race (Baker, 2002; Snyder & Mitchell, 2006). Intellectual disabilities were a primary target under the notion of "feeblemindedness [that] came to operate as an umbrella concept that linked off-white ethnicity, poverty, and gendered conceptions of lack of moral character together and that feeblemindedness thus understood functioned as the signifier of tainted whiteness" (Stubblefield, 2007, p. 162; see also Trent, 1994). The efforts of this movement, for what Baker (2002) described as "population quality control," had mixed results, although as I explain in the next section, they have transmogrified into new discourses in which the govern-mentality of deviance continues to evolve. Lowe (2000) identified five areas of educational policy and practice that were deeply influenced by eugenic ideas: testing, differential treatment, quality of home life and mothering, transmission of opinions through children's books and school texts, and the planning of educational buildings. It is likely some of these influences had consequences for the racialization of disability.

Disability and racial laws were enacted largely through visual identification, which suggests, in Roach's (2001) terms, that "skin is the principal medium that has carried the past into the present" (p. 102). The intermingling of social class, disability, disease, and racial segregation drilled leaks in the taxonomic economy of deviance and disease, due in part to the reliance on White subjects to determine visually the other's identity essence. Hence, racial and other forms of segregation have constituted a "complex fabric of structural ambiguity" (Cell, 1982, p. 3). A key consequence of this state of affairs has been that skin color is both a legal status and a performance (Schweik, 2009).

People inhabiting more than one identity category, however, created problems for this system, which had two major consequences. First, disruptions in the application of these categorical identities prompted additional managerial resolutions. This likely explains the proliferation of "ugly" ordinances in the late 1800s that tackled the interrelated categories of Black, immigrant, disabled, beggar, and diseased (Schweik, 2009). Second, the legal apparatus demanded a positivist logic that, despite the ambiguous nature of race and disability, relentlessly compelled White enforcers to make unambiguous decisions. The question arises as to whether the increasing density of managerial solutions and the positivist requirements in enforcement systems influenced professional practices in schools to produce and maintain the racialization of disabilities.

Despite the variability among these laws, some of which were still in effect as late as the 1970s, it is important to note that they were founded in a quintessentially American ideology, namely, individualism, which located disability, race, and begging as problems rooted in the individual. The historical intertwining of race and disease reported by Schweik (2009) and Krieger (2011) constitutes a narrative of visual exclusion and of (Foucauldian) discursive formation that unveiled how bodies were normalized in the laws and the means through which aesthetic conceptions of beauty were systematically associated with poverty, disease, and race (Foucault, 2005). These are important insights, not only because of the moral repercussions of the ideological work attained with these laws but also because they disrupt mainstream historical accounts of these ordinances as solely concerned with disability, that is "ungendered (that is, male), unraced (that is, white), without a nationality (that is, American), and unsexualized (that is, heterosexual, but only in default)" (Schweik, 2009, p. 18).

To conclude, many efforts to change educational inequities and enhance opportunities rest on problematic assumptions and values about race and ability differences and have been informed in part by the ideologies of meritocracy and individualism. Critiques of these efforts gain new depth and texture when placed in the historical contexts in which the traditional axes of difference—race, disability, poverty, disease—have been defined, and in which those at the wrong end of the axes have been regulated and have struggled "against the 'government of individualization'" (Foucault, 1982, p. 781). Scientific, legal, and policy discourses, with their attendant rhetorical and analytical tools and their monitoring and compliance technologies have played a key role in such govern-mentality. As I explain below, this state of affairs can create conditions for struggles against "subjection" (i.e., forms of subjectivity[1] and submission) that are tied to markers of difference such as race and disability (Foucault, 1982) and that can end up reifying a symbolic economy of difference.

Race and disability in contemporary education: the equity vagaries of naming and ordering

Although the discourses and practices that intertwined race and ability with other dimensions of difference took place at a distant time, they are well and alive in current educational policy and practice. A mosaic of narratives maintains the currency of the race–ability binomial ontology. Examples include "quality," "risk," "safety," and even "equity," and they are embedded in policies and practices associated with No Child Left Behind (NCLB), inclusive education, Response to Intervention (RTI), and the monitoring of racial disproportionality in special education. Each of these narratives and their intersections create what Baker (2002) termed *outlaw ontologies*—"a way of being or existing that is thought outside the normal and as such to need chasing down" (p. 674). This state of affairs has fostered the contemporary govern-mentality (Foucault, 1982) of the race–disability binomial ontology.

I use NCLB as a point of departure to show how, through the management of (racial and ability) *differences*, this policy embodies a case of what Epstein (2007) calls the "inclusion-and-difference paradigm."[2] He used the term to describe the politics of difference in medical research. I use it to describe the work that NCLB does to intertwine "the meaning of biological difference [with] the status of socially subordinated groups . . . [through the articulation of] a distinctive way of asking and answering questions about the demarcating of subpopulations of patients and citizens" (Epstein, 2007, p. 18). Thus, NCLB promises accountable educational systems for students with disparate backgrounds and ability levels, through the disaggregation of outcome data for subgroups of marginalized students such as racial and linguistic minority and disabled learners. In other words, this contemporary educational equity project erases difference (i.e., same outcomes for all subgroups of students), while it also reinscribes difference (i.e., a surveillance system organized by subgroups of students). The principal means for enacting the policy include regulations to improve teacher quality, increase student achievement (which is monitored through testing), and increase educational choice.

This form of "biopolitical paradigm" demands the inclusion of various forms of difference in delivering the promise of educational equity through outcome tracking for underserved groups (e.g., defined through membership in race, language, or ability groups). I adapt Epstein's use of the notion of "biopolitical paradigm." He relies in part on Foucault's work to describe the "frameworks, ideas, standards, formal procedures, and unarticulated understandings that specify how concerns about [learning, education] . . . and the body are made the simultaneous focus of [evidence-based educational interventions] and state policy" (Epstein, 2007, p. 17). It is a biopolitical model because the subgroup definitions are partly embedded in assumptions about identity purportedly framed by biological differences (e.g., race, disability).

On the other hand, there are crucial dimensions of *representation* embedded in this policy. Like the inclusion-and-difference model in medical research, NCLB offers representation in *social visibility* and *political* terms—that is, the requirement for outcome reporting by subgroup gives marginalized communities an opportunity to disrupt their historical invisibility in systems' accountability, and the subgroup disaggregation of outcome data indexes an equity focus for these underserved groups. We could construe NCLB, therefore, as fostering new forms of *biopolitical citizenship* in which membership in the various subgroups purportedly promises access to resources, status, and affiliations that afford social mobility (Epstein, 2007)—that is, a high-quality educational system in which everybody excels. Specifically, NCLB promises that the educational system will be accountable to all students; otherwise, the pledge is that schools will be closed, teachers fired, and/or students transferred to better schools. However, this emerging biopolitical citizenship might end up reinscribing the historical deficit narrative about race and disability.

Note that a complex though subtle process of *categorical alignment* (Epstein, 2007) takes place under NCLB so that administrative, sociohistorical, and scientific categories come to be overlaid as if they had the same meanings. "The marker of successful categorical alignment work is that it becomes invisible in hindsight" (Epstein, 2007, p. 92). Let us consider, for instance, NCLB's requirement to report outcome data for students with disabilities. In this case, the *sociohistorical* meanings of disability, which weave together a social movement, racialized assumptions, and exclusion, are implicitly aligned in this policy with the administrative classifications of disability, despite the substantial variability of definitions and operationalizations across geographical regions (Donovan & Cross, 2002). Similarly, scientific constructions of disability, with their historical sedimentations of definitional and measurement changes and intersections with racial classifications, are purportedly aligned through the requirement of achievement outcome reports for students with disabilities. This way, NCLB implicitly promises to address a major technical and political problem—overhauling the educational system—along with a justice project—leveling the playing field of educational outcomes.

Categorical alignment has also served as a scaffold for the emergence of *niche standardization,*

> a general way of transforming human populations into standardized objects available for scientific, political administration, marketing, or other purposes that eschews both universalism and individualism and instead standardizes at the level of the social group—one standard for men, another for women, one standard for blacks, another for whites, another for Asians; one standard for children, another for adults; and so on. (Epstein, 2007, p. 135)

NCLB seems to have bought into the niche standardization model used in contemporary medical research, through the subgroup reporting practices. However, as I explain in the next section, categorical alignment and niche standardization have negative consequences, particularly for students embodying multiple identity categories (race/disability).

Consequences of the inclusion-and-difference paradigm in a policy-saturated world

The implementation of NCLB has been neither smooth nor uncontested. Darling-Hammond (2007) reported that

more than 20 states and dozens of school districts have officially pro-
tested the Act, voting to withdraw from participation, withhold local
funding for implementation or resist specific provisions. One state and
a national teachers association have brought lawsuits against the federal
government based on the unfunded costs and dysfunctional side-effects
of the law. Members of the Congressional Black Caucus, among other
federal legislators, have introduced bills to place a moratorium on high-
stakes standardized testing . . . withhold school sanctions until the bill
is fully funded and require progress toward adequate and equitable educational opportunities for students in public schools. And the Harvard
Civil Rights Project, along with other advocacy groups, has warned that
the law threatens to increase the growing dropout and push-out rates
for students of color, ultimately reducing access to education for these
students. (p. 246)

This is the case partly because of the policy's theory of action and its implementation idiosyncrasies and because of the policy saturation of the education
field. Indeed, NCLB intersects with other major policies and reform strategies,
further compounding contradictions, tensions, and ambiguities in educational
practice, all of which affect the subgroups of students expected to benefit from
this policy. The most salient ripple effects are unintended consequences associated with multiple niche standardizations.

The structural consequences of black-boxing
educational achievement

The implementation of NCLB without consideration of structural inequities (e.g.,
uneven access to financial and personnel resources) has had unintended consequences that hurt the very students that were expected to benefit from it. Nichols
and Berliner (2007), for instance, documented the collateral damage caused by the
testing craze associated with NCLB. Examples of such damage are schools' devot-
ing inordinate amounts of time to practicing test-taking skills and teaching to the
test, differential allocation of resources to students who are on the cusp of reaching the test score threshold that would move up a school's accountability report,
and cheating practices to make test results look better. Valli and Buese (2007)
also documented the impact of the accountability movement on teacher–student
relations, which are affected because most students in low-performing schools
are shuffled throughout the school day between remedial programs and interventions as a means to increase their test performance. Moreover, these researchers
unveiled teachers' declining morale and sense of professional well-being in light
of the accountability movement's disregard for teacher professional knowledge
and clinical decision making.

Again, the most affected have been students living double-bind identities such
as racial minority disabled students. For instance, "the chances that a school would

be designated as failing increased in proportion to the number of demographic groups served by the school" (Novak & Fuller, 2003). Moreover, because of the racial segregation of schools around the nation, schools with the largest concentration of minority students living in poverty who already underperform on standardized tests have the greatest chance of having their federal funding further reduced, which in turn will impinge upon improvement efforts (Darling-Hammond, 2007). A perverse repercussion of the policy is that expected yearly progress will be greatest for the lowest performing schools that are already badly strapped financially and serve large concentrations of students considered vulnerable (Darling-Hammond, 2007). These consequences set off a spiral of additional negative developments that worsen these high-need schools. For example, as funding cuts undermine performance gains in adequate yearly progress reports, schools are labeled "failing," which will cause the best teachers to move to other schools or stay away from the failing ones (Darling-Hammond, 2007). Therefore, NCLB's original justice project is subverted by the structural consequences of its implementation, which Darling-Hammond has called "diversity penalty." Meanwhile, there is a push to expand the percentage of students with disabilities who take alternate accountability assessments. Aside from the negative consequences that this decision would have on students with disabilities, it might also alleviate the accountability pressures on schools through the placement of racial minority students in special education, thus contributing to the racialization of disability.

The faces of justice in a policy-saturated world: leaks in niche standardization

Niche standardization has several appealing features that could potentially benefit NCLB's agenda, including a commitment to representation of various groups and attention to within-group variability. On the other hand, setting accountability requirements by subgroups suggests a reductionist logic that purports that background traits have a main effect on test performance. Furthermore, NCLB's niche standardization is fraught with paradoxes that end up undermining its initial promises. Specifically, just as the act requires monitoring outcomes by subgroups, it also can erase some of these groups from the final auditing. Students with disabilities can be tested with alternate assessments, and these results could be regarded as nonproficient; the test results could also be excluded from accountability reports "if they apply to fewer than 2% of all test-takers" (Darling-Hammond, 2007, p. 250). In other instances, some of the very social groups used to challenge the assumption of a universal learner in the niche standardization architecture of NCLB are defined in such a way that makes it implausible to attain the original goals of the act (Darling-Hammond, 2007). A case in point is the group of students labeled *limited English proficient* (LEP), a definition that entails the inability to attain proficient levels. As these students acquire the label *English proficient*, they migrate out of the LEP category, and thus their test performance is not accounted for in the LEP accountability report, which creates a self-perpetuating cycle of underperformance for the subgroup. In certain localities, LEPs do not shed the label but add a disability identity (Artiles, Rueda, Salazar, & Higareda, 2005).

Other parallel reforms and policies strive to achieve equity in educational processes and outcomes that could conceivably advance NCLB's work. Nevertheless, as I explain below, these reforms and policies rest on comparable niche standardization schemes, and their overlaying with the NCLB accountability world is eroding the attainment of justice goals and tightening the race–ability knot. Two such efforts are RTI and IDEA's requirements for reporting and monitoring of special education placement patterns by student racial subgroups.

RTI aspires to strengthen the interface between general and special education, with particular attention to students with learning disabilities and to a lesser extent with emotional/behavioral disorders (Vaughn & Fuchs, 2003). It offers nothing less than reframing responses to struggling learners, using a public health lens in which prevention, early intervention, and ongoing data-based performance monitoring are the hallmarks. Tiers of increasing intensity and individualization are built into the educational system, and students move through the tiers depending on their lack of responsiveness to interventions. Tier 1 encompasses instructional strategies for all students, with the use of systematic screening and ongoing monitoring of performance to identify struggling learners who might need attention in Tier 2—which entails a more intense form of intervention in small-group formats, ranging between 8 and 16 weeks of treatment. The last step on the ladder (Tier 3) is special education. To succeed, interventions must be delivered with a high level of fidelity. "A central assumption is that responsiveness to treatment can differentiate between two explanations for low achievement: poor instruction versus disability" (Fuchs, 2002, p. 521). RTI also offers to reduce the longstanding racialization of disability through better (and instructionally valid) identification technologies. "In summary, RTI promises to improve the distribution of valued resources (evidence-based instruction) and address misrecognition injustices through more precise identification procedures" (Artiles, Bal, & King-Thorius, 2010, p. 252).

Despite the well-intentioned aspirations of RTI, this model subscribes to a universal learner perspective since it tends to rely on standardized instructional protocols and assessment measures with no apparent regard for cultural or linguistic variability. These practices create tension with RTI's purported commitment to reduce the racialization of disability, although on closer examination, they represent a color-blind commitment in which the race–disability knot will be untied through technical solutions—that is, more accurate diagnostic decisions.

It could be argued that RTI is concerned with an alternative version of niche standardization. While NCLB defines subgroups a priori to track the impact of educational interventions, RTI rests on an inductive approach when defining subgroups in order to enact its version of niche standardization. Specifically, NCLB black-boxes student movement across subgroups; it only regulates how to manage the outcome data for the already formed subgroups. In contrast, all students presumably enter RTI as standard learners. Through the screening of discrete skills, subgroups of students become new kinds, namely, at risk (or struggling) and non–at risk. Movements to different spaces of the educational system are required as these student ontologies morph, so that, for example, at-risk learners move to small-group intensive intervention settings. Yet others eventually become disabled, thus moving to new instructional ecologies.

It is not yet clear what will be the consequences of the intersections of accountability practices with RTI implementation strategies, with their different versions of niche standardization. Emerging evidence about the implementation of RTI suggests that this model may be taking on narrower and problematic meanings and functions across regions of the country. For example, it has been reported that some districts and schools in the Southwest are now "referring students to RTI" (Orosco & Klingner, 2010) or that certain students in the Northeast are being "RTIed" (E. Fergus, personal communication, January 2011). The emerging evidence on RTI troubles also comes from the federal level. In a recent memo disseminated by the U.S. Department of Education's Office of Special Education Programs (OSEP), state directors of special education were informed of the following:

> It has come to the attention of [OSEP] that, in some instances, [local education agencies, or LEAs] may be using [RTI] strategies to delay a timely initial evaluation for children suspected of having a disability. States and LEAs have an obligation to ensure that evaluations of children suspected of having a disability are not delayed or denied because of implementation of an RTI strategy. (Memo to state directors from OSEP, January 21, 2011)

This memo excerpt raises questions about the interface between RTI and special education and how niche standardizations may be creating tensions and contradictions. On the one hand, it is assumed students move through RTI tiers based on the analysis of performance data. This ought to be done carefully and thoughtfully to avoid misidentification, particularly for racial minority and poor students. In this context, what constitutes "delay [of] a timely initial evaluation"? Is the problem observed at Tier 2, where small-group interventions might be extended beyond the time protocol stipulated for the chosen treatment? Or are the delays happening in Tier 1? If so, is the expectation that struggling students in Tier 1 skip Tier 2 and go straight into Tier 3? How are practitioners expected to interpret this message in light of RTI's promise to reduce the disproportionate representation of racial minority students?

Consideration of the enforcement of IDEA's provisions related to racial disproportionality in special education further contextualizes the contemporary intertwining of race and disability. Although disability identification under federal law grants distinctive rights and triggers various procedural safeguards and timelines to protect individuals, there is a longstanding concern with the disproportionate placement of racial minority students. The persistent and compelling nature of this evidence has led to questions about systemic bias (see Table 1).

All in all, the available evidence defies simplistic interpretations that oscillate between individual (e.g., poverty and its concomitant developmental deficits) and structural (e.g., institutional racism) explanations (Artiles, Kozleski, Trent, Osher, & Ortiz, 2010). This 43-year-old problem triggered two National Research Council reports in a 20-year period, along with several other reform efforts, including amendments to IDEA. OSEP is responsible for enforcing and monitoring the 2004 IDEA disproportionality provisions.[3] OSEP's regulations to implement these provisions call for states to identify LEAs with racial disproportionality resulting from *inappropriate identification.*[4] Racial disproportionality is examined in special education and related services (Indicator 9) and by disability category (Indicator 10). According to Albrecht et al. (in press), OSEP created a dual monitoring system to enforce these IDEA provisions

> based on two parts of the statute. First, Section 616 makes "disproportionate representation of racial and ethnic groups in special education . . . to the extent the representation is the result of inappropriate identification" a monitoring priority area and the primary source for states to report to the Secretary and to the public under Indicators 9 and 10. Second, Section 618 requires that each state collects and analyzes data to determine if "significant disproportionality based on race and ethnicity is occurring in the state and the [LEAs] of the State" with respect to identification, placement and discipline, and if so, these LEAs must spend 15% of their Part B funds on coordinated early intervening services. (Albrecht, Skiba, Losen, Chung, & Middelberg, in press)

These provisions and regulations seem intent on maintaining a clean typology in which race and disability are kept apart. As a way to enforce the categorical alignment that characterizes niche standardization in the special education field, these policies send the message that racial differences trump ability differences (i.e., "Do not confuse racial status with disability status"). In contrast, NCLB seems to endorse the view that disability trumps race since achievement outcomes for disabled students can be treated differently.

Emerging evidence suggests that these policy tools designed to track inequality, disentangle race and disability, and enhance educational opportunities are being appropriated in ways that distort their original meanings and purposes. For example, Table 2 represents the number of states reporting *zero* districts with racial disproportionality levels in special education and by disability category that resulted from inappropriate identification over a four-year period. The evidence suggests that the number of states in the nation that were "disproportionality free" increased substantially in this short time period. Table 3 shows that the majority of states reported no change or slippage in disproportionality that resulted from *inappropriate identification* for Indicators 9 and 10 between 2007 and 2009.

Moreover, because OSEP did not create indicators to monitor how *significant* disproportionality is implemented (Albrecht et al., in press), it is not surprising to

Table 2 States' monitoring of disproportionality in special education and by disability category, 2005–2009

School Years	Number of States Reporting Zero School Districts With Disproportionality Due to Inappropriate Identification	
	Special Education (Indicator 9)	*Disability (Indicator 10)*
2005–2006	27	21
2006–2007	39	27
2007–2008	42	35
2008–2009	43	34

Note. Data are from U.S. Department of Education (2011).

Table 3 Number of states reporting no change or slippage in the number of districts with disproportionality due to inappropriate identification in special education and by disability category, 2007–2009

State Reports on Disproportionality Due to Inappropriate Identification	Special Education (Indicator 9)	Disability Category (Indicator 10)
Number of states reporting no change in the percentage of LEAs with disproportionality due to inappropriate identification from 2007 to 2008	41	31
Number of states reporting slippage in the percentage of LEAs with disproportionality due to inappropriate identification from 2007–2008 to 2008–2009	5	10

Note. LEA = local education agency. Data are from U.S. Department of Education (2011).

see considerable variability and some concerning trends in this respect. Figure 1 summarizes the various cutoff scores required to determine disproportionality and the number of states that use them. The majority of states (*n* = 32) require that racial minority students be between two and three times as likely to be identified as their peers if the identification is to count as disproportional. Twenty of the 39 reporting states expect risk ratios of 3 and above. About one third (*n* = 12) of the reporting states have a multiple-year requirement for LEAs to be identified as having significant disproportionality; 6 of these states require two consecutive years, and another 6 states require three consecutive years before any state education agency (SEA) action is triggered.

Data spanning a longer period of time are needed before conclusive generalizations can be made. Nevertheless, the evidence suggests that a substantial proportion of states do not have any racial disproportionality and that an even greater proportion of states were free of disproportionality that resulted from *inappropriate* identification. Although the U.S. Department of Education recently concluded that the available evidence represents "a numerical improvement over previous

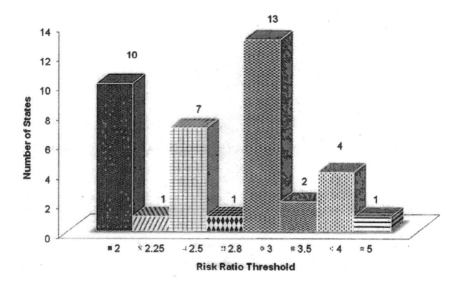

Figure 1 Relative risk ratio thresholds for disproportionality by number of states. Data are from U.S. Department of Education (2011)

years" (as quoted in Albrecht et al., in press), these data do not prove that racial disproportionality was eliminated. In fact, it is conceivable that a sizable proportion of racial minority students are placed in special education, but what makes a difference is *what counts as* disproportionality. The data on relative risk ratios suggest that about half of the states are setting disproportionality thresholds at substantially high levels (to the tune of 300% or greater). This creates an accountability buffer for these states since a considerable number of racial minority students can still migrate to disability categories without any disproportionality policy consequences while nevertheless raising the probability of improving the state's test performance report. An irony embodied in this state of affairs is that the niche standardization encoded in these equity monitoring policies is preserved; that is, states are free of racial disproportionality, and the race–disability link is left intact. States can continue to place racial minority students in these programs without penalties from NCLB or IDEA.

But the rising threshold for the disproportionality index is also connected to other reasons, such as resource availability and ideologies circulating in the institutional cultures of educational systems. For instance, a senior staff member from an SEA recently explained at a meeting of a national advisory group that her state had to use a very high disproportionality index because otherwise most of the LEAs in the state would show up as having disproportionality levels, and their scarce human and financial resources would not allow them to respond appropriately to such a scenario. Another SEA special education staff member from a different state suggested at the same meeting that his state could not afford to lose

15% of its special education funds to correct or prevent disproportionality, given the current fiscal crisis affecting his state.

To conclude, it looks as though justice has multiple faces across and even within NCLB, RTI, and disproportionality monitoring systems. Across these initiatives, justice means the distribution of instructional resources and opportunities for all learners, the elimination of the conflation of race with disability, and the accurate placement of students in special education. Each of these justice messages brings incentives and deterrents for local actors.

NCLB accounts for who is represented in the system through a reliance on background markers but misses the processes and practices taking place in educational spaces that shuffle student identity across categories. In this niche standardization economy, some kinds of accountability are more consequential than others; thus we are witnessing, among other things, a number of gaming practices that shift students across identity boundaries as a means to pass the accountability tests. RTI, in turn, juggles a narrower constellation of identities in its version of niche standardization. RTI focuses on an academic dimension to define identities typically framed in binary terms—for example, at risk/not at risk, treatment responder/treatment resistor, learning disabled/nonlearning disabled. Student race is dissolved in the RTI grammar. As with NCLB, gaming strategies related to student identity have been observed in RTI implementation (e.g., delays). Finally, the monitoring system for the racialization of disability is concerned with students wearing double-bind identities, and although it has the potential to account for processes and practices that lead to inequities, in a move reminiscent of *Brown v. Board of Education's* handling of school racial desegregation, it leaves states and districts the power to define what Counts as inequity and how to document it. One consequence is that measurement gaming strategies gain currency, oftentimes as a means to cope with the demands stemming from NCLB, other times because of local (financial, human resource) constraints. Common to these reforms (and their impact) is that they constitute the exercise of power on race and disability, for "power [is about] a question of government" (Foucault, 1982, p. 789). The analysis of the disruptions and contradictions created at the interstices of these reforms make visible the govern-mentality of racial and ability differences, because the policies "structure the possible field of action" (p. 790) of certain kinds of students.

Toward interdisciplinary research on educational equity: notes on the study of the racialization of disability

The contradictions and disruptions forming at the intersections of NCLB, RTI, and racial disproportionality monitoring systems are creating chronotopes that are bending and redefining the racialization of disability. The preceding analysis leads me to identify four assertions to consider in future educational equity research:

1   A historical perspective is necessary to understand the changing, seemingly symbiotic intertwining of race and ability differences and to identify the

effects of policies and practices on educational equity for students inhabiting double-bind identities. These insights should inform intervention efforts to address such inequities.

2   Space must be overlaid in this line of analysis. Attention to space sheds light on the regulation of social and public spaces for disabled people, including those from racial minority backgrounds, in the late 1800s and in the contemporary gaming strategies of the education field that shuffle identities across programmatic spaces. This perspective enables researchers to examine technical, cultural, and ideological dimensions of the racialization of disability.

3   The examination of the ideological underpinnings of policies, legal decisions, and cultural practices is an imperative for future equity research. This way, equity analyses can place the role of *power* center stage. The work on White innocence applied to legal decisions and educational reforms illustrates this point, although power can also be examined in practices situated in institutional contexts (i.e., implicit or official regulations, procedures, and practices; Foucault, 1982).

4   The interdisciplinary study of equity in relation to the intersection of race and ability differences calls for a double analytic focus. Indeed, the historical analysis outlined above illustrates the critical importance of understanding the connection between local practices and larger sociohistorical processes, which in turn requires a simultaneous focus on multiple analytic scales.

Based on these assertions, I outline guiding ideas for the interdisciplinary study of the racialization of ability differences.

Chronotopes of practice: a research program on re-mediating differences and enabling geographies

We need an analytic framework that integrates attention to the temporal, spatial, and sociocultural dimensions of the human experience (Soja, 2010; Young, 1990). When this *triple dialectic* is examined through a cultural prism, we reframe the study of the racialization of disability from *the equitable hunt for disabilities* or *the identification of structural determinants of stigma* to an "understanding of the phenomena surrounding the state of affairs called 'disability'" (Tremain, 2005, p. 1).

The perspective I propose benefits from the growing interest in the spatial turn (Soja, 2010). This work has enabled us to gain a greater understanding of the role of space in the production of inequities. There is considerable evidence in epidemiology, educational policy studies, and urban sociology (e.g., Krieger, 2011; Lipman, 2002; Lobao & Hooks, 2007) about the spatiality of injustices that affect access to and the distribution of state or city (e.g., health, education, mass transportation, crime prevention) and other forms of private and semiprivate services and resources (e.g., food, employment, housing). These spatially distributed inequities disproportionally affect racialized communities. Nevertheless, Said (1993) and Soja (2010) remind us of the duality of inequities, as both oppressive *and* potentially empowering. The spatial justice perspective I draw from avoids traditional limits of justice paradigms that stress an exclusive attention to *outcomes* (e.g., income level, racial proportions in special education) at the expense of understanding the *processes* that produce them (Soja, 2010; Young, 1990). This is an important consideration since entire systems are built on this perspective of justice, including the legal system.

Time is another key dimension of this approach. The examination of equity questions at various spatial scales is situated at particular points in time so that the historical nature of the analysis is not lost. I rely on Vygotsky's elegant model to understand the ongoing refashioning of human nature across multiple time scales through which mental activities are historicized. Scribner (1985) revised the model to include the study of human development at the moment-to-moment, life-history, cultural historical, and phylogenetic levels. The model has been used in cultural and developmental psychology (Cole, 1996; Dien, 2000; Lemke, 2000) and special education (Artiles, 2003), among other fields.

Re-mediating differences that make a difference

We integrate attention to temporal, spatial, and sociocultural dimensions in our work with education leaders about the racialization of disabilities. Because of the ambiguities surrounding disability identification processes and the historical deficit views of communities of color sedimented in educational policy and practice, educators need to re-mediate (Cole & Griffin, 1983) their understandings of the racialization of disabilities. Inspired by cultural historical theory (Cole, 1996), my colleagues and I have used a two-pronged approach to reframe and re-mediate understandings and solutions to this problem, namely through artifact design and the orchestration of social spaces to re-mediate educators' understandings of the problem as a means to produce solutions inspired by new visions of educational futures for these children and youth. We are inspired by cultural historical intervention work and its argumentative grammar (Engeström, 2011).

First, we design artifacts that reframe the analysis of the racialization of disabilities, debunk deficit explanations of the problem, and challenge meritocratic and distributive views of justice underlying research and policy on this phenomenon. Specifically, we produce visual representations of evidence that portray (dis)abling and (en)abling influences (e.g., placement rates in schools by race, teacher quality, and other markers) through the use of geographic information system (GIS) maps and other visual representations (Artiles, Kozleski, Waitoller, & Lukinbeal, 2011; Kozleski & Artiles, in press). We re-present this evidence at the cultural historical level for regions, states, cities, or school districts. For instance, a simplistic argument blaming poverty and some of its correlates as the only cause of the racialization of disability has been used persistently to explain this phenomenon. Poverty is correlated with poor health, substandard housing, high crime rate, and the like. Lead paint in public housing is still common in old, poor sections of cities around the nation where many racial minority families live.

306

Exposure to lead paint has negative consequences for child development that can ultimately cause intellectual disabilities. But when we contrast the geographical areas in a city like Chicago that have concentrations of children exhibiting high lead paint toxicity with the city areas where African American students are disproportionally represented in the intellectual disability category, we observe little overlap between these two data sets. This way, we disrupt simplistic explanations about the role of certain structural forces in the racialization of disabilities (Artiles, 2009).

The reframing allowed by these artifacts is also used to understand how the categorical alignment that is embedded in the notion of disability enables the emergence of niche standardization to normalize at the level of the social group (Epstein, 2007). This way, disability is standardized by type (e.g., learning, emotional, intellectual) as well as by race, social class, and so on. Because niche standardization work related to disability is concerned with multiple purposes (administrative, political, scientific), we use GIS maps, tables, and figures to call attention to the ways in which disability constitutes an *ideal boundary object.* These objects

> have different meanings in different social worlds but their structure is common enough to more than one world to make them recognizable, a means to translation. The creation and management of boundary objects is a key process in developing and maintaining coherence across intersecting social worlds. (Star & Griesemer, 1989, p. 393)

An ideal boundary object "does not accurately describe the details of any locality or thing" (p. 410); it is "abstracted from all domains and may be fairly vague" (e.g., the notion of species; p. 410). This means that disability, as an ideal boundary object, is adjustable to local conditions and implies the erasure of idiosyncratic circumstances. Let me illustrate this point.

A complex management system has been institutionalized across states to maintain the niche standardization of disabilities (referral, assessment, diagnostic practices). However, the data in Table 4 suggest that such a system rests on the orchestration of disability identification practices as ideal boundary objects. African American students, for instance, have disparate chances of being identified for intellectual disabilities, depending on where they live. This is the case despite the standardization of disability definition and identification practices. GIS map evidence at the city level further contextualizes this point, as it shows that the disproportionate representation of African American students in Chicago, for example, is observed in areas of the city with concentrations of high-poverty, but also low-poverty, schools. Moreover, it is found in areas of the city where high-and low-poverty schools are in close proximity (see Artiles, 2009).

This evidence defies simplistic explanations that place greater emphasis on technical or sociopolitical models. The evidence forces the educational leaders we work with to examine the convergence of technical, cultural, and ideological

Table 4 Comparison of states with highest and lowest disproportionality: relative risk ratios for African American Students (compared with students of other races) in the category of intellectual disability, 2006–2007

State	Relative Risk Ratio
Highest	
South Carolina	3.77
Tennessee	3.75
Kansas	3.67
North Carolina	3.66
Delaware	3.39
New Hampshire	3.33
New Jersey	3.22
Illinois	3.19
Louisiana	3.16
Florida	3.14
Lowest	
Washington	2.15
Pennsylvania	2.13
Rhode Island	2.11
Connecticut	2.09
Maine	2.02
New Mexico	1.81
California	1.78
Kentucky	1.66
West Virginia	1.49
Alaska	1.35

Note. Data are from National Center for Culturally Responsive Educational Systems (2003).

forces that help explain the work of disability as boundary object. This means shifting the analytic lens from individuals or groups of students to constellations of influences that forge local actors' decisions about who is able and disabled. These artifacts also enable us to raise questions about power relations germane to what Foucault (1982) described as "systems of differentiation" and the "means of bringing power relations into being" that are used in schools and districts (e.g., assumptions about ability, consequences applied to such differences).

The GIS maps portray the *outcomes* of opportunities and inequities in various domains, and we can enrich this evidence with data that have enabling potential (e.g., community assets). Sociological research on collective efficacy (Sampson, Morenoff, & Gannon-Rowley, 2002) and civic engagement can be integrated to examine the spatial distribution of these assets alongside racial disproportionality in disability categories across neighborhoods and city regions. The notion of collective efficacy adds to our understanding of the role of social processes in neighborhood effects. Collective efficacy entails the "linkage of mutual trust and the shared willingness to intervene for the public good" (Sampson et al., 2002, p. 457). Analysis of equity related to the racialization of disability can include mapping collective efficacy in neighborhoods with high and low school disproportionality patterns, through the identification of neighborhood socioeconomic resources and residential stability patterns. How do collective efficacy resources and practices spill over to school–family interactions? How can such permeability be facilitated and used to engineer school initiatives that make the curriculum more responsive to neighborhoods' histories, needs, and assets? How can neighborhood collective efficacy be used to revisit and reframe the schools' assumptions and technologies about competence and disability? An important point to remember is that collective efficacy has a positive impact not only on neighborhood residents but also on residents in other geographical areas (Sampson et al., 2002). In short, this line of research aims to understand the connection between spatial and social processes in the production of educational opportunities and inequities.

The histories of opportunity distributions in the affected regions across the education, labor, health, and other sectors can be brought to bear in the design of artifacts as well (e.g., teacher quality, school and residential racial segregation). The work of John A. Powell on maps of opportunities represents a promising alternative. This work aims to

> understand the dynamics of "opportunity" within metropolitan areas. The purpose of opportunity mapping is to illustrate where opportunity rich communities exist (and assess who has access to these communities) and to understand what needs to be remedied in opportunity poor communities. Opportunity mapping builds upon the rich history of using neighborhood based information and mapping to understand the challenges impacting our neighborhoods. (Kirwan Institute for the Study of Race and Ethnicity, "GIS Mapping," 2011)

This way, a range of relevant data can be examined as a means to understand the processes that led to the outcomes represented in the maps. Attention to these aspects empowers us to examine the "relations of strategy" present (or potentially available) to engage relations of power in those spaces (Foucault, 1982).

With regard to the creation of social spaces, we use the described artifacts with educators in leadership positions at the LEA or SEA levels to address racial disproportionality in special education. We build on Hedegaard's (2002) notion of "double move" to learn content (from personal knowledge to scientific knowledge) to engage participants in *triple moves* in which we compel leaders (or teachers) to compare and contrast their (a) everyday experiences with disproportionality with (b) the existing research evidence and (c) the evidence that reframes the problem (our GIS maps, data tables and figures). Contradictions are identified among these three types of knowledge, and the search for simplistic or binary explanations evolves into reexaminations and reformulations of educators' lived experiences with racial minority communities, which in turn can forge reconceived educational futures for these learners.

Tate and Hogrebe's (2011) work using visual representations of opportunities and constraints with GIS maps as a means to inform visions for the future of African American male students constitutes an alternative approach in this envisioned research program. Comparable to our re-mediation work with teams of educators, they proposed a visual political literacy project to support capacity building and civic engagement initiatives for African American students with city and educational leaders and community residents. These researchers relied on GIS maps of St. Louis to represent the distribution of African American students categorized by educational attainment in relation to the location of biotechnology company clusters as a way to gauge the geospatial distribution of opportunities and constraints. Visual representations of these kinds of distributions can offer insights into (a) students' levels of preparedness for jobs related to science, technology, engineering, and mathematics; (b) who benefits from economic activities in science and technology in various regions of cities; and (c) structural barriers to accessing opportunities (e.g., transportation systems). Ultimately, Tate and Hogrebe expect that the use of these tools will nurture coalition-building and mobilization efforts that enhance the educational opportunities of African American students.

Tate and Hogrebe's (2011) proposal can be enriched to shed light on the placement patterns of racialized students in special education through the representation of social and civic organizations and institutions in cities and neighborhoods that might enhance educational opportunities. This is an important strategy, particularly when working in economically depressed neighborhoods; Johnson (2010) recently concluded that "the measures most important to the estimation of educational differences between the most and least advantaged [neighborhood] areas are of resources rather than poverty" (p. 567). Lipman's (2002) work on types of educational programs available in different sections of Chicago is exemplary in this regard. Other examples include after-school programs that offer educational enrichment for students and/or peer support initiatives that enhance student socioemotional resiliency. Neighborhood associations and formal and informal youth or community clubs are additional examples. Again, attention to these resources is critical since they have been largely neglected in the research about the educational experiences of racialized students. Conversely, linking these data with school evidence such as special education placement patterns can add to our understanding of neighborhood effects (see Artiles et al., 2011).

The proposed interdisciplinary research program can be enriched with studies that focus on different time scales, specifically biographical and moment-to-moment temporal lines. Ethnographic portraits of student trajectories traveling across ideologically charged situations, events, or places can illustrate how educators, students, and families use ideal boundary objects (e.g., disabilities) in the "key situations" of school and everyday life to reproduce or contest the racialization of disability. Equity dilemmas and challenges crystallize when professionals struggle in such gatekeeping encounters to balance local constraints and resources with the stratification demands embedded in policies and practices. There is research that can guide these efforts (Rueda & Mehan, 1986; Varenne & McDermott, 1999). This research examines the cultural processes though which students are positioned in different categories across social and physical spaces with important consequences for student competence constructions. A few studies have documented student trajectories over time and dissected critical moments in which identities are irreversibly changed by institutional practices, such as disability identification. This work offers an important component of the envisioned program of research because it adds time scales in the study of equity processes and outcomes, brings forth an emic lens, enables researchers to trace the emergence of equity through heterochronic processes (Artiles, 2003), and opens the possibility of documenting the "forms of institutionalization" and "the degrees of rationalization" used in power relations (Foucault, 1982, p. 792).

Conclusion

The interdisciplinary examination of the racialization of disability promises to transcend substantial limitations of previous equity research in terms of how difference is theorized; the unit of analysis used in this literature; the role of culture, power, and history in institutional practices; and the systematic juxtaposition of culture, space, and time. The framework demands a shift from the traditional examination of equity as a *consequence* of technical processes and practices (e.g., Does the differential access or distribution of resources cause inequitable conditions?) to a research paradigm that also documents the very *production* of inequity and is braided with interdisciplinary intellectual traditions. This is an equity perspective that decenters individual traits and sameness as the main pillars of justice. It resonates with Dewey's (1976) vision of equality as "moral, a matter of social justice secured, not of physical or psychological endowment" (p. 299). Considering the legacies of stratification in U.S. society, we as educational researchers are required to practice our craft within epistemic cultures that are deeply mindful of equity. The proposed framework promises to contribute to an approach in the study of educational inequities that takes into account the dynamic, culturally situated, and historically produced nature of difference and its consequences. Students inhabiting double-bind identities have historically existed in heterotopias of deviance bounded by regimes of order (Foucault, 1986).

> The history of the order imposed on things would be the history of the Same—of that which, for a given culture, is both dispersed and related, therefore to be distinguished by kinds and to be collected together into identities. (Foucault, 2005, e-library location 457 of 8465)

Our challenge is to "re-vision" these forms of difference by grappling with questions such as, How do we productively engage with race–ability difference heterotopias that juxtapose incompatible spaces—the promise of educational rights and cultural recognition along with exclusionary and oppressive consequences? This is hard, complicated work, but we must remain "prisoner[s] of hope" (West, 2008, p. 41).

Notes

I acknowledge the support of the Equity Alliance at Arizona State University under Office of Elementary and Secondary Education Grant No. S004D080027. I am grateful to the Center for Advanced Study in the Behavioral Sciences at Stanford University for the residential fellowship that allowed me to do the research for the theoretical model and analysis outlined in this article. I benefited from the feedback and suggestions of Mike Gerber, Kris Gutiérrez, Elizabeth Kozleski, Joanne Larson, Dan Losen, Allan Luke, Joe Tobin, and Stan Trent on earlier versions of this article. I am responsible, however, for the limitations of the manuscript.

1 Foucault's (1982) use of the term "subject" includes "subject to someone else by control and dependence; and tied to his own identity by a conscience or self-knowledge. Both meanings suggest a form of power which subjugates and makes subject to" (p. 781).
2 As I finish writing this analysis, important changes to this policy are being proposed in the U.S. Senate that include the elimination of the adequate yearly progress report, waivers to increase flexibility for states in addressing accountability requirements, and greater state discretion in devising accountability systems. These changes would undoubtedly have an impact on educational equity, and civil rights groups are already raising such questions. The analysis presented in this article would have to be updated if the proposed changes crystallize.
3 These provisions also include requirements for reporting on disciplinary disparities by race and ethnicity; however, I focus only on disability identification disproportionality, because of space constraints.
4 Evidence from the U.S. Department of Education (2011) shows that states use qualitative strategies for determining inappropriate identification as follows: self-reviews (21 states), state monitoring processes (19 states), both (8 states), and not reported (4 states).

References

Albrecht, S. F., Skiba, R. J., Losen, D. J., Chung, C., & Middelberg, L. (in press). Federal policy on disproportionality in special education: Is it moving us forward? *Journal of Disability Policy Studies.*

Artiles, A. J. (2003). Special education's changing identity: Paradoxes and dilemmas in views of culture and space. *Harvard Educational Review, 73,* 164–202.

Artiles, A. (2009). Reframing disproportionality: Outline of a cultural historical paradigm. *Multiple Voices, 11*(2), 24–37.

Artiles, A. J., Bal, A., & King-Thorius, K. (2010). Back to the future: A critique of Response to Intervention's social justice views. *Theory Into Practice, 49,* 250–257.

Artiles, A. J., Kozleski, E., Dorn, S., & Christensen, C. (2006). Learning in inclusive education research: Re-mediating theory and methods with a transformative agenda. *Review of Research in Education, 30,* 65–108.

Artiles, A. J., Kozleski, E. B., Trent, S. C., Osher, D., & Ortiz, A. (2010). Justifying and explaining disproportionality, 1968–2008: A critique of underlying views of culture. *Exceptional Children, 76,* 279–299.

Artiles, A. J., Kozleski, E. B., Waitoller, F., & Lukinbeal, C. (2011). Inclusive education and the interlocking of ability and race in the U.S.: Notes for an educational equity research program. In A. J. Artiles, E. B. Kozleski, & F. Waitoller (Eds.), *Inclusive education: Examining equity on five continents.* Cambridge, MA: Harvard Education Press.

Artiles, A. J, Rueda, R., Salazar, J. J., & Higareda, I. (2005). Within-group diversity in minority disproportionate representation: English language learners in urban school districts. *Exceptional Children, 71*, 283–300.

Baker, B. (2002). The hunt for disability: The new eugenics and the normalization of school children. *Teachers College Record, 104*, 663–703.

Cell, J. (1982). *The highest stage of White supremacy: The origins of segregation in South Africa and the American South.* Cambridge, UK: Cambridge University Press.

Christensen, C., & Dorn, S. (1997). Competing notions of social justice and contradictions in special education reform. *Journal of Special Education, 31*, 181–198.

Cole, M. (1996). *Cultural psychology.* Cambridge, MA: Harvard University Press.

Cole, M., & Griffin, P. (1983). A socio-historical approach to remediation. *Quarterly Newsletter of the Laboratory of Comparative Human Cognition, 5*(4), 69–74.

Darling-Hammond, L. (2007). Race, inequality and educational accountability: The irony of "No Child Left Behind." *Race, Ethnicity and Education, 10*, 245–260.

Dewey, J. (1976): Individuality, equality, and superiority. In J. A. Boydston (Ed.), *John Dewey: The middle works, 1899–1924* (Vol. 13, pp. 295–300). Carbondale: Southern Illinois University Press.

Dien, D. S. (2000). The evolving nature of self-identity across four levels of history. *Human Development, 43*, 1–18.

Donovan, S., & Cross, C. (Eds.). (2002). *Minority students in special and gifted education.* Washington, DC: National Academy Press.

Engeström, Y. (2011). From design experiments to formative interventions. *Theory & Psychology, 21*, 598–628.

Epstein, S. (2007). *Inclusion: The politics of difference in medical research.* Chicago: University of Chicago Press.

Erevelles, N., & Minear, A. (2010). Unspeakable offenses: Untangling race and disability in discourses of intersectionality. *Journal of Literary and Cultural Disability Studies, 4*, 127–146.

Farley, A. P. (2002). The poetics of colorline space. In F. Valdes, J. M. Culp, & A. P. Harris (Eds.), *Crossroads, directions, and a new critical race theory* (pp. 97–158). Philadelphia: Temple University Press.

Ferri, B. A., & Connor, D. J. (2005). Tools of exclusion: Race, disability, and (re)segregated education. *Teachers College Record, 107*(3), 453–474.

Foucault, M. (1982). The subject and power. *Critical Inquiry, 8*, 777–795.

Foucault, M. (1986). Of other spaces. *Diacritics, 16*, 22–27.

Foucault, M. (2005). *The order of things: An archaeology of the human sciences.* London: Taylor & Francis e-Library.

Fraser, N. (2007). Re-framing justice in a globalizing world. In T. Lovell (Ed.), *(Mis)recognition, social inequality, and social justice* (pp. 17–35). London: Routledge.

Fuchs, L. (2002). Three conceptualizations of "treatment" in a responsiveness to treatment model. In R. Bradley, L. Danielson, & D. Hallahan (Eds.), *Identification of learning disabilities: Research to practice* (pp. 521–529). Mahwah, NJ: Lawrence Erlbaum.

Gotanda, N. (2004). Reflections on *Korematsu, Brown*, and White innocence. *Temple Political and Civil Rights Law Review, 13*, 663–674.

Hammonds, E. M., & Herzig, R. M. (Eds.). (2008). *The nature of difference: Sciences of race in the United States from Jefferson to genomics.* Cambridge, MA: MIT Press.

Harry, B., & Klingner, J. (2006). *Why are so many minority students in special education? Understanding race and disability in schools.* New York: Teachers College Press.

Hedegaard, M. (2002). *Learning and child development: A cultural-historical study.* Aarhus, Denmark: Aarhus University Press.

Johnson, O. (2010). Assessing neighborhood racial segregation and macroeconomic effects in the education of African Americans. *Review of Educational Research, 80,* 527–575.

Kirwan Institute for the Study of Race and Ethnicity. (2011). GIS mapping. Retrieved from http://www.kirwaninstitute.org/research/opportunity-communities/gis-mapping/

Kozleski, E. B., & Artiles, A. J. (in press). Technical assistance as inquiry: Using activity theory methods to engage equity in educational practice communities. In G. Canella & S. Steinberg (Eds.), *Critical qualitative research reader.* New York: Peter Lang.

Krieger, N. (2011). *Epidemiology and the people's health: Theory and context.* New York: Oxford University Press.

Lemke, J. L. (2000). Across the scales of time: Artifacts, activities, and meanings in ecosocial systems. *Mind, Culture, and Activity, 7,* 273–290.

Lipman, P. (2002). Making the global city, making inequality: The political economy and cultural politics of Chicago school policy. *American Educational Research Journal, 39,* 379–419.

Lobao, L. M., & Hooks, G. (2007). Advancing the sociology of spatial inequality: Spaces, places, and the subnational scale. In L. M. Lobao, G. Hooks, & A. R. Tickamyer (Eds.), *The sociology of spatial inequality* (pp. 29–61). Albany, NY: SUNY Press.

Lowe, R. (2000). Eugenics, scientific racism and education: Has anything changed in one hundred years? In M. Crotty, J. Germov, & G. Rodwell (Eds.), *"A race for a place": Eugenics, Darwinism, and social thought and practice in Australia* (pp. 207–220). Newcastle, Australia: University of Newcastle Press.

Mills, C. W. (1997). *The racial contract.* Ithaca, NY: Cornell University Press.

National Center for Culturally Responsive Educational Systems. (2003). Data maps: Disproportionality by race and disability. Washington, DC: Department of Education. Retrieved from http://nccrest.eddata.net/maps/index.php?fl=2006–2007

Nichols, S. L., & Berliner, D. (2007). *Collateral damage.* Cambridge, MA: Harvard Education Press.

Novak, J., & Fuller, B. (2003). *Penalizing diverse schools? Similar test scores but different students bring federal sanctions.* Berkeley, CA: Policy Analysis for California Education.

Orosco, M. J., & Klingner, J. (2010). One school's implementation of RTI with English language learners: "Referring into RTI." *Journal of Learning Disabilities, 43,* 269–288.

Rizvi, F., & Lingard, B. (1996). Disability, education and the discourses of justice. In C. Christensen & F. Rizvi (Eds.), *Disability and the dilemmas of education and justice* (pp. 9–26). Buckingham, UK: Open University Press.

Roach, J. (2001). Deep skin: Reconstructing Congo Square. In H.J. Elam & D. Krasner (Eds.), *African American performance and theater history: A critical reader* (pp. 101–113). New York: Oxford University Press.

Ross T. (1990). The rhetorical tapestry of race: White innocence and Black abstraction. *William and Mary Law Review, 32,* 1–40.

Rueda, R., & Mehan, H. (1986). Metacognition and passing: Strategic interactions in the lives of students with learning disabilities. *Anthropology and Education Quarterly, 17,* 145–165.

Said, E. (1993). *Culture and imperialism.* New York: Vintage Books.

Sampson, R. J., Morenoff, J. D., & Gannon-Rowley, T. (2002). Assessing "neighborhood effects": Social processes and new directions in research. *Annual Review of Sociology, 28,* 443–478.

Schweik, S. M. (2009). *The ugly laws: Disability in public.* New York: New York University Press.

Scribner, S. (1985). Vygotsky's uses of history. In J. V. Wertsch (Ed.), *Culture, communication, and cognition* (pp. 119–145). New York: Cambridge University Press.

Skiba, R. J., Simmons, A. B., Ritter, S., Gibb, A. C., Rausch, M. K., Cuadrado, J., et al. (2008). Achieving equity in special education: History, status, and current challenges. *Exceptional Children, 74*, 264–288.

Snyder, S., & Mitchell, D. T. (2006). *Cultural locations of disability.* Chicago: University of Chicago Press.

Soja, E. W. (2010). *Seeking spatial justice.* Minneapolis: University of Minnesota Press.

Star, S. L., & Griesemer, J. (1989). Institutional ecologies, translations, and coherence: Amateurs and professionals in Berkeley's Museum of Vertebrate Zoology, 1907–1939. *Social Studies of Science, 19*, 387–420.

Stubblefield, A. (2007). "Beyond the Pale": Tainted Whiteness, cognitive disability, and eugenic sterilization. *Hypatia, 22*, 162–181.

Tate, W., & Hogrebe, M. (2011). From visuals to vision: Using GIS to inform civic dialogue about African American males. *Race, Ethnicity and Education, 14*, 51–71.

Tremain, S. (2005). Foucault, governmentality, and critical disability theory. In S. Tremain (Ed.), *Foucault and the governmentality of disability* (pp. 1–24). Ann Arbor, MI: University of Michigan Press.

Trent, J. W (1994). *Inventing the feeble mind.* Berkeley: University of California Press.

U.S. Department of Education. (2009). *Children with disabilities receiving special education under Part B of the Individuals with Disabilities Education Act* (Office of Special Education Programs, Data Analysis Systems, OMB No. 1820–0043). Washington, DC: Author.

U.S. Department of Education. (2011). 2010 Part B SPP/APR [state performance plan/annual performance report] analysis document (Office of Special Education Programs). Washington, DC: Author. Retrieved from http://therightidea.tadnet.org/assets/1684

Valli, L., & Buese, D. (2007). The changing roles of teachers in an era of high-stakes accountability. *American Educational Research Journal, 44*, 519–558.

Varenne, H., & McDermott, R. (Eds.). (1999). *Successful failure: The school America builds.* Boulder, CO: Westview Press.

Vaughn, S., & Fuchs, L. S. (2003). Redefining learning disabilities as inadequate response to instruction: The promise and potential problems. *Learning Disabilities Research and Practice, 18*(3), 137–146.

West, C. (2008). *Hope on a tightrope.* Carlsbad, CA: Hay House.

Young, I. M. (1990*). Justice and the politics of difference.* Princeton, NJ: Princeton University.

36

"TELLING IT LIKE IT IS: THE ROLE OF RACE, CLASS, AND CULTURE IN THE PERPETUATION OF LEARNING DISABILITY AS A PRIVILEGED CATEGORY FOR THE WHITE MIDDLE CLASS"

Wanda J. Blanchett

Source: *Disability Studies Quarterly*, 30, 2, 2010.

Abstract

For more than 40 years, the American educational system has used mild disability special education categories to sort students on the basis of perceived disability, race, culture, language, and social class. Accordingly, African American and other students of color have the highest risk ratio for being placed in special education and they received the most segregated special education placements (Blanchett, Mumford, & Beachman, 2005; Dunn, 1968; Losen & Orfield, 2002; Mercer, 1973). How the social constructions of mild disabilities and learning disabilities, in particular, perpetuate learning disability as a privileged category for the White Middle Class while marginalizing students of color has been largely missing in the disability studies and disproportionality debates. The purpose of my paper is to commemorate and revisit Sleeter's seminal work while contextualizing it within contemporary debates by address the following four questions: (1) What is the historical context of the treatment of African American and other students of color in special education?; (2) Is learning disabilities a category of privilege for the privileged?; (3) What is the social cultural context of learning disabilities in the 21st century?; and (4) In what ways do students who receive the same label of LD have very different in-school and post-school experiences based upon the intersection of race and class with LD?

"Telling it like it is: the role of race, class, and culture in the perpetuation of learning disability as a privileged category for the white middle class"

Few researchers and scholars in education as a whole and even fewer in special education have sought to explore and grapple with issues pertaining to the social context that has both given birth to and continues to maintain the social constructions of mild disabilities in the American culture. To be clear, some scholars (e.g., Dunn, 1968; Mercer, 1973) have long questioned the social constructions of mild disabilities and the practice of sorting children on the basis of the intersections of race, culture, socio-economic status, and perceived ability. However, with the exception of scholars such as Dr. Asa G. Hilliard, III, few of these early pioneer scholars linked these sorting practices to larger social and societal phenomenon that were at work and that were intentionally designed to prevent the integration of black and white children. Legal mandates paved the way for children to be physically present in the same schools, but special education identification practices became the way to ensure that they were not in the same classrooms. While some of the early pioneers who called attention to this method of segregating (i.e., separate special education classrooms) African American and Hispanic children in supposedly integrated American schools were white themselves, naming the social phenomenon that was likely at play (i.e., racism, white supremacy, white dominance, white privilege) was usually the responsibility of African American and other scholars of color.

This, however, changed in 1987 when a young, white, former special education teacher from Oregon employed her acquired formal education in multicultural education, her insider experiences as a white person living in America, and her personal commitment to social justice to examine the socio-cultural context that gave birth to the disability category of learning disabilities. She named the socio-cultural context surrounding the creation and maintenance of the disability category of learning disabilities in very bold terms.

As the Guest Editors of this special issue Drs. Connor and Ferri have asserted,

> It has been just over 20 years since the publication of Christine Sleeter's, "Why is There Learning Disabilities? A Critical Analysis of the Birth of the Field of Special Education in its Social Context." In this seminal publication, Sleeter argues that the category of LD emerged to fulfill a particular political and economic purpose during the Cold War threats to U. S. supremacy. (2010)

Sleeter provided an explanation for why learning disabilities emerged as a disability category that shocked many, but that few have been able to successfully refute. In her own words in the introduction of the chapter, Sleeter (1987) states that:

> This chapter offers a different interpretation for why learning disabilities exist. It argues that the category emerged for a political purpose: to

317

differentiate and protect White middle class children who were failing in school from lower class and minority children, during a time when schools were being called upon to raise standards for economic and military purposes. Rather than being a product of progress, the category was essentially conservative in that it helped schools continue to serve best those whom schools have always served best: the White middle and upper-middle class. (p. 212)

Given that this special issue provides an opportunity for us to both commemorate and revisit Sleeter's seminal work while also contextualizing it within contemporary debates, the purpose of my paper is to address the following four questions: (1) What is the historical context of the treatment of African American and other students of color in special education? (2) Is learning disabilities a category of privilege for the privileged? (3) What is the social cultural context of learning disabilities in the 21st century? and (4) In what ways do students who receive the same label of LD have very different in-school and post school experiences based upon the intersection of race and class with LD? To begin to address these questions I will first attempt to situate the treatment of these students within the context of the larger American educational system and its treatment of children on the basis of the intersection of race, culture, language, and class.

Historical context of the treatment of African American and other students of color in special education

Prior to the development of learning disabilities as a disability category and shortly after the courts ordered schools to desegregate and began enforcing desegregation plans in the years following the *Brown* decision, it became apparent that significant percentages of African American children and Mexican-American students in New York and California, respectively, were being labeled as mildly mentally retarded and placed in segregated classrooms (Dunn, 1968; Mercer 1973). In working with poor inner-city students in New York, Dunn noted that African American students' representation in programs for students identified as having mild mental retardation exceeded rates that would be expected given their relative size in the general population of school-aged children. Specifically, Dunn called attention to the fact that African American children were labeled as mildly mentally retarded and their white peers where not labeled at all, even when the white children evidenced more significant levels of mental retardation than the African American students. Mercer (1973) noted similar patterns in California among Mexican-American students who were new immigrants and English language learners or non-speakers. The work of these researchers and others was the basis for *Larry P. v. Riles* which helped to end the use of intelligence tests as the sole basis for determining special education eligibility and played a role in securing some of the safeguards guaranteed by IDEA today (Blanchett, 2009). Additionally, this research provided the legal basis for parents and advocates to challenge special education referral, evaluation, and placement decision-making and led to the establishment of several national committees to study the disproportionate representation of African American and other students of color in special education. Over the last couple of decades, we have seen the Harvard Civil Rights Project play an ongoing role in studying this issue, two National Academy of Science (NAS) studies commissioned, and the development of a lengthy list of recommendations for addressing this issue introduced by Dunn and Mercer. However, despite all of these noteworthy efforts, overrepresentation and disproportionate representation of African American and other students of color has persisted for more than 40 years. As stated above, the initial concerns related to disproportionality were centered on African American and Mexican American's placement in mild mental retardation classrooms at disproportionate rates. However, as other socially constructed disabilities categories (e.g., Learning Disabilities, Emotional and Behavioral Disabilities) have been developed and incorporated into legislation, similar trends of disproportionality have been associated with them as well. More importantly, it seems that while learning disabilities may have been developed, as Sleeter states, as a disability category to protect while middle class children from school failure, the American educational system and our society has not missed any opportunity to use it to continue a sorting system for children on the basis of race, ethnicity, culture, and social class and to re-segregate students of color. African American students have the highest risk ratio for LD (the risk of identification in comparison to white students) with a risk ratio that ranges from 1.1 to 2.85 and Hispanic students have a risk ratio of .57 to 1.97 (NCCRESt, 2009). Though a larger number of students with learning disabilities are placed in general education classrooms than those with other disabilities, African American students labeled with disabilities (a high percentage who are labeled with LD), even today, have some of the most segregated placements (27th Annual Report to Congress, 2005). For example, with regard to general education, or least restrictive environment placements (LRE) less than 40% of the day, African American students have a risk ratio range of .97 to 3.62 (NCCRESt, 2009). It is important to note that the category of learning disabilities has changed drastically with regard to race/ethnicity and social class since Sleeter wrote her paper about white students receiving the LD label while children of color received the MR label. Today, African American children and other children of color are identified with LD labels more frequently than white students, and, once identified, have a risk ratio of up to 3.62 times white children of being placed in segregated classroom settings (NCCRESt).

Learning disabilities: a category of privilege for the privileged

For many years the disability category of learning disabilities was primarily comprised of males (Valdes et al., 1990) with an overwhelming percentage of white males. In fact, "boys outnumber girls by about three to one in the learning disabilities category" (Hallahan & Kauffman, 2006, p. 175). While there are varying levels of privilege that exist in American society, white male privilege and white middle class privilege are very prominent in many American institutions, including education (Kivel, 2004). Thus, Sleeter's argument that learning disabilities was developed to protect white middle class children from school failure and to ensure that they were deemed more intellectually superior to their black and brown peers remains a valid argument. I do not know if it is strictly coincidental, or if it was a part of the original intent, but from its inception as a disability category, an overwhelming majority of the students (i.e., the white middle and upper class students) labeled with LD (a disproportionate percentage of whom are males) have been treated in privileged ways when compared to other socially constructed mild disability categories (e.g., emotional and behavioral disorders). Some scholars have argued that males being overrepresented in these categories might be the result of the fact that females are underrepresented, and/or that an overwhelming female teaching force may be more inclined to refer males for special education services base upon a wide range of factors such as behavior and maturation (Harmon, Stockton, & Contrucci, 1992). While there may be some validity to these arguments, they do not explain why middle- and upper class white students with LD receive accommodations and modifications within the general education classroom setting while students of color with the same labels are educated in self-contained settings.

Although the Individuals with Disabilities Education Act (IDEA) requires that states report on the implementation of IDEA in terms of the race and ethnicity of students served under each disability category, surprisingly, these data do not provide a breakdown of the gender, socioeconomic status, and placement for each disability category. However, NCCRESt's 2007 data by state illustrates that white children with LD represent from 1.6–5.2% of the school age population of White children, compared to African American children with LD representing from 1.8–14.9% of the total population of African American children. More importantly, it appears that white students with LD may be privileged in terms of their access to the general education classroom, rates of high school graduation, postschool outcomes, and overall societal acceptance. With regard to placement, during the 1989–90 school year as reported by the Advocacy Institute (2002), 21% of students with LD spent less than 20% of their in-school time outside of the regular classroom. However, data for 1998–99 illustrated that 45% of students with LD spent less than 20% of their time outside of regular classrooms, meaning that twice as many students with LD were educated in regular classrooms between 1989–90 and 1998–99.

Students labeled as having a learning disability are by the codified federal definition of a learning disability deemed intellectually superior or privileged compared to their peers because they are reported to have average or above intelligence, which sets them aside from students identified with developmental disabilities, who are reported to have significantly lower levels of intellectual ability (National Dissemination Center for Children with Disabilities (NICHCY), 2009). For example, according to NICHCY, ". . . Researchers think that learning disabilities are caused by differences in how a person's brain works and how it processes information. Children with learning disabilities are not 'dumb' or 'lazy.' In fact, they usually have average or above average intelligence. Their brains just process information differently" (p. 1). Although the way in which LD is identified today is evolving as a result of the Reauthorization of the Individuals with Disabilities

Education Act of 2004, as illustrated above by the language used to define LD and to differentiate LD from developmental disabilities, white students with LD are more normalized. And as a result, they appear to be more privileged in our society than are students of color with LD and students who are identified with developmental disabilities due to the social construction of the LD category and the overwhelming continued reliance on the medical model even today in the diagnoses of developmental disabilities including mental retardation and autism. The privileging of LD is reflected in special education introductory textbooks (e.g., Smith, 2004) that often give a vignette of someone with incredible creativity or ability that experts in the field of learning disability now believe might have had a learning disability even though the term LD had not been socially constructed during many of these individuals' lifetimes. In addition to illustrations of individuals with learning disabilities in textbooks that depict them as being very creative and intelligent, but who struggle in school, even recent publicity campaigns for dyslexia (i.e., a learning disability characterized by reading difficulties) highlight individuals like Piscasso, Leonard Da Vinci, Tom Cruise, Thomas Edison, Richard Branson, Jay Leno, and Whoopi Goldberg as famous people with dyslexia (Dyslexia Online, 2009). While this is undoubtedly a creative and talented group of individuals, it is interesting to note that they are primarily white men and may not be representative of students who are labeled LD today.

It seems that regardless of where illustrations of learning disabilities occur (e.g., textbook, website), they are designed to help the reader begin to understand how special or intelligent individuals with learning disabilities are. Such illustrations start to "normalize" students with LD among educators and our society as a whole, portraying them as a unique and talented heterogeneous group of learners who struggle in school. As Erevelles (2005) has argued, this is likely the case because as a society we seem to be far more accepting of individuals with a disability that do not look very different from us, and we also make assumptions about cognitive ability based upon what we perceive to be "normal." In fact, we have been conditioned in American society to primarily see students with learning disabilities as being just like us with a couple of extra challenges in learning. However, much to the detriment of individuals with developmental disabilities, as a normalized society, we too often see them as being drastically different from us when they too are just like us with a few extra challenges. To be sure, I am arguing that everyone with a disability should be seen as "just like us," or better yet, there should be no "us and them." And as such, all individuals with disabilities should be valued and respected without the perception of the need to "fix them" — not just those with LD.

In addition to being a privileged disability category in terms of the perception of their intellectual superiority and creativity, as stated previously, individuals identified with learning disabilities are often privileged in terms of the services that they receive once identified and in their access to the general education classroom and to all other aspects of life when compared to individuals with developmental or intellectual disabilities (i.e., mental retardation, autism). When the privilege conferred by the LD label is compounded by the privilege of whiteness and social class privilege, it greatly advantages those students. However, when LD intersects with lower socio-economic status or class and with being African American or of color, the privileges described above that are often associated with LD are denied these students.

The social cultural context of learning disabilities in the 21st century

As of Fall 2004, learning disabilities was the largest disability category and accounted for 46.4 percent of all students ages 6 through 21 receiving special education and related services under IDEA (28th Annual Report to Congress on the Implementation of Individuals with Disabilities Education Act, 2009). While there has been little overall change in the percentage of students served in most IDEA protected disability categories over the last ten years, from 1993–2003 students receiving services in LD increased from 4.1 percent in 1993 to 4.3 percent in 2003 (27th Annual Report to Congress, 2005). Although the category of learning disabilities might have been, as Sleeter argues, developed for white middle- and upper-class school-aged children, as students of color failed to qualify for special education under other disabilities categories (e.g., Mental Retardation), we have seen an increase in the number of them labeled LD. For example, nationally, 56.6% of all Hispanic students receiving special education services received them in LD, 53.3% of American Indian/Alaska Natives, 44.8% of black, 44.1% of white, and 38.4% of Asian/Pacific Islander (28th Annual Report to Congress on the Implementation of Individuals with Disabilities Education Act, 2009).

In addition to learning disabilities accounting for the largest percentage of students served ages 6–21 in the national data across all ethnic groups, American Indian/Alaska Native students had the highest risk ratio for LD at 1.79 followed by black students at 1.42, Hispanic 1.15, white .80, and Asian/Pacific Islander .40 (28th Annual Report to Congress on the Implementation of Individuals with Disabilities Education Act, 2009). These national data suggests that American Indian/Alaska Native and black students are 1.8 times and 1.4 times more likely, respectively, than their non-American Indian/Alaska and non-black peers to be identified as having a learning disability. However, as illustrated earlier, the national aggregates do not give a clear picture of what occurs at the state level and nor does it capture the variability across states in the identification and labeling of students with learning disabilities. Using the NCCRESt data for the 2006–07 academic year, African American students risk ratio ranges from 1.11 in Kentucky to 2.85 in Iowa, American Indian from .58 in Mississippi to 2.82 in Washington state, Hispanics from .57 in Louisiana to 1.97 in Minnesota, and Whites from .40 in Hawaii to 1.26 in Vermont.

These disaggregated state data highlight the importance of not just looking at the national aggregates. Also, when examining the state disaggregates it is important to taken into consideration that a lot of variance remains in how states identify students with learning disabilities. Further, the disaggregated state data shows disproportionality among racial/ethnicity groups that are concentrated in specific regions and states that does not show up in the national aggregate data. It is also important that any discussion of students' risk for LD take into consideration the role that the historical context of racism, white privilege, and classism in the American educational system and society as a whole has played and continues to play in these students' perceived or actual risk for disability identification. Once students of color are identified as having LD, they seem to have very different experiences from their white peers with the same label. These differences appear to be in access to the general education classroom, quality of services provided, postsecondary education, and in overall outcomes and quality of life.

Same LD label: different experiences on the basis of race and social class

In recent years, 50% of all students with disabilities have been educated in the general education or inclusive classroom alongside their peers without disabilities (27th Annual Report to Congress, 2005). Students labeled with speech or language impairments make up of the majority of students who are educated in general education classrooms followed by those with learning disabilities. For example, in 2003, 49.9% of all students with disabilities ages 6–21 who received special education services were educated outside of the general education classroom for less than 21% of their total school day and 48.8% of students with learning disabilities spent less than 21% of day outside of general education classroom (27th Annual Report to Congress, 2005). These percentages reflect a welcomed trend toward educating students with learning disabilities in general education classrooms. However, when it comes to educational placements, not all students with learning disabilities are afforded equitable access to general education or to inclusive classrooms where they will be educated with their peers without disabilities. In fact, recent data shows that "compared to students with disabilities from other racial/ethnic groups, black students with disabilities were the least likely to be educated in the regular classroom for most of the school day (38.6 percent). White students with disabilities were the mostly likely to be educated in the regular classroom for most of the school day (54.7)" (27th Annual Report to Congress, 2005, p. 48). The same report finds, "Black students with disabilities were more likely than students with disabilities from other racial/ethnic groups to be educated *outside the regular classroom more than 60 percent of the day* (28.1 percent). They were also more likely to be educated in *separate environments* (5.2 percent)" (27th Annual Report to Congress, 2005, p. 48). Whether students with disabilities are placed in general education or segregated special education classrooms has been associated with decreased graduation rates, increased dropout rates, diminished secondary education options, and a negative overall post-school experience.

During the 1998–99 academic year, students with LD had a 63.3% graduation rate, significantly higher than the graduation rate for all students with disabilities as whole at 57.4%. Though race and ethnicity data were not available for graduation rates, as stated above, according to the Advocacy Institute (2002), ". . .Given the large proportion of students with SLD in the overall population of students with disabilities, this data would suggest that the graduation rates for students with SLD vary significantly by racial/ethnic group" (p. 3). However, dropout data was available on the basis of race/ethnicity. For this same academic year, students with LD had a 27.1% dropout rate compared to a 28.9% dropout rate for all students with disabilities, 44% for American Indian/Alaska Native, 33.7% for black, 32.3% for Hispanic, 26.9% for white, and 18.8% Asian/Pacific Islander (Advocacy Institute, 2002). These data suggest some differences in types of placement, graduate rates, and dropout rates on the basis of race and ethnicity with White students with learning disabilities and other disabilities appearing to fare much better than American Indian, black, and Hispanic students. As stated previously, available data does not provide an ethnic/racial breakdown for each disability category in terms of type of placement, gender, social class, dropout rate, percentage of students who receive a regular high school diploma versus a nonregular diploma, and percentage of students that enter postsecondary education. However, given the data that is available it is highly likely that these data would, as the Advocacy Institute (2002) indicated, ". . .Vary significantly by racial/ethnic group" (p.3).

The intersection of race and social class seems to impact students' risk ratio, identification, type and quality of placement, and graduation and dropout rates. Additionally, the intersection of race and social class impacts the postsecondary outcomes of all students labeled with disabilities and specifically those labeled with learning disabilities' postsecondary education outcomes. For example, according to the National Longitudinal Transition Study (2009),

> . . .The differences for youth related to household income were significant. Youth from households earning more than $50,000 were more likely than youth from households earning $25,000 or less to have held a job over the time since leaving high school (81 percent vs. 61 percent). . .At the time of the interview, 63 percent of White youth were employed, compared with 35% of African American youth. The percentages of these youth who have been employed since leaving high school also differed significantly, with 80 percent of White youth having been employed since high school compared with 47 percent of African American youth. (Newman, Wagner, Cameto, & Knoke, p. 50)

As the statistics above clearly indicate, race and class continues to play a significant role in who is identified and placed in the special education category of learning disability, their risk ratio for being identified, their access to the general education classroom, and ultimately their overall in-school and post school experiences. To be sure, once students of color enter the American educational system, regardless of whether they are placed in general or special education or labeled with a learning disability or mental retardation, they have quantitatively and qualitatively different experiences from their white peers, and this is exacerbated in urban settings. To make matters worse, our current educational climate is in many ways much like the one Sleeter describes in the 1950s and 1960s. Like the supposed focus on improving educational standards after Sputnik, today, through the No Child Left Behind Act of 2000, we have witnessed the massive watering down of already sub-standard curriculum and the removal of sound pedagogy from our classrooms, especially in those urban schools serving some of our historically most under-served students (Fusarelli, 2004; Kozol, 2009). All of this is happening at a time when we (Americans) are focused on globalization and preparing American students to compete in a globally diverse and interconnected world. Yet, we are continuing to fail to tap the potential of thousands of urban children (a disproportionate percentage whom are African American and other students of color) as they sit in segregated classrooms waiting for someone to throw them lifelines. Instead, as a society, we seem to be about business as usual — American supremacy.

As I have stated previously (Blanchett, 2009), contrary to what some believe, the struggle to desegregate schools and special education programs in particular and to ensure that all children receive an equitable education is much larger than simply wanting students of color and white students to sit next to each other and to be educated in the same environment. While it makes sense that we would expect public schools to be reflective of the diversity that exists in our society and for children to be educated in racially, culturally, and linguistically diverse settings, integrated and equitable schools offer the potential for other opportunities as well. For many poor parents of color and some middle-class parents, especially those in urban settings, integrated, equitable schools are their only hope for their children receiving high-quality educational opportunities. In fact, research has illustrated that schools attended primarily by African American and/or Latino students are often schools that are deemed high-poverty schools, have high turnover of the teaching and instructional staff, high number of uncertified or provisionally licensed teachers, limited access to technology, few educational specialists (e.g., math and reading specialists) and resources (e.g., accelerated curriculum for all students), limited extracurricular opportunities, and dilapidated physical environments (Ayers & Ford, 1996; Blanchett, 2009; Blanchett, Mumford, & Beachum, 2005; Kozol, 1992). Moreover, in recent years and with the implementation of the No Child Left Behind Act of 2000 (NCLB), the school described above is more likely to be identified as a "failing school" or a school "in need of improvement," despite the obvious lack of financial, human, and educational resources provided other schools.

On the other hand, schools that have a majority white student body are often viewed as just the opposite of those attended by a majority of African American and/or Latino students. They are often located in suburban or rural areas and are touted and labeled as "high performance" schools. Many of their teachers and instructional staff hold graduate degrees, receive higher salaries, have access to state of the art technology and science labs, accelerated, honors, and/or Advanced Placement curriculum, newer or renovated physical structures, and a waiting list of teachers who would like to become employed with the school. Despite numerous calls for local, state, and federal policy makers to be responsive to the fiscal needs of students in large metropolitan areas (a large percentage of whom live in poverty and are students of color), the funding in many of these schools continues to be insufficient. Middle-class parents, a disproportionate percentage of whom are white, have actively opposed tax increases and other proposals to augment funding of urban schools. These actions are the result of an effort to ensure the success of majority white schools often attended by their children, and ultimately, to maintain educational privilege (Brantlinger, 2003). Many researchers have cited the overt underfunding of urban schools and the lack of societal ownership and responsibility for the success of these students as the newest form of structural racism and discrimination (Kozol, 1992; Losen & Orfield, 2002). More importantly, the failure to provide students in urban settings, a disproportionate number of whom are poor and students of color, with a high-quality equitable education has been identified as a major contributing factor to the overrepresentation of students of color in special education. Majority white schools' use of special education placement to re-segregate students of color in racially homogeneous separate special education classrooms also contributes to disproportionality (Losen & Orfield, 2002). While the initial overrepresentation of African American and Mexican students was associated with mild mental retardation, shortly after the conception of the learning disability as a category of privilege for the privileged, it too quickly became a dumping ground for children of color who did not "qualify" for mild mental retardation or other developmental disabilities. As time has illustrated, not all students with the label of learning disability would receive the same high quality services and access to the general education classroom and subsequently to postsecondary opportunities. In fact, the privileges associated with the category of learning disabilities would only be afforded to some and not to all who shared the LD label.

Conclusion

Sleeter asserts that the disability category of learning disability was conceived and formed to respond to political, military, and economic pressures to supposedly increase educational standards for all American children in an effort to ensure America's dominance and supremacy in the world while also protecting White middle- and upper-class children from school failure. If you are like me and you see the merit in Sleeter's argument, you have to face the fact that even at that time (during the 1950s and 60s) when America was focused on raising the standards for all children, not all children were REALLY included. Does this sound familiar? As I have already stated (e.g. Blanchett, 2006), the American educational system has a long and sordid history of not educating ALL of its children — the reasons offered for this intentional neglect differs from scholar to scholar — however, racism, white privilege, and white dominance and supremacy are rarely mentioned as the primary culprits. The American educational system and society as a whole has

326

purported to launch initiatives that are in the best interest of the "public good" to secure the American public's support for these initiatives, while in reality the initiatives that are implemented often do just the opposite. While I am not a believer in conspiracy theory per se, I agree with Sleeter that developing and instituting a way to explain White middle and upper class students' failure during a period of increasingly higher educational standards was a deliberate move to ensure and protect white middle class intellectual supremacy. More importantly, as illustrated above, this system of privilege pertaining to LD that Sleeter uncovered is still securely in place today and has been coupled with new initiatives and legislation that is devastating many urban communities and the potential of children of color.

Writing a paper that named the social-cultural context surrounding the creation and maintenance of learning disabilities would have been gutsy at any point in her career, but to do so as a little-known untenured assistant professor was courageous and risky to say the least. To have done so more than 20 years ago is almost unheard of, let alone to have done so in a manner where what was written then is still so groundbreaking and seminal that researchers and scholars are still trying to make meaning of it and to operationalize it into educational research, policies, and practices that support the major tenets of the argument. The person who did provided a framework, which I and others can employ to examine the special education category of learning disabilities, is indeed a woman of great conviction and a scholarly friend. More importantly, she is a human being who saw practices that were not adequately described and explained in the professional literature at the time, and she could not ignore it. Today, even in retirement, Dr. Christine Sleeter is still pushing the academy and our society to think more deeply about issues of social justice and the importance of social context in educational research, policy, and practice. If we embrace Sleeter's (1987) article and see the validity of her arguments, we would move swiftly to create a social context and employ a social justice lens to uncover and eradicate differential and inequitable treatment of ALL children — those labeled as having learning and other disabilities, those who languish in urban areas, and those from diverse racial, ethnic, class, and linguistic backgrounds. More importantly, we would have the conviction of Sleeter to conduct research and to make scholarly contributions that "attempt to correct so many generations of bad faith and cruelty, when it is operating not only in the classrooms but in society" (James Baldwin, 1963 as cited in Ayers, Ladson-Billings, Michie, & Noguera, 2008, p. XIII).

Works cited

Advocacy Institute. (2002). *Students with Learning Disabilities: A National Review*. Retrieved December 6, 2009 from http://www.ncldtalks.org/content/interview/detail/1154/.

Ayers, W., & Ford, P. (1996). Chaos and opportunity. In W. Ayers, & P. Ford (Eds.), *City kids city teachers: Reports from the front row* (pp. 81–90). New York: The New Press.

Ayers, W., Ladson Billings, G., Michie, G., & Noguera, G. (2008). *City Kids, City Schools: More Reports from the Front Row*. The New Press: New York.

Blanchett, W. J. (2009). A Retrospective Examination of Urban Education: From Brown to the Resegregation of African Americans in Special Education — It Is Time to "Go for Broke." *Urban Education, 44*(4), 370–388.

Blanchett, W. J. (2006). Disproportionate Representation of African Americans in Special Education: Acknowledging the role of White Privilege and Racism. *Educational Researcher, 35*(6), 24–28.

Blanchett, W. J., Mumford, V. & Beachum, F. (2005). Urban School Failure & Disproportionality in a Post-Brown Era: Benign Neglect of Students of Color's Constitutional Rights. *Remedial and Special Education, 26*(2), 70–81.

Brantlinger, E. (2003). *Dividing classes: How the middle class negotiates and rationalizes school advantage*. New York: RoutledgeFalmer.

Connor, D. J. & Ferri, B. A. (2010). "Why is There Learning Disabilities?" — Revisiting Sleeter's Socio-political Construction of Disability Two Decades On. *Disability Studies Quarterly.*

Dunn, L. M. (1968). Special education for the mildly retarded: Is much of it justifiable? *Exceptional Children, 35*, 5–22.

Dyslexia Online. (2009). Retrieved December 20, 2009 from http://www.dyslexiaonline.com/famous/famous.htm

Erevelles, N. (2005) Reconceptualizing curriculum as "normalizing" text: Disability studies meets curriculum theory. *Journal of Curriculum Studies, 37*(4), 421–439.

Fusarelli, L. D. (2004). The Potential Impact of the No Child Left Behind Act on Equity and Diversity in American Education. *Educational Policy, 18*(1), 71–94.

Hallahan, D. P. & Kauffman, J. M. (2006). Exceptional Learners: An Introduction to Special Education (10th Ed.). Boston, MA: Pearson Education.

Harmon, J. A., Stockton, T. S., & Contrucci, V. J. (1992). *Gender disparities in special education*. Madison, WI: Wisconsin Department of Public Instruction.

Individuals with Disabilities Education Improvement Act of 2004 (IDEA 2004) H.R.1350. Retrieved November 20, 2006, from http://thomas.loc.gov/cgibin/query/z?c108:h.1350.enr:

I Teach I Learn (2009). Gender as a Factor in Special Education Eligibility. Retrieved from http://www.iteachilearn.com/uh/meisgeier/statsgov20gender.htm

Kivel, P. (2004). The Culture of Power. In F. W. Hale, Jr. (Ed.), *What makes racial diversity work in higher education: Academic leaders present successful policies and strategies.* (pp. 25–31). Virginia: Stylus Publishing.

Kozol, J. (2009). University of Missouri Kansas City Rosa Parks Distinguished Lecture Series. Kansas City, MO. 11/../09.

Kozol, J. (1992). *Savage inequalities*. New York, NY: Harper Collins Publishers.

Larry P. v. Riles, 343F. Supp. 1306 (N.D. Cal. 1972), aff'd 502 F. 2d 963 (9th Cir. 1974); 495 F. Supp. 926 (N.D. Cal. 1979) aff'd 793 F. 2d 969 (9th Cir. 1984).

Losen, D. J. & Orfield, G. (2002). *Racial inequity in special education*. Cambridge, MA: Harvard Education Press.

Mercer, J. R. (1973). *Labeling the mentally retarded*. Berkeley: University of California Press.

National Center for Culturally Responsive Educational Systems. (2009). *Data Maps*. Retrieved December 20, 2009 from http://nccrest.eddata.net/maps/index.php

National Dissemination Center for Children with Disabilities (2009). Retrieved December 19, 2009 from http://www.nichcy.org/Disabilities/Specific/Pages/LD.aspx

Newman, L., Wagner, M., Cameto, R., & Knoke, A-M. (2009). The Post-High School Outcomes of Youth with Disabilities up to 4 Years After High School. A Report of Findings from the National Longitudinal Transition Study-2 (NLTS2) (NCSER 2009–3017). Menlo Park, CA: SRI International. Available at http://www.nlts2.org/reports/2009_04/nlts2_report_2009_04_complete.pdf.

No Child Left Behind Act of 2001, Pub. L. No. 107–110, 115 Stat. 1425, 20 U.S.C.A. §§ 6301 et seq. (2002 Supp.).

Sleeter, C. E. (1987). Why is there learning disabilities? A critical analysis of the birth of the field with its social context. In T.S. Popkewitz (Ed.), *The formation of school subjects: the struggle for creating an American institution.* (pp. 210–237). London: Palmer Press.

Smith, D. D. (2004). *Introduction to special education: teaching in an age of opportunity* (5th Ed). Needham Heights, MA: Allyn & Bacon.

U. S. Department of Education. (2009). Office of Special Education and Rehabilitation Services, Office of Special Education Programs, *28th Annual Report to Congress on the Implementation of the Individuals with Disabilities Education Act*, 2006, vol.1, Washington, D.C.

U. S. Department of Education. (2008). Office of Special Education and Rehabilitation Services, Office of Special Education Programs, *27th Annual Report to Congress on the Implementation of the Individuals with Disabilities Education Act, 2005, vol. 1,* Washington, DC.

Valdes et al., (1990). The National Longitudinal Transition Study of Special Education Students: Statistical almanac (Vol. 1). Menlo Park, CA: SRI International.

37

THE SONG REMAINS THE SAME

Transposition and the disproportionate representation of minority students in special education

Gregg D. Beratan

Source: *Race Ethnicity & Education*, 11, 4, 2008, 337–354.

The disproportionate representation of minority students in special education has long been recognised as a problem in the United States. It is, however, only with the 2004 authorisation of the Individuals with Disabilities Education Improvement Act (IDEA) that Congress has tried to prescribe a remedy for this. Beginning with a deconstruction of the case law, public law and policy interpretations built around IDEA, this paper will first use an understanding of the concept of 'institutional ablism' as it has been developed within disability studies, to challenge the widely accepted view of IDEA as civil rights legislation. Drawing on Critical Race Theory, the article will then offer a further deconstruction of IDEA focusing on the IDEA'S attempt to address the disproportionate representation of minority students in special education. The analysis of the law illustrates the use of a mechanism that I will call *transposition:* the use of the legally accepted segregation of special education to maintain the effects of the unacceptable and illegal segregation by race. The analysis will make the case that the development of special education in the United States offers yet another example of interest convergence, specifically that of the marginal disability rights gained with the creation of special education converging with the white interest of recouping the losses of the US Supreme Court's historic *Brown v. Board of Education* desegregation decision.

Introduction

We must recognise and acknowledge (at least to ourselves) that our actions are not likely to lead to transcendent change and, despite our best efforts, may be of more help to the system we despise than to the victims of that system that we are trying to help.

(Bell 2004, 192)

This statement by Derrick Bell is not intended to remove all hope of progress in the fight against discrimination. Bell is taking note of the historic lessons of the civil rights movement; a history in which all victories or progress have been almost immediately undermined through systemic mechanisms that serve to maintain existing discrimination. It is meant to take note of the power of institutional racism to create racist outcomes out of even seemingly strong stands against racism, such as the ruling in *Brown v. the Board of Education*.[1] As Bell (1992, 92) notes, 'Understanding the true nature of racism would equip us to weather its myriad harms'.

The intersection of disability and race as a means of discrimination in the United States has a long history dating back to the beginnings of the eugenics movement (Reid and Knight 2006; Selden 1999; Valencia 1997). It is a juncture that is most prominent today in the disproportionate representation of minority students[2] in special education.

The disproportionate representation of minority students in special education is as clear an example of a racist outcome as one can find. The Individuals with Disabilities Education Improvement Act of 2004 (IDEA) formally recognises such disproportionate representation as a problem in special education.

(12)

(A) Greater efforts are needed to prevent the intensification of problems connected with mislabeling and high dropout rates among minority children with disabilities.

(B) More minority children continue to be served in special education than would be expected from the percentage of minority students in the general school population.

(C) African-American children are identified as having mental retardation and emotional disturbance at rates greater than their White counterparts.

(D) In the 1998–1999 school year, African-American children represented just 14.8 percent of the population aged 6 through 21, but comprised 20.2 percent of all children with disabilities.

(E) Studies have found that schools with predominately White students and teachers have placed disproportionately high numbers of their minority students into special education.[3]

The disproportionate representation of minority students in special education is not a new issue. Overrepresentation was addressed in the 1997 reauthorisation of IDEA and has been identified as an issue for almost 40 years (Artiles et al. 2002; Losen and Orfield 2002; Tomlinson 1982).

331

This article focuses on the way the Individuals with Disabilities Education Improvement Act of 2004 (IDEA 2004) and a combination of *institutional ablism* and *racism* are used to discriminate against students – a violation of the stated intent of the law. First, I define institutional ablism. Then, I deconstruct the meanings and understandings of disability contained within US case law, public law, and policy interpretations that have been built around IDEA. I then illustrate how the very components of the law that prohibit discrimination against disabled and minority students, in fact, actively contribute to and maintain existing discrimination. Further, I demonstrate that this is a mechanism for transposing societally and legally acceptable ablist outcomes for less acceptable racist goals. Lastly, I will use two concepts developed by critical race theorists, 'retrenchment' and 'interest convergence', to offer an explanation of why this has occurred in the way it has.

Institutional ablism

I believe that the body of scholarly work to be discussed in this section collectively establishes the existence of what I refer to as 'institutional ablism'. Specifically, I contend that discriminatory structures and practices, as well as uninterrogated beliefs about disability that are deeply ingrained within educational systems, subvert even the most well-intentioned policies by maintaining the substantive oppression of existing hierarchies.

I would argue that scholars within both disability studies and inclusive education – without coining the term 'institutional ablism' – have begun over the last quarter-century to make an argument for the existence of such a mechanism in relation to disability. Vic Finkelstein (1980), Mike Oliver (1981, 1983) and Irving Kenneth Zola (1981, 1982), for example, were among the first to apply an understanding of the social model of disability to larger societal practices and structures, illuminating a multitude of the barriers encountered by disabled people in US and British society.

In 1982, Sally Tomlinson looked at the materialist structures and policies that artificially constructed West Indian students in England as educationally subnormal. Tomlinson's *A Sociology of Special Education* is arguably the first major disability studies in education text and was also one of the first books to challenge the belief that disabled students' inequitable position within the education system is the result of their individual and inherent deficits.

Barton (1986) examined the underlying politics and unquestioned beliefs that shaped educational policies and practices in England, arguing that they served as a built-in obstruction to more traditional educational pathways – a 'safety valve for the mainstream system' (283). This was an early development within a much larger body of work (e.g., Barton 2003, 1999, 1988; Barton and Slee 1999) that focused upon identifying intended and unintended discrimination and oppression built into educational systems. This task has been furthered by a number of researchers, most notably Roger Slee (1999a, 1996, 1993) and Gillian Fulcher (1999). Ainscow (1989) and Clough (1988) both charted the ways in which discrimination is built into curriculum.

This was an important step as, until this point, the inclusive education/ integration/mainstreaming[4] debate had largely focused on the issue of location as the main institutional barrier to disabled people accessing education. Since this time, research has begun to elaborate on the discriminatory effects of pedagogy (Allan 1999a, Benjamin 2002; Vlachou 1997), education reform (Bowe, Ball, and Gold 1992; Peters 2002; Slee 1993), management practices (Clough 1998; Armstrong 1998), school funding practices (Marsh 1998), and teacher education (Barton 2003; Booth 2003; Nes and Strømstad 2003). Collectively, this body of work establishes the existence of what I refer to as 'institutional ablism': the collective failure of an organisation to provide an appropriate and professional service to people because of their disability. It can be seen or detected in processes, attitudes and behavior that amount to discrimination through unwitting prejudice, ignorance, thoughtlessness and ablist stereotyping which disadvantage disabled people.[5] This is the idea that there are discriminatory structures and practices and uninterrogated beliefs about disability deeply ingrained within societal systems and institutions that subvert even the most well intentioned policies and maintain the substantive oppression of existing hierarchies.

Critical Race Theory, deconstruction, and disability studies

In 1967, Stokely Carmichael and Charles Hamilton first posited that racism operated in more complex and covert ways than just explicit and deliberate hatred and discrimination. Over the years, a number of scholars have refined the concept of institutional racism. In 1999, the United Kingdom's official inquiry into the murder of Stephen Lawrence[6] defined the phrase as:

> The collective failure of an organization to provide an appropriate and professional service to people because of their colour, culture, or ethnic origin. It can be seen or detected in processes, attitudes and behaviour which amount to discrimination through unwitting prejudice, ignorance, thoughtlessness and racist stereotyping which disadvantage minority ethnic people. (Macpherson 1999, 28)[7]

The importance of the concept of institutional racism lies not only in its recognition that racism is more than just individual prejudice, but also in its understanding that individual intent is irrelevant. Even if an institution attempts to eradicate racist outcomes, if it does not succeed it is still institutionally racist.

In reaction to institutional racism, many scholars of race and racism turned to the burgeoning field of 'Critical Race Theory' as a means of interrogating this phenomenon (Gillborn 2008; Ladson-Billings 1998). Critical race theorists deconstruct meanings and understandings of race embedded within both case and common law to better understand *how* those meanings and understandings create existing inequities (Crenshaw 1995; Ladson-Billings 1998; Parker and Stovall 2004).

One of the ways that critical race theory can serve this end is to generate informed perspectives designed to describe, analyze and challenge racist policy and practice in educational institutions. The connection between critical race theory and education would entail linking teaching and research to general practical knowledge about institutional forces that have a disparate impact on racial minority communities. (Parker and Stovall 2004)

Critical Race Theory formalises the application of a number of practices and uses them to place understandings of race at the centre of the analysis of particular policies (Ladson-Billings and Tate 1995; Ladson-Billings 1998; Parker and Stovall 2004). None of these practices are exclusive to critical race theory; in fact, are all used extensively throughout social science research. Narrative/counter-narrative has been employed in relation to class, race, and gender by the likes of Michael Apple (1999) and bell hooks (2000). Deconstruction has been used by a range of theorists and researchers, from philosophers such as Jacques Derrida (1982) to feminist theorists such as Hélène Cixous (1986).

Disability study scholars have also begun to utilise these same means to place disability at the centre of a number of areas of theory and research. The work of Jenny Morris (1989, 1991) and Carol Thomas (1999) uses the narratives of disabled women to gain an understanding of their experiences of both disability and oppression. Marian Corker (1999) uses deconstruction as a way of understanding competing discourses within disability studies, while Felicity Armstrong (2003) deconstructs the meanings and understandings of 'inclusion' and 'exclusion' to gain new insight into the positioning and experience of disabled people within the English and French educational systems. It has been argued that such deconstructive strategies allow for an understanding in which both macro and micro level perspectives become clear.

Deconstructing IDEA

I would like to deconstruct the ways in which the meanings of disability embedded within IDEA 2004 actively construct disabled students' marginalised positioning within schools. Derrida expands upon both the analytical and the transformative power of deconstruction:

[W]hen I first met, I won't say 'deconstructive architecture' but the deconstructive discourse on architecture, I was rather puzzled and suspicious. I thought at first that this was an analogy, a displaced discourse, and something more analogical than rigorous. And then . . . I realised that on the contrary the most efficient way of putting deconstruction to work was by going through art and architecture. As you know, deconstruction is not simply a matter of discourse or a matter of displacing the semantic content of the discourse, its conceptual structure or whatever.

> Deconstruction goes through certain social and political structures, meet-
> ing with resistance and displacing institutions as it does so. I think that
> in these forms of art and in any architecture, to deconstruct traditional
> sanctions – theoretical, philosophical, cultural – effectively you have to
> displace . . . I would say 'solid' structures, not only in the sense of mate-
> rial structures but 'solid' in the sense of cultural, pedagogical, political,
> economic structures. (Derrida 1989 quoted in Armstrong 2003, 75–76)

While Derrida is speaking in relation to his own examination of art and architecture, I apply deconstruction to the structures, institutions, mechanisms, and
discourses built around IDEA. I have no delusions of this process displacing
structures, as Derrida suggests, but hope that some understandings and perceptions of IDEA will be troubled; this may be a necessary first step in the wider
process of critical reform.

Since its inception, IDEA has been portrayed as an anti-discrimination law in
the same vein as the civil rights laws of the 1960s:

> [F]or far too long children with disabilities were closed out of those
> kind of opportunities, trapped in a system without guideposts, influ-
> enced by stereotypes, dominated by assumptions that people like Josh
> couldn't take the course that he just enumerated. In 1975 Congress
> began to change that when the IDEA was enacted. It has meant the right
> to receive an education that all children deserve. It has given children
> who never would and never have had it, the right to sit in the same
> classrooms, to learn the same skills, to dream the same dreams as their
> fellow Americans. And for students who sat next to them in those class-
> rooms, it has also given them a chance to learn a little something. To get
> rid of the baggage of ignorance and damaging stereotypes, and to begin
> to understand that what we have in common is far more important than
> what divides us.[8]

IDEA may be about civil rights, but can it be called anti-discriminatory? It is an
improvement on the non-educational institutions and asylums it was designed to
replace, but being an improvement on institutionalisation is hardly a grandiose
claim. What does it do, and how does it do it?

The 1975 passage of IDEA was a case of the government trying to catch
up with the law. In 1971 and 1972, US district courts agreed to two consent
decrees which declared that in states guaranteeing a right to education, denying
disabled students an education amounted to a violation of the equal protection
clause of the 14th amendment. IDEA formalised the right to education that
the courts had recognised, and attempted to fund it (Gilhool 1997; Rothstein
2000).

IDEA is a funding bill. States accepting money under it are required to adhere
to certain principles. There were five principles in the original act:[9]

1) All children with disabilities, regardless of the nature of their disability, have a right to and must be provided with a free appropriate public education (FAPE).
2) All children with a disabilities will have a right to and must receive an Individual Education Program (IEP) that is tailored to address the child's unique learning needs.
3) Children with disabilities must be educated in the least restrictive environment (LRE) with their nondisabled peers to the maximum extent appropriate.
4) Students with disabilities, must a have access to all areas of school participation.
5) Children with disabilities and their families are guaranteed rights with respect to non discriminatory testing, confidentiality and due process.[10]

Because of the limits of space in this paper, I focus only on the principle of least restrictive environment (LRE) as a significant factor in the institutional ablism within the US public school system. This is not to imply that the other requirements are not deeply involved in embedding ablist discrimination within the law. In other work I have found institutional ablism at work in the structures and requirements of the Individualized Education Program (IEP) as well as in IDEA'S due process requirements (Beratan 2006). The LRE provision, however, is very much the cornerstone of the law; it is the main reason that IDEA is seen as civil rights legislation and, as I will demonstrate in the next section, it plays a dominant role in enabling discrimination.

The least restrictive environment and its qualifiers

While IDEA does not specifically mention the concept of inclusive education, the principle of LRE has been taken by many to imply it. As stated in the 2004 authorisation, LRE requires:

(5) LEAST RESTRICTIVE ENVIRONMENT

(A) To the maximum extent appropriate, children with disabilities, including children in public or private institutions or other care facilities, are educated with children who are not disabled, and special classes, separate schooling, or other removal of children with disabilities from the regular educational environment occurs only when the nature or severity of the disability of a child is such that education in regular classes with the use of supplementary aids and services cannot be achieved satisfactorily.[11]

The view that IDEA encourages or promotes inclusive education originates in this definition of LRE, which implies preference for educating disabled students in the same environment as non-disabled students. While much of the literature has focused on the meaning and interpretation of 'least restrictive environment' (e.g., Crockett and Kaufman 1999; Daugherty 2001; Lipton 1997), the words that dominate the clause are 'to the maximum extent *appropriate*'. The word 'appropriate' serves as a qualifier that overshadows the rest of the section. The law itself does not say what is appropriate. As Henderson (1993, 94) has pointed out:

> This term is much broader than mainstreaming in that the LRE for a student with a profound or multiple disability might be a self-contained special class located in a neighborhood elementary or secondary school. The key here is the term 'appropriate', which requires an individually designed educational program (IEP) based on the child's specific educational needs. If the IEP can only deliver the needed resources by means of special classes staffed by special educator and related service personnel . . . then *that* becomes the LRE for that child.

The importance of the word 'appropriate' comes in the implication that what the law refers to as 'the regular educational environment' is not appropriate to the same level for all children. This is important, for a number of reasons, not the least of which is the implicit assimilationist intent implicit within IDEA. In other words, the onus is on disabled students who, given the necessary 'supplementary aids and services', must find a way to fit into 'the regular educational environment'. This is by no means exclusive to IDEA. Slee (1999b, 127) has described the same phenomenon within the Australian context:

> Predominantly unchanged practices are described in new terms. Inclusion is practiced by the same people who presided over exclusion. The aim is to have 'othered' children fit schools we provide with a minimum of fuss and without disrupting the institutional equilibrium. This is assimilation.

One of the problems with an assimilationist approach is that it establishes an instant hierarchy between those being assimilated (in this case, disabled students) and those students for whom the system was designed. This hierarchy is reflected in a reading of the least restrictive environment clause, which ends with a statement to the effect that if a disabled student cannot reasonably fit into the existing system, then it is acceptable to segregate them. There are a number of things built into IDEA that serve to complement and augment this hierarchy. Most notable is the law's definition of disability:

(B) CHILD AGED 3 THROUGH 9.

The term 'child with a disability' for a child aged 3 through 9 (or any subset of that age range, including ages 3 through 5), may, at the discretion of the State and the local educational agency, include a child –

(i) experiencing developmental delays, as defined by the State and as measured by appropriate diagnostic instruments and procedures, in 1 or more of the following areas: physical development; cognitive development; communication development; social or emotional development; or adaptive development; and (ii) who, by reason thereof, needs special education and related services.[12]

This definition operates wholly from within a deficit model understanding of disability. The conflation of impairment and disability[13] is something that has long been criticised within both disability studies and disability politics (Corbett 1996; Oliver 1990; UPIAS 1976). Proponents of the social model of disability argue that by not distinguishing between impairment and disability, disabled people become constructed as problematic. Deficit understandings do not account for or recognise disability as socially constructed; rather, disability is conceptualised as an internal deficit located solely within the individual (Altman 2001; Oliver 2004, 1990).

A number of social model theorists argue that the act of problematising individuals amounts to a form of oppression (Abberly 1996; Swain, French, and Cameron 2003; Oliver 2004). In adopting deficit model understandings of disability, institutions and laws privilege this oppression (Oliver 1990). Embedded within IDEA is a conception of disabled people as 'less than' in comparison to non-disabled people, and therefore not always worthy of equal treatment under the law. Looking again at the phrase 'to the maximum extent appropriate', it becomes clear that its intended interpretation is to the maximum extent appropriate *to an individual's deficit*. This is one example of how IDEA establishes a form of ablism into the educational system, regardless of the intent of the individuals within that system.

Case law interpreting the LRE clause has been inconsistent (Henderson 1993; Rothstein 2000). While almost all of the LRE cases have determined that the law implies that the regular educational environment is not always the least restrictive environment, there have been significant disagreements in the courts over how and on what basis this is to be determined. Case law interpretation is important because it is the court interpretation of the meaning of IDEA from which schools and school districts must take their cue. Just as the actual wording of IDEA has constructed ablist institutions, so has the judicial interpretation of IDEA.

In *Board of Education of the Hendrick Hudson Central School District* v. *Amy Rowley*, the Supreme Court, focusing upon the free appropriate public education requirement (FAPE), expounded on what they saw as the proper interpretation of the term 'appropriate'. Justice Rehnquist wrote on behalf of the majority:

Thus if personalized instruction is being provided with sufficient supportive services to permit the child to benefit from the instruction, and the other items on the definitional checklist are satisfied, the child is receiving a 'free appropriate public education' as defined by the Act.

The ruling establishes the bare minimal standard of educational *benefit* as the final arbiter of appropriateness. Rehnquist argues that this interpretation stems directly from legislative intent:

> By passing the act, Congress sought primarily to make public education available to handicapped children. But in seeking to provide such access to public education, Congress did not impose upon the states any greater substantive educational standard than would be necessary to make such access meaningful. Indeed Congress expressly 'recognized that in many instances the process of providing special education and related services to handicapped children is not guaranteed to produce any particular outcome.' ... Thus the intent of the act was more to open the door of public education to handicapped children on appropriate terms than to guarantee any particular level of education once inside.

It is important to remember that Supreme Court rulings are the law of the land regarding how any particular law is to be interpreted. This ruling says that states need only meet a standard of educational *benefit* for a program to be deemed appropriate. The ruling also reinforces a hierarchy between disabled and non-disabled students whose education is held to a higher standard, particularly in light of recent standards-based reforms such as *No Child Left Behind*.[15] While the ruling does not prohibit states from holding a higher standard, very few states have attempted to do so.

It is worth noting that the dissenting opinion, offered by Justice White, considered the majority's opinion akin to unequal treatment. In fact, Justice White disputed Rehnquist's interpretation of legislative intent:

> [I]f there are limits not evident from the face of the statute on what may be considered an 'appropriate education', they must be found in the purpose of the statute or its legislative history. The Act itself announces that it will provide a 'full educational opportunity to all handicapped children'. . . . This goal is repeated throughout the legislative history in statements too frequent to be 'passing references and isolated phrases' . . . These statements elucidate the meaning of 'appropriate'. According to the senate report for example the Act does 'guarantee that handicapped children are provided equal educational opportunity'. . . . Indeed, at times the purpose of the act was described as tailoring each handicapped child's educational plan to enable the child 'to achieve his or her maximum potential'.

If Justice White's assertion is believed,[16] it becomes clear that the majority opinion embeds yet another layer of ablism within IDEA by allowing schools to provide lesser standards of education for disabled students than for non-disabled students.

Other cases have affirmed the interpretation that the regular education environment is not always appropriate (e.g., *Walter* v. *Roncker* 1983; *Daniel R.R.* v. *State Board of Education*, 5th Cir. 1989), while still other cases have determined *who* gets to determine what is appropriate. For example, in *Hartman* v. *Loudon County Board of Education*, the 4th Circuit Court of Appeals determined that responsibility for determining the appropriate placement belonged to the school's IEP team rather than to the courts. The significance of this is in its recognition of the privileging that IDEA gives to professional expertise. It is noteworthy that 'expertise' does not apply to the entire IEP team; only the professionals on the team who have the 'right to apply their professional judgement', not the students or their family members.

This privileging was recently formalised even further in *Schaeffer* v. *Weast* (2005), when the court determined that if a student's family wishes to challenge an IEP team's decision the burden of proof lies with the family; the school's determination is presumed to be correct until proven otherwise. This creates yet another hierarchy, in which professional expertise is officially valued more highly than the knowledge and expertise of disabled students and their parents. A large body of work within disability studies has examined the oppressive nature of this hierarchy of expertise (Biklen 1992; Corbett 1996). For many of these professionals, their professional identity is strongly tied to the deficit understandings of disability discussed earlier (Reiser and Mason 1995).

It is clear that ablist understandings and mechanisms are firmly entrenched within IDEA. I have focused only on one clause within the law; however, I would suggest that ablism runs throughout IDEA. Its level of involvement in the LRE clause alone should raise alarms for anyone concerned with equity. The remainder of this article will focus on the interplay between institutional ablism and institutional racism in IDEA'S attempts to address racial disproportionality in special education.

Disproportionality and the transposition of racist outcomes?

Institutional ablism alone is insufficient to understand the disproportionate identification of minority students under IDEA. An understanding of institutionalised racism must also be brought into the picture. The importance of the concept of institutional racism lies not only in its recognition that racism is more than just individual prejudice, but also in the understanding that individual intent is irrelevant, even if an institution attempts to eradicate racist outcomes. If it does not succeed, it is still institutionally racist.

In relation to disproportionality, institutional ablism (as will be discussed shortly) is very much a factor; however, it is impossible to take institutional racism out of the equation. It is difficult to find a more clearly racist outcome than the disproportionate segregation of minority students from general education. If ablism alone were involved, one could expect to find similar levels of representation across racial and ethnic groups. The combination of institutional ablism and institutional racism serves to make both stronger than they would be on their own. In effect, society's willingness to perceive discrimination against disabled people as being the result of individual deficiencies is used to make racism more palatable. As Reid and Knight (forthcoming) point out:

> To explain overrepresentation of minority students in special education, we first reveal US historical conditions that have made institutionalized racism, classism, and sexism seem natural and just through their conflation with *disability*, a form of oppression based on ablism.

Much of the focus on institutional racism in education has been around the resegregation of public schools through a variety of covert mechanisms, including white flight (Johnson and Shapiro 2003), testing (Brown et al. 2003; Gillborn and Youdell 2000), 'color-blind' policies (Bonilla-Silva 2003) and pedagogy (Gillborn 1990; Sleeter 2004). However, the use of ablist segregation of special education allows for a legal, overt, and systematised means of achieving the same end. IDEA, legally and overtly, achieves the racially segregated system that the courts attempted to do away with in the *Brown* decision.

The 2004 incarnation of IDEA expands upon the attempts of earlier versions to address disproportionality. Whereas the 1997 version of IDEA stopped at requiring local education agencies (LEAs) to report, review and, if necessary, revise policies, practices and procedures aimed at preventing the disproportionate representation of minority students in special education, the 2004 version of IDEA mandates LEAs

> ...to reserve the maximum amount of funds under section 613(f) to provide comprehensive coordinated early intervening services to serve children in the local educational agency, particularly children in those groups that were significantly overidentified under paragraph (1).[17]

This full-funding trigger, located in section 618 d (B) of IDEA, is written in a way to suggest that it is intended to give more funds to LEAs for the purpose of fighting existing disproportionality. Although there is no reason to question this intention, an understanding of both institutional ablism and racism means that intentions are irrelevant and there is a need to focus on outcomes. While it is too soon to determine the consequences of this clause, there is enough evidence to speculate upon possibilities.

Anything that triggers maximum funding for a school or local education agency is an incentive. In this case, rather than discouraging the disproportionate identification of minority students as disabled, the clause serves as a *bounty* that actively encourages overidentification as a means to higher funding levels. Greene and Forster (2002, 7) found that bounty funding systems in special education led to far greater growth in special education than lump sum funding systems (no incentives):

The average special education enrollment rate for states that had lump-sum systems at any time during the study period grew from 11.1% in the 1991–92 school year to 12.4% in the 2000–01 school year, an increase of 1.3 percentage points. In the same period, the average special education enrollment rate for states that maintained bounty systems for the entire study period grew from 10.5% to 12.8%, an increase of 2.3 percentage points.

Although Greene and Forster (2002) focused upon the effects of bounty systems on the identification of special education students, there is no reason to suggest that a bounty targeting minority students would have a different outcome.

It could be argued that any incentive would be nullified by additional costs related to a student being identified as needing special education services. Greene and Forster (2002, 4) have also answered this claim by pointing out that there is actually a relative *benefit* tied to increased identification of students:

> Some services that a school would have provided to a particular child no matter what can be redefined as special education services if the child is placed in special education; these services are not truly special education costs because they would have been provided anyway. For example, if a school provides extra reading help to students who are falling behind in reading, the school must bear that cost itself. But if the same school redefines those students as learning disabled rather than slow readers, state and federal government will help pick up the tab for those services. This is financially advantageous for the school because it brings in new state and federal funding to cover 'costs' that the school would have had to pay for anyway. Furthermore, there are many fixed costs associated with special education that do not increase with every new child. For example, if a school hires a full-time special education reading teacher, it will pay the same cost whether that teacher handles three students a day or ten. However, the school will collect a lot more money for teaching ten special education students than it would for teaching three.

The funding mechanisms in terms of both funding received and relative benefits becomes an institutionalised mechanism of inequity.

Is this a form of institutional ablism or institutional racism? It is both. In this instance, the two are indistinguishable. Neither offers sufficient explanation on its own. Kimberlé Williams Crenshaw (2003, 23) argues in her analysis of the intersections of race and sex that focusing on either construction as discrete from the other

> . . .creates a distorted analysis and sexism because the operative conceptions of race and sex become grounded in experiences that actually represent only a subset of a much more complex phenomenon.

Disability and race are similarly conjoined in IDEA's disproportionality clause. It is ablist, in that students' opportunities and experiences are being limited by mechanisms and structures built around constructions of disability; but it is also institutionally racist in the way it targets students by their membership in racial and ethnic minority groups. *The racist outcomes could not be achieved without the ablist mechanisms.* Returning to a focus on outcomes, racism would seem to be the primary operative. I put forward an argument similar to that identified in ongoing research by D. Kim Reid and Michelle G. Knight (see quotation above), that an ablist mechanism (in this case IDEA's full-funding trigger) has been transposed to create the racist outcome of disproportionate representation of minority students in Special Education.

The Merriam-Webster Dictionary defines the word 'transpose' as: 'to write or perform (a musical composition) in a different key' (p. 761); the main effect of this being that, while the sound changes, the song remains the same. In this case, racism was the original key, and it was replaced by the form of discrimination that was the least assailable: the legally accepted ablism of IDEA. The deficiency changes, but the inequality remains the same.

The accessibility of ablism as a means of maintaining racial discrimination is not merely a debatable matter of perception, but a legal distinction mandated by the supreme court. In *City of Cleburne v. Cleburne Living Centre, Inc.* (473 US 432, 1985). The United States Supreme Court held that mental retardation and other types of disability are not a suspect class and therefore are not entitled to a 'strict' or even 'heightened' scrutiny standard of review under the equal protection clause of the 14th Amendment; there must only be a rational basis for exclusion to occur. What this means is that it is legal to discriminate against disabled people, as long as there is a rational basis for the discrimination (Blanck et al. 2004; Colker and Tucker 2000; Minow 1990). When this is compared with racial discrimination that is held to a strict scrutiny standard, it is clear that discrimination against disabled people is far more acceptable and accessible in US society.[18] This makes disability the perfect conduit for the transposition of racial discrimination.

History would also seem to support this analysis. It is no coincidence that the initial push to recognise that disabled people have a right to education began in the early 1960s, as states were immersed in addressing the desegregation mandate of *Brown v. the Board of Education.* Many would identify, and have identified, this development as a natural attempt by disabled people to build on the civil rights gains made by African Americans (Ferri and Connor 2006). In fact, Attorney John W. Davis, while arguing for the state of South Carolina in *Brown*, made this connection:

> May it please the court, I think if the appellants' construction of the Four-teenth Amendment should prevail here, there is no doubt in my mind that it would catch the Indian within its grasp just as much as the Negro. If it should prevail, I am unable to see why a state would have any further right to segregate its pupils on the ground of sex or on the ground of age or on the ground of *mental capacity.* (Friedman 2004, 51, emphasis added)

While there is little question that much of the motivation for the activists fighting to extend the principles of desegregation to disabled people were inspired by the success of the civil rights movement in *Brown*, disabled people's success in achieving this extension may be tied to *Brown* in a very different way, as I explain in the following section.

Interest convergence: retrenchment and disability rights

Ferri and Connor (2006) trace a shift from discourses of race to discourses of ability following the *Brown* decision. They argue that this shift has allowed the resegregation of schools that we see today (Bell 2004; Clotfelter 2004; Orfield and Eaton 1996). How and why did this happen? The answer may lie in two concepts that have been developed within the scholarship of Critical Race Theory; the concepts of 'interest convergence' and 'retrenchment'.

Retrenchment is a concept that was developed by Kimberle Williams Crenshaw (1995). It describes the process by which any civil rights gains are almost immediately nullified, either through the political process or through the execution of the very policy or court rulings that are meant to provide those gains. It is a process that has been documented extensively by critical race theorists such as Derrick Bell (1987, 1992, 2004) and Richard Delgado (2003).

In his (2004) book, *Silent Covenants: Brown v. Board of Education and the Unfulfilled Hopes for Racial Reform*, Derrick Bell argues that the permanence of racism in American life has led to the use of a myriad of methods to undermine and undo the progress represented by the stated intent of the *Brown* decision.

The need for a retrenchment of the gains offered by *Brown* was a driving force behind the development of our system of special education. Special Education presented an opportunity for what Derrick Bell (1980, 2004, 2005) has termed 'interest convergence'. As Bell (2005, 35) articulates it:

> [T]his principle of 'interest convergence' provides: the interest of blacks in achieving racial equality will be accommodated only when it converges with the interests of whites.

In the case of special education, the need for retrenchment was the perceived white interest; and it converged, not with the black interest of racial equality, but with interests of disability activists and parents of children with disabilities who wanted the principles of *Brown* extended to disabled people.

It is no coincidence that Congress first established a Federal Office of Special Education in 1966, 11 years after *Brown*, just as foot-dragging over desegregation was beginning to show segregationist approaches to 'all deliberate speed' for the obstructionism that it was. Ferri and Connor (2006) have argued that the gradualism represented by states' approaches to *Brown's* 'all deliberate speed' mandate enabled the shift from a discourse of race (under which segregation was prohibited) to one of ability (under which it was maintained):

Unfortunately the various reactions to Brown demonstrate how gradual-ism has been used to subvert the original intent of the law. It is important to remember that although IDEA mandates a free and appropriate public education and stresses an environment as close to general education as possible, it does not mandate inclusion. This, in and of itself, allows a perpetual state of gradualism to exist. (Ferri and Connor 2006, 70)

When seen as part of this overarching shift from discourses of race as deficit to discourses of deficit of ability, the development of special education can be seen as primarily serving the white interest of reformalising segregation; the disabled interest in a right to education becomes merely a useful conduit.

This offers not only a glimpse of interest convergence at work, this time against the interest of minority students, but also another example of transposition. What becomes clear is that the *Brown* decision made the discourse of race legally unac-cessible, and so the more readily accessed and unquestioned discourse of ability was used to maintain the segregation.

Conclusion

The institutional ablism built into IDEA's LRE clause serves to legalise the discrimination that it was intended to alleviate. With this legal and accessible discrimination at its disposal, the special education system offers the general education system a means of maintaining the discrimination that *Brown v. the Board of Education* made illegal. The disproportionate identification of minority students as disabled becomes the means of transposing disability discrimination in place of racist discrimination. Understanding this makes it easier for us to rec-ognise the explicit connection between the development of special education and white America's interest in recouping its losses from the *Brown* decision.

IDEA's attempts to address the disproportionate representation of minority students in special education today presents us with a glimpse of how policy itself serves to maintain inequities within the education system, even when those inequities are seen as unacceptable, inaccessible and illegal. Mechanisms such as transposition enable alternate routes of access. Understandings of race and dis-ability as being wholly detached from one another enable a sleight of hand within the policy that serves the dominant interest of maintaining the inequality.

In the macro policy context in which IDEA was created, discrimination against disabled people is scrutinised far less, and is therefore much more accessible than discrimination based on race. In transposing ablist mechanisms to achieve rac-ist outcomes, IDEA has created a powerful institutionalised inequity. Society's acceptance of disability discrimination enables the acceptance of the otherwise unacceptable racial discrimination. Camouflaged in the language of good inten-tions, IDEA is protected against charges of either racism or ablism.

Transposition is a context-specific mechanism that can occur in multiple ways at many levels of policy execution and interpretation. In other research (Beratan

2005), looking at the micro (school) level, we see that in a situation where ablist mechanisms had been made inaccessible to teachers, racism, sexism, and class-based discrimination (all of which received less scrutiny and were therefore more acceptable in the particular context) were utilised to achieve the same ends. In merging the outcomes of both institutional ablism and racism, IDEA has created a powerful institutionalised inequity.

Society's acceptance of disability discrimination enables the acceptance of the otherwise unacceptable racial discrimination. Camouflaged in the language of good intentions, IDEA is protected against charges of either racism or ablism. It is necessary for researchers in disability studies and Critical Race Theory to cross borders and engage with this interaction in order to address the inequities. As long as there is insularity between the fields, neither will be adequate to the task.

Acknowledgements

I would like to thank Claudine Rausch and Nicola Rollock for feedback that helped clarify my thinking about transposition.

Notes

1 *Brown v. the Board of Education* is the landmark civil rights case widely credited as ending formally segregated education in the United States. A detailed history of the case can be found in Kluger (1975).
2 This is IDEA's terminology rather than my own. It is used consistently throughout the law. The law refers to minority groups, minority children, children with disabilities from minority backgrounds, and racial and ethnic groups. All of these terms appear to be used interchangeably within the law. There is little recognition that disproportionate representation affects some minority groups and not others, although African Americans are mentioned as one group significantly impacted by disproportionality. There is no mention of the historical context of racism in public education that has contributed to this. It is not even asserted that disproportionality is not a natural result of individual deficiency. The law merely asserts that disproportionality is something that needs to be queried to determine causality.
3 P.L. 108–446 (2004) The Individuals with Disabilities Education Improvement Act, p. 5.
4 Different writers have used these terms in a variety of ways. At times, they have been used interchangeably; at other times, they have been argued as distinct from one another. While throughout this paper I focus on inclusive education, and use it as distinct from mainstreaming and integration, in this sentence I am highlighting the blurring of the terms within the overarching debate.
5 I have closely adapted this definition, from the definition of institutional racism offered by the Macpherson report on the inquiry into the death of Stephen Lawrence.
6 The Stephen Lawrence Inquiry was the official investigation into the mishandling of the investigation into the murder of Stephen Lawrence, a young black man who was murdered by seven white youths while waiting for a bus in London. The Inquiry's report represented the first time that the existence of institutional racism was recognised by the UK government. For more information, see Macpherson, 1999.

7 It should be noted that the Stephen Lawrence Inquiry's definition of institutional racism has been criticised by some as too narrow a definition. John Solomos (1999, 3) has argued that 'the report is in many ways not concerned with defining the meaning of institutionalised racism in any depth' and that the definition offered the commission a means of condemning the actions of the murderers while at the same time absolving them of the crime of intent.

8 President Bill Clinton, 4 June 1997, on the re-authorisation of IDEA.

9 Other requirements have been added in the subsequent re-authorisations (including two significant additions in the 2004 act that focus on attorney fees and the reduction of paperwork).

10 P.L. 94–142 (1975). The Education for all Handicapped Children Act.

11 P.L. 105–17 (1997). The Individuals with Disabilities Education Act, p. 30.

12 P.L. 108–446, pp. 6–7.

13 The distinction between disability and impairment has emerged largely out of the disability rights movement and the field of disability studies (for more, see Barnes 1996; Finkelstein 2004; Oliver 1990; UPIAS 1976).

14 The social model of disability emerged largely as a criticism of the medical model. Proponents of the social model of disability argue that disability is a socially constructed oppression (rather than an individually located problem) in which various impairments are used by society as the basis for group marginalisation (Barnes 1996; Finkelstein 2004; Oliver 1990; UPIAS 1976).

15 *No Child Left Behind* is the law passed by the Bush administration in 2001. It is based on the belief that a standardised testing regime will hold schools accountable and thus lead to an improved education system. It was been widely criticised, not only for its rationale (Hursh 2005; Darling-Hammond 2004), but also for discriminating against many groups of students (Fusarelli 2004; Giroux and Schmidt 2004).

16 White's opinion was joined by joined by Justices Brennan and Marshall. The . . . within the quote represents citations from the congressional record, which White uses far more extensively than Rehnquist in making the case for legislative intent.

17 P.L. 108–446, p. 94.

18 It should be noted that several legal and critical race scholars (Delgado 2003; Delgado and Stefancic 2005) have also begun to take note of an eroding of this strict scrutiny standard as it applies to race; but the doctrine of the court does still say that a strict scrutiny can be applied in relation to race, which does make disability as determined by Cleburne much more accessible.

References

Abberly, P. 1996. Work, utopia and impairment. In *Disability and society: Emerging issues and insights*, ed. L. Barton, 61–82. London: Longman.

Ainscow, M., ed. 1989. *Special education in change.* London: David Fulton.

Allan, J. 1999a. *Actively seeking inclusion: Pupils with special needs in mainstream schools.* Philadelphia: Falmer Press.

Altman, B. 2001. Disability definitions, models classification schemes, and applications. In *The handbook of disability studies*, ed. Gary Albrecht, Katherine Seelman and Michael Bury, 97–122. London: Sage Publications.

Apple, M. 1999. *Power, meaning, and identity* (vol. 109). New York: Peter Lang.

Armstrong, F. 1998. Curricula, 'management' and special and inclusive education. In *Managing inclusive education – from policy to experience*, ed. P. Clough, 48–63. London: Paul Chapman Publishing.

——. 2003. *Spaced out: Policy difference and the challenge of inclusive education.* Dordrecht, The Netherlands: Kluwer.

347

Artiles, A.J., B. Harry, D.J. Reschly, and P.C. Chinn. 2002. Over-identification of students of color in special education: A critical overview. *Multicultural Perspectives* 4, no. 1: 3–10.

Barnes, C. 1996. Theories of disability and the origins of the oppression of disabled people in western society. In *Disability and society: Emerging issues and insights*, ed. L. Barton, 43–60. London: Longman.

Barton, L. 1986. The politics of special educational needs. *Disability, Handicap and Society* 1, no. 3: 273–290.

———. 1988. The politics of special educational needs. In *The politics of special educational needs*, ed. L. Barton. Philadelphia: Falmer.

———. 1999. *Difference and difficulty: insights, issues and dilemmas*. Sheffield: University of Sheffield.

———. 2003. *Inclusive education and teacher education: A basis for hope or a discourse for delusion?* London: Institute of Education.

Barton, L., and R. Slee. 1999. Competition, selection and inclusive education: Some observations. *International Journal of Inclusive Education* 3, no. 1: 3–12.

Bell, D. 1980. Brown v. Board of Education and the interest convergence dilemma. *Harvard Law Review* 93: 518–33.

———. 1987. *And we are not saved: The elusive quest for racial justice*. Philadelphia: Basic Books.

———. 1992. *Faces at the bottom of the well: The permanence of racism*. New York: Basic Books.

———. 2004. *Silent covenants: Brown v. the Board of Education and the unfulfilled hopes for racial reform*. New York: Oxford University Press.

———. 2005. Brown v. the Board of Education and the interest convergence dilemma. In *The Derrick Bell reader*, ed. R. Delgado and J. Stefancic, 33–39. New York: New York University Press.

Benjamin, S. 2002. *The micropolitics of inclusive education*. Philadelphia: Open University Press.

Beratan, G. 2005. Who they think you are: Pedagogy and the transposition of disabled identities. Paper presented to the American Educational Research Association annual conference, April 11–15, in Montreal, Canada.

Beratan, G.D. 2006. Institutionalizing inequity: Ablism, racism, and IDEA 2004. Paper presented to the American Educational Research Association annual conference, April 7–11, in San Francisco.

Biklen, D. 1992. *Schooling without labels*. Philadelphia: Temple University Press.

Blanck, P., E. Hill, C. Siegal, and M. Waterstone. 2004. *Disability civil rights law and policy*. St. Paul: West.

Bonilla-Silva, E. 2003. *Racism without racists: Color-blind racism and the persistence of inequality in the United States*. Boulder, CO: Rowman and Littlefield.

Booth, T. 2003. Views from the institution: Overcoming barriers to inclusive education. In *Developing inclusive teacher education*, ed. Kari Nes Marit Stromstad and Tony Booth, 33–58. London: RoutledgeFalmer.

Bowe, R., S.J. Ball, and A. Gold. 1992. *Reforming education and changing schools: Case studies in policy sociology*. London: Routledge.

Brown, M.K., M. Carnoy, E. Currie, T. Duster, D.B. Oppenheimer, M.M. Shultz, and D. Wellman. 2003. *Whitewashing race: The myth of a color-blind society*. Berkley, CA: University of California Press.

Cixous, H. 1986. Sorties. In *The newly born woman*, ed. H.C.C. Clement, 66–79. Minneapolis: University of Minnesota Press.

Clotfelter, C.T. 2004. *After Brown; The rise and retreat of school desegregation*. Princeton, NJ: Princeton University Pres.

Clough, P. 1988. Bridging the gap between 'mainstream' and 'special': A curriculum problem. *Journal of Curriculum Studies* 20, no. 4: 327–338.

———., ed. 1998. *Managing inclusive education: From policy to experience*. London, Paul Chapman Educational Publishing.

Colker, R., and B.P. Tucker. 2000. *The law of disability discrimination*. Cincinnati, OH: Anderson Publishing.

Corbett, J. 1999. Inclusive education and school culture. *International Journal of Inclusive Education* 3, no. 1: 53–61.

Corker, M. 1999. New disability discourse: The principle of optimization and social change. In *Disability discourse*, ed. M. Corker and S. French, 192–209. Philadelphia: Open University Press.

Crenshaw, K.W. 1995. Race, reform, and retrenchment: Transformation and legitimation in antidiscrimination law. In *Critical race theory: The key writings that formed the movement*, ed. N. Gotada, K. Crenshaw, G. Peller, and K. Thomas, 103–122. New York: The New Press.

———. 2003. Demarginalizing the intersection of race and sex: A black feminist critique of antidiscrimination doctrine, feminist theory and antiracist politics. In *Critical race feminism: A reader*, ed. A.K. Wing, 23–33. New York: New York University Press.

Crockett, J.B., and J.M. Kaufman. 1999. *The least restrictive environment: Its origins and interpretations in special education*. London: Lawrence Erlbaum & Associates.

Darling-Hammond, L. 2004. Standards, accountability, and school reform. *Teachers College Record* 106, no. 6: 1047–85.

Daugherty, R.E. 2001. *Special education law: A summary of the legal requirements, terms and trends*. London: Bergin & Garvey.

Delgado, R. 2003. *Justice at war: Civil liberties and civil rights during times of crisis*. New York: New York University Press.

Delgado, R., and J. Stefancic, eds. 2005. *The Derrick Bell reader*. New York: New York University Press.

Derrida, J. 1982. *Margins of philosophy*. Trans. A. Bass. Chicago: University of Chicago Press.

———. 1989. Jacques Derrida in discussion with Christopher Norris. In Deconstruction 11, ed. A.C. Papadakis,. London: Academy Editions.

Ferri, B.A., and D.J. Connor. 2006. Reading resistance: Discourses of exclusion in desegregation and inclusion debates. New York: Peter Lang.

Finkelstein, V. 1980. *Attitudes and disabled people: Issues for discussion*. New York: World Rehabilitation Fund.

———. 2004. Representing disability, In *Disabling barriers, enabling environments* (2nd ed.), ed. S. French, J. Swain, C. Barnes, and C. Thomas, 13–20. London: Sage Publications.

Friedman, L. 2004. *Argument: The oral argument before the supreme court in Brown v. Board of Education of Topeka*. New York: Chelsea House.

Fulcher, G. 1999. *Disabling policies? A comparative approach to education policy and disability*. Sheffield: Phillip Armstrong Publications.

Fusarelli, L.D. 2004. The potential impact of the No Child Left Behind Act on equity and diversity in American education. *Education Policy* 18, no. 1: 71–94.

Gilhool, T.K. 1997. The events, forces and issues that triggered the Education for All Handicapped Children Act, 1975. In *Inclusion and school reform: Transforming America's classrooms*, ed. D.K. Lipsky and A. Gartner, 263–273. Baltimore, MD: Paul H. Brookes.

Gillborn, D. 1990. *Race, ethnicity and education: Teaching and learning in multi-ethnic schools*. London: Unwin Hyman.

——. 2008. *Racism and education: Coincidence or conspiracy?* New York: Routledge.

Gillborn, D., and D. Youdell. 2000. *Rationing education: Policy, practice, reform and equity*. Philadelphia: Open University Press.

Giroux, H.A., and M. Schmidt. 2004. Closing the achievement gap: A metaphor for children left behind. *Journal of Educational Change* 5, no. 3: 213–28.

Greene, J.P., and G. Forster. 2002. Effects of funding incentives on special education enrollment. *Civic Report* 32 (December), 1–13.

Henderson, R.A. 1993. What is the least restrictive environment in the United States? In *Is there a desk with my name on it?*, ed. R. Slee, 93–105. London: Falmer Press.

hooks, b. 2000. *where we stand: class matters*. London: Routledge.

Hursh, D. 2005. The growth of high-stakes testing in the USA: Accountability, markets and the decline in educational equality. *British Educational Research Journal* 31, no. 5: 605–622.

Johnson, H.B., and T.M. Shapiro. 2003. Good neighborhoods, good schools: Race and the 'good choices' of white families. In *White out: The continuing significance of race*, ed. A.W. Doane and E. Bonilla-Silva, 173–188. New York: Routledge.

Kluger, R. 1975. *Simple justice: The history of Brown v. Board of Education and black America's struggle for equality*. New York: Alfred A. Knopf.

Ladson-Billings, G. 1998. Just what is critical race theory and what's it doing in a nice field like education? *International Journal of Qualitative Studies in Education* 11, no. 1: 7–24.

Ladson-Billings, G., and W.F. Tate. 1995. Toward a Critical Race Theory of education. *Teachers College Record* 97, no. 1: 47–68.

Lipton, D. 1997. The full inclusion court cases: 1989–1994. In *Inclusion and school reform: Transforming Americas' classrooms*, ed. D.K. Lipsky and A. Gartner, 299–314. Baltimore: Paul H. Brookes.

Losen, D., and G. Orfield. 2002. Introduction. In *Racial inequity in special education*, eds D.J. Losen and G. Orfield, xv–xxxvii. Cambridge: Harvard Education Press.

Macpherson, W. 1999. *The Stephen Lawrence inquiry*. CM 4262–1. London: HMSO.

Marsh, A. 1998. Resourcing inclusive education: The real economics. In *Managing inclusive education: From policy to experience*, ed. P. Clough, 64–77. London: Paul Chapman Publishing.

Minow, M. 1990. *Making all the difference: Inclusion, exclusion and American law*. Ithaca: Cornell University Press.

Morris, J. 1989. *Able lives: Women's experience of paralysis*. London: The Women's Press.

——. 1991. *Pride against prejudice*. London: The Women's Press.

Nes, K., and M. Strømstad. 2003. Creating structures for inclusive development in teacher education. In *Developing inclusive teacher education*, ed. K. Nes, M. Stromstad and T. Booth, 116–129. London: RoutledgeFalmer.

Oliver, M. 1981. Disability, adjustment and family life. In *Handicap in a social world*, eds A. Brechin, P. Liddiard, and J. Swain. London: Hodder and Stoughton.

——. 1983. *Social work and disabled people*. London: Macmillan.

——. 1990. *The politics of disablement*. London: Macmillan.

———. 2004. If I had a hammer: The social model in action. In *Disabling barriers, enabling environments* (2nd ed.), ed. S. French, J. Swain, C. Barnes, and C. Thomas, 7–12. London: Sage Publications.

Orfield, G., and S.E. Eaton. 1996. *Dismantling desegregation: The quiet reversal of Brown v. Board of Education.* New York: New Press.

Parker, L., and D.O. Stovall. 2004. Actions following words: Critical race theory connects to critical pedagogy. *Educational Philosophy and Theory* 36, no. 2: 167–182.

Peters, S. 2002. Inclusive education in accelerated and professional development schools: A case-based study of school reform efforts in the USA. *International Journal of Inclusive Education* 6, no. 4: 287–308.

Reid, D.K., and M.G. Knight. 2006. History in the present: Disability as justification for educational exclusion of minority students. *Educational Researcher* 35, no. 6: 18–23.

Reiser, R., and M. Mason. 1995. *Disability equality in the classroom: A human rights issue.* London: Disability Equality In Education.

Rothstein, L. 2000. *Special education law*, 3rd ed. New York: Longman.

Selden, S. 1999. *Inheriting shame: The story of eugenics in America.* New York: Teachers College Press.

Slee, R., ed. 1993. Inclusive learning initiatives: Educational policy lessons from the field. In *Is there a desk with my name on it?: The politics of integration*, ed. R. Slee, 185–200. London: Falmer Press.

———. 1996. Inclusive education in Australia? Not yet? *Cambridge Journal of Education* 26, no. 1: 19–32.

———. 1999a. Policies and practices? Inclusive education and its effect on schooling. In *Inclusive education*, ed. H. Daniels and P. Gamer, 194–206. London: Kogan Page.

———. 1999b. Special education and human rights in Australia. In *Disability, human rights and education: Cross-cultural perspectives*, ed. F. Armstrong and L. Barton, 119–131. Philadelphia: Open University Press.

Sleeter, C.E. Critical multicultural education and the standards movement. *English Teaching: Practice and Critique* 3, no. 2: 122–138. http://education.waikato.ac.nz/joumal/ english_joumal/ uploads/files/2004v3n2diall.pdf

Solomos, J. 1999. Social research and the Stephen Lawrence inquiry. *Sociological Research Online* 3, no. 1. http://www.socresonline.org.uk/socresonline/4/lawrence/solomos.html.

Swain, J., S. French, and C. Cameron. 2003. *Controversial issues in a disabling society.* Philadelphia: Open University Press.

Thomas, C. 1999. *Female forms: Experiencing and understanding disability.* Philadelphia: Open University Press.

Tomlinson, S. 1982. *A sociology of special education.* London: Routledge and Kegan Paul.

UPIAS. 1976. *Fundamental principles of disability.* London: UPIAS.

Valencia, R.R. 1997. *The evolution of deficit thinking: Educational thought and practice.* London: Falmer Press.

Vlachou, A.D. 1997. *Struggles for inclusive education.* Philadelphia: Open University Press.

Zola, I.K. 1981. *Missing pieces: A chronicle of living with disability.* Philadelphia: Temple University Press.

———. 1982. Social and cultural disincentives to independent living. *Archives of Physical Medicine and Rehabilitation* 63, no. 8: 394–7.

38

SMARTNESS AS PROPERTY

A critical exploration of intersections between Whiteness and Disability Studies

Zeus Leonardo and Alicia A. Broderick

Source: *Teachers College Record*, 113, 10, 2011, 2206–2232.

Background/Context: Two scholars who each primarily identify as a scholar of Critical Race/Whiteness Studies and a scholar of Disability Studies, respectively, engage in this article in a purposeful dialogue that responds to the invitation put forth by Baglieri, Bejoian, Broderick, Connor, and Valle to engage with the construct of inclusive education, writ large. Through purposeful engagement with one another's discourse communities, the authors explore both the challenge and the tremendous promise of more theoretically integrated efforts toward abolishing ideological systems of oppression in schooling.

Purpose/Objective/Research Question/Focus of Study: This article explores "smartness" as an ideological system and particularly explores the ways in which it intersects with Whiteness as ideology. Using Cheryl Harris's analysis of Whiteness, the authors argue that smartness works as a form of property, with all the advantages that come with membership in the group.

Research Design: Analytic essay.

Conclusions/Recommendations: Analogous to Roediger's claim about Whiteness, the authors argue that smartness is nothing but false and oppressive, and as such, attempts to theoretically rearticulate or rehabilitate smartness may serve to illuminate, but ultimately fail to dissolve, the normative center of schooling.

Baglieri, Bejoian, Broderick, Connor, and Valle (2011, this issue) have invited us to join them in "unravel[ing] the myth of the normal child" to participate in exploring the ways in which multiple complex ideological systems operate in constituting the "normative center of schools" and to work with them toward "dissolving the normative center" of schooling. Thus, as scholars who each primarily identify as a scholar of Critical Race/Whiteness Studies and a scholar of

Disability Studies, respectively, we have elected to explore theoretical intersections not between particular issues or groups of people (e.g., students of color and disabled students), but rather, between ideologies—specifically, the ways that the construct of "smartness"[1] intersects both race and ability as ideological systems. This collaborative article documents but a small sliver of the generative discussions we have shared on this topic in the past several years. We explore the theoretical dilemmas inherent in "going it alone" in this work from a single critical conceptual standpoint (e.g., Whiteness Studies or Disability Studies) and, through purposeful engagement with the other and with one another's discourse communities, explore both the challenge and the tremendous promise of more theoretically integrated efforts toward abolishing ideological systems of oppression in schooling, and thereby dissolving the normative center of schooling.

In seeking points of intersection between Whiteness Studies and Disability Studies, perhaps the most obvious issue to address is the overrepresentation of students of color in special education (Artiles, 2008; Blanchett, 2006; Harry & Klingner, 2006)—particularly what Fierros and Conroy (2002) have referred to as the "double jeopardy" of students of color not only being overrepresented in special education service provision generally, but also being overrepresented in the most restrictive or segregated of special education placements. We acknowledge the usefulness and necessity of the work that has been done thus far in exploring these particular issues; however, in attempting to engage deeply with the intersectionalities of the constructs of race and ability, we hope also to avoid the theoretical pitfalls that are often evident when one approach or the other (foregrounding of race or foregrounding of ability) dominates. For example, the very construct of "overrepresentation" of students of color has been acknowledged and explored in the literature for over four decades (see Dunn, 1968, for an early, explicit engagement with this issue), within both educational discourse communities concerned with issues of disability, and those concerned with issues of race. We wish to shift our gaze in this piece away from that which is clearly illuminated through this discursive representation, and toward that which is obscured by it. Rhetorically, to conceptualize the "problem" as the statistical overrepresentation of a particular group of students within the bureaucratic systems of special education leaves unquestioned the legitimacy of that system or the problematic ways in which it operates beyond the question of overrepresentation. Indeed, the very conceptualization of the "problem" of "*over*representation" may rhetorically suggest that if the number of students of color in special education were "representative" of the percentage of students of color in the educational system as a whole, then a significant part of the "problem" would therefore have been addressed. By conceptualizing the problem as one of overrepresentation, there is risk of tacit reification and legitimation of the naturalness and neutrality of the bureaucratic system of special education as a whole and, by extension, of the deficit-driven and psychological understandings of "ability" and "disability" within which it is grounded. Of course, few, if any, of these scholars would argue that equal racial representation in special education amounts to equitable distribution of power. Many other conditions would need to be met. But our concern here takes a different tack at the issue of representation as we peer into the politics of signification within schooling in response to Baglieri et al.'s (2011, this issue) invitation to work to unravel the myth of the normal child.

In short, we examine the meanings underlying the constitution of a central facet of the valued, normative center of schools, particularly the construct of "smartness" that many otherwise insurgent scholars fail to interrogate. Here we theorize the problem of representation from another angle, arguing that the *politics of representation* within both Whiteness and Disability Studies function as discourses that regulate the fields under study. In other words, like race, ability is a relational system. In terms of race, the category, White, cannot exist without its denigrated other, such as Black or people of color generally; in terms of ability, constructs such as smartness only function by disparaging in both discursive and material ways their complement, those deemed to be uneducable and disposable. In both cases, the privileged group is provided with honor, investment, and capital, whereas the marginalized segment is dishonored and dispossessed. And each of these ideological systems (of Whiteness and of smartness) tends to operate in symbiotic service of the other in their mutual (though not exclusive) constitution of "the normative center of schools" (Baglieri et al.).

The ideology of whiteness

Theories about Whiteness are making an impact on education and allied disciplines. Strictly speaking, Whiteness Studies belongs within a larger engagement of race relations. More traditional race studies focused on the experiences of people of color with structures of racism and could be regarded as interventions of color within Whiteness or, more accurately, White racism. In contrast, as a form of neo–race theory (Leonardo, 2002), Whiteness Studies is an intervention within race, unmasking the nature of racial privilege. Whereas the former was, by and large, a knowledge production of color, the latter is generally a White-led innovation. In schooling, Whiteness Studies is conceived as a "pedagogy of the oppressor" (Allen, 2005), demystifying what passes as educationally natural, normal, and valorized. In effect, Whiteness Studies is an intervention in race theory; it focuses on the strongest form of investment in race relations (Lipsitz, 1998), namely the protection and perpetuation not only of White myths but also perhaps of raciology itself (Gilroy, 2000). To be clear, minorities also invest in race—a certain possessive investment in color—but this is mainly a defensive posture, a reaction to the power of Whiteness. When people of color assert their histories of resistance, pride in their culture, and purpose in life as bound up with a search for freedom, they do so within a logic premised on the first fact of Whiteness. Otherwise, such claims to minority power in its own right would be unnecessary. Without injecting more power into Whiteness, one is compelled to avoid giving it less.

Given this state of affair, it behooves educators to pin down what they mean by "Whiteness," lest it become a floating signifier with neither utility nor precision.

As we invoke it, Whiteness is defined as an ideology untied to certain bodies, but an articulation of disparate elements—some racial, some not—in order to build a racial cosmology that benefits Whites in absolute ways and minority groups relative only to one another. Whites recruit class, gender, and sexual interests into the general phenomenon of race contestation and specifically into the logic of Whiteness. For instance, White women, working-class Whites, gay and lesbian Whites, and disabled Whites—groups that suffer in their own right despite their Whiteness—are consoled by the power and promise of Whiteness, what Du Bois (1935/1998) earlier called Whites' psychological and public wages (see also Roediger, 1991). As such, there is no essence to Whiteness, which is a contingent category that morphs and shifts according to context and history (Prashad, 2000). It has no ultimate loyalty to this or that group belonging to Whiteness proper. Its membership changes over time and may include as brethren two groups with longstanding ethnic animosities toward one another, such as the English and Irish within a U.S. understanding. Like capitalism, Whiteness has no ultimate sense of loyalty and cares primarily about perpetuating race relations with Whiteness at the top of the hierarchy. Whiteness may revoke a group's membership when it is deemed necessary, such as the increasingly anxious relation that Arabs have with Whiteness post-9/11.[2] It may, as was the case in South Africa, promote a group as "honorary White" as a way of disciplining other non-Whites to stay in line, and quell large-scale confrontations. In the case of U.S. race relations, Bonilla-Silva (2004) suggested that the nation approaches a tripartite racial hierarchy that mimics the racial structure in Latin America, with a "buffer" group that stands between the collective White and Black. Whiteness's only stable investment is ideological power and material advantage, synonymous with the continuation of Whiteness as long as it remains a social fact.

As Cheryl Harris's (1995) seminal essay on critical race theory argued, Whiteness functions as a form analogous to property. First, Whiteness becomes property through the objectification of African slaves, a process that set the precondition for "propertizing" human life (Harris, p. 279). Whiteness takes the form of ownership, the defining attribute of free individuals that Africans did not own. Second, through the reification and subsequent hegemony of White people, Whiteness is transformed into the common sense that becomes law. As a given right of the individual White person, Whiteness can be enjoyed, like any property, by exercising and taking advantage of privileges coextensive with Whiteness. Third, like a house, Whiteness can be demarcated and fenced off as a territory of White people that keeps Others out. Thus, calling a White person "Black" was enough reason, as late as 1957, to sue for character defamation; the same could not be said of a Black person being mistaken for "White." This was a certain violation of property rights, much like breaking into someone's house. In all, Whites became the subjects of property, with Others as its objects.

If our definition of Whiteness as ideology smacks of a certain orthodoxy that flies in the face of recent rehabilitations of the concept of ideology, it is worthwhile to recount ideology's pejorative history. Since Marx's operationalization of ideology as a form of distortion and dissimulation of economic relations, the concept has gone through permutations in efforts to avoid the pitfalls of a mystifying move that claims its opposite: science (see Leonardo, 2003a). Assumed to transcend partiality, a scientific analysis is able to shed contextual embeddedness to arrive at universal laws of social life and history (Althusser, 1971). Much like Thales's discovery of mathematics and Galileo's of physics, Marx is said to have uncovered the general laws of history through historical materialism. Scientific knowledge was purported as a possibility while also avoiding being ensnared by ideology's distortive effects. In a more general sense, ideology was not a property of unscientific individuals, but of an entire social formation, such as capitalism (Eagleton, 1991). Since then, ideology has been rescued from its status as a derogated concept and is now often regarded as a generally descriptive term that serves an integrative function (Ricoeur, 1986), a culturally based necessity (Geertz, 1994), and even a source of inspiration for mass mobilization (Gouldner, 1976). In the first moment, Ricoeur suggested that ideology offers society a blueprint, a plan without which a people would be without direction; in the second, Geertz offered anthropological support for ideology as a cultural system of tropes necessary for communication (see also Giroux, 1981; Hall, 1996); in the third, Gouldner recast ideology as having the capacity to galvanize people into action, such as the crusades. We note that Gouldner's engagement represents the complete opposite of ideology's pejorative history. From this short account of the concept of ideology, we avoid its reductive definition as something hopelessly caught up in distortion. So why return to theoretical orthodoxy with respect to Whiteness?

Whiteness as a social grouping

As a social grouping, Whiteness does not have essential features. Its hue spans across the palest Scandinavian to brown Semites. Its members have hailed from Europe and parts of Asia, Africa, and Latin America. Its status as a social marker is guided by the common sense of its times, as uncovered by the case of Thind, an Asian Indian man who argued that he was White by the geographical standards of Whiteness as originating from the Caucasus mountains (Lopez, 2006; Omi & Winant, 1994; Wu, 2002). In 1923, the U.S. sued Thind in order to revoke his citizenship. In this case, the court argued that although Thind was indeed Caucasian, he was a *non-White* Caucasian by the standards of common sense. Thus, the court ruled against the "scientific" evidence of the time, which followed Blumenbach's racial anthropology that classified people as either Negroid, Caucazoid, or Mongoloid according to their physical traits. The court justified its decision based on the assumption that any reasonable American would deem Thind non-White by virtue of his appearance. Thind's case followed an earlier case filed by Osaka, a man of Japanese descent who, just months before Thind, sued for citizenship on the basis of being more culturally White than many recent White immigrants. He was judged to be non-White by way of geographical considerations; that is, Japan is not a land of White people. So, whereas Osaka lost because of geography, Thind's geopolitics were correct, but his phenotype was not. In Osaka's case, "science" won out over common sense. From this contradictory history, the capriciousness of Whiteness is clear. It is flexible and appropriates commonsensical and scientific arguments to serve its purpose. Many decades later, it is more than a bit of irony that Asian Americans today are being labeled "probationary Whites," "honorary Whites," or "almost White." It is an even crueler irony that the same Justice wrote the opinion for both Thind and Osaka, separated by a mere few months. In the case of Mexican Americans, the courts ruled that Mexicans were White in order to observe treaty rights with Mexico (Martinez, 1997). But when, in 1954, the same year as *Brown v. Board of Education of Topeka*, Hernandez tried to reverse his murder conviction because there were no Mexicans on the predominantly White jury that convicted him in *Hernandez v. State*, the court asserted his Whiteness and that he was fairly judged by his peers: "Through this discourse on the Mexican-American, Anglo Americans also reformulated their white selves. Anglo judges, as we have seen, did the same thing, ruling that Mexicans were co-whites when this suited the dominant group—and nonwhite when necessary to protect Anglo privilege and supremacy" (p. 212).

This egregious arbitrariness speaks to the moving target known as White ideology. It reserves the right to exclude any person or group for the purposes of racial domination. "White" is whatever Whites make it to be, using whatever ideological reasoning happens to be available at the time. It confirms Roediger's (1991, 1994) charge that Whiteness, as an ideology, has a violent history.[3]

Whiteness as a tool for stratification

As a normative marker, Whiteness exists for the sole purpose of stratification. It led David Roediger (1994) to announce that "whiteness is *nothing but* false and oppressive" (p. 13; italics in original). As fruitful as Descartes's statement, "I think therefore I am," Roediger's "whiteness is not only false and oppressive, it is *nothing but* false and oppressive" has been the subject of generative interpretations. From our perspective, it marks a correct beginning for a critical, if not accurate, understanding of Whiteness. First, Roediger did not write that "Whites are nothing but false and oppressive." We are warranted immediately to infer that he is speaking of Whiteness at the plane of ideology. That is, he recognized the distinction that Whites—as people—have performed acts against Whiteness; they are what Ignatiev and Garvey (1996) called "race traitors." Treason to Whiteness is not only loyalty to humanity, as Ignatiev and Garvey reminded us, but equally, solidarity with color. That is, White race traitors arguably function through an ideology of color to the extent that they act against the distortions of Whiteness. They are bodies that look White but act like people of color. Whites may benefit from Whiteness even as they act against it, which speaks to the power of racial ideology. Second, this distinction disrupts the commonsense notion of Whiteness as equatable with White identity; rather, it is an interpellating system that encourages subjects (most of whom are considered Whites, but not all) to act on behalf of Whiteness. There were no White people to speak of, before the arrival of an interpellation called Whiteness. If Roediger, Ignatiev, and Garvey are correct (and we believe that they are), then White people do not constitute an ontologically real category, but only become social facts with the birth of the ideology known as Whiteness. It took the ideology of Whiteness to turn "white" bodies into White people. Of course, by ideology, we do not suggest Whiteness as purely ideational, but side with Althusser's (1971) insight that ideology's modes of existence are real (see also Leonardo, 2005). Whites are only real insofar as social institutions like education, and formidable processes like common sense, recognize certain bodies as White.

Third, that Whiteness is nothing but false and oppressive means that it exists only as a tool for oppression. When Whites act against racism, they do not reconstruct Whiteness through their action. Whiteness does not reappear as virtuous because Whites behave differently. When this happens, as an ideology, Whiteness is not resignified into something, but nothing; it ceases to exist. Just as it is difficult to reimagine fascism, the history of Whiteness betrays it as violent and bogus. The more frequently Whites act against racism, the more they increase the chances that Whiteness may disappear. When Whites fight against racism, they are not just dismantling racist relations; they are arguably abolishing Whiteness, whose existence depends on maintaining racial stratification. That is, the end of racism foreshadows the end of Whiteness as we know it. It undercuts the lifeline of the otherwise abstract category of Whiteness, which was created for the sole purpose of denigrating and dispossessing people of color. It was an invention that turned white bodies into White people roughly 500 years ago. What are Whites but people who think they are Whites (and therefore better), as Baldwin once provoked (as cited in Roediger, 1994)? Synthesizing Descartes, Roediger, and Baldwin, we may say that for certain subjects, it is accurate to recast the *cogito* as, "I think I am White therefore I am." Although we do not have to rehearse the limitations of Cartesian dualism between the mind and body here, a case can be made that Whites exist because they, along with people of color, believe certain bodies are White; furthermore, the reification of Whiteness into a social fact positions Whites as superior. As Baldwin further noted, as long as Whites think they are White, there is no hope for them. We would like to extend this insight by including the idea that as long as people of color also think that Whites are White, there is no hope for any of us. Having established this perception, it follows that socioeducational arrangements ensue, from the naturalness of Eurocentric curricula (despite challenges from multiculturalism), to the assumption of White smartness, and finally, to the purging of most race-conscious analysis of the educational system from official knowledge (Apple's phrase, 1979/2000). That we think some people are White often goes without saying, and saying that this or that literary character is "White" actually becomes a form of transgression, whereas people of color become known precisely because books signify them as such (Morrison, 1993). Moreover, what does it mean to be White *sans* the racial privilege? Just as capitalists who fail to exploit workers are no longer the bourgeoisie, Whiteness that functions contrary to its modus operandi withers away. The circle between ideology and material practice has been broken.

To the extent that racial supremacy is taught to White students and to students of color, it is pedagogical. Insofar as it is pedagogical, there is the possibility of critically reflecting on its manifestations in order to disrupt them. The hidden curriculum of Whiteness saturates everyday school life, and one of the first steps to articulating its features is coming to terms with its specific modes of discourse (Leonardo, 2004). There is thus a good deal of compelling scholarship that explores the ways that Whiteness operates as an ideology in curriculum, in educational policy, and in broader social and cultural life (Gillborn, 2005, 2006; Leonardo, 2009). We wish now to explore the ways that a particular facet of dis/ability ideology, "smartness," operates simultaneously to construct a center of normative privilege and domination as well as a periphery of nonnormative marginalization and subjugation within schools and society. Of particular interest to us are the ways that the ideology of smartness operates in the service of the ideology of Whiteness and vice versa. The discourse of minority overrepresentation in special education frames the issue as a racial problem, and we attempt to advance it by interrogating the additional ideological layers of the bureaucratic system in which these racial inequities are embedded—the ideological systems of ability and disability, competence and incompetence, smartness and not-so-smartness. This is where we turn next.

The ideology of smartness

A substantial part of the ideological work of schooling constructs and constitutes some students as "smart," while simultaneously constructing and constituting other students as "not-so-smart"—that is, some students are taught their intellectual supremacy and concomitant entitlement to cultural capital, whereas others are taught their intellectual inferiority and concomitant lack of entitlement to both an identity as a "smart" person, and the cultural and material spoils that such an identity generally affords. Analogous to our earlier claim regarding Whiteness, we likewise argue that to the extent that intellectual supremacy and inferiority are taught, they are pedagogical. Insofar as smartness is pedagogical, there is the possibility of critically reflecting on its manifestations in order to disrupt them. And, as is the case with Whiteness, the hidden curriculum of smartness saturates everyday school life, and one of the first steps to articulating its features is coming to terms with its specific modes of discourse. We next review two bodies of literature that explicitly engage in theoretical critiques of smartness, and explore their theoretical potential as tools for supporting the work of "dissolving the normative center" of schools. Each of the bodies of work—one grounded more firmly in race studies, and the other in Disability Studies—we argue, is theoretically inadequate to the task before us, each offering tools to rehabilitate or rearticulate, rather than dissolve, smartness as an ideological system at the heart of the normative center of schooling.

Ideological critique of smartness (sans critical perspective on disability)

We are all undoubtedly familiar with the myriad ways that schooling practices, from a very early age, construct, and therefore constitute, some people as "smart" while similarly constituting others as "not-so-smart." Teachers routinely characterize some students as "bright," "smart," "a real star," "academically gifted," and so on, and the academic opportunities afforded to students so constituted are rarely commensurate with the opportunities afforded to their peers who are alternately characterized as "dull," "slow," "lazy," or simply not very "bright" or "smart." Hayman (1998) argued that "we make some people smarter than others, by rewarding the smartness of some people and ignoring the smartness of others. We make some people smart, in short, just by choosing to call them that" (p. 26). Drawing an analogy to an earlier point in our analysis—what is smartness absent of privilege? Just as Baldwin once complained, What are Whites but people who think they are Whites? so, too, might we ask, What are smart people but people who think they are smart? We argued earlier that, as a normative marker, Whiteness exists for the sole purpose of stratification, a point that led David Roediger (1994) to announce that Whiteness is nothing but false and oppressive. Indeed, Hayman would seem to be making an analogous point to Roediger's assertion—that smartness is *nothing but* false and oppressive—when he asserted that, "except as a tool for promoting hierarchy, it is hard to see the utility of the concept [of intelligence]" (p. 272). We may thus offer a synthesis of Descartes and Hayman by recasting the *cogito* as, "I think I am smart, therefore I am." But what is smartness in the absence of its stratifying privilege? What are smart people *sans* their advantage? Indeed, like our analysis of Whiteness, when we interrogate smartness—as an ideology and material practice—it withers away as a conceptual category.

Hayman (1998) and others (Gould, 1981/1996; Kincheloe, Steinberg, & Villaverde, 1999) have offered cogent critiques of the general constructs of "intelligence" and "IQ" particularly in the wake of Herrnstein and Murray's (1994) *The Bell Curve*. All these critiques have made explicit the problematic relationships between cultural constructs of intelligence, as a reified form of ability, and cultural constructs of race. Hayman pointed out that "in America . . . the cultural construction of "intelligence" . . . has been inextricably intertwined with the construction of 'race.' 'Intelligence' was defined by one race and defined in racial terms; 'race,' in turn, was defined in substantial part through 'intelligence,' through intellectual inferiority and superiority" (p. 294). Similarly, Kincheloe et al. suggested that

> One of the key ways to rethink intelligence is to expand the boundaries of what can be called sophisticated thinking. When such boundaries are expanded, those who had been excluded from the community of the intelligent seem to cluster around categories based on race (the nonwhite), class (the poor), and gender (the feminine). (p. 7)

It is curious that Kincheloe et al. did not notice what for us seems a another obvious, and significant, group of those who have often been excluded from the "community of the intelligent": the disabled. Hayman made no such omission when he observed that "white men without disabilities, it seems, are almost always in charge of everything. They must be really smart. Smarter, on average, than black folks or other racial minorities. Smarter, on average, than women. Smarter, on average, than people with disabilities" (p. 220). Disputing and rejecting the mythology of intelligence requires, according to Hayman, "a determination to dispute the peculiar *ideology* of intelligence" (p. 262).

Although a comprehensive review of this literature is beyond the scope of this article, there is nevertheless a compelling body of extant literature that critically explores smartness as ideology, and indeed that critically implicates Whiteness as ideology in the mutual constitution of those subject positions. Nevertheless, despite Hayman's (1999) observation that people with disabilities are less likely than nondisabled people to be characterized as "smart" (a clear indication of how smartness operates ideologically), he nevertheless excepted a particular group of disabled people from his analysis when he asserted that

> some people are less "smart" than others for identifiable physiological reasons. Neurological disorders often have direct effects on cognitive ability; sometimes these disorders may so affect a cognitive ability that we will say that the person is cognitively impaired. If the impairment is spread among a wide enough range of cognitive abilities, it may be possible to say that—in most cultural contexts—the person will be less smart than the norm. Here, however, a certain note of caution is in order: in some discrete contexts, our cognitively impaired person may be quite smart after all—smart, that is, at some things, if not at most. (p. 21)

Although Hayman (1999) put forth the proposition that intelligence and smartness operate as ideologies, he simultaneously used constructs such as "cognitive ability," "cognitive impairment," and even "cognitively impaired person," suggesting that there may be a certain point at which "smartness" may be more reflective of a realist ontology than an act of ideology (despite his urging of "caution" in such cases). Most critical thinkers who have critiqued ideologies of intelligence or smartness—indicting the ways that they intersect with ideologies of Whiteness and urging their expansion to become more inclusive and democratic—have failed to engage at all as it concerns the experiences of people who have been judged to have significant intellectual disabilities, and they seem to leave open the possibility that there are exceptions to their treatment of smartness as ideological. Thus, we may applaud Hayman for acknowledging the theoretical conundrum posed by the notion of intellectual disability (the corollary construct of intellectual ability, or smartness), even if we remain disappointed at his retreat from the realm of ideological critique in this instance, citing this exception to his analysis: that rare instance in which some people are *really* "less smart." Thus, the ultimate suggestion of Hayman, Kincheloe et al. (1999), and others seems to be to rehabilitate theoretically the concept of intelligence, to democratize it to be somewhat inclusive of other kinds of abilities (yet still exclusive of those judged to be *really* [biologically, neurologically] not smart). They did not appear to consider our proposed corollary to Roediger's assertion about Whiteness: that *smartness* is nothing but false and oppressive, a move that aligns them with the argument that rearticulates Whiteness in an apparently analogous attempt to rearticulate smartness or intelligence.

Social constructionist critique of smartness
(sans critical perspective on race)

There is another body of literature—located within the tradition of critical Disability Studies—that disputes and challenges notions of "intelligence" and "smartness," primarily through direct critical engagement with the corollary construct of "mental retardation" (or "intellectual disability," or "cognitive impairment"). Blatt, as cited in Taylor and Blatt (1999), referred to mental retardation as both a "myth" and a "metaphor," as well as an "unnecessary story" that is "always abusive" (p. 86; cf. Roediger's assertion above). Borthwick and Crossley (1999) asserted that "the time may be approaching when the burden of proof will . . . shift from those who cast doubt on the explanatory power of the concept of intellectual disability to those who wish to justify it" and that "'mental retardation' may be, both in any given case and in its wider conceptualization, inadequate as an explanatory concept, undefinable as a scientific entity, and unhelpful as a clinical diagnosis." Similarly, scholars such as Kasa-Hendrickson and Ashby (2008) have suggested that we "completely discard the idea of mental retardation as it is not a useful way to capture human intelligence" (p. 15).

The bulk of this scholarship is conducted within the theoretical tradition of social constructionism and argues that dominant notions of ability, competence, and intelligence (and their corollaries of inability, incompetence, and mental retardation) are socially constructed and thus are not real (ontologically), objective (epistemologically), or useful (clinically). This scholarship is largely informed by a body of qualitative research that actively solicits and foregrounds the testimony and experiences of individuals who have been regarded, labeled, and therefore materially constituted as "mentally retarded" or "intellectually impaired" (Biklen, 1990; Biklen & Burke, 2006; Biklen & Kliewer, 2006; Bogdan & Taylor, 1989/1992; Broderick & Kasa-Hendrickson, 2001, 2006; Kasa-Hendrickson & Ashby, 2008; Kliewer, 1998).

Despite this originating focus on critical analysis of the organizing construct of mental retardation or intellectual disability, much (though not all) of this work has logically and necessarily evolved into a more general, and much more radical, critique of the corollary construct of intellectual ability, or "smartness"—a critique that is somewhat marginalized even within the discourse community of critical Disability Studies. Indeed, Biklen and Kliewer (2006) noted,

At this point our analysis becomes radical, for it directly questions not simply degrees of intelligence or degrees of literacy, but the very definition of intelligence and mental retardation. Here we enter into an area about which the Disability Studies field has not been very vocal—we suspect that critical academics' relative silence on matters of mental retardation relates to concerns about their own claims to smartness. (p. 177)

Indeed, though we concur that collectively, this body of work is politically quite radical, we argue that the critique it offers is nevertheless theoretically insufficient to our task of dissolving the normative center of schooling.

First, Biklen and Kliewer (2006) offered what they called "a social constructionist way of thinking about competence":

Neither autism nor mental retardation, and not any perceived combination of the two—they are often conflated—is natural or real. They are, rather, socially constructed. This is by way of saying that disability categories are *not* "given" or "real" *on their own.* Rather, autism, mental retardation, and competence are what any of us make of them. (p. 182)

Similarly, Kasa-Hendrickson (2005), in a qualitative study designed to document the ways in which teachers do come to recognize competence in their students officially designated as incompetent, noted, "It was my desire to emphasize the socially constructed nature of reality, keeping in mind that ideas like autism, ability and mental retardation are understood not to exist in an objective state, but are understood only through society's cultural, historical perspectives, and in practices that create and reproduce them" (p. 57). By locating "mental retardation," "competence," or "smartness" primarily as social constructions rather than systems of ideology that operate to constitute and sustain unequal relations of power, there is an as of yet incomplete exploration of the oppressive and mystifying ways in which power and privilege operate. Like Whiteness, these notions exist in their modes of practice, or, as Althusser (1971) may suggest, in their ideological state apparatuses (Leonardo, 2005). Likewise, smartness may be socially constructed, but this fact alone does not explain how the relation exists in real and institutional forms. Abdicating the critique to the weak moment of "social construction" (at once helpful and insufficient) does nothing for the stronger moment of ideology critique. Although these differences are not real on the ontological plane, they are real on the existential plane of lived experiences, and we argue that ideological critique is necessary to begin to dissolve these complex systems of oppression.

Second, although the bulk of this work does explicitly and critically engage with the broader constructs of smartness, ability, and intelligence, there are some data within this body of literature that would appear to reify traditional conceptualizations of intellect, smartness, or competence even as they attempt to disrupt, destabilize, and discard the notion of mental retardation. For example, Broderick and Kasa-Hendrickson (2006) critically reflected on their own normative ideological assumptions in the process of engaging in inquiry with students who had been previously regarded as "retarded" or "incompetent" or "not smart" as these students managed radical shifts in their own and others' perceptions of them in the process of gaining access to complex expression through typing. Among the students' stories related through the data, we heard Lucy Harrison describe her experience:

> I used to be retarded but I am real normal now and I am being treated as a believable talker. I want to explain the retarded girl I was and I was not thinking I want to be real and I want to tell you that I am smart but I was thinking no one would ever know I was smart. (p. 180)

Similarly, Franklin Wilson deftly described the ways in which the ideology of smartness manifested materially in his own experience:

> I was thought to be retarded and I was not and when I was typing the people said I was smart and I am. So each time we do it and was smart it was good and bad. It was bad because I got angry how some assholes thought I was retarded. (p. 181)

The authors did frame Franklin's story as an example of "agency and resistance to the powerful cultural and ideological assumptions that contributed to constructing, and indeed constituting, him as 'retarded' for so many years" (p. 181). Nevertheless, although the authors[4] did point to the ideological and discursive basis of the construct of "retardation," they failed to fully extend that ideological analysis to the construct of competency, intelligence, or "smartness."

Admittedly, people's need to assert their intellectual competence is hardly surprising and is quite understandable in the face of their experience first of having been regarded and oppressively treated as "mentally retarded" for years, sometimes decades, and subsequently of having professionals continue to doubt their competence even after they have finally gained independent access to a sophisticated system of augmentative or alternative communication. In some ways, it is difficult to understand the vehemence and vitriol with which some professionals have continued to deride many of these individuals as "retarded," failing to even grudgingly admit to the ideologically conservative interpretation of these individuals' experiences as "exceptions" to the rule. The fervor is more easily understood when one explicitly recognizes (as many of these professionals apparently seem to) the ideological critique at work. This is no mere "social construction"; each assertion that "I am smart, too" contributes to the dismantling of an ideological state apparatus. Borthwick and Crossley (1999) documented one such example of the vehement professional opposition to recognizing the competence of individuals who have been described and regarded as "mentally retarded": "People are trying to brainwash us into believing, as they seem to, that there is no real difference between the mentally handicapped and the rest of us, but there is. . . . How do we combat these seductive but pernicious ideas?" (Rimland, 1993, p. 3, as cited in Borthwick & Crossley, 1999). Rubin cogently sized up this "pernicious" idea when she stated, simply, "They think we are not as smart as they are" (Rubin et al., 2010, p. 427).

Notwithstanding this good faith effort, it nevertheless can be understood as a case of what Audre Lorde (2007) called dismantling the master's house with the master's tools, of validating as "smart" people who have been derogated by the same concept. This is similar to the limitations of asserting the humanity of people of color within the standards of a White-centered hierarchy that recognizes what it means to be human. The standards are set by the master's terms. In these examples, one is reminded of Harris's (1995) theoretical treatment of Whiteness as property, enjoyed by its subjects who have enough privilege to be granted keys to the house, and it seems that smartness can likewise be regarded as property, asset, and commodity. Similarly, we argue that smartness functions as a form of property that its "owners" exercise to their enjoyment and privilege. The contradiction becomes clear when we understand that smartness and Whiteness are relations with a denigrated portion: the unintelligent and people of color, respectively. This property only has value as a commodity if there are others who continue to be denied access to its possession.

Parents habitually tell their children how smart they are. In a stratified society, who could blame them, particularly those from oppressed communities? It is understandable that people who have been denigrated as retarded would desire to accrue smartness as property, capital that has historically been vehemently denied to them with dire material consequences (including complete exclusion from mainstream schooling experiences). It is equally understandable, for example, that a colleague of ours, who is a parent of a male child of color, would welcome her son's school's initiative to label her son as "gifted and talented," particularly given that his previous school had sought to label him "emotionally disturbed" and to exclude him from mainstream classroom membership. Despite her own misgivings about the antidemocratic nature of the gifted and talented educational program at his school, diverting resources and rich academic opportunities and experiences to a select few that she felt deserved to be distributed among all the children in the school, she nevertheless accepted this piece of smartness as property as some small measure of protection for her son, a talisman against growing up in a racist educational system.

But our concern here includes the costs that marginalized communities bear when appropriating such benign-seeming tropes. As a fact of the matter, just as Whiteness is parasitic on blackness or colorness, smartness requires its dialectical opposite and cannot exist without the cursed population of so-called low intellect. For smart students to buoy themselves above the general population, their dialectical alibi of not-smart people has to be denigrated. Like the derogation of people of color under White supremacy, smart supremacy derides the "intellectually disabled" figure. The discourse of derision is daily for both marginalized groups. In race terms, the preference for lightness within communities of color is a well-documented phenomenon (Hunter, 2002, 2005). The upshot is that people of color distinguish themselves *within* their group according to skin tone to establish distinction while approximating Whiteness. Similarly, disabled people (as well as nondisabled parents, teachers, and members of society in general) often perform hierarchies whereby they denigrate certain exceptionalities as having lower status and in the process valorize others, such as the cultural preference for Asperger syndrome over autism, or "high-functioning" over "low-functioning" autism (generally accepted popular cultural codes for "smart" and "not-so-smart" autistics). Often, these strategies develop as learned defensive responses against the larger and threatening presence of Whites in the case of race, or the normate in the case of ability. That being said, they unwittingly reproduce the system of stratification responsible for their degradation.

A final critique of this body of literature relates to a theoretical conundrum posed by its central, and most politically radical, pedagogical maxim: the presumption of competence (Biklen, 1990, 1999, 2000; Biklen & Burke, 2006; Biklen & Kliewer, 2006; Kasa-Hendrickson, 2005). Simply stated, in presuming competence,

> the observer's obligation is not to project an ableist interpretation on something another person does, but rather to presume there must be a rationale or sympathetic explanation for what someone does and then to try to discover it, always from the other person's own perspective. Thus the presumption of competence does not require the teacher's ability to prove its existence or validity in advance; rather it is a stance, an outlook, a framework for educational engagement.
>
> (Biklen & Burke, p. 168)

This stance is not unlike the stance of culturally relevant pedagogy, in which students' interests, experiences, desires, and cultures are understood to be relevant, rich, and valuable resources, and the onus is placed on the educator to enact curriculum and pedagogy in culturally relevant ways. According to Rubin et al. (2001), "Our view is that competence should always be presumed, with the burden upon teachers and others around the person to find ways of helping the person communicate" (p. 427). If one cannot imagine capacity in a child, one is unlikely to endeavor to educate that child. In this very basic sense, then, a presumption-of-competence stance may be understood as a necessary precondition for educating all children.

Our concern lies with the theoretical difficulty of presuming that everyone is competent. As discussed previously, if competence or smartness is understood as cultural capital, commodity, or property (rather than as some objective cognitive or neurological state), it is theoretically untenable that everyone could attain access to these material spoils of such an ideological system—just as in a capitalist system, everyone cannot, by definition, be wealthy (and if they are, the conditions cease to be capitalist). Competence, or intellect, or smartness are but halves of conceptual binaries—the "haves" require the "have nots," or they become meaningless constructs. What is Whiteness sans privilege? What is smartness sans a denigrated not-so-smart Other? Conceptually, the category withers away.

As progressive and politically radical as the stance of presuming competence is, we nevertheless believe that this stance can be read and enacted in a potentially problematic way. If the presumption-of-competence stance is not coupled with an explicit critical engagement of the ways in which smartness (or competence) is inextricably bound up with other oppressive ideologies (such as Whiteness), it runs the risk of operating at some level as a mystifying mythology. Materially, there is more at work in the constitution of people as incompetent than ableist ideologies; there are also racist, classist, sexist, and so on, ideologies that come into play. Likewise, there is more at work in the constitution of people as competent, or smart, than ableist ideologies, and these must be explicitly interrogated with an eye to their abolition for the presumption-of-competence stance to become an emancipatory narrative for all, and more, to work as an effective tool in the dissolving of the normative center of schools.

For example, it can be observed that when the individuals with significant disabilities in this body of research, who have historically been regarded as mentally retarded, successfully contest their relegation to this category, many, if not most— through no small amounts of political and legal advocacy—do manage to secure for themselves more equitable access to opportunities in both school and the wider society. However, the roles of ideological privilege (such as Whiteness and class privilege) are rarely discussed in documenting such individuals' resistance to the oppressive ideology of smartness, and this undertheorization remains a significant limitation of this body of work. As Freire (1993) may suggest, they become sub-oppressors in an oppressive system, and rather than challenge it, they are content with sharing in its spoils. We must realize that oppression is a bundled set of relations that reinforce one another, so there is little to suggest that advantages in terms of one relation necessarily contradict the enforcement of another relation. There has been very little explicit engagement within this body of literature regarding the ways in which these educational "success" stories, although perhaps resisting and transgressing ideologies of smartness, may nevertheless actually *rely* on ideological acts of Whiteness and of class privilege in the process. Erevelles (2002a) pointed to the class privilege at play, without explicitly engaging in the possible acts of Whiteness that such success also may rest on:

> It could be argued that . . . the users of Facilitated Communication enjoy class privilege—a distinction that also separates them from most persons with disabilities who often live under conditions of abject poverty. In fact, it is because of their class privilege that this populations [sic] of persons labeled autistic had access to the sophisticated technologies as well as facilitators to enable them to communicate. (p. 32)

It could also be argued that many (though not all) users of facilitated communication who have successfully gained access to academic curricula in their schooling also enjoy White privilege and therefore benefit from White ideology. Similarly, Blanchett (2006) explicitly noted the ways that White privilege and racism operate in concert with the bureaucratic structures of special education to ensure that students of color with identified disabilities are much more likely to be placed in segregated classrooms and schools, whereas their White peers with identified disabilities are much more likely to have access to "inclusive," or at least integrated, classrooms and schools. It would seem likely that, for many White students considered to be significantly disabled, efforts at transgressing and resisting ideologies of smartness so as to escape the impoverished curricula and segregation of special education may actually be aided by the ideological work of Whiteness, of what Du Bois (1935/1998), and later, Roediger (1991), once called the "public and psychological wages of whiteness."

Toward the abolition of whiteness and smartness

Thus, we argue that both of these extant bodies of literature that critically engage the construct of "smartness" have made significant contributions to the project of working to illuminate the normative center of schools. Nevertheless, although we take theoretical and political strategies from each, we argue that the work of either discourse community on its own is theoretically and politically incomplete. The first engages critically with race and locates smartness as ideology, rather than a mere "social construction," but leaves the experience of "severely" disabled individuals outside the realm of their theoretical analysis. The analysis leaves open the position that there are limits or exceptions to this analysis and that some [severely disabled] people *really* are not smart, thus retreating at the most pivotal moment from the emancipatory potential of a radical ideological critique. The latter engages critically with the experiences of the significantly disabled who have been regarded as mentally retarded, but framing intelligence and mental retardation, competence and incompetence, and smartness and not-so-smartness as social constructions largely fails to engage with smartness/intelligence as an ideological system and further largely declines to engage with the ideological system of Whiteness (and in many ways actually may rest on ideological acts of Whiteness and of class privilege in order to "free" some significantly disabled people from the oppressive positioning of "mental retardation"). Hence, both a Whiteness studies critique of smartness (in the absence of a Disability Studies critique of smartness) and a Disability Studies critique of smartness (in the absence of a Whiteness Studies critique of smartness) are inadequate and incomplete, and the theoretical pursuit of each in isolation may actually (however unwittingly) continue to rest on and reify other ideological systems of oppression, and therefore continue to contribute to the oppression of certain groups of individuals. It unwittingly reinforces an oppressive relation and betrays a conciliatory posture toward a bogus ideology.

That Whiteness is nothing but false and oppressive means that it exists only as a tool for oppression. Likewise, that smartness is nothing but false and oppressive means that it, too, exists only as a tool for oppression. Whites and smart people are only real insofar as social institutions like education, and formidable processes like common sense, recognize certain bodies as White and certain people as smart. Historically and materially, these ideologies have operated not in isolation from one another, but as inextricably intertwined systems of oppression and exclusion. Theoretical and political efforts to address one system of oppression without simultaneously addressing the other (as well as other inextricably interwoven oppressive ideologies, such as patriarchy, capitalism, and heterosexism) are incomplete at best and actively (however unwittingly) oppressive to others at worst. Thus, we join with scholars such as Erevelles (2002b), Erevelles, Kanga, and Middleton (2006), Baker (2002a, 2002b), Ferri and Connor (2005a, 2005b), Kliewer, Biklen, and Kasa-Hendrickson (2006), and Baglieri et al. (2011, this issue) who have called for more integrated efforts to transgress and dismantle interlocking ideologies of oppression in schools and in society. As challenging as such work is, we argue that such theoretically integrated efforts to act in material solidarity against oppression of *all* kinds is nothing less than an ethical imperative.

How, exactly, do we propose to proceed with such work? We are not convinced by efforts from within our respective discourse communities to rearticulate either Whiteness or smartness. For instance, efforts to reform or rearticulate Whiteness are correct to argue that its abolition will not win over many Whites to join the cause. The abolition of Whiteness faces grim prospects for success; for many Whites, it is a nonstarter. That said, its proponents are convinced that reinventing Whiteness is a coping strategy with an oppressive category that has known no other way to exist; it is doomed from the start. Rearticulating Whiteness has greater chances for success if by "success" we mean that more Whites will buy into it. But if the history of race has taught us anything, it is that the actions of Whites are not a reliable gauge for combating racism. Likewise, efforts from within the field of Disability Studies that have sought to rescue the construct of intelligence through Gardner-esque, relativistic calls for a celebration of "multiple" intelligences similarly fail to adequately address that some forms of "intelligence" are still more highly culturally valued than others and thus continue to be used as (perhaps less thinly veiled) mechanisms of oppression (see Kincheloe, 2004, for a cogent critical discussion of multiple intelligences theory and its ideological functions). We suggest, rather, a different strategy: the abolition of both Whiteness and intelligence.

We acknowledge that this position is not very intuitive for many scholars and activists. To suggest a strategy of abolition of Whiteness is to simultaneously suggest an abolition of a racial identity, and such a move is likely to encounter almost equal opposition from people of color and from Whites. It is not an illogical conclusion to suggest that this move implicates race abolition, which in turn involves non-White identities—for the abolition of Whiteness is the repudiation of an entire social relation, something extending well beyond the problem of what it means to be White, but equally what it means to be a racial being (Leonardo, 2010). Similarly, to suggest an abolition of smartness as an ideological system is likely to encounter equal opposition from both those who currently enjoy the privilege of that status, and from those who have historically been excluded from those privileges yet who may aspire to attain them and thereby benefit from the very ideological system that actively marginalized and oppressed them (such as those previously labeled as mentally retarded). We concur with Biklen and Kliewer's (2006) assertion that not very many academics—even those in the field of Disability Studies—seem particularly eager to engage in this conversation, nor even seem to imagine engaging in it.[5] Academics are almost exclusively people who have identities that are fairly solidly bound up in being smart people, and it is not an aspect of their identity that they are eager to part from—nor are teachers, in our experience, particularly open to interrogating the ways that their classroom discourse serves to actively constitute some students as smart and other students as not-so-smart. We already know that they constitute who is White and who is not.

Yet this is precisely why this interrogation needs to take place at the locus of cultural ideology. "Smartness" is not an inherent physical feature of individual brains, not a "stuff" or a "quantity" that some people have more of than others, no more so than "Whiteness" is an inherent physical feature of white bodies. Yet the ideology of smartness is inextricably intertwined in the creation of Smart people (as an identity), just as the ideology of Whiteness is inextricably intertwined in the creation of White people (as an identity). We understand smartness to be a performative, cultural ideological system that operates in the service of constructing the normative center of schools and of societies, an ideological system that is nonetheless materialist not in any biological or neurological way, but rather in that developing an identity as either "smart" or "not-so-smart" is to have very real material consequences vis-à-vis one's access and sense of entitlement (or not) to opportunities, privileges, and myriad forms of cultural capital—to smartness as property.

We would like to return to one of our previous assertions. To the extent that both racial and intellectual supremacy are taught, they are pedagogical. This is the great promise of this work—that of pedagogical possibility for the disruption of oppressive ideological systems such as smartness. However, as we hope we have begun to illustrate in this analysis, meaningful disruption must necessarily involve complex interrogation of multiple, interlocking ideological systems of oppression in schools and of exploring the complex ways in which, for example, cultural ideologies such as "smartness" (as well as other ableist ideologies—of goodness, beauty, sanity, and so on) may be performed as intersecting acts of Whiteness, of class privilege, of heterosexist privilege, of patriarchy, and so on. We offer the purposeful and deliberative unpacking of the ideologies of smartness and Whiteness as one possible avenue through which to forge alliances with other radical educators seeking more inclusive, and hence more socially just, cultural practices of schooling.

Notes

1 We argue that there are multiple ideologies operating within the broader umbrella of ableist ideologies, including ideologies of smartness, of beauty, of physical ability, of goodness, and of sanity, among others. Interestingly, the ideology of Whiteness intersects with each

370

of these ideologies of dis/ability in compelling and underexamined ways. Nevertheless, the focus of this essay will remain on the intersections between the ideologies of Whiteness and of smartness.

2 According to the U.S. Census, Arabs are classified as Whites.

3 Here we use ideology not in the terms of a pure ideality, but as having material modes of existence. Ideas are not mental categories as such, but exist in institutional forms (see Leonardo, 2003b).

4 Note that the first author of this cited piece (Broderick & Kasa-Hendrickson, 2006) is the second author of the present manuscript. Thus, much of the critique being levied is self-reflexive.

5 Indeed, at the AREA session where we first publicly shared these ideas with colleagues (Leonardo & Broderick, 2009), one of us metaphorically likened the experience of an early attempt to have critical discussions about the abolition of smartness with academic colleagues to "poking a stick in a beehive and swirling it around."

References

Allen, R. (2005). Whiteness and critical pedagogy. In Z. Leonardo (Ed.), *Critical pedagogy and race* (pp. 53–68). Malden, MA: Blackwell.

Althusser, L. (1971). *Lenin and philosophy* (B. Brewster, Trans.) New York: Monthly Review Press.

Apple, M. (2000). *Official knowledge: Democratic education in a conservative age* (2nd ed.). New York: Routledge and Kegan Paul. (Original work published 1979)

Artiles, A. (2008). Special education's changing identity: Paradoxes and dilemmas in views of culture and space. *Harvard Education Review, 73*, 164–202.

Baglieri, S., Bejoian, L. M., Broderick, A. A., Connor, D. J., & Valle, J. W. (2011). [Re]claiming "inclusive education" toward cohesion in educational reform: Disability studies unravels the myth of the normal child. *Teachers College Record, 113*(10).

Baker, B. (2002a). The hunt for disability: The new eugenics and the normalization of school children. *Teachers College Record, 104*, 663–703.

Baker, B. (2002b). Disorganizing educational tropes: Conceptions of dis/ability and curriculum. *Journal of Curriculum Theorizing, 18*(4), 47–80.

Biklen, D. (1990). Communication unbound: Autism and praxis. *Harvard Educational Review, 60*, 291–314.

Biklen, D. (1999). The metaphor of mental retardation: Rethinking ability and disability. In H. Bersani Jr. (Ed.), *Responding to the challenge: Current trends and international issues in developmental disabilities: Essays in honor of Gunnar Dybwad* (pp. 35–52). Cambridge, MA: Brookline Books.

Biklen, D. (2000). Lessons from the margins, narrating mental retardation: A review essay. *Mental Retardation, 38*, 444–456.

Biklen, D., & Burke, J. (2006). Presuming competence. *Equity and Excellence in Education, 39*, 166–175.

Biklen, D., & Kliewer, C. (2006). Constructing competence: Autism, voice and the "disordered" body. *International Journal of Inclusive Education, 10*, 169–188.

Blanchett, W. (2006). Disproportionate representation of African Americans in special education: Acknowledging the role of White privilege and racism. *Educational Researcher, 35*(6), 24–28.

Bogdan, R., & Taylor, S. J. (1992). The social construction of humanness: Relationships with severely disabled people. In P. M. Ferguson, D. L. Ferguson, & S. J. Taylor (Eds.),

Interpreting disability: A qualitative reader (pp. 275–294). New York: Teachers College Press. (Original work published 1989)

Bonilla-Silva, E. (2004). From biracial to triracial: The emergence of a new racial stratification system in the United States. In C. Herring, V. Keith, & H. Horton (Eds.), *Skin/deep: How race and complexion matter in the "color-blind" era* (pp. 224–239). Urbana: University of Illinois Press.

Borthwick, C., & Crossley, R. (1999). Language and retardation. *Psycoloquy, 10*(038). Retrieved June 16, 2010, from http://www.cogsci.ecs.soton.ac.uk/cgi/psyc/newpsy?10.038

Broderick, A., & Kasa-Hendrickson, C. (2001). "Say just one word at first": The emergence, of intentional speech in a student labeled with autism. *Journal of the Association for Persons With Severe Handicaps, 26*, 13–24.

Broderick, A., & Kasa-Hendrickson, C. (2006). "I am thinking that speech is asinine": Narrating complexities and rethinking the notion of "independence" in communication. *Equity and Excellence in Education 39*, 176–186.

Dunn, L. M. (1968). Special education for the mildly retarded—Is much of it justifiable? *Exceptional Children, 35*, 5–22.

Du Bois, W. E. B. (1998). *Black reconstruction in America, 1860—1880.* New York: Free Press. (Original work published 1935)

Eagleton, T. (1991). *Ideology.* London: Verso.

Erevelles, N. (2002a). Voices of silence: Foucault, disability, and the question of self-determination. *Studies in Philosophy and Education, 21*, 17–35.

Erevelles, N. (2002b). (Im)material citizens: Cognitive disability, race, and the politics of citizenship. *Disability, Culture and Education, 1*, 5–25.

Erevelles, N., Kanga, A., & Middleton, R. (2006). How does it feel to be a problem? Race, disability, and exclusion in educational policy. In E. Brantlinger (Ed.), *Who benefits from special education? Remediating [fixing] other people's children* (pp. 77–99). Mahwah, NJ: Erlbaum.

Ferri, B., & Connor, D. (2005a). Tools of exclusion: Race, disability, and (re) segregated education. *Teachers College Record, 107*, 453–474.

Ferri, B., & Connor, D. (2005b). In the shadow of *Brown:* Special education and overrepresentation of students of color. *Remedial and Special Education, 26*, 93–100.

Fierros, E. G., & Conroy, J. W. (2002). Double jeopardy: An exploration of restrictiveness and race in special education. In D. J. Losen & G. Orfield (Eds.), *Racial inequity in special education* (pp. 39–70). Cambridge, MA: Harvard University Press.

Freire, P. (1993). *Pedagogy of the oppressed* (Revised 20th anniversary ed.). New York: Continuum.

Geertz, C. (1994). Ideology as a cultural system. In T. Eagleton (Ed.), *Ideology* (pp. 279–294). London: Longman.

Gillborn, D. (2005). Education policy as an act of White supremacy: Whiteness, critical race theory and education reform. *Journal of Education Policy, 20*, 485–505.

Gillborn, D. (2006). Public interest and the interests of White people are not the same: Assessment, education policy, and racism. In G. Ladson-Billings & W. F. Tate (Eds.), *Education research in the public interest: Social Justice, action, and policy* (pp. 173–195). New York: Teachers College Press.

Gilroy, P. (2000). *Against race.* Cambridge, MA: Belknap Press of Harvard University.

Giroux, H. (1981). *Ideology, culture, and the process of schooling.* Philadelphia: Temple University Press.

Gould, S. J. (1996). *The mismeasure of man.* New York: W. W. Norton & Company. (Original work published 1981)

Gouldner, A. (1976). *The dialectic of ideology and technology.* New York: Seabury Press.

Hall, S. (1996). The problem of ideology: Marxism without guarantees. In D. Morley & K. Chen (Eds.), *Stuart Hall* (pp. 25–46). London: Routledge.

Harris, C. (1995). Whiteness as property. In K. Crenshaw, N. Gotanda, G. Peller, & K. Thomas (Eds.), *Critical race theory* (pp. 276–291). New York: New Press.

Harry, B., & Klingner, J. (2006). *Why are so many minority students in special education? Understanding race and disability in schools.* New York: Teachers College Press.

Hayman, R. L. (1998). *The smart culture: Society, intelligence, and law.* New York: New York University Press.

Herrnstein, R., & Murray, C. (1994). *The bell curve: Intelligence and class structure in American life.* New York: Simon and Schuster.

Hunter, M. (2002). "If you're light you're alright": Light skin color as social capital for women of color. *Gender and Society, 16,* 171–189.

Hunter, M. (2005). *Race, gender, and the politics of skin tone.* New York: Routledge.

Ignatiev, N., & Garvey, J. (1996b). Abolish the White race: By any means necessary. In N. Ignatiev & J, Garvey (Eds.), *Race traitor* (pp. 9–14). New York: Routledge.

Kasa-Hendrickson, C. (2005). "There's no way this kid's retarded": Teachers' optimistic constructions of students' ability. *International Journal of Inclusive Education, 9,* 55–69.

Kasa-Hendrickson, C., & Ashby, C. (2008, March). *Rethinking smart: Challenging the construct of mental retardation.* Paper presented at the annual meeting of the American Educational Research Association, New York, NY.

Kincheloe, J. (Ed.). (2004). *Multiple intelligences reconsidered.* New York: Peter Lang.

Kincheloe, J., Steinberg, S., & Villaverde, L. (Eds.) (1999). *Rethinking intelligence: Confronting psychological assumptions about teaching and learning.* New York: Routledge.

Kliewer, C. (1998). *Schooling children with Down syndrome: Toward an understanding of possibility.* New York: Teachers College Press.

Kliewer, C., Biklen, D., & Kasa-Hendrickson, C. (2006). Who may be literate? Disability and resistance to the cultural denial of competence. *American Educational Research Journal, 43,* 163–192.

Leonardo, Z. (2002). The souls of White folk: Critical pedagogy, Whiteness studies, and globalization discourse. *Race Ethnicity and Education, 5*(1), 29–50.

Leonardo, Z. (2003a). *Ideology, discourse, and school reform.* Westport, CT: Praeger.

Leonardo, Z. (2003b). Reality on trial: Notes on ideology, education, and utopia. *Policy Futures in Education, 1,* 504–525.

Leonardo, Z. (2004). The color of supremacy: Beyond the discourse of "White privilege." *Educational Philosophy and Theory, 36,* 137–152.

Leonardo, Z. (2005). Through the multicultural glass: Althusser, ideology, and race relations in post-civil rights America. *Policy Futures in Education, 3,* 400–412.

Leonardo, Z. (2009). *Race, Whiteness, and education.* New York: London.

Leonardo, Z. (2010, September 10). After the glow: Race ambivalence and other educational prognoses. *Educational Philosophy and Theory.* doi:10.1111/j.1469-5812.2010.00645.x

Leonardo, Z., & Broderick, A. (2009, April). *Whites as normates: Intersections between Whiteness and disability studies.* Paper presented at the annual meeting of the American Educational Research Association, San Diego, CA.

Lipsitz, G. (1998). *The possessive investment in Whiteness.* Philadelphia: Temple University Press.

Lopez, I. H. (2006). *White by law.* New York: New York University Press.

Lorde, A. (2007). *Sister outsider.* Berkeley, CA: Crossing Press.

Martinez, G. (1997). Mexican-Americans and Whiteness. In R. Delgado & J. Stefancic (Eds.), *Critical White studies* (pp. 210–213). Philadelphia: Temple University Press.

Morrison, T. (1993). *Playing in the dark: Whiteness in the literary imagination.* New York: Vintage Books.

Omi, M., & Winant, H. (1994). *Racial formation in the United States: From the 1960s to the 1990s* (2nd ed.). New York: Routledge.

Prashad, V. (2000). *The karma of brown folk.* Minneapolis: University of Minnesota Press.

Ricoeur, P. (1986). *Lectures on ideology and utopia* (George Taylor, Ed.). New York: Columbia University Press.

Roediger, D. (1991). *The wages of Whiteness.* London and New York: Verso.

Roediger, D. (1994). *Toward the abolition of Whiteness.* New York: Verso.

Rubin, S., Biklen, D., Kasa-Hendrickson, C., Kluth, P., Cardinal, D., & Broderick, A. (2001). Independence, participation, and the meaning of intellectual ability. *Disability and Society, 16*, 413–429.

Taylor, S. J., & Blatt, S. D. (Eds.). (1999). *In search of the promised land: The collected papers of Burton Blatt.* Washington, DC: American Association on Mental Retardation.

Wu, F. (2002). *Yellow.* New York: Basic Books.